Your Unselfish Kindness

T0294234

Also by Mary Edmond-Paul

Lighted Windows: Critical Essays on Robin Hyde (ed.)
Her Side of the Story: Readings of Mander, Mansfield & Hyde
Gothic NZ: The Darker Side of Kiwi Culture
(ed. with Misha Kavka and Jennifer Lawn)

Your Unselfish Kindness

Robin Hyde's Autobiographical Writings

Edited by
Mary Edmond-Paul

Otago University Press

Published by Otago University Press
PO Box 56 / Level 1, 398 Cumberland Street,
Dunedin, New Zealand
F: 64 3 479 8385
E: university.press@otago.ac.nz
W: www.otago.ac.nz/press

First published 2011
Introduction, annotations and
volume copyright © Mary Edmond-Paul 2011
ISBN 978 1 877578 21 2

Publisher: Wendy Harrex
Cover design: Fiona Moffat

Printed in Aotearoa New Zealand by
PrintLink Ltd, Wellington

CONTENTS

Dedicated to Derek and Ellynne Challis

ACKNOWLEDGEMENTS

First, my most sincere thanks to Derek and Ellyne Challis, who made available Hyde's manuscripts and gave their time, knowledge and hospitality over a decade of visits. Thanks, too, to Alison Hunt, whose findings in her extensive doctoral research have proved complementary to my own, and whose work should be consulted by anyone wanting more detail on Hyde's psychiatric experience and further contexts for her other writing. I am most grateful for Alison's support of this publication. And thank you to Lisa Docherty for the first transcription of the '1934 Auotbiography' manuscript, to my wonderful colleagues Michele Leggott and Patrick Sandbrook as co-initiators of the Marsden funded project which began this project and for the inspiring examples of their work, and to Pat particularly for his ongoing interest and generosity in the late stages of this project (of which initially he was to be co-editor). Profound thanks go to all other Hyde scholars and students whose insights have informed my commentary: from the 1980s scholars Linda Hardy, Gillian Boddy, Phillida Bunkle and Jacqueline Matthews, to the authors of essays in *Lighted Windows*: Susan Ash, Nadine Attewell, Diana Bridge, Alex Calder, Renata Casertano, Megan Clayton, Michelle Elleray, Jolisa Gracewood, Nikki Hessell, Alison Hunt, Alison Jeffreys, and Brigid Magner. Also thanks to Hyde enthusiast Mark Hanson, who often rang me to find out how the book was proceeding and regularly sent maps and documents. My gratitude, too, to manuscript librarians past and present at Auckland Central City Library – Georgia Prince, Kate de Courcy and Iain Sharp – for their continuing custodianship of the '1934 Autobiography' and the typed copy of the '1935 Journal', and more recently to librarians at the Alexander Turnbull Library, where the Hyde papers previously held by her son Derek Challis now reside.

I am grateful to the Royal Society Marsden Fund and the Victoria University Stout Centre (and its director Lydia Wevers) for support in early stages of research, including Marsden support of Lisa Docherty as doctoral researcher. Latterly, a Massey University MURF Grant and funding from the School of English and Media Studies for research assistance and relief of teaching, and from the College of Humanities and Social Sciences for assistance with publication, allowed completion of the project.

As readers, I have appreciated the enthusiasm and encouragement of Sarah Grimes and Rose Lovell-Smith; the support and comments of colleagues, particularly Jack Ross and Jenny Lawn, in the former School of Cultural Studies, Massey University. My thanks also to the Massey Albany past principal Ian Watson and his wife and fellow academic Patsy, who expressed enthusiasm for this project at its inception; and to other senior academics who have encouraged it: Mike O'Brien, Peter Lineham, Michael Belgrave and John Muirhead. Many thanks to Catharina van Bohemen for her engaged investigative enthusiasm in proofing and making contributions to annotations of the '1934 Autobiography'. Thanks to Jackie Liggins for suggestions on my brief history of psychiatry, to Peter Hughes, Librarian at UNITEC, for historical assistance with people and places, to Pat Sandbrook, again, of Massey University, for organising photography of manuscripts and for his own photographs of the Lodge, and to Anne Zimmerman for her work on ordering the '1934 Autobiography', and again to Pat Sandbrook for help in applying Zimmerman's series. For advice in later stages of writing the introductory essay, my thanks to Charlotte Paul, Jacob Edmond, Michael Fletcher and Pat Baskett; for hospitality on research leave: in Wellington, Michael Nicholson and Jane Paul; in Honolulu, Anne Kennedy and Robert Sullivan; in London, Gwynne Somerville, Christine and Julian Wallace; and in Crief, Scotland, Jean Ann Scott-Millar.

Finally, thanks to my publisher Wendy Harrex for her dedication to New Zealand publishing and to the recuperation of Robin Hyde, whose work she first brought back into print in the 1980s through New Women's Press, with commissioned introductions by feminist scholars. This book has a long history, having been worked on intermittently, and has required a great deal of patience and acumen to pull together the parts and to unify the text. The process of turning these manuscripts into a published book has been challenging: as manuscripts, they required much interpretation and translation, but printed and in chronological sequence, as they now are, they are lucid and moving – in a way that I always hoped they would be. Thank you to my publisher Wendy Harrex for trusting that they would have this quality and for trusting that I could interpret them. Wendy's own interest in history has meant she has asked very useful questions above and beyond the exceptional editorial contribution she has made. Readers will also notice her hand in the book's design, making it echo the typographical style of the 1930s – even to the use of Times New Roman, a typeface invented in 1932.

Earlier versions of the introductory essay were presented as conference papers at the 'Paradise' SHARP Regional Conference, Wellington, 27–30 January 2005 and the Stout Centre, Victoria University Wellington in June 2005, and revised as talks given at University of Hawai'i at Manoa and the New Zealand Studies Centre, Birkbeck College, London, in May 2009.

MARY PAUL

CHRONOLOGY

1906 19 January: Iris Guiver Wilkinson, later known as Robin Hyde, is born in Capetown.

1907 16 February: The Wilkinsons leave South Africa, settling in South Wellington at Melrose.

1910 Nelly Wilkinson takes children to Australia. On return, Wilkinsons move to Newtown: Russell Tce. then Waripori St.

1922 26 April: First poem ('Flanders Poppies') published in *Free Lance.*

1923 February: Children's Page Editor for *Farmers Advocate*, a *Dominion* publication, until March 1924.

1924 18–21 April: Visits Harry Sweetman in Auckland.
April–December: Hospitalised in Wellington for right knee inflammation; given morphine for pain relief. Permanent lameness.

1925 Resumes work on *Dominion* as social page reporter and correspondent for *Women's Mirror* (Auckland).
25 June: Attends Ladies' Press Gallery to write parliamentary column as 'Novitia' (June–October). Lives in central Wellington.
25 October: Harry Sweetman sails to England via New York and Boston.
Late 1925–early 1926: Holiday in Rotorua. Meets Frederick de Mulford Hyde. Knee worsened by hospital treatment. Resumes work on *Dominion*. Suspects pregnancy.

1926 13 May: Harry Sweetman dies in Manchester.
28 May: Iris departs for Sydney from Wellington on *Marama.*
[July–September]. Christopher Robin Hyde stillborn or died at birth in Stanmore, Sydney. Iris writes: 'Robin died at birth when I was twenty *and six months.*' (JL 21, 23 October 1937. Italics represent holograph insertion in typed letter naming de Mulford Hyde as child's father.)
16 September: Nelly Wilkinson departs for Sydney from Wellington on *Maheno.*
17 November: Frederick de Mulford Hyde marries Alice Algie at St Barnabas church, Auckland.

30 November: Iris and Nelly Wilkinson return to Auckland from Sydney on *Ulimaroa*.

Christmas: Gwen Hawthorn given fair copy MS book of poems, including 'C.R.H.' (Christmas 1926).

December 1926–early 1927: Iris visits Rotorua. Breakdown and hospitalisation in Hamilton and Palmerston North, followed by nursing at home in Wellington.

1927   22 April: First poem ('Conflagration') published using 'Robin Hyde' nom de plume in Christchurch *Sun*.

7 May: Admitted to Queen Mary Hospital, Hanmer Springs.

7 September. Begins correspondence with Schroder after poems are published in Christchurch *Sun*.

8 October: Leaves Hanmer for Christchurch, meets Schroder. Back in Wellington freelancing and working for the Publicity Bureau until March 1928. Meets C.A. Marris.

19 December: News of Harry Sweetman's death received from his brother Hardy.

1928   September–December: Works for *NZ Truth* newspaper, Wellington.

1929   May: Hyde appointed Lady Editor on *Wanganui Chronicle*. Meets Henry (Harry) Lawson Smith (1895–1982), journalist on Marton newspaper and married. In November first book (poems) *The Desolate Star* published.

1930   April: A pregnant Hyde is given leave of absence from *Chronicle* for fictitious 'heart condition'. Three weeks in Christchurch (May).

June: Boards on D'Urville Island, then in Picton (July–October).

Mid-October: *Chronicle* terminates weekly column (possibly because of news of pregnancy).

29 October: Derek Arden Challis born in Picton. His father is Henry Lawson Smith.

Mid-November: Hyde returns to parents at Northland Rd. Derek boards in nursing home.

1931   Late January: Accepts McLean's invitation to become Lady Editor on *New Zealand Observer*. Moves to Auckland. Derek in Palmerston North.

1932   Derek boards in Auckland with Ben and Alive (Ivy) Hutson until 1939.

1933   2 June: Hyde attempts suicide. Arrested and held in police cell at Public Hospital.

20 June: Admitted to Auckland Mental Hospital as voluntary patient in extramural ward (the Lodge) under care of Drs Buchanan and Tothill.

25 July: Transferred to the main hospital's Wolfe Home until 20 August after failed attempt to smuggle morphia into Lodge.

28 September: Discharged from hospital. Stays with Nelly at Hutsons'. First meeting with Rosalie and Gloria Rawlinson, 1 October.

4 December: Magistrate's court appearance: Hyde is discharged. Breaks down 5 December and requests readmission to Lodge. Tothill takes over care 12 December.

1934   January–February: Autobiography written at Tothill's suggestion.

April–May: C.A. Marris selects and submits on Hyde's behalf a seventy-page poetry MS to AP Watt, London literary agent.

April–May: *Journalese* begun at Tothill's suggestion, completed August, published late October. Begins researching *Check to Your King* at Rosalie Rawlinson's suggestion.

1935   February: Begins 1935 Journal. Intermittent entries to 29 July.

March: Begins first version of *The Godwits Fly*. Works March–April on 'Bronze Outlaw' (*Passport to Hell*).

November: *Conquerors* published through Macmillan, London. *Passport to Hell* accepted for publication by Hurst & Blackett. Resubmits short-story collection 'Unicorn Pasture' to Macmillan (rejected).

1936   23 April: *Passport to Hell* published.

25 August: Accepts Stewart's invitation to visit Dunedin at his expense.

2 December: Returns by air to Wellington after meeting Nelly Wilkinson in Nelson. Hyde returns to Lodge before Christmas.

1937   1 January: Gilbert Tothill takes up position as Medical Superintendent at Tokanui Hospital, moving with family to Te Awamutu.

13 February: Three-week stay at Whangaroa Harbour. Rents cabin, typing final draft of *The Godwits Fly*. Overnight trip to Spirits Bay and Ninety-Mile Beach with Percy Mitcalfe.

8 March: Self-discharged from Lodge after disagreement with doctors. Rents bach at Waiatarua in the Waitakere ranges until Easter (late March). Drafts autobiographical fragment, published in 1984 as *A Home in This World*.

17 June: Hurst & Blackett draw contract for *Persephone in Winter*.

July: Her articles about eviction of Orakei Maori appear in *Observer.*

27 October: Publication of *Persephone in Winter.*

November: Copies of *Wednesday's Children* arrive in NZ.

1938   18 January: Departs from Auckland on *Awatea* bound for Sydney. Begins using 'China Notebook' Jan–April for travel notes from Sydney to Hankow.

22 January: Departs from Sydney on *Changte* bound for Hong Kong via Brisbane, Cairns, Thursday Island and Manila.

Early February: Connection to Kobe delayed. Stays a week in Hong Kong and decides to visit mainland China to gather material for book.

17 February: Departs for Shanghai on *Aramis*. Posts bulk of papers to AP Watt in London before leaving Hong Kong.

19 February: Arrives in Shanghai, occupied by Japanese since Nov 1937. Stays a week at Great Eastern Hotel. Shown around Shanghai by Rewi Alley.

15 March: Departs for Hong Kong on *Kaiser-I-Hind,* commissioned by *Far Eastern Mirror* to report from Canton war-zone.

19 March: Day trip to Macao from Hong Kong with James Bertram.

7–9 April: Train journey from Canton to Hankow. Stays at Lutheran Mission, first with Edith Epstein then in top-floor room.

10 May: Japanese aerial bombardment of Hsuchow begins. Lunghai railway line cut 14 May.

19 May: Japanese occupation of Hsuchow. Hyde remains with American missionaries.

30 May: Unsuccessfully attempts to leave Hsuchow by walking out on Lunghai line. Returned by Japanese to Hsuchow about 2 June.

16 June: Leaves Hsuchow walking along northern railway line. Later escorted on troop train to Tsingtao.

22 June: Taken to British Consulate in Tsingtao by Japanese authorities. Stays a week with consul, arriving in Shanghai 5 July. Receives a copy of newly published *Nor the Years Condemn.*

11 July: Arrives in Hong Kong on *Tjinegara.* Collapses. Taken to War Memorial Hospital and diagnosed with sprue.

11 August: Departs from Hong Kong on *Serooskerk.* Hospitalised briefly in Singapore.

26 August: Leaves Singapore on *Johan van Oldenbarnevelt* bound for

Southampton via Manila, Belewan, Sabang, Columbo, Suez, Port Said, Genoa, Villefranche, Algiers.

18 September: Arrives at Southampton. Stays briefly in London before renting caravan at Pope's Hall in Kent, late October. Begins drafting *Dragon Rampant*.

11 November: *The Godwits Fly* published. Buchanan visits caravan, voices concern about conditions.

1939   January: Hurst & Blackett accept *Dragon Rampant*. Hyde returns to Idris House, involved with China Campaign, United Front and Left Book Club. Health deteriorating. Meets Douglas Lilburn.

8 March: Stays briefly in caravan at Pope's Hall, Kent. Scheduled for admission to hospital for Tropical Diseases in London 15 March.

30 March: Works on dramatisation of *Wednesday's Children* for Heron Carvic and Phyllis Neilson-Terry. Bertram continues to help with content checking of *Dragon Rampant*. He sails for China on 12 April.

5 June: Returns to London. Rents attic room at 1 Pembridge Square, Notting Hill.

29 June: Brasch visits Pembridge Square, leaves for New York 30 June.

30 June: Hyde inscribed a copy of *Dragon Rampant* for mother and father.

13 August: Spends day with Sylvia Pankhurst, writing article for *New Times and Ethiopia News*.

23 August: Commits suicide by benzedrine poisoning. Is buried at Kensington New Cemetery, Gunnersbury.

This chronology is adapted from the more extensive version in Michele Leggott's collection *Young Knowledge: the Poems of Robin Hyde* (Auckland: Auckland University Press, 2003). For a diagrammatic record of when Hyde was working on each of her books and manuscripts, see Patrick Sandbrook's PhD thesis, 'Robin Hyde: A Writer at Work' (1985). For information on the time and place of poetic composition, see Michele Leggott's introduction to *Young Knowledge*. Also helpful is Alison Hunt's 'A Bibliography of the Published Works of Robin Hyde (Iris G. Wilkinson, 1906–1939)' (2004), which updates previous bibliographies.

Other sources for this chronology include Archives New Zealand, Gloria Rawlinson and Derek Challis's *The Book of Iris, The Dictionary of New Zealand Biography,* Lisa Docherty's PhD Thesis, '"Do I Speak Well?" A Selection of Letters by Robin Hyde 1927–1939' (2000), and the AP Watt Archives. The biography *The Book of Iris* (2002) is the most comprehensive source for biographical information.

Other chronologies important to Hyde studies include: the history of the ownership and location of manuscripts; the history of the writing of the biography; and also of Gloria Rawlinson's ordering of Hyde's papers, and editing of the poetry. For these, see particularly *Young Knowledge* (29–30) and Derek Challis's 'The Fate of the Iris Wilkinson Manuscripts'. Both Hunt's bibliography and Challis's essay can be found on the New Zealand Electronic Poetry Centre website: http://www.nzepc. auckland.ac.nz.

ABBREVIATIONS

Works by Robin Hyde

Disputed Ground: Disputed Ground: Robin Hyde, Journalist, ed. and introd. Gillian Boddy and
    Jacqueline Matthews (Wellington: Victoria University Press, 1991).

A Home: A Home in this World, Introd. Derek Challis (Auckland: Longman Paul, 1984).

Houses by the Sea: Houses by the Sea & The Later Poems of Robin Hyde, ed. and introd. Gloria
    Rawlinson (Christchurch: Caxton Press, 1952).

Works relating to Robin Hyde

Iris

Challis, Derek and Gloria Rawlinson, *The Book of Iris: A Life of Robin Hyde* (Auckland:
    Auckland University Press, 2002).

Lighted Windows

Mary Edmond-Paul (ed.), *Lighted Windows: Critical Essays on Robin Hyde* (Dunedin: Otago
    University Press, 2008),

'Cage'

Hunt, Alison. '"The Cage with the Open Door": Autobiography and Psychiatry in the Life and
    Works of Robin Hyde'. (PhD: University of Auckland, 2008).

'Robin Hyde'

Sandbrook, Patrick. 'Robin Hyde: A Writer at Work' (PhD: Massey University, 1985).

Young Knowledge

Leggott, Michele (ed.). *Young Knowledge: The Poems of Robin Hyde* (Auckland: Auckland
    University Press, 2003).

INTRODUCTION
A Fortuitous Moment

Iris Wilkinson, better known as Robin Hyde, had two major mental breakdowns – the first in 1926–27 when she was twenty, another in 1933 – and arguably a third leading up to her death in 1939. She also sustained, continuously, a writing career: from the time she left school (at sixteen), when she started work as a cadet reporter on *The Dominion* newspaper in Wellington, until her death in August 1939 in London, where her seventh book, *Dragon Rampant*, had just been *The Times* newspaper's 'Book of the Month' for July.

From her own accounts and her son's quotation from her patient notes,* it appears that Hyde's collapses were severe, involving fits of uncontrollable crying and anger, despair, suicidality, self-harming, not eating, self-medication and a (possibly drug-induced) sense of other-worldly possession – a state in which her imaginary world was more real than the real. However, on the whole, and fortunately for her, these states of mind and behaviours were treated professionally as hysterical, borderline or neurasthenic, and as having been precipitated by life events, loss, grieving and physical pain, the modern world, or even bad behaviour. Apart from eight weeks in 1933, she escaped the incarceration in the main ward of an asylum that befell many distressed women and men, and notably another prominent New Zealand writer, Janet Frame (ten years later).

Hyde's unique situation as (albeit secretly) a single mother who was also a well-known working journalist and poet (her fiction career began after 1933) was a factor in her experiencing psychiatric care at all – as well as it being in two institutions specifically designed for borderline recoverable conditions. She first became a patient at Queen Mary Hospital at Hanmer in 1927 for five months. Then in 1933 she lived at the Lodge (or Grey Lodge, as she called it), a voluntary villa in the grounds of Auckland Mental Hospital at Avondale, for more than three years. These were times when she was so incapacitated mentally and physically that she was unable to continue her career and needed somewhere to live, as well as financial and emotional support. Had Hyde been the non-working daughter of a wealthier and

---

* See *Iris*, 219–22.

more established family, rather than the second and most successful of four daughters of immigrant parents, she might have been able to turn to extended family or other resources at crisis points in her life (for example, fellow New Zealand writer Frank Sargeson was able to stay on his uncle's farm to escape gossip and regain confidence after a court case in Wellington).[*] When she jumped off the wharf at the bottom of Queen Street in Auckland on 2 June 1933, she might have been scooped into the privacy of that family or given extended private nursing care, instead of being taken to the *Delirium tremens* cells at Auckland Hospital and thence to the Lodge.

The fragility of her family's finances, especially in the Depression years, and their anxiety and at times judgmental attitudes (she was partially estranged from her parents, especially her father) meant that while her mother did offer some support it was not sufficient, and her collapses provoked medical intervention and therefore diagnoses, and perhaps even symptoms designed consciously or unconsciously to solicit help. Hyde's long-term financial independence (by 1933, she had been a working journalist for over ten years) meant that she needed to find a solution independent of her family; informed agency was involved both times she became a patient in facilities designed for borderline recoverable conditions. Her commitment to an asylum in 1927 was prevented by her own plea to see a locum whom she had met when she was pregnant with Robin, combined with her father's insistence; similarly in 1933 she strenuously resisted any suggestion that involved being admitted and committed to the main wards at Avondale Mental Hospital, asking to be guaranteed that this would not happen.[†]

It also happened that Hyde's breakdowns coincided with the opening of new voluntary wards, at Queen Mary Hospital at Hanmer – a first women's ward – and at Auckland Mental Hospital at Avondale – the Lodge – staffed with doctors whose

---

[*] Sargeson, then Norris Davey, was persuaded to 'dob in' an older lover, who was charged with corrupting him in a criminal case against homosexual sex acts, while Davey was given a suspended sentence on a charge of indecent assault. Following this incident in 1929 he retired from his law career, to spend eighteen months at his uncle's farm in the King Country before emerging with a new name to settle in Devonport, Auckland, where he pursued a writing career. See Michael King, *Frank Sargeson: A Life* (Auckland: Viking, 1995), 94, 96, 98, 107.

[†] 'Hyde opted for voluntary admission under the Mental Defectives Act (1911) by signing a form requesting treatment and agreeing not to leave without giving notice, after which she could legally be detained by her doctors for no more than seven days (part V, 39 (1)).' Alison Hunt, '"The Cage with the Open Door": Autobiography and Psychiatry in the Life and Works of Robin Hyde' (PhD: University of Auckland, 2008), 57.

tolerance of mental breakdown and attitudes to recovery were extremely useful to her. Twice she found a place to live and be cared for where her experience was validated and her work as a writer encouraged. At this time, what had previously been regarded as disturbances of behaviour with an organic (bodily or physical) explanation and treatment were beginning to be thought of by some as 'riddles of a disordered mind'* – riddles worth exploring because they were able to be disentangled in conversation and 'analysis' with specially trained mind doctors. Both of her stays in mental health facilities were positive. In five months at Hanmer in 1927 she was allowed to recover in a calm environment and wrote sequences of poems, published in the Christchurch *Sun* and collected in her first volume of poetry, *Desolate Star.* Then in 1933 at the Lodge she trusted her psychiatrist, Dr Gilbert Tothill, who advised her to write autobiographically in order to discover the source of her fear and anxieties. Her writing development was supported from then on for more than three years, with the provision of a spacious single room and eventually an attic study, parole to do research in libraries, as well as an available reader of her manuscripts (her doctor), who supported her recording her therapy and experience as part of a shared programme to humanise mental illness.

Published here for the first time after half a century and more in manuscript are two major documents written at the Lodge: the first her life story that Hyde was encouraged to write for therapeutic purposes ('1934 Autobiography') and, second, her fluent and analytical account of being there ('1935 Journal'). These documents can now be seen to be the raw material for the themes in Hyde's fiction and poetry (particularly the effects of childhood psychological damage, gender relations, and a punitive society), discussed in the second part of this Introduction, 'The Opening Door: The Writing'. Both documents, as well as the other shorter pieces included here, were written between late 1933 and 1936. These records of the success of Hyde's relationship with her psychiatrist and of her gradual recovery are examples of a humanising of mental problems that is relevant in our own times, when once again we emphasise bodily (chemical rather than nervous) disorders and when treatment has become predominantly psychopharmacological. They require us to think generally about how mental illness expresses itself and is regarded and treated at different times and in different societies. This is the task of this first part of the Introduction.

---

* Janet Oppenheim, *'Shattered Nerves': Doctors, Patients and Depression in Victorian England* (Oxford: Oxford University Press, 1991), 311.

Fear of the Asylum

The Auckland Mental Hospital at Avondale (like those in Britain) was a village of many facilities, including a farm, gardens, and church, situated on an elevated site overlooking the inner harbour. However, also as in Britain, by the 1920s and '30s it was overcrowded: in the main hospital the ratio of doctors to patients was extremely low and organisational matters took precedence over treatment. Fear of the asylum had been felt by the middle classes since the invention of the asylum system;* for Hyde, admission to an asylum would have represented a fall from her precarious professional status and a final disappointment to her mother's continuous attempts to protect and better the social status of the family. She also feared that if she was consigned to an asylum she would never come out, a not-unfounded fear, as, once committed, patients were often lost in the crowd and worsened in repetitious regimes. In many cases, they could remain patients for their whole lives and even if released were stigmatised in a way that made returning to a normal life impossible.

Specific origins of Hyde's fear of asylums are given in Chapter 6 of the '1934 Autobiography', where she describes how Olga (her pseudonym for the older sister of her best friend Gwen Hawthorn)† was committed to the asylum nearest Wellington, Porirua Hospital, as a rape victim rejected by her father, while in Chapter 9 she recalls a woman neighbour, who had attempted suicide by jumping out a window, being taken away 'to Porirua and she died'. And it was in Porirua that Hyde was almost a patient in 1927, when her father had torn up the committal papers before the doctor she requested referred her to a genuinely therapeutic hospital, the Queen Mary at Hanmer.

As Janet Oppenheim suggests of Virginia Stephen's treatment by her doctor George Savage,‡ diagnosis, the names and ideas of treatment, and the available facilities combined with factors of class and background to influence what happened to a life. Significantly, Savage treated Stephen (later Woolf):

as a neurasthenic who needed tranquillity, rest, sleep, and nourishment, not as a lunatic. Her official diagnosis was loss of nerve force, not loss of reason. … a working class patient would

---

* See Elaine Showalter's summary, *The Female Malady: Women, Madness and English Culture 1830–1980* (New York: Pantheon Books, 1985), 27.

† Later Mitcalfe. Hyde calls her 'Simone' in *Godwits* and in the '1934 Autobiography'.

‡ Oppenheim is commenting on what feminist critic Elaine Showalter saw as evidence of the tyranny exercised by Edwardian psychiatrists over women (*'Shattered Nerves'*, 107).

have quickly been admitted to a public asylum. Many were for less serious symptoms.[*]

The explanation for Robin Hyde's experience has a similar complexity. Roy Porter observes that mental health stories generally are a question not so much of good and bad psychiatry, as this history is often written, but of synchronicities of individual patients with individual doctors – 'the complex range of encounters'.[†] While Hyde's collapse in Auckland was fortuitously coincident with new moves in psychiatry and the interest at that time of Dr Gilbert Tothill and his colleague Dr Kathleen Todd[‡] in the use of talking (and life writing) therapy, it was also guided by her meeting with a particular Wellington general practitioner, by the enthusiastic Dr Buchanan (Medical Superintendent of Auckland Mental Hospital), who felt that the regime and doctors at the Lodge could help her (and who visited her six times in two weeks in June 1933 at Auckland Hospital, urging her to become a voluntary boarder), and by Buchanan's choice of Dr Tothill, his senior Medical Officer of Health who took over as her psychiatrist – a sympathetic, imaginative and non-judgmental character.[§] As an articulate and well-known young woman journalist who already knew something of the theory of repression and neurosis that Tothill and Todd were drawing on for 'borderline patients', Hyde was a perfect candidate for treatment, but she was also a sensitive and intelligent young woman who interested her doctors and who engaged with them in research into the mind and emotions.

The Auckland Hospital *Delirium Tremens* cells where Hyde was taken immediately

---

* Oppenheim, *'Shattered Nerves'*, 107–08.
† My thanks to Alison Hunt, who has drawn this point out of the encounter, quoting Roy Porter's claim that, although the 'history of psychiatric ideas and practices has conventionally been written as a saga of good versus bad psychiatry', in actuality 'the real protagonists are the doctors and patients, and the real subject the complex range of their encounters.' Roy Porter, *A Social History of Madness: The World Through the Eyes of the Insane* (New York: Weidenfeld and Nicholson, 1987), 231. Alison Hunt, 'Angel-Guarded Liar in a Pleasant, Quiet Room: Robin Hyde's Experiences in the New Zealand Mental Health System of the 1930s', *Lighted Windows*, 143.
‡ Although Todd is mentioned only once in Hyde's writings, her history is very interesting. See p. 48 for further discussion of the therapists working with Hyde, especially Dr Kathleen Todd.
§ For the most detailed and recent research relating to the treatment regimes favoured by Dr Henry Buchanan and his second, Dr Gilbert Tothill, Hyde's primary carer at the Lodge, see Hunt, 'Cage'. Also see Warwick Brunton, 'A Choice of Difficulties: National Mental Health Policy in New Zealand, 1840–1947' (PhD: University of Otago, 2001). More is yet to be discovered about psychiatry in New Zealand at this time.

after she was rescued from the Waitemata Harbour were primarily intended for men withdrawing from alcohol after binge drinking. The building holding these cells was situated on the edge of the Auckland Hospital, where it abuts the Domain, a large park in which the War Memorial Museum is also situated. The building, an annexe to a casualty department, was described by a nurse who had once worked there as:

> a barbaric out-house known as 'the cells'. The rooms had strong doors and small grills. To these rooms we admitted, on a temporary basis, alcoholics and other patients in various states of dementia. ... The bunch of keys and the small wire grills, and the noise of those poor patients will remain in the memories of many of us. The conditions of the annexe frequently hit the headlines in the daily newspapers, until a much improved observation unit was created down the hill in old ward 10.[*]

In spite of this unappealing environment, Hyde found some respite here, indicating how difficult her life had become. In the two weeks she spent in the cells, she wrote poems and sent them for publication to the *Auckland Star* and also received visitors, including upsettingly her editor-employer John Gordon McLean, and her chemist friend 'Father Time' or 'Joe', while Rosalie Rawlinson and her poet-daughter, Gloria, who revered Hyde as a writer (though they had never met her) sent a bunch of irises.[†] Hyde was anxious about the possibility of a criminal conviction for attempting suicide (although by this time such convictions were uncommon) and it seems that her employer was concerned that her drug use could be revealed, bringing her newspaper, the *New Zealand Observer,* into disrepute and identifying her chemist-friend supplier.[‡] She thought he was alarmist but was reluctant to leave the cells and had few better alternatives. Returning to work was impossible: McLean had sacked her or threatened to sack her on the day she jumped into the harbour and it was clear she had lost her Lady Editor status. Another possibility, a private nursing home, was beyond her means. She didn't want to return to her family and it was also financially impossible. The worst prospect of all – the one she terribly feared – was being committed to an asylum, in this case to the Auckland Mental Hospital at Avondale.

---

[*] Thelma Bollard, nursing in the old main building in the 1940s. David Scott (ed.), *The Story of Auckland Hospital 1847–1977* (Auckland: Medical Historical Library Committee of the Royal Australasian College of Physicians in New Zealand, 1977), 34–8.

[†] See '1934 Autobiography', p. 171.

[‡] Hunt discusses Hyde's drug use in both her illness and diagnosis ('Cage', 231–42). She also outlines a use of drug 'therapy' in the Lodge that may have contributed to distortions of the mind ('cross-over'), including auditory and visual hallucinations ('Cage', 230–1).

Failure of the Asylums

The history of the asylums and their doctors – known as 'mad doctors', 'alienists' and only later (by the early twentieth century) as 'psychiatrists' – is a significant part of the larger picture of how insanity and mental breakdown were understood and treated by the 1930s. Asylums such as Avondale Mental Hospital, when built in the second half of the nineteenth century, were inspired (like their British counterparts) by the revolutionary belief that good environment and exemplary regimes of behaviour and moral management could explain behaviour and reform the mad and 'break with the crude coercion of the past'.[*] The asylums were ideologically framed as 'home-like mental institutions that would tame and domesticate madness and bring it into the sphere of rationality'.[†] Their optimistic philosophy was tested in focused British innovations as early as the late eighteenth century, such as the York Retreat, but the 'chimera of the curative asylum'[‡] came to be pursued on a vast scale partly as a result of legislation in 1845 that made all counties in Britain responsible for the care of the insane.

Colney Hatch, the largest and most costly asylum in England, was opened in Middlesex in 1851, in the same year as the Great Exhibition and comparable to that great celebration of the British Empire in scale and intent. The high point of Victorianism was expressed by the building of these palaces: Colney Hatch featured 'a spectacular Italianate facade a third of a mile long' with all manner of ornamentation, six miles of wards and corridors, and was planned to hold 1250 patients. Included in its grounds were 'a chapel, a stable, a farm and a cemetery'.[§] These villages were typically built on elevated and healthy sites. In New Zealand's case, similar developments were in coastal areas on the edges of townships; their edifices still

---

[*] Andrew Scull, *The Most Solitary of Afflictions: Madness and Society in Britain, 1700–1900* (New Haven and London: Yale University Press, 1993), 379.

[†] Showalter, *The Female Malady,* 17: 'domesticate' is a term she takes from Andrew Scull. The building of asylums was also designed to clean up the previous degradation and neglect that those mentally disturbed or unable to work had suffered, particularly the very poor and working classes, to remove as Dickens wrote: 'the chains, straw and filthy solitude' of Bedlam (Showalter, 97).

[‡] Andrew Scull, *Hysteria: The Biography* (Oxford: Oxford University Press, 2009), 63. For a full study of this extremely complex history of changes in the 'cultural meaning of madness' and the innovations and developments in nineteenth-century treatments and ideas, see also Scull, *The Most Solitary of Afflictions*.

[§] Showalter, *The Female Malady,* 23.

stand today either as crumbling ruins or revitalised as educational facilities – even in one case as a horror theme park – and their attractive names resonate with sad histories: Seacliff, Sunnyside, Avondale, Oakley, Porirua, Kingseat, Tokanui.

These palaces of beneficence to the poor and infirm, the mad and the disabled did not live up to expectations. The idea of a therapeutic community was to allow patients to recover in an orderly, productive and tranquil setting, but the needs of the authorities and the population directed otherwise. For complex reasons – poor families keen to have their infirm or confused family members looked after,[*] authorities wanting vagrants confined and the insane accounted for – the asylum population exploded, so that almost immediately there was severe overcrowding. In Britain, where – after decades of warfare, emigration and industrialisation – there were more women than men in the population and considerable feminisation of poverty, female patients outnumbered men, while in New Zealand the population was more male so the reverse was true, at least until the early twentieth century.[†] And in Britain, many of those who under the old poor laws would have been supported briefly were now detained or made incapable for life.

Almost as soon as these great clean-up and think-big projects to build asylums throughout the land were launched, their failure was being proclaimed. However, in spite of the publicised and researched discovery that asylums were serving more as detention centres than retreats for respite and that cure rates were falling, there was no move towards the closing of the asylums or treatment in the community. Instead, their poor performance was laid at the door of hereditary and incurable conditions.[‡] Andrew Scull argues that physical and hereditary degeneracy then began to be touted

---

[*] See Scull, *The Most Solitary of Afflictions*, 332.

[†] See Judith Holloway, '"Unfortunate Folk": A study of the Social Context of Committal to Seacliff 1928–1937' in Barbara Brookes and Jane Thomson (eds), *'Unfortunate Folk': Essays on Mental Health Treatment 1863–1992* (Dunedin: University of Otago Press, 2001). At Seacliff, apart from in 1935–7, men outnumbered women: 'For men, as for women, the way in which they manifested their mental distress revealed much about the pressures exerted upon them to realise their gender roles. In an era of social change and economic depression the internal contradictions of these were heightened.' (165) For example, men were expected to provide but couldn't if they were out of work.

[‡] 'Prominent English alienists', including Henry Maudsley and Andrew Wynter (founder of the *British Medical Journal),* were amongst the critics of asylums. Scull, *The Most Solitary of Afflictions,* 318. His section, 'The Critics of Asylumdom' 315–33, links the failure of asylums and the late nineteenth-century shift to ideas of innate degeneracy.

as an explanation of why certain groups (or classes) of people were powerless and in penury.[*] The late nineteenth-century fear of reverse-evolutionary tendencies in society and in the population, and of racial and national degeneracy, became linked to the treatment of insanity and social policy generally in both Britain and the United States, a tendency which morphed in the inter-war years into a fully fledged theory of eugenics that was influential in many European and colonised countries. New Zealand followed this pattern in its organisation and sequestering of different groups; in the period during which Robin Hyde was hospitalised, and concurrent with the opening of hospitals and clinics for recoverable cases, psychopaedic hospitals were established for those children considered to be innately mentally degenerate.[†]

Borderline Recoverable?
From nervous breakdown to mood disorders

The Lodge to which Hyde agreed to be admitted[‡] in July 1933 and again in December of that year had been built some twenty years before as a hospital superintendent's home (most recently Superintendent Buchanan's) and was renovated for patients in 1931, only two years before Hyde's admission, as part of a response to the problems of the asylum system. It was a free-standing homestead at the top corner of the site, with a view of the sea and overlooking the extensive grounds of the Auckland Mental Hospital at Avondale. It is now part of a polytechnic (first Carrington, now UNITEC) that has utilised the asylum buildings and grounds since they were decommissioned in the early 1990s. The Lodge had two storeys and an attic. On the ground floor were living and dining rooms, a service wing and some nurses' accommodation; an imposing main staircase with plenty of woodwork to be polished led up to a wide landing, which featured stained-glass windows, and off that landing were several large dormitory-like bedrooms, a closed verandah also with

---

[*] Similar fears of degeneration also emerged as British recruits from the industrial working classes for the Boer War failed their health examinations and as ideas of social Darwinism became more prevalent and 'In the wake of the disastrous Boer War fears for national standards of physique reached a peak'. Anna Davin, 'Imperialism and Motherhood', *History Workshop Journal* 5, Spring 1977, 10.

[†] A contemporary of Hyde, and survivor of the Templeton Psychopaedic Hospital near Christchurch, Norm Madden, was the subject of a 1997 documentary, *Out of Sight, Out of Mind* (Frank Film). He was taken to the hospital aged five years when found stealing a pie and unable to write his own name.

[‡] See Hunt, 'Cage', 43–67, and 'Angel-Guarded Liar', *Lighted Windows*, 143–50.

beds, and two single bedrooms, housing in all about twenty-three women patients. The house was approached by a circular driveway, enclosing (as Hyde describes) fragrant flowerbeds. Behind the house were tennis courts and a croquet ground, more gardens tended by the patients, as well as gardens and treed grasslands leading down to a creek – with views thenceforth to the coast. While the voluntary men's ward (the Wolfe Home) was purpose-built and part of the admission ward, the Lodge was separate in appearance and street address (37 Gladstone Road, now Carrington Road) and offered some disguise to patients, which Hyde utilised regularly in her correspondence.

The Lodge was seen as a ward for nervous disorders and for patients who were rational if highly disturbed. It was part of the public health system; although patients were asked to pay board, there was a clear understanding that should a patient not be able to pay (this was during the Great Depression) they would still be treated and able to stay on. On the other hand, there was vigilance in identifying free-loaders.[*]

The terminology and explanations of borderline conditions are relevant to Hyde's experience as they record the complex and often contradictory social and medical inheritance of the time. The Lodge, the men's voluntary ward in the Wolfe Home and another smaller house/ward adjacent (a back-up for extremely nervous patients who needed strict bed rest) were described interchangeably as being for 'borderline', 'neuropathic' or 'neurasthenic' patients. The terms neuropathic and neurasthenic indicated an explanation of nervous collapse that predicated much of the treatment at the Lodge and its bodily emphasis. Since the mid-nineteenth century, neurological research and explanations had set the scene for talking about anxiety and depression and various other mood changes. And from the 1860s 'neurasthenia' had mostly replaced 'hysteria' or 'hysteric' as the term to indicate a physical explanation. The idea of hysteria being explained by a link with the uterus had 'lost all credibility by the Georgian [pre-Victorian] era', but in the early nineteenth century medicine 'still credited the uterus with a formidable power to disrupt the workings of the nerves'.[†] However neurasthenia, by pertaining to both men and women, moved diagnosis on from the notion of a condition that women were specifically liable to get. It was the 'discovery' or coinage of Charles Beard, a New York neurologist, which built on older ideas of susceptibility to nervous disorders, especially amongst the educated,

---

[*] Hunt, 'Cage', 57.
[†] Oppenheim, *'Shattered Nerves'*, 187.

and included a wide range of symptoms that it was supposed would be identified in brain lesions as more became known of that organ's inner workings.

Beard put most emphasis on neurasthenia as a problem of challenging, stressful and competitive modern times, and its sufferers as sensitive casualties of 'the dynamism of American life'[*] (and of other similarly developed societies). The idea that sensitive and ambitious types were particularly likely to use up their reserves of nervous energy gave some scope to patients, as it suggested that willpower and balanced regulation of everyday life could aid in avoiding nervous collapse. The proposed diagnosis was neurological and therefore physical, with physical or somatic treatments, and no suggestion of mental or psychological responses.

The best approach to neurasthenia was thought to be in the Weir Mitchell[†] cure, which consisted of withdrawal from home, bed-rest and feeding-up. Aspects of this treatment were first applied to Hyde in early 1927, when her father was asked to move out of their Wellington house while she was nursed, and later in the same year when she was removed to the seclusion of Queen Mary Hospital in Hanmer Springs. Similarly, at the Lodge, Hyde was at first confined to bed, not allowed to go outside at night for the first year, and was fed a milk and high-iron diet. Indeed, special diets were prescribed throughout her residency and even afterwards: in 'A Night of Hell' she describes, for example, the black pudding diet she is obliged to follow.[‡]

Ben Shephard, who traces the history of treatments in his *A War of Nerves: Soldiers and Psychiatrists in the Twentieth* Century, explains that the Weir Mitchell cure was 'advertised' as 'entire rest' and felt to be particularly effective for female patients: men might respond better to 'fresh air and foreign cruises'.[§] While this neurologist's diagnosis and cure was initially advertised and designed for private middle-class patients, it 'lost its class specificity'[¶] as it spread to other countries and societies, like New Zealand, where 'doctors worked for the state'. It also became a useful category for alienists (asylum doctors) grappling with what to do with

---

[*] Ben Shephard, *A War of Nerves: Soldiers and Psychiatrists in the Twentieth Century* (Cambridge, Mass.: Harvard University Press, 2001), 9.

[†] Silas Weir Mitchell was a 'nineteenth-century American neurologist and novelist' who invented a 'famous rest cure' and 'grew rich on the proceeds from the hundreds of hysterics who annually crowded into his Philadelphia consulting rooms' (Scull, *Hysteria,* 6–7).

[‡] 'A Night of Hell', published in *A Home in this World* (Auckland: Longman Paul, 1984).

[§] Shephard, *A War of Nerves*, 10.

[¶] Shephard, 10.

borderline patients.[*]

Shephard identifies the continuity of these ideas into the Edwardian age, when Hyde was a child. Then, 'nervous breakdown' was still a popular term and a condition that literary people, in particular, were seen as 'prone to'; 'there is scarcely an Edwardian writer who did not have one', he writes, including Oscar Wilde, Virginia Woolf and Rupert Brooke in his list.[†]

However, Janet Oppenheim, an historian of depression, suggests in her book 'Shattered Nerves' that by the beginning of the twentieth century a complex social shift in the conception of heredity and evolution turned the concept of neurasthenia around, giving it a more sinister resonance than initially, and disrupting its favourable connection with earlier, particularly eighteenth-century, ideas: 'No longer an essentially admirable quality marking a superior sort of person, the late Victorians and Edwardians feared that such delicacy might be nothing less than an agent of racial degeneration and national decline'.[‡] And in The Female Malady, Elaine Showalter observes that the 'most characteristic and revealing metaphor of Darwinian psychiatry was that of the "borderland," the shadowy territory between sanity and madness which sheltered "latent brain disease" and the "seeds of nervous disorders."'[§]

This shift in reputation of 'nervous' sensitivity is significant for Hyde because it means that while she did at times see her own excitableness and fragility as allying her with artists from Shelley to Wilde and beyond, she was also anxious at the suggestion of degeneracy and inherited flaws in both her and her family. Fears of degeneracy were particularly discoursed around the family – so intense was this that for many doctors 'the family was demarcated not so much by shared values and memories as by the morbid traits circulating amongst its members'.[¶] This discourse of anxiety is clearly evident in Hyde's family portrait in her bio-fictional novel The Godwits Fly. Feminism and women's education, homosexuality and male sexuality were also implicated in the panic about decline in the quality of the population.

---

[*] 'Borderline' is a term used since the nineteenth century to suggest 'on the borders of insanity' or in another terminology 'neurotic' rather than 'psychotic'. It seems to be distinct from the diagnostic phrase 'borderline personality disorder'.

[†] Shephard, 10.

[‡] Oppenheim, 'Shattered Nerves', 273–4.

[§] Showalter, The Female Malady, 105.

[¶] Oppenheim, 'Shattered Nerves', 277.

Oppenheim writes: 'Medical literature abounded with tragic tales of intelligent young women rendered invalids (if not corpses) by their determination to obtain academic honours intended for men'.[*]

But there is another element that we need to examine in order to understand this complex of mental health ideas prevailing by the 1930s – specifically, the development of the ideas of psychotherapy and psychoanalysis.

Psychotherapy and Psychoanalysis

In the late nineteenth century, there being no neurological breakthrough in finding physical explanations for depression, anxiety, anorexia, and other behaviours and experiences we now think of as mood disorders, another approach was evolving. Beginning with Charcot's experiments in hypnosis and Freud's treatment of young female hysterics, a theory was developed that nervous or mental breakdown was not a consequence of depleted nervous energy (or other physical causes) but of unconscious habits and repetitions of the mind which resulted from difficult, often love or libidinal, experiences and that these habits could be investigated, understood and remedied by specially trained medical specialists. At the *fin de siècle*, however, more than one psycho-therapy was being promulgated. There were also objections to the negativity of psychoanalysis as allowing 'men and women to wallow in the very miseries that obsessed them'.[†] James Crichton-Browne was arguing that 'in a vast number of cases it should be the aim of a rational psycho-therapy to withdraw the patient's mind from the contemplation of an objectionable and painful past and from ferreting out various reminiscences, and to occupy it with prospective duties, and wholesome pursuits, and sure and certain hopes'.[‡] Eventually a version of Freud's ideas took precedence: Dean Rapp writes that Freudian ideas were 'circulating in academic circles' in Britain from 1900, and were, 'minus the sexual theories', 'accepted in broad terms by the intellectual community, if not the psychiatric establishment.'[§] Commenting on the application of Freud's ideas during and post

---

[*] Oppenheim, *'Shattered Nerves'*, 195.

[†] Oppenheim, *'Shattered Nerves'*, 307.

[‡] Quoted in Scull, *The Most Solitary of Afflictions*, 387 n.42.

[§] Dean Rapp, 'The Discovery of Freud by the British General Public, 1912–1919', in *Social History of Medicine,* vol. 3, no.2 (August 1990), 217–43, cited in Jennifer Styles, 'Men and the Development of Psychiatry in New Zealand in the 1920s and 1930s' (MA: University of Canterbury, 1997), 56

World War I, he wrote that it was the extreme nature of war that was the new element: 'The conditions that the soldiers had to endure were at the heart of psychic conflict that caused distress and "flight" into illness'.[*]

During World War I, Sigmund Freud turned his attention to 'shell-shock'. He and others (including the well-known Scottish psychiatrist Rivers)[†] found that a system of talking and uncovering suppressed memories and naming war experiences explained and relieved what Freud called 'conversion symptoms' (symptoms such as paralysis, mutism, and screaming fits) that he argued were the consequence of unconscious and irresolvable mental conflicts being converted to physical behaviours.

The significance of the success of this treatment was that these patients were previously sane and capable young men who appeared to have no inherited debility but became mentally incapacitated as a consequence of experiential or mental trauma. Their diagnosis and recovery was an argument that insanity/sanity was not a binary but a diagnosis of a state on a continuum, which could befall anyone. This new awareness of the possibility of previously well and moral citizens suffering mental crises from which they could recover led to the integration of what were previously regarded as extreme or irrelevant Freudian ideas of psychoanalysis into mainstream psychiatric medicine.

But while mental and psychological explanations slowly became influential, their adoption was by no means systematic; new approaches sometimes overlapped earlier, even contradictory, ideas – such as the physical treatment discussed earlier and 'moral regimes' of behaviour modification. The 'talking cure' that Freud had developed with young women hysterics (the famous young hysteric Anna O coined the phrase),[‡] and that now extended into the treatment of soldiers, was only intermittently taken up in ongoing and civilian treatment. Andrew Scull suggests it was only ever popular amongst the 'chattering classes' in Britain, a superficial change confined to the middle class that he contrasts with the United States, where psychoanalysis was embraced and became standard treatment in individual, private and state contexts by the 1930s and especially post World War II. Hyde's 'Essay on Mental Health' included in this book (p. 295) refers to United States writers and

---

* Rapp quoted in Styles, 'Men and the Development of Psychiatry in New Zealand', 56.
† W.H.R. Rivers, an army doctor who worked with traumatised soldiers, is known beyond the world of psychiatry and medical history because of the dramatisation of his methods in the *Regeneration Trilogy* by novelist Pat Barker, specifically the first novel *Regeneration* (1991).
‡ Scull, *Hysteria*, 135.

contexts because that was where research and psychoanalytic therapy was taking place; almost certainly it was written with United States publication in mind. Andrew Scull also emphasises 'it would be easy to construct a link between recognition of shell-shock's psychogenic origins and a more understanding "kinder" therapy'. But he corrects, 'Easy, but wrong'.[*] Janet Oppenheim cautions in a similar way against seeing the use of some Freudian ideas of conversion and conflicted-ness in the treatment of shell-shock in Britain as a sign of a revolution in treatment generally.[†]

The uneven adoption of Freudian ideas was perhaps even more so in New Zealand. Theodore Gray, Director General of the Mental Hospitals Department,[‡] visited mental institutions overseas in 1927. This didn't change his view that the 'causation of mental disorder' was hereditary and/or poor upbringing in unwholesome surroundings.[§] He thought, contrary to the theories about trauma being applied in Britain, that shell-shocked servicemen must already have been inferior types, and was said to have resisted the new ideas and language of psychoanalysis, which he described as 'bosh'.[¶] His opinions are typical of the degeneracy hypothesis or fears that Oppenheim describes for this period.

---

[*] Scull, *Hysteria*, 168. He suggests that extreme and physical techniques used to punish and get soldiers back to their regiments were more common. The idea of psychological causes, if not combined with an idea of the unconscious, caused fears of malingering. There was no wholesale abandoning of a regime of behaviour modification, or of the idea that symptoms were a failure of will that justified 'the infliction of painful, almost sadistic, remedies' (Scull, 168), where soldiers had paralysed arms shocked or electrodes applied to the pharynx to force speech (Scull, 171). These 'techniques were bitterly resented by troops and their families' but it was only in Germany, where a regime was defeated, that briefly there was 'revolutionary fever' against such treatment and 'neurologists were chased from their offices' with 'dark talk of revenge' (Scull, 173).

[†] The tendency to see abrupt (rather than blended) changes in social and medical ideas is illustrated by Elaine Showalter in *The Female Malady*. Showalter divides her study (of English expression and treatment of female hysteria) into three periods: psychiatric determinism, psychiatric Darwinism and psychiatric modernism, seeing the development from Victorianism to Darwinism as facilitated by the failure of asylums, and the move from Darwinism to modernism by male hysteria/shell-shock.

[‡] From 1928 to 1947, and before that between 1924 and 1927.

[§] From Gray's 'Draft Report on Visits of Inspection to Various Institutions in Great Br, America and the Continent', quoted in Styles, 'Men and the Development of Psychiatry in New Zealand', 66.

[¶] Styles, 'Men and the Development of Psychiatry in New Zealand', 65.

In his tour report, Gray's solutions to possibly borderline or neurotic disturbances seem to be the 'good sunlight and fresh air' formula that was the 'ubiquitous' solution in New Zealand social and educational policy in the 1920s.[*] As mentioned earlier, Hyde was not allowed to go out at night – 'I never saw the moon', she says (she couldn't see it from her room).[†] Lying on the grass watching the stars and moon was clearly not a favoured activity, although it was one of her favourites; there was also a set bed-time and Hyde was often reprimanded for reading after the 9 pm lights-out.[‡] Gray's report suggests neurological diagnosis and somatic treatment, combined with moral hygiene and good behaviour: 'I returned more convinced that in the treatment of recent and recoverable mental disorders, our main resources are to be found in providing the elementary requirements, namely fresh air, sunshine, hydrotherapy … suitable diet, exercise, recreation, rest and sleep, everything indeed conducive to the establishment of active, regular, daily habits and the restoration of the full enjoyment of the daytime – thus inducing the organism to the normal reaction of sound and refreshing sleep at night.'[§]

Despite the disparagement of the new, and sometimes considered weirdly sexual, diagnoses and talking cures being explored in Britain and in European clinics at that time (where the interest was turning to psychoses), the idea of employing specially trained doctors in specially designed hospitals and clinics for borderline cases was one of the few innovations directly developed from Freudian ideas that really took root in both Britain[¶] and New Zealand by the 1920s and '30s.

Hyde's young psychiatrist Gilbert Tothill trained in Britain between the wars. There, by 1939, 100 centres for neurasthenic ex-servicemen and civilians had been set up, to which general practitioners were directed by the Ministry of Pensions to refer patients. Practitioners were trained in psychotherapy and the 'mainstream medical literature included a much wider range of material on the treatment of the

---

[*] Styles elaborates: '[t]hat the New Zealand environment was inherently more salubrious than life in the cities of the "old world" was an enduring piece of colonialist propaganda' (35).

[†] 'For a little more than a year, I never saw the moon. I can't from this room, and I wasn't allowed out'. '1935 Journal', 2nd entry 11 pm, p. 192.

[‡] '1934 Autobiography', Chapter 8, p. 93. Hunt, 'Cage', 188.

[§] From Gray's 'Draft Report on Visits of Inspection to Various Institutions in Great Br, America and the Continent', quoted in Styles, Men and the Development of Psychiatry in New Zealand, 36–7.

[¶] Oppenheim, 'Shattered Nerves', 311.

neuroses'.* Tothill's training for a diploma in psychological medicine was at Long Grove Mental Hospital, where there were options to specialise in psychopathology and psychotherapy.†

In New Zealand, even the most sceptical of administrators and doctors (like Gray) were able to preside over national changes that were designed to separate recoverable from incurable cases.‡ The development of separate facilities was initially in response to the situation of returned servicemen: not only was the discovery being made that their insanity was induced by trauma, but it was also argued that it was disrespectful to throw men who had served 'King and Country' into the mainstream asylums or mental hospitals. Queen Mary Hospital at Hanmer, originally opened for returned soldiers in 1916 and transferred to the Department of Health in the early 1920s, was a state facility. Private mental hospitals were few in number, Ashburn Hall in Dunedin, founded in 1882, being one of these.

In 1911, the committal legislation was adjusted to allow for voluntary admissions to mental hospitals: the change from 'asylum' to 'hospital' was an associated move to lessen the stigma of admission and encourage the afflicted to seek help. Structural changes to the process of admission and treatment, the physical layout of institutions, and an increased emphasis on the role of the mental hospital as a specialist hospital with associated laboratories occupied the pages of the asylum doctors' *Journal of Mental Science*.§

Overall, the consensus of researchers seems to be that the real impact of shell-shock on the practice of psychiatry in New Zealand was in the growing emphasis on differentiating between 'acute' and chronic cases of mental illness. The development of the 'villa' system, the establishment of outpatient services at the major general

---

* Styles, 'Men and the Development of Psychiatry in New Zealand', 58.
† Hunt, 'Cage', 159.
‡ The other extreme, of the least recoverable, were also separated at this time with the opening (for example) of psychopaedic hospitals. Styles comments, 'The patient population was rigorously classified in the early twentieth century' (33) 'Extensions that were advocated for "early" cases or sufferers of incipient insanity were paralleled by the development of farm colonies for the chronically incapacitated … moved further from the main centres of population (34).
§ Styles, 'Men and the Development of Psychiatry in New Zealand', 34. For example T.E. Knowles Stansfield, 'The Villa or Colony System', *The Journal of Mental Science*, vol. LX, no. 248 (1914), 30.

hospitals and of 'admission cottages or wards at the mental hospitals'[*] bring us to the other name by which the Lodge was known.

Voluntary Villas

As we have seen, the villa system arose partly out of the psychological challenge to neurologists' theories of borderline insanity and was largely a development of the private and clinical specialities. In New Zealand the small facilities were government funded, whereas in Britain they were often private. When the Lodge opened in 1931, it was as part of New Zealand's policy of creating voluntary villas akin to private nursing homes, staffed by psychiatrists, matrons and nursing staff paid for by the national mental health system. These villas were intended to be very different from the big asylums or 'mental hospitals' (as they were by then re-named): they were located at some remove from these institutions and they treated small numbers of patients under specialist psychiatric care.

Both the Lodge and Wolfe Home at Avondale (a wing of which was the men's voluntary ward) were opened as a consequence of these new policies, as were similar wards at the other mental hospitals. The intention was to remove stigma, and to allow for recovery and time away from home without institutionalisation actually worsening the patient's condition. No longer were people in mental distress to be taken to prison while awaiting examination; they were 'to be spared the distress and humiliation of being treated as delinquents or criminals'.

In 1927, police officers were told they must not wear uniform nor use police vans to escort patients to mental hospitals. All patients were to be transported by taxi, no matter how disturbed or difficult. Once at the mental hospitals, new patients were not to be brought within sight of the main asylum building or the inmates. Immediately on arrival, they were to go instead to 'an attractive home-like entry lodge or other suitable place out of sight of the main institution'.[†]

In these wards/lodges/villas for the borderline nervous patients, the 'volunteers' were allowed to wear their own clothes and to follow recreational pursuits, as well as help to run and clean the house, and take some parole. From 1935, occupational therapy added to this approach, but was probably in effect quite similar to the practice

---

[*]   Wendy Hunter Williams, *Out of Mind, Out of Sight: the story of Porirua Hospital* (Porirua: Porirua Hospital, 1987), 66–7.

[†]   Williams, *Out of Mind, Out of Sight*, 89, is describing Porirua under Truby King.

at the Lodge from its opening – Buchanan was an early proponent of OT. However, without radically altered ideas of treatment, some of this approach must have seemed like window dressing; similar regimes of good behaviour, reward and punishment probably prevailed in the main wards. For example, Hyde didn't like the matron at the Lodge, who, she thought, felt she had special privileges and should be cleaning the floor rather than writing, suggesting that the matron had an idea of appropriate behaviour for a female patient that did not include writing and reading.

One of the Last Great Divas

Robin Hyde comes late to the list of women artists and thinkers who have suffered mental illness and been claimed as acting out feminist protest. She would also easily rank in the genealogy descending from Mary Wollstonecraft that features in Elaine Showalter's *Inventing Herself: Claiming a Feminist Intellectual Heritage.*[*] Not that all of the women discussed by Showalter suffered mental collapses, but of those who do their episodes are viewed as feminist protest and unconscious expression of the social conflicts of femininity.[†]

Writing in 1995, Janet Oppenheim argued with what she saw as particular orthodoxies being created about women's history and takes Showalter's approach as exemplary:

> In recent years the paramount psychological theory with regard to nineteenth-century women has fastened on the concept of rebellion. The conclusion now almost unquestioned amongst feminist scholars that is middle-class Victorian women subconsciously turned to illness to vent their rage against limited unsatisfactory lives, devoid of personal significance and imposed on them by the tyranny of a male-dominated society. Through sickness, the argument claims, their rebellion allowed them to escape from endless service to others by forcing others to serve them, while society could not condemn a form of insubordination that confirmed standard expectations of female weakness.[‡]

Her assertion is about the nineteenth century but the orthodoxy she speaks of has been widened to include many cases of mental breakdown, especially of prominent women thinkers and artists who have come to be seen as a gallery of those who acted out their rebellion in the only way allowed to women, by illness. In her account,

---

[*] New York: Scribner, 2001.

[†] Her interpretation followed on from her development of this idea in her 1985 work, *The Female Malady*.

[‡] Oppenheim, *'Shattered Nerves'*, 225.

Oppenheim specifically quotes and refutes Elaine Showalter's assertions in *The Female Malady*, explaining Showalter's claim thus:

> It was the refusal of these women 'to adjust to the "inevitable" conditions of their lives' and their 'rebellion against their sex roles' that 'led to an unprecedented wave of nervous disorders' in the second half of the nineteenth century.

Oppenheim's contention is that the specificity of each case is obscured in this large, gestured generalisation, but she seems particularly concerned at the implicit use of Freud in the mix, and the suggestion that women unconsciously turned to illness, which can replicate a picture of women as different and passive. Her rejoinder is that:

> The encounters with depression that scarred, or terminated, the lives of these women seem to demand due acknowledgment that an entire cultural milieu can potentially contribute to nervous breakdown. The problem was not just that the boredom and emptiness of many women's lives, spent without intellectual stimulation or meaningful work could end in melancholy, apathy and physical malaise, as many contemporaries, both male and female, pointed out before World War I. It was that attempts to rectify the situation involved struggles against social expectations, cultural stereotypes and social practices, which left the fighter physically exhausted and mentally depressed thereby earning the diagnosis of nervous collapse.*

Oppenheim's clarification sits well with the case of Hyde. Although her social milieu was different – she lived and worked as one of the first generation of career women – she did struggle against social expectations (in both revelation and concealment), as Oppenheim describes.

Another way to see this discussion is in terms of mental illness always having an expression in relation to its time and society. If Showalter's argument is that the explosion and then disappearance of hysteria shows that it was a sign symbolising the relation between society and the individual, it would also be possible to argue that the expression of mental states has a niche in every age – and not just for women. Some conditions are solved by treatment, some get re-named according to fashions in terminology, but one can also argue that the range of expressable symptoms is socially determined because of changing fashions in how extremes of emotion and mental states are expressed (linguistically and narratively) to meet a possible diagnosis.

Showalter is explicit about the political motivation of feminist orthodoxy when she records that 'hysteria', a term that had denigrated women and biologised their

---

* Oppenheim, *'Shattered Nerves'*, 225.

behaviour, was reclaimed by feminists from the 1970s on as the first step on the road to feminism;[*] feminist historians and literary critics have been very interested in it partly as a sign symbolising the relationship between society and the individual.

However, Scull and Oppenheim's words caution against what this political generalisation might obscure. The specifics of how Hyde's mental illness developed, and the mental pain she suffered, tend to support Oppenheim's contention that she was suffering mental and physical fatigue from struggling against social conventions. When Hyde said 'I needed madness if I were to survive',[†] she seems to have meant both that madness gave her a place to live and write, and that it gave her time in a newly positive social environment.

Modern Woman: Gender in the inter-war years

Those familiar with Robin Hyde's work will know this summary of her soon-to-be out-of-datedness from *A Home in this World*:

> … so in time will an Iris Wilkinson, knocking her head on the ground and her bleeding knuckles on the door, seem extremely queer to those who have learned to be happy without self-consciousness.

> Just the same, I will carry my skinned knuckles and sometimes abject countenance through life, and so will a good many other women. If another generation is allowed to do the same thing, I say, more fools men: for a woman can be a pretty thing when she is happy, and a soul, like a cloth, becomes heavy to carry when it is sodden through with tears.[‡]

What was it about life in the early part of the twentieth century that she was referring to? Hyde's sense was that women's lives were changing profoundly and that stigma around the expression of female sexuality and female emotions would soon become outdated. She was also alluding to the sombre, judgmental mood of the family and society in which she grew up: 'No mercy, only a thin soupy trickle of "charity" was ever preached to us. If we have practised better, it is because we have learned the art for ourselves. I can laugh now at the comicality of distressing myself over the little things that happened in my life …'.[§]

When Hyde turned twenty in 1926, women's suffrage had been a reality for

---

* Elaine Showalter, *Hystories: Hysterical Epidemics and Modern Media* (New York: Columbia University Press, 1998), 10.
† *A Home*, 94.
‡ *A Home*, 28.
§ *A Home*, 12.

thirty years, but political change had not necessarily altered structures or prevailing social attitudes to support the emergence of the 'new woman'. As in other countries, the post-war period in New Zealand was a time when the problems that intelligent women faced in combining the challenges of career and personal life became obvious. Indeed in the United States, following the unity of the suffrage movement, 1925 was seen as the moment when the women's movement collapsed and factionalised.[*] From this time, issues for women came to be framed differently: 'progress, or lack of it, was to be measured in individual terms',[†] with 'a new emphasis on psychology, personal fulfilment and the problems of the individual psyche'.[‡]

Another New Zealand novelist, Jane Mander, obliged to return from New York to her home in Auckland in the 1930s, made blunt comments on finding set gender roles that she considered were already challenged earlier in the century, describing New Zealanders as 'mentally and spiritually one of the most backward peoples on earth'.[§] Her opinion suggests, too, that post World War I and as the depression of the 1920s became the Depression of the 1930s, New Zealand society switched to an unmodulated and compulsory domesticity for women, in line with local settler society ideas of psychology and personal fulfilment.

Like the women writing in New York in the 1920s, Hyde sometimes rejected women's past public gains: her comments on women in politics or social work positions tend to be impatient; she wanted a lighter approach to the world than a do-gooder one and preferred the tricks of the male politicians to the stuffiness of the female office-holders. At times she was also suffocated by the prospect of traditional married life; her personal aspirations included a career, a sexual life and maternity. Perhaps the latter is especially preoccupying in her work because of the natalist (or child-bearing) emphasis in government and public policy in most European and developed countries that was characteristic of the inter-war period, contradictory

---

* Elaine Showalter (ed.), *These Modern Women: Autobiographical Essays from the Twenties* (New York: The Feminist Press, 1978), 9.

† Showalter, *These Modern Women,* 10. In her introduction to this collection of autobiographical essays by a group of successful professional women originally published in the periodical *The Nation* in New York in 1926 and 1927, Elaine Showalter comments that the women were of the generation that still called themselves feminists, but they were like those who followed in seeing structural change as over, and issues as now individual.

‡ Showalter, *These Modern Women,* 8.

§ Quoted by Lawrence Jones, 'The Novel', in Terry Sturm (ed.), *The Oxford History of New Zealand Literature* (Auckland: Oxford University Press, 1991), 124.

though it often was with what was happening.

Writers and bohemian women in metropolitan centres were risking different sorts of lives, but to the respectable and upwardly mobile middle and lower-middle classes they were also a terrible spectre of social failure, probably more so in newer societies where the idea of the 'New Woman' sparked animosity. New Zealand historian Barbara Brookes, writing on shame, suggests that there was a social consensus at this time that being an unmarried mother once (if the baby was adopted out) could be accommodated and a new relationship and marriage could take place but to be an unmarried mother twice was beyond the social pale. Relatedly, she comments: 'A "shameless" woman who had given birth to more than one illegitimate child was unlikely to be received sympathetically'.[*] Janet Oppenheim maintains that the sexual theories about neurosis put forward by Freud increased a feeling of shame about breakdown and depression. The sexualised mocking of women writers in this period, internationally, was part of the new freedom to name and interpret women's sexual motivations,[†] while fear and anxiety about the New Woman may have contributed to the development of that ubiquitous figure in film noir and other cultural texts post World War II, the femme fatale.

Lisa Appignanesi goes further, in seeing 'disturbances of love' as characteristic of these times, both as women were freed to think of themselves as having a sexuality, and as psychological discourse employed sexuality as the mystery to be diagnosed:

> It is hardly surprising if the conflict between new liberties and old laws played itself out in both symptoms and diagnoses. Erotomania [in] its newly amplified guise, compounded with persecutory delusions, … reflected some of the disorder of the times, the contradictory liberties, demands and prohibitions which tugged at women's minds and emotions, as well as a fraying class system and its attendant resentments.[‡]

'Freud's psychoanalysis had its origins in the idea that psychic disorders were prompted by conflicts related to sexuality', conflicts that were generated by the necessary and contradictory rules of civilisation; its solution was to give the adult 'a space in which to remember, re-enact and work though blockages that the drama

---

[*] 'Shame and Its Histories in the Twentieth Century', *Journal of New Zealand Studies,* Issue 9 (Oct 2010), 48.

[†] The gendered attack of the male poets ('the mob' referred to in the opening sentence of the '1934 Autobiography') was permissible, even fashionable, in this new psychological climate.

[‡] Lisa Appignanesi, *Mad, Bad and Sad: Women and the Mind Doctors* (New York: Norton & Co., 2008), 254.

of family life had created'.[*] But, as Appignanesi puts it, in the 'consulting room, Freud's child was always a creature of memory'.[†] Women analysts were the first to deal with the living child analytically and to think about approaches and plans to free childhood repression. Hyde's concerns in her essay about the hospital,[‡] which explores patterns of recrimination, self-blame and despair, and imagines a new type of child rearing, echo those of Melanie Klein, one of these early women analysts, and her first article in the *International Journal of Psychoanalysis*.[§]

Hyde's criticism of the impact of a restrictive society on child development (both in these writings and in her novels, particularly *Passport to Hell*) is also typical of the sophisticated and radical commentary of the times internationally. It could be paralleled with August Aichhorn's *Wayward Youth,* published in Vienna in 1925, which 'set out to show a repressive, militaristic society that delinquents were not criminals but children whose inner development had gone awry'.[¶] Transference – deep love for and attachment to one's therapist – is such an important idea, Freud claims, because its existence is evidence that the symptoms of psychic trouble are to do with libidinal problems. This idea led post World War II into a theory of attachment, the theory of the crucial importance of an infant's attachment to their parent or care-giver in the development of their capacity to love. Hyde's telling of her own stories emphasises a family disaffection that anticipates this idea – one that she would no doubt have made good use of.

---

* Appignanesi, *Mad, Bad and Sad*, 272.
† Ibid.
‡ 'Essay on Mental Health', p. 295.
§ 'We can spare the child unnecessary repression by freeing – first and foremost in ourselves – the whole sphere of sexuality from the dense veils of secrecy, falsehood and danger spun by a hypocritical civilization upon an affective and uninformed foundation.' Melanie Klein cited in Appignanesi, *Mad, Bad and Sad,* 274.
¶ Appignanesi, *Mad, Bad and Sad,* 277.

The Opening Door:
The Writing

The principal part of Robin Hyde's autobiographical writing consists of three substantial documents: the '1934 Autobiography' (about 40,000 words), the '1935 Journal' (about 30,000 words), and *A Home in this World* (about 40,000 words). The last of these was written after Hyde left the Lodge in 1937 and published (with 'A Night of Hell', an autobiographical fragment now identified as a chapter discarded from the novel *Nor the Years Condemn*) in 1984. The first two have remained unpublished until now. Besides these principal texts, there exist a few journal fragments and diary entries written at the Lodge, where Hyde lived from late 1933 until April 1937, between the age of twenty-eight and thirty-one.

Taken together, these documents comprise all of Hyde's personal writings – no other journals or diaries exist or have survived apart from limited personal jottings made alongside political and travel records in her China Notebook;* this means that Hyde does not appear to have kept journals or diaries in her younger years, nor in the last two years of her life. Thus it would seem that her autobiographical writing was motivated by the intensity and opportunity of her 'exile' in the voluntary ward of the mental hospital and also, given its explorative content, that this experience of writing from life and of living as a writer led to her development as a major fiction writer.

These texts are published in this book in their entirety for the first time. They are reproduced as the author handwrote or typed them, with any uncertainties being indicated. Also published here are two other items: 'The Cage with the Open Door', an autobiographical short story, and Hyde's 'Essay on Mental Health'. There are seven chapters. In each, a detailed introduction precedes each text, describing its character and provenance. This section of the introduction is a general discussion of the two principal texts, the '1934' Autobiography' and the '1935 Journal'.

All but one of the autobiographical writings are now in public collections. The two hitherto unpublished substantial documents have been available in the Special Collections of the Auckland Public (now Auckland Central City) Library for many

---

* This handmade notebook was gifted to Hyde by printer Ron Holloway in October 1934. Its first entry, the poem 'Incidence', was written immediately but apparently it was then put aside for Hyde's travels in China and to London. Its last entry is April 1938.

decades – the handwritten '1934 Autobiography' since 1964 and a typescript of the '1935 Journal' since 1990. The original manuscript of the '1935 Journal', and other writings previously in the collection of Hyde's son Derek Challis, are in the Alexander Turnbull Library, acquired in 2009.* The one item that cannot be located in the Turnbull – the untitled essay known as 'Essay on Mental Health', or '1936 Mental Health Essay' – is not there. A copy (presently in my possession) will be lodged once this book is published.

While the documents in the Auckland Central City Library have been consulted many times by researchers, particularly during the past fifteen years, they have remained unpublished; their particular character has never been interpreted or commented on, nor indeed have they been appreciated in their entirety. When they have been quoted, it has been to support biographical essays or thematic work on Hyde's poems and novels.† The publication of this book makes it possible to consider these texts in their own right.

It has become clear that these documents are very different in character from each other: the 'Autobiography' is a therapeutic account with an abruptly broken-off ending that is significantly cathartic, and the 'Journal' is a record of recovery which displays and ponders a different way of being-in-the-world, built on an understanding of the context of the treatment. What story can help us to understand the mood of these manuscripts? As literary theorist Paul Ricoeur suggests, all reading is a process of conjoining discourses: finding something in the writing sends one back to another discourse to interpret it. The interesting route by which the two texts came into the same public collection is a tempting history to conjoin with Hyde's unpublished autobiographical work – a history that in the first instance seems to suggest romance. We know both the 'Autobiography' and the 'Journal' were written at the Lodge and

---

* Challis, Derek Arden, 1930–. Papers relating to Robin Hyde [ca 1910–2000]. MS-Group-1648.
† Alison Hunt's 2008 thesis makes a similar claim. My 'reading' first promulgated at a 2005 conference presentation concurs very much with hers and is complemented by her detailed research. Hunt argues that the '1934 Autobiography' 'functioned as Hyde's defence to Tothill against potential charges of social impropriety, but it also created a confessional intimacy between them, which intensified on her part to a deep bond of love expressed in many of her texts, but particularly in her '1935 Journal'. There she professed her affection openly, alongside a discussion of the psychoanalytical phenomenon of transference, which enables a new critical attitude to be adopted towards this problematic attachment' ('Cage', 5). See also Anne Barbara Zimmerman, 'Godwitting and Cuckooing: Negotiations and Legitimations of Cultural Identity in New Zealand Literature' (PhD: University of Berne, 1996).

both are addressed to Hyde's psychiatrist Dr Gilbert Tothill. They came into the possession of the Auckland Central City Library in very different ways.

The '1935 Journal'

Following Hyde's death in London in August 1939, pronounced suicide by benzedrine poisoning,* the office of the New Zealand High Commissioner (who had, just days before, offered Hyde, in straitened circumstances, a fare home), arranged for her funeral and burial. They also collected all of her papers from her Notting Hill address – including the typewriter with its last note – and consigned them to an Auckland solicitor and friend of Hyde, W.R. Edge, whom Hyde had named as her business executor in her 1935 will and who happened to be in London. He in turn shipped them to her mother, Nelly Wilkinson, in Northland, Wellington, where they were held with papers Hyde had previously left there. Some further papers were sent from the Avondale Mental Hospital. The '1935 Journal' may well have been amongst these latter papers, although it is possible that it could have been amongst the papers Hyde travelled with. While it is not listed as such,† we know she did take many papers with her, including the manuscript that became *A Home in this World*.

Following the death in late 1944 of Hyde's parents Nelly and Edward Wilkinson, both just five years after their daughter, her papers were sent (in May 1945) back to Bill Edge in Auckland. This was despite the fact that by this time it had been ascertained from Hyde's letters that a later codicil to her 1935 will named her schoolfriend Gwen Mitcalfe (née Hawthorn) and Nelly Wilkinson as joint literary executors, and despite

---

* According to Roy Porter, benzedrine was new and one of 'the dangerous amphetamines widely used, clinically and officially as well as experimentally, in the 1930s'. See *Madness: A Brief History* (Oxford: Oxford University Press, 2002), 205. It would shortly be prescribed to soldiers and airmen – British, American and Japanese – in combat, and experimented with by writers and artists as various as Graham Greene, Lee Miller and Allen Ginsburg. Hyde was using it for probably the first or second time; its toxicity in large doses and its side-effects of inducing paranoia were not well known. An account of the inquest into Hyde's death, 'Authoress Took New Brain Drug', in the *London Star* on 25 August 1939, reported the pathologist concluding 'Death was due to acute pulmonary oedema, due to cerebral poisoning, consistent with poisoning by Benzedrine.'.

† Derek Challis, 'The Fate of the Iris Wilkinson Manuscripts' (University of Auckland: New Zealand Electronic Poetry Centre, 2002) http://www.nzepc.auckland.ac.nz/authors/hyde/challis.asp. Accessed 1 September 2011. This is a 'corrected form' of the earlier essay of the same name published in the *Journal of New Zealand Literature* 16 (1998), 22–32.

the fact that there had been disputatious correspondence between Nelly Wilkinson and the Rawlinsons.* (The rightful owner of the papers, Hyde's son Derek Challis, was at this time fourteen years old and living in an orphanage, with no contact with her family or friends.) As it was, it was lucky the papers survived, as Edna, Hyde's sister, asked Edge, 'Do you want them otherwise I will destroy them?', apparently oblivious to the value of the work.† Edge was a lawyer, friend of the Rawlinsons, and partner of Rosalie Rawlinson. Gloria, Rosalie's daughter, was a young poet, and both had been Hyde's friends, and by this time mother and daughter were living with Edge in his house in the suburb of Greenlane, in Auckland. Thus by dint of association, in Derek Challis's words, 'the *de facto* literary executorship had effectively passed into the Rawlinsons' hands'‡ and Gloria Rawlinson proceeded to sort the papers and plan projects, beginning by editing a collection of poetry (*Houses by the Sea*, 1952), writing essays, typing up manuscripts (including the '1935 Journal') and generally ordering Hyde's papers. Her devotion to the idea of a biography and the later sharing of that project with Derek Challis kept Hyde's work intact and alive where it might well have been lost.§

In 1954 Derek Challis went to live in a 'bach' in the Rawlinsons' garden; although ownership of Hyde's papers had officially passed to him in 1952, at the age of twenty-one, they had physically remained with Gloria while he was away serving in the navy. When Challis married and left the Rawlinsons in 1962, he deposited some papers in the University of Auckland Library and took others, including 'all the autobiographical writings', which included the original manuscript of the '1935 Journal', with him. However, in 1965 he and Gloria began cooperating on a biography and he returned papers in his possession to her.¶

Rawlinson's typescript copy of the '1935 Journal' now held in the Auckland Central City Library was not deposited until 1990, apparently through Geoff Walker

---

* For a more detailed discussion of this issue see the account given by Challis, 'The Fate of the Iris Wilkinson Manuscripts'.

† Ibid. Other papers survived thanks to Hyde's older sister Hazel.

‡ Ibid.

§ For more on the manuscripts, and the composition and abandonment of the biography, see Derek Challis, 'Introduction', *The Book of Iris: A Life of Robin Hyde* (Auckland: Auckland University Press, 2002), xvii–xxii. Also see Michele Leggott, 'Introduction', *The Book of Nadath* by Robin Hyde (Auckland: Auckland University Press, 1999), xi, and 'Introduction', *Young Knowledge: The Poems of Robin Hyde* (Auckland: Auckland University Press, 2003), 6.

¶ Challis, 'The Fate of the Iris Wilkinson Manuscripts'.

of Penguin Books.* It must have been made – if Derek Challis's account is correct – either before 1962 or after 1965. We do know that in the early 1960s Challis had shown the manuscript of what became *A Home in this World* (most probably already re-typed and titled by Gloria) to Hamilton publisher Blackwood Paul of Paul's Book Arcade, who wanted to publish it, but with a biographical essay that Challis or Gloria felt pre-empted their planned biography.† In a letter to Gwen Mitcalfe, Gloria Rawlinson suggested that Hyde's papers included several autobiographical and very publishable pieces, describing these as 'some of the best writing Iris ever did.'‡ The original of the '1935 Journal' had remained in the possession of Derek Challis and was acquired by the Alexander Turnbull Libray in 2009.

The '1934 Autobiography'

This document came to the Auckland Central City Library by a much more direct route than the typescript of the 'Journal'. It was Dr Gilbert Tothill, Hyde's psychiarist, who deposited the autobiography around the time of his retirement in 1964, when he was sixty-six years old. Here we have a late middle-aged man, recently retired as superintendent of New Zealand's biggest psychiatric hospital – Oakley, previously Avondale – a position which he had taken up in 1952, bringing a manuscript addressed to him thirty years earlier. When he gifted the 'Autobiography' to the library, it had been in his possession from immediately after Hyde completed it in early 1934 (albeit with a break during some of the decade 1935–45) until thirty years later. He requested that it be embargoed for some fifteen further years, to allow the biography to be written.§ In the '1935 Journal' entry for 22 March, Hyde willed items of writing to various people, including 'Dr. G. M. T. the papers he has (my lame-duck autobiography,)'. However, it appears he returned the manuscript to her to use as material for *The Godwits Fly,* and it came back to him again only when Hyde's papers were distributed in 1945 after the deaths of her parents. Certainly, it never went to Bill Edge or the Rawlinsons, as did the other papers.¶

In the '1935 Journal' (which Tothill would not have seen but which is the record

---

* This suggests Challis had left it with this publisher at some earlier stage.
† *Iris,* xv and n†.
‡ Gloria Rawlinson to Gwen Mitcalfe, April 1965. See Challis, 'The Fate of the Iris Wilkinson Manuscripts.'
§ For the most complete synthesis of information on this provenance, see Hunt, 'Cage', 182–3.
¶ See Hunt, 'Cage', 182.

of the success of his treatment and of the Lodge environment), Hyde wrote many entries about him, how he inspired her, how she admired him, and how she was guided by him:

> I am afraid, and of such childish things. Of <u>seeming</u> to 'let you down', in the classic phrase of the Avondale Mental Hospital: of showing myself as the cheap sentimental little fool I am – 'for from him that hath not shall be taken away also even that little he hath –'*

And in the next entry:

> – nobody in the world but you can give me peace – and now I can stop being a forlorn sort of deathbed letter to you and go on in the natural sequence of a diary. I'm happier – Every word you say means something – Thank you: and goodnight.[†]

And later:

> It's very queer to love anyone as much as I do you – and in so many different ways. Through my work, through the deepest possible sense of reserve and confidence, even through a kind of humour. I like you to laugh at me – to see the funny side – it makes me feel befriended. And yet the laughter of others can leave me raw – a ridiculous limping figure.[‡]

And shortly after:

> I doubt that many of them had peace, as whatever the petty tempests outside, I have had from your unselfish kindness,

> I shan't die (willingly) unless I lose that peace – unless the funny little figure obscures the other whose work you have helped.[§]

She also wrote about how she loved him but didn't want to embarrass him with this love:

> I love you, with all the stupid useless love of which I am capable. I suppose you know it, but I'll never put it into words so it can't hurt you. But all the time I'm torn with the dread of losing the little I do see of you altogether – you might go elsewhere, or I be sent away. Five minutes in a day, sometimes less – But when I don't see you, all the rest is dust and ashes. Today I didn't think you'd be here so I went out, and you did come up with my manuscript and looked for me.[¶]

Given both the existence of all these tender addresses and the provenance of the manuscript, one can see how tempting it is to picture a special love relationship between doctor and patient. One might question: was Tothill just a very good doctor

---

* '1935 Journal', 5 April, p. 231.
† '1935 Journal', 6 April, p. 231.
‡ '1935 Journal', 28 July, p. 257.
§ Ibid.
¶ '1935 Journal', 29 April, p. 243.

able to inspire his patients to recovery? or, because we are unable to find anything to the contrary from his side, can we infer more? The relationship was made intimate by her telling him so much – but then again that's just what such a patient–doctor relationship requires. But could the intelligence, humour and worldliness of this attractive young woman have been more than usually compelling? Did Dr T. admire her in return? Did he love her? Was some kind of 'boundary breaking' going on as scholar Michele Leggott suggested early in her writing on Hyde's poetry, whereby Hyde could acknowledge a conflicted 'dangerous (exquisite)' love 'for a figure of authority'?[*] The occasion of Tothill visiting the city library, treasured manuscript in hand, is resonant and continues the theme; it even resembles scenes from Robin Hyde's own novel *Wednesday's Children*, having those poignant elements of local history, thwarted romance and haunting. The hero Bellister of that novel was, like Dr Gilbert Tothill, from England. And this gentleman, Bellister, was in love with the protagonist Wednesday, whom he found an interesting mix of fragility and deviance; he wanted to become part of her life, as well as being a philosopher of life, someone to whom she could talk about personal matters. Alison Hunt draws similar paralells between Tothill and the hero of Hyde's unpublished novel.[†]

I want to suggest, however, from looking further into the autobiographical writings and into the treatment ideas emerging at the time, that Hyde's love for Tothill was not as ordinary or as potentially rocky ('problematic' as Hunt puts it) as a love affair or flirtation.[‡] This is not to say that Hyde had not had a love-life; we know from both her own and others' accounts about her young love for would-be writer Harry Sweetman; a gorgeous physical love amongst the lupins with newspaper editor Mac Vincent;[§] the relationships/affairs she had with the fathers of her children (younger fellow journalist Mary Smee described her as 'warm and generous' and a 'very passionate woman'[¶]). But she was very conflicted about these experiences. She explains in *A*

---

[*] Leggott, 'Introduction', *The Book of Nadath*, xxii.
[†] Hunt comments: 'The recognition that she consciously played out transference fantasies partially resolves the critically disturbing manifestations of Hyde's love for Tothill, such as his representation as the lover of Hyde's alter-ego Echo in "The Unbelievers"' ('Cage', 307).
[‡] Hunt, 'Cage', 5. Poetry critics Michele Leggott and Megan Clayton have also made a version of this shift in emphasis, though remaining more interested in textual ambiguity than in ideas of attachment. *Young Knowledge*, 14, and Clayton, 'Thoroughly Modern Malory: Robin Hyde's Poetic Ciphers and Camelot Codes', *Lighted Windows*, 113–5.
[§] See *Iris*, 133–4.
[¶] Mary Smee (later Dobbie) quoted in *Iris,* 353, 355.

Home in this World that she was well suited for love, but also for the self-doubt, shame, and sense of social stigma resulting from her first love affair and the birth and death of Robin.* This confliction, also evidenced in apologies for her love-life in the '1934 Autobiography', was a driving component in her breakdowns.

When she became a patient at the Lodge, Robin Hyde was suffering mentally and physically; as a part of the psychotherapeutic and to an an extent psychoanalytic philosophy there, her doctor seems to have offered his kindness and allowed himself to be loved. The idea of this treatment also opposed conventional mores, was non-judgmental and was interested in her mental illness as an example of the effects of her upbringing and experiences. (Her distrust of other people, described at the end of the '1934 Autobiography', intensified by the intervention of officially judgmental, institutional authority in her life, was actually, for the most part, countered by the humanity and acceptance that she experienced at the Lodge). In the parlance of transference, because she was able to develop trust and love for her psychiatrist, she could receive his treatment ideas, and identify and relieve her own patterns of desire for approval, fear of rejection, suicidality, and self-harming that had been triggered rather than solved by her romantic experiences.[†]

Understood in this way, the '1934 Autobiography' and '1935 Journal' record attachment to, and attention from, Dr Tothill – and advice and reassurance which calmed her anxiety and dignified her intelligence and humanity. There are references within the writing to their conversations and to his reading her manuscripts, but clearly the writing was a major means of communication. Hunt postulates that they were a means of treatment when doctors were so over-worked.

The Therapists and the Writing

Both Tothill and Buchanan appear to have encouraged Hyde's career. They made sure that she had the privacy and time for writing – and appropriate spaces: a generous single room, a garden, even eventually an attic study. Both men are notable figures in New Zealand medical history. Dr Henry Buchanan (1884–1974) was born

---

* *A Home*, 12.

† As in Leggott's work on Hyde's collected poems, *Young Knowledge*, Alison Hunt's doctoral thesis ('Cage') settles not on a conflicted romantic love but on the idea of transference to explain the significance of Hyde's love for her doctor. Leggott orders and titles her sections of poems under the names 'Analyst' and 'Analysand', and speaks of transference in her introduction. Hunt is even clearer on the evidence for this interpretation.

and educated (in general medicine) in Edinburgh (his employer Theodore Gray, Director-General of Health, and the well-known Sir Truby King were also Scottish-trained), arriving in New Zealand in 1913 to be Medical Superintendent at Hokitika Mental Hospital. Buchanan then served as Lieutenant-Colonel for the New Zealand Medical Corps from 1914–18, earning an OBE and transferring subsequently to the role of Medical Superintendent at Seacliff near Dunedin, before becoming Medical Superintendent at Auckland Mental Hospital at Avondale (Kingseat was also in his compass later) from 1929 until his retirement in 1952. As early as 1925, he began to extend the prevailing moral regime in the treatment of mental illness of work and rational occupation into the more professionalised concept of occupational therapy 'that had originated in the United States as part of the medical and rehabilitation services' for World War I soldiers. He 'acknowledged the benefits of handicrafts and music for those "more or less intelligent beings" unsuited for work gangs' and particularly for women, who seldom worked outdoors.' By 1935, he was using volunteers to implement OT at Avondale.[†] Occupational therapist Hazel Skilton described him as 'bluff and friendly'.[‡]

As Buchanan's Senior Medical Officer, Dr Gilbert Tothill was the most senior practising doctor at the hospital and Hyde's primary carer at the Lodge. Like Hyde, he had been born in Capetown, but he studied medicine in Edinburgh and at Long Grove Mental Hospital in England took a diploma in psychological medicine.[§] When he arrived in New Zealand in 1928, he was (Derek Challis suggests) 'possibly the first professionally qualified psychiatrist to practise' in the country.[¶] In 1937 he became Medical Superintendent at Tokanui; other positions followed before he returned to Avondale in 1952 to take over from Buchanan. Another Medical Officer of Health at the Lodge, Dr Kathleen Todd, may be (Alison Hunt suggests) a missing link in explaining the use of psychotherapy there. She was a New Zealander who studied medicine at the University of Otago, had travelled to the United States and studied psychiatry in London. She was working briefly at the Lodge in 1934 before travelling to London again to do specialist training in psychiatry. Hunt has found that

---

*   Brunton, 'A Choice of Difficulties', 377.

†   Beth Gordon, Sunny Riordan, Rowena Scaletti and Noeline Creighton, *Legacy of Occupation: Stories of Occupational Therapy in New Zealand 1940–1972* (Auckland: Bush Press, 2009).

‡   Quoted in Hunt, 'Cage', 77.

§   Hunt, 'Cage', 159.

¶   *Iris,* 217.

she used writing therapy in at least two cases and that she provided a publication on psychology to a patient to read. Hyde mentions Todd's children's psychological clinic in the city. When Todd died in 1968, she was lauded as a "'an intellectually gifted and compassionate psychiatrist", one of the few "who believed that the psychological approach to the study and treatment of psychiatric illness was an essential part of the speciality".' Hunt speculates that Todd's presence at the Lodge may have influenced Tothill's practice, and that one could extrapolate the treatment climate of the Lodge through the presence of these two enthusiastic young specialists.*

It also seems that Buchanan and Tothill collaborated on Hyde's case. Dr Buchanan set the scene, with both policies that helped her and facilities being made available to her (and he kept in touch after she left the hospital, even visiting her in Britain). His belief in a regime of work and other activities (including housework, sewing, gardening and games), which preceded his being the first doctor in New Zealand to introduce occupational therapy in 1945, extended in Hyde's case to her writing. Thus when Hyde was prescribed the physical care and seclusion of a neurasthenic, like Virginia Stephens (later Woolf), she was not, as Woolf famously was, ever forbidden to write.

However, Dr Gilbert Tothill became Hyde's primary carer. From the '1934 Autobiography' and its direct address to him, and the '1935 Journal' and its descriptions, we can see how he guided and reassured her, making sure that she was ready for adversities and that she didn't exaggerate them. As she recovered, Hyde also felt engaged in a joint project with Tothill to expose the consequences of sexual ignorance and repression for young women; he shared her plans and hesitations about publishing both the 'Autobiography' and the untitled essay later known as 'Essay on Mental Health' or '1936 Mental Health Essay'.† The fact that in the description of her will on 22 March in the '1935 Journal', she hoped that any money from the share in her writings that she left to G.M.T. might go to his 'beloved psychological clinics', increases this sense that they shared a philosophy.

The '1935 Journal' also shows that Hyde was well aware of the typicality and therapeutic purposes of loving her doctor, and that she saw herself as similar to all the other patients in needing a cure by love. Indeed, by the time she wrote the entry from the '1935 Journal' printed below, she was also able to imagine herself in the role

---

* Hunt, 'Cage', 161–2.
† Hunt, 'Cage', 180. For essay, see p. 295.

of the psychiatrist, although she didn't think she could fulfil it well. Her comments here also indicate a knowledge of the recent history of psychological/pyschoanalytic debate: the query 'in far-gone cases, can such transference be of any use?' is the same question Eugen Bleuler was asking in Switzerland at the Burghölzli Institute (where Gustav Carl Jung was his student) around 1908, and a question that Freud responded to in the discussion of Bleuler's new category of illness: schizophrenia.* These are Hyde's ponderings:

> Dr. Palmer is now the psychological father of Mrs Bramley, and one for whom she has all the respect, fear and love of which a madwoman is capable. Query: in far-gone cases, can such transference be of any use? Further query: even if it could, will they give it a chance? Oh, I wish I understood instead of groping in this blind ignorance – But the case bears out my own theory, which I worked out independently of Freud or any other. The entire native power of these broken and disconnected lives is love – when love can be evoked in them the first step has been taken. The psychiatrist who is afraid of that leech-like love must fail – he has to work straight through its embarrassing physical and emotional presentments until the clay gives way to enduring marble. Worth doing? Yes – if only because it takes courage – it is what I should have done, but am too emotional and easily swayed to do, with Gloria Rawlinson, Starkie and others.†

To say that Hyde's love for her doctor was professionally guided is not designed to over-simplify our understanding of the experience. Transference does imply doubling, in that the doctor/analyst allows him or herself to stand in for all the failures in love or loved ones of the patient without becoming really involved with the patient (and counter-transference is possible because the humanity of the doctor on a terrain with the patient is part of the cure). Jung's love affair with Sabina Spielrein is well known, and she has been seen not only as having been taken advantage of in an uneven power relationship but also as having been 'a pawn in a relationship between two dominant, doctoring males' when Jung, fearing scandal, gave up his role as her analyst and handed her over as a patient to his mentor Sigmund Freud.

Robin Hyde, however, is now better known as a writer and thinker than her doctors, something not true of Sabina Spielrein, in spite of her becoming an analyst and initiating analytic concepts. Fortunately for Hyde, her love seems to have been treated professionally and her awareness of power relations and the negative consequences of her first sexual relationship when, as she describes, she was 'almost a child'‡ were countered rather than reinforced.

*   Appignanesi, *Mad Bad and Sad*, 206, 216.
†   '1935 Journal', 6 April, p. 231.
‡   *A Home*, 29.

Letters Freud wrote to Jung at the time of the affair with Sabina explain the importance of the transference process:

You are probably aware that our cures are brought about through the fixation of the libido prevailing in the unconscious (transference), and that this transference is most readily obtained in hysteria. Transference provides the impulse necessary for understanding and translating the language of the ucs. [unconscious]; where it is lacking, the patient does not make the effort or does not listen when we submit our translation to him. Essentially, one might say, the cure is effected by love. And actually transference provides the most cogent, indeed the only unassailable proof that neuroses are determined by the individual's love life.*

A later letter cautions against seeing 'the cure through love ... [as] an actual love affair'.†

The end of the '1934 Autobiography' throws more light on the question of a nuanced reading and confirms this interpretation of an underlying theme of therapeutic love. It enacts a drama that illustrates Hyde's perilously fragile state of mind and her culturally induced sense of shame, in this case triggered when she is filled with regret at having given the impression of being a good and loveable young woman to Dr Buchanan when in fact she is (as she perceives it) hopelessly tainted and deserving rejection. The narrative culminates in an apology for a consequent incident (further elaborated in the '1935 Journal') of trying to have morphine smuggled into the Lodge in order to end the confusion (and to show how 'bad' she really is) and her quarrel with the Superintendent, Dr Buchanan, after this was discovered.

In the final paragraph she describes how she anticipated the doctor's anger (it makes sense here to read 'you' as Dr Buchanan rather than Tothill): 'you were to be frightened and angry and send me away. The wilderness is wide enough.'‡ This culminating incident was not independently documented until Derek Challis read his mother's case notes and published the story in the 2002 biography, *The Book of Iris*; even so, an understanding of the incident is not evident in the biography.

Hyde describes a smuggling incident at the Lodge in July 1933, when she had written a note asking her chemist friend (a Queen Street pharmacist), whom she always referred to as 'Joe', or 'Father Time', to smuggle morphine tablets into the Lodge. The message and probably its delivery were intercepted and a box of chocolates was delivered without the enclosed morphine. Subsequently, she was

---

* Quoted in Appignanesi, *Mad Bad and Sad*, 215.
† Lisa Appignanesi's paraphrase, *Mad Bad and Sad*, 217.
‡ '1934 Autobiography', Chapter 23 Many Waters, p. 174.

punished with a six-week transfer to the Wolfe Home – the admission ward for the main hospital (although part of it was also the voluntary ward for male patients) – before being returned to the Lodge and discharging herself from there in September. She then travelled to Wellington and on to a writing assignment in North Auckland before her appearance in the magistrate's court in Auckland on 4 December 1933 to answer the charge of trying to take her own life. The next day she had another nervous collapse (apparently at a tram stop) and asked to be taken back to the Lodge, specifically to the care of Dr Tothill, because, as she writes later to him: 'you were very patient, a host of phrases and sentences built up into certain reality. Unknown to me you must at the time have healed some wound a little.'*

The powerfulness of a therapeutic relationship is in its ability to get a patient to tell with affect and to discover new insights in the telling. In some ways, most of the account in the '1934 Autobiography' does not display this quality – it tells a story most evocatively and serves its purpose as a diagnostic tool. As Alison Hunt argues, the narrative identifies for Dr Tothill incidents of her life in terms of key relationships (fitting with the Freudian stress on the libidinal) and often serves to justify and defend her actions from moral approbrium.[†] As mentioned earlier, Hunt also argues that the suggestion of writing an autobiography, also made to several other patients by both Dr Tothill and Dr Kathleen Todd, was in the first place to supply a history for the doctors, partly because they had so little time. (Even the idea of carefully recording a history was relatively new and it was newer still to take into consideration the patient's story).[‡]

It seems that the emotional work (the impact of divulging, which is designed to lead to some catharsis) may have gone on in conversation, and there are some episodes in the '1934 Autobiography' where a piece of information is left out that had perhaps been told (the reference to 'the monkey' is one example). However, to trigger some unconscious connections and open up new self-knowledge/insight by writing is difficult. How could the highly rational act of authoring, assembling in sequence, describing action and creating characters (with events grouped, as Hunt suggests, around self defence against accusations of drug use, promiscuity, etc.) let this happen? In making a book (organised from the beginning into chapters), Hyde

---

* '1934 Autobiography,' Chapter 18 City of Trees, p. 143. This page is part of a new ordering of this chapter as suggested by Anne Barbara Zimmerman, in her MA thesis. See p. 63.

† Hunt, 'Cage', 208–10.

‡ Hunt, 'Cage', 165.

tells about her first baby, Robin, and his conception and birth quite openly but at the end the writing reveals how painful this telling has been, what it has cost her and how impossible it had been previously to tell almost anyone about these incidents. The catharsis is produced only at the very end, when the trajectory of the story meets the almost-present (her initial admission and her falling out with Buchanan), the disclosure of which has been made by the tolerance and acceptance of Dr Tothill. As she relates being taken to the hospital and invited to the Lodge, she breaks into apology and upset. At this point it is the superintendent of the hospital Dr Buchanan she is talking about – not Dr Tothill – describing him as 'your colleague', she calls him 'Dr B'. Hyde is explaining that she couldn't bear to disappoint the kindly doctor and gentleman who fancied her a 'perfectly nice young woman',* and who had rescued her from the cell in the public hospital and taken her to such a comfortable, reassuring place as her room in the Lodge. She could not bear to break this illusion by telling him that she had had not only one baby, Derek (here called 'Gerard'), but an earlier baby, Robin.

Relatedly, it was Oscar Wilde who first made the quip in *The Importance of Being Ernest*: 'To lose one parent, Mr Worthington, may be regarded as a misfortune, to lose both looks like carelessness',† a neat summary of social attitudes that still prevailed in the 1930s. Hyde also uses the words 'promiscuity' and 'nymphomania' – the possibility of such labels haunts her because they stigmatise – 'other' – a person, and take away their identity. By divulging not one but two babies, she fears she will allow those words power over her and the possible consequences:

> Oh dear! The locked cupboards, and that which I wouldn't and couldn't put into words. You may have guessed worse of me, or better. 'Promiscuity is death.'‡

The account of this significant incident (of perceived duplicity, shame, desire to self-harm and punishment for it) is fragmented and difficult to follow, signs again of that necessary catharsis. Taking a lead from the analysts, one could say that this is the incident which enacts Hyde's obsessive feelings and therefore was able to give her some new knowledge about herself and make her open to therapy.

On her admission to the Auckland Hospital cells, Hyde had received a visit from Dr Buchanan, who was running an outpatient clinic at the hospital for returned

---

* '1935 Journal', 22 March, p. 224.
† Oscar Wilde, *The Importance of Being Ernest*, Act 1.
‡ '1934 Autobiography', Chapter 23, p. 173.

servicemen. He subsequently visited her five times in two weeks, trying to persuade her to go as a voluntary boarder to the Lodge (she was reluctant even to leave the hospital) and reassuring her she would not be sent to the main wards of the mental hospital. Subsequently at the Lodge, it seems that she felt she had deceived the superintendent: she perceived him as a father figure and guardian angel, whose approval she felt she had gained by posing duplicitously as an innocent young woman, not telling many (hardly any) truths about herself, and especially not about Robin or her desperation and dreams.*

> Most vital of all, I never told about my secret child. About Gerard, yes, as very occasionally, in bravado or when in a corner, I told some other, but not about Robin. In fact, I told nothing and came here to a pleasant, quiet room, a smiling, re-assured, angel-guarded liar. I forgot to tell you.†

Then, as the '1934 Autobiography' recounts, when she did try to tell him, she felt his response as rejection – a rejection which she couldn't recover from and which made her want to disappear into another world, to suicide or perhaps just resolve the problem by showing how bad she was. Whether his was a real or perceived rejection, it had the same effect:

> More clumsily than any silent lips have ever told their secret, the secret which was essential me, I did blurt out some parody of the truth at last. I who can remember so clearly, remember not at all what I said. Just, probably that Gerard was a second child, there's been another — But I <u>do</u> remember the soft monosyllable, 'oh!' the tone like the drawing away of a steady hand. And the question of my own mind came to me to dwell there, 'Am I mad, or merely unclean?'‡

Just over a year later in a 22 March entry in the '1935 Journal', Hyde throws more light on the incident of the drugs, showing how crucially important the process of telling and having her story accepted without judgment was for her peace of mind, for her very existence. G.M.T. was second best – not the doctor she fell for and whose judgment and possible consequences haunted her – but the trustworthy one whom she came to love. Dr Tothill knew her story but it didn't make a difference, he accepted her and believed her capable of recovery.

---

* Hunt, 'Angel-Guarded Liar', *Lighted Windows*, 150, and 'Cage', 43–67, draws on files she has located – Hyde's 1933 admission papers from the Psychiatric Clinic at Auckland Hospital – and comes up with a very similar interpretation; she emphasises particularly Hyde's fear of Dr Buchanan's power to commit her to a institution from which she may never escape.
† '1934 Autobiography,' Chapter 23, p. 173.
‡ Ibid.

Then it occurred to me how much, how stupidly much, I'd like to leave something to Dr. Buchanan as well. And I can't. He is superintendent here. It was he who fished me out of that hideous cell, and laughed, and lent me old French books, and broke all rules and regulations by coming to see me here everyday. Only the unexpected thing was that, sick and three-quarters mad as I was, I couldn't bear him to learn the truth about me. I wanted his regard as I didn't then want food or drink. That was that. I wrote an insane letter to a chemist who was always trying to become my lover, begging him to send me enough morphine to end it – He did, it was intercepted, I was very properly chucked into the outer darkness of the extremely grim Wolfe Home. Of course I couldn't explain, and anyhow it was such a lunatic explanation – I don't think he ever forgave me. Certainly never gave the old friendliness back again – and do I blame him. That loss all but killed me. I don't know why it didn't – and I gave away what I was suffering, but never after I'd regained even the beginnings of self-control. For more than a year now, on the very rare occasions when he puts in an appearance, I've been what Mr Dernford Yates calls 'Good old 'ard and bright.' Of course the worst is all over – Dr.Tothill built up a sort of trust and understanding that in the end became more than all the lost things in my life – more than Harry Sweetman, or Frederick, or – perhaps not more than Robin, who is my life – more than any silly desire to pose as a perfectly nice young woman before a cheery Scot. How women hoard their old griefs! Of course now that I'm no longer a wilted lily or an embarrassment or anything but a fool who chooses to live and work here, that scrawled chapter is closed – I made a fool of myself and it's forgotten – But if I could only do or give something to make up for disappointing a friend who didn't deserve it.

~~Forgive me for the unrequited debt of faith betrayed, or gratitude unmet –~~

Oh this is purely maudlin – and if only Dr. Tothill were here I wouldn't think of it. Goodnight.*

This conflicted apology shows the mixture of fear and bravado that was Hyde's reaction to the privacy and denial of the society she lived in. Her fears about the consequences of breaking silence were often justified. There were many secrets in her life: her mother only recently knew of her second baby, her father seems never to have known of either (and never met Derek), her youngest sister knew of Derek only after her mother's death, the journalists she worked with didn't know about him either,[†] friends she met didn't know she lived at the Lodge, and so on.[‡] Society in general valued stoicism – socially unacceptable relationships couldn't be acknowledged or, if lost, grieved for; such relationships and losses were shocking and if known about were probably 'talked down' – it was best to 'get on with it'.

* '1935 Journal', 22 March, pp. 223–4.
† Mary Smee, quoted in *Iris*, 354.
‡ See *Iris,* 207, for the family knowledge and lack of it.

Telling the truth is not simple either: Hyde blames herself at the end of the '1934 Autobiography' because she feels either she should have kept quiet about Robin or she should have told straightforwardly (been either 'silent' or 'lucid' are her words), but instead she told indirectly – by taking the baby's name and thus the name of his father – by outing herself in code.

Hyde's autobiographical writings convey her sense of herself as created out of the dissonances of her time, strength, sensuousness, gentility, secrecy – mixed. Perhaps her sense of herself was so grand, and for posterity, because it was dissociated through trauma and unresolved suffering, and lack of 'attachment' as a child; she was more full of longing, more multiple than most of us. We can't find the real Robin Hyde, but we can respect her extraordinary understanding of society and psychology, and her ability to use her own life symbolically, and recognise with thankfulness that she was able to do this therapeutically and go on to write so much poetry and fiction in consequence.* Derek Challis's very moving introduction to the co-authored biography *The Book of Iris: A Life of Robin Hyde,* that he rewrote from Gloria Rawlinson's 1971 manuscript, shows how alive the question of 'to-tell' or 'not-to-tell' family secrets remained after her death and in the correspondence between her family and Gloria Rawlinson. That Hyde probably knew this would be the case makes her insistence on being recognised as an intelligent individual cognisant of social norms and fears, and not a casualty or a tragic figure, even more of a social commentary.

As an incident in the history of the mental health system in New Zealand, this is an unusually happy outcome. Dr Gilbert Tothill's training, and his ideas about treatment were an important component.† Hyde was not the only patient whom he and his New Zealand colleague Dr Kathleen Todd encouraged to write autobiographically,‡ but this was not a direction that Tothill particularly pursued: his later account of his career places no emphasis on narrative or psychoanalytic methods.§ What we seem to have is the fortuitous coincidence of a new emphasis on voluntary care, early intervention

---

* Megan Clayton in her doctoral thesis takes a similar line of argument, exploring the poems written at the Lodge and Hyde's China writing from this perspective: 'Iris, Read and Written: A New Poetics of Robin Hyde' (PhD: University of Canterbury, 2001). A synthesis of this argument is made in her 'Thoroughly Modern Malory', *Lighted Windows,* 107–18.
† Roy Porter, *A Social History of Madness*, 231.
‡ Hunt, 'Cage', 15.
§ *New Zealand Herald* interview, '40 Years Helping the Mentally Ill', 21 December 1964, sec 1: 6.

in nervous cases, experimental talking cures, and an enthusiastic newly qualified doctor (perhaps encouraged by his equally young colleague Kathleen Todd) getting the opportunity to assist an intelligent, sensitive, well-read and psychologically acute patient who had already experienced psychological treatment at Queen Mary Hospital at Hanmer Springs and was able to recover and use her discoveries, offering her own work in thankfulness for his 'unselfish kindness'.*

Grief and Trauma

It was Freud who first used the term 'grief work' and who identified stages of grieving and stated desired recovery outcomes. In terms of practice, though, psychiatrists are bound to absorb the culture of the time; in the 1930s, it is clear that certain grief was disenfranchised. Grieving for a perinatal death or for a child who died at birth (especially by an unmarried mother) was less serious grief than other forms. However, the practice of Hyde's doctors, Dr Chisholm at Hanmer and Dr Tothill at Avondale, suggests they did take on board the consequences of the loss of her first baby.

Another characteristic of the Freudian and older models of grief is their emphasis on recovery by 'letting go', the patient's tasks being:

- to accept the reality of loss;
- to work through pain and grief;
- to adjust to an environment in which the deceased is missing;
- to emotionally release the deceased and move on with life.[†]

More recent psychological (psychotherapeutic) theory and practice has emphasised the importance of actually holding on to the relationship – 'being able to feel that there is an important relationship even after the loss has occurred'.[‡] Grieving, it is argued, is not so much a process of severing ties as maintaining those ties despite

---

* '1935 Journal', 28 July, p. 257: 'Yet I've nothing to offer, in return for all you have done for me, except my work. It seems to me that has to be protected – so I have to take risks, to abandon the human discretion of not making a fuss.' That work was substantial: while at the Lodge, Hyde wrote two collections of poems, a book about her career as journalist, most of five published novels, pieces of journalism, reviews, short stories, and much unpublished work.

† Although Freud does argue for introjection or internalisation, but perhaps as getting worse before getting better. 'Mourning and Melancholia', Vol. 14, *The Standard Edition of the Complete Psychological Works* (London: Hogarth, 1953–74), 237–60.

‡ Neil Thompson, Introduction, *Loss and Grief: a Guide for Human Services Practitioners* (Basingstoke: Palgrave, 2002), 9.

the loss. However, this legitimation in theory has only gradually permeated into practice: 'as recently as the late 1990s people who have received counselling and read umpteen books on the bereavement, have nowhere received permission to find a place for their dead. Everywhere the message they heard was "Let go. Leave behind. Move on."'[*]

Despite the cultural assumptions of the time, the tolerance of Hyde's doctor seems to have given her permission to do this kind of integration – finding a place for those she loved and who had died, by writing about them and for them. Our contemporary vocabulary around grieving speaks of solace and positive memory – storytelling and so on; Hyde seems to have stumbled on this.

Trauma theory is also very applicable and has implications for thinking about Hyde the person and about the patterning of her work – and is perhaps even more suggestive than ideas about grieving. In both German and English, the word trauma comes from the Greek for physical wound (and is still used like that, of course) but has more often come to be associated with a wound of the mind. Significantly, Freud began the study of trauma at the time of the World War I atrocities ('Beyond the Pleasure Principle' was published in 1922), looking at survivors of an accident or sudden loss. In his definition, a trauma is something that the person is never ready for and is seen as having a quite specific psychological consequence (not like ordinary neurosis, in which Freud saw dreams, for example, as the attempted avoidance of unpleasant conflict – wish fulfilments or repressed desire, things he was really more interested in). In a case of a war experience or accident, the incident keeps returning in dreams and hallucinations. The idea of repetition compulsion in trauma is explained as the need of the sufferers to repeat the experience in order to be ready for it, because they were not ready the first time. This seems to speak to the string of accidental losses that Hyde suffered – and to her need to remake the world again and again in fiction and narratives. Cathy Caruth terms this, as in the title of her book, 'unclaimed experience': a wound which is experienced too soon, too unexpectedly to be fully known and is therefore not available to the conscious mind until it imposes itself repeatedly in the nightmares and repetitive actions of the survivor.[†]

---

[*] Tony Walter, *On Bereavement: the Culture of Grief* (Buckingham: Open University Press, 1999), quoted in Thompson, *Loss and Grief,* 9.

[†] 'What returns to haunt the victim is not only the reality of the violent event but also the reality of the way its violence has not yet been fully known.' Cathy Caruth, *Unclaimed Experience: Trauma, Narrative and History* (Baltimore: The John Hopkins University Press, 1996), 6.

Healing and Serenity

Allen Curnow, poet and Hyde's contemporary, editorialised on her poetry to the effect that it improved as she came to know her country; this idea of geographical cure is rather typical of settler society's preference for externalisation of mental states. What Hyde's record suggests is that her writing improved as she discovered a language for talking about mental states, a language that normalised her feeling of alienation from society as a psychological and cultural effect of living where and when she did.

Another way to talk about Hyde's discoveries is in terms of aesthetics and personal development. This is an approach that has been taken by Megan Clayton, who charts a movement in Hyde's work from images and stories of thwarted desire and loss, misery and bitterness, that play out in her early Malorian-inflected poems (whose ghost is Harry Sweetman, her first love who left her to travel and who died young in England), expressing a struggle for ownership of memory and of self. Around 1935, a new influence, a contemplative wisdom Hyde found in the translations by Arthur Waley of Japanese and Chinese poetry, is apparent. Clayton identifies this new style as conveying a new mindfulness and an acceptance of opposites: 'a kind of internal stillness that comes from the dignity of deliberate action mindfully undertaken, and the observation of the perpetual movement, the continual changing, of the surrounding landscape'.* From this point of view, Freud's suggestion that it is necessary to fully re-experience the horror of loss in dreams and action to become serene enough to live an ordinary difficult life matches Hyde's journey through the stages of her poetry. Its themes of loss, infidelity, drowning and betrayal when first at the Lodge develop by 1935, influenced by the mood of Waley's translations, into a new expression of serenity, where similar losses are encountered but differently.

As an alternative but it seems also compatible view, Alison Hunt suggests that Hyde's heroines progressed, as she did, away from the gravitational pull of the Freudian death wish towards a sense of purpose within the common community of humankind. Concluding her thesis, she writes:

> She was initially fascinated with that existential median, metaphorically the hinge in the door between life and death that is the stepping off point for the suicide .... But, finally, she determined that a network of social bonds, as opposed to conventional, discrete relationships, could steer the suicide from despair to new life.†

---

* Clayton, 'Iris, Read and Written', 196.

† Hunt, 'Cage', 307.

What better place to leave this discussion then, than with the internal stillness, observation and sense of global community of the last page of Hyde's story 'The Cage with the Open Door':

> The gardeners have planted a circular bed of night-scented stock in front of the house. The night is perfectly clear, and heavy on it, sweet beyond words, lies the fragrance. House a cage, street a cage, world a cage, body a cage. The moon, half-crescent, floats in the indigo, attended by stars. Do you remember those old blue-painted watering-carts, always drawn by white horses, which ~~used to xxx lumber~~ *[lumbered]* solemnly along the hot little streets, laying the dust with jets of sparkling water? We used to run behind the carts and splash the water over our faces, our bare arms and legs. The old drivers cracked their whips at us, but they were not seriously offended. The streets were cool, the dust, it seemed, had fallen never to rise again. Now all the dust of the world is somehow swept out of the way, it is dark, and everything is miraculously clean and cool. Something has done this for us, I do not know what. I say to it, 'Let me be yours ... let me belong to you, not to anything else at all,' knowing in my heart that I belong to every littleness, like the rest of my kind. Only <u>that</u> is not little, perhaps tonight, among all those who sing and are triumphant, an Italian soldier is weeping at Adowa. *[Italy invaded Abyssinia October 1935]**

---

* See pp. 289–90.

I

1934 Autobiography

NZ MS 412A, Special Collections, Auckland Central City Library (formerly Auckland Public Library). Donated by Dr Gilbert Tothill on 10 February 1965.

DESCRIPTION: This is a manuscript of approximately 190 pages handwritten in blue ink on loose-leaf foolscap paper, with a change in paper type in Chapter 14 from 'blue-lined, 34-line foolscap resembling paper used for patient records and scrap at Auckland Mental Hospital' to 'a poor-quality notepaper, possibly letter pad'.*

PROVENANCE: The manuscript was written in early 1934 (between January and probably March), addressed to Dr Gilbert Tothill, Hyde's psychiatrist, and gifted to him. It was actually given or returned into his possession only after Hyde's death. He gifted it to the Auckland Public (now Central City) Library on his retirement in 1965, with an embargo of sixteen years to protect work on the biography (eventually published as *The Book of Iris*).† The handwritten manuscript of the '1934 Autobiography' was first transcribed by Lisa Docherty as part of the Marsden Fund project that also produced *The Book of Iris* and *Young Knowledge*: that version has been refined and corrected for this publication.

The manuscript is arranged in 23 chapters, but is missing Chapter 1, the beginning of Chapter 2 and the end of Chapter 16, as well as at least the beginning of Chapter 17 (although some of this chapter has been re-instated from mis-ordered pages). It is possible that there were more pages and that the ending may not be the original ending. In 1980 the manuscript was bound out of sequence, so that it is difficult to determine where there are pages missing. Two parts of a poem, 'Sodom', previously bound in different places, were the initial clue to reinstating some of the original order. In the following text, the end of Chapter 16 and part of what is probably Chapter 17 have been re-ordered by Mary Edmond-Paul and Patrick Sandbrook according to the suggestions made by Anne Zimmerman in her 1991 MA thesis

---

* Hunt, 'Cage', 311.

† For further information, see Patrick Sandbrook, 'Robin Hyde: A Writer at Work' (PhD: Massey University, 1985), 364, and Hunt, 'Cage', 310–11.

incorporated as research notes in her 1996 Doctorate.* Zimmerman's series C, F, A have been placed in Chapters 16–17; however, another suggested series has not been applied as we considered additional re-ordering would further complicate the problems of sequence. Similar suggestions for re-sequencing this manuscript have been made by Alison Hunt in her 2008 doctoral thesis.

Three poems – 'The Last Ones'; 'Sand'; 'Descendants'† – are bound at the end of the manuscript but not reproduced here. Pencil notes on the verso of 'Descendants' mention '54 Woburn Rd' and 'Bellevue Hotel', the date '19th', with partial directions and possibly telephone numbers.

The '1934 Autobiography' was written at the suggestion of Robin Hyde's psychiatrist, Dr Gilbert Tothill, when she first became a patient at the Lodge, a voluntary ward of Auckland Mental Hospital at Avondale. She wrote it quite quickly in the summer of 1933–34, beginning before the New Year and finishing, probably, by or before the end of March. (Readers will notice that the only dated entries are around 31 January and early February.) Hyde bequeathed this autobiography to Dr Gilbert Tothill and he presented the manuscript at the time of his retirement, along with his signed copy of Hyde's bio-fictional novel *The Godwits Fly*.‡

The manuscript is missing its first chapter and some pages of Chapter 2, which must have recounted the earliest years of Hyde's childhood story, but it is not difficult to follow the subsequent narrative. The opening paragraph, on 'the Mob', is an aside on a group of young New Zealand poets who were then beginning to dominate the literary scene; the personal story then resumes. The incident where her father quarrelled with a landlord, 'got himself into an amusing scrape with a lady who was not one', and then sent frantic telegrams to Australia to call his wife and children home, took place when Hyde was about four years old.

After and including Chapters 16 and 17, it is difficult to restore order to some fragmentation, owing to the missing pages and because Hyde moves between incidents at the Lodge, taking place as she writes, and the account of events in her life that precipitated her breakdowns. The fact that she does not tell the life story

---

* Anne Barbara Zimmerman, 'Godwitting and Cuckooing: Negotiations and Legitimations of Cultural Identity in New Zealand Literature', (PhD: University of Berne, 1996), Addenda D: 'A Philological Analysis of Robin Hyde ms "Autobiography", Research Notes', 1991, 303–11.

† *Young Knowledge,* 232–4 – all versions from '1934 Autobiography'.

‡ See Introduction, pp. 45–61.

chronologically complicates the matter. However, if the reader follows the main strands of present events at the Lodge, the incident of the girl who runs away to see her mother and is in danger of being sent to the main hospital, and Hyde's own story of being transferred summarily to the main hospital (the Wolfe Home), it is easier to follow.

The whole narrative, except for one example in the final pages, is addressed to Dr Tothill and from time to time refers to conversations with him. It is a diagnostic and explanatory piece of writing, as Hyde tries to understand and explain both to herself and her doctor the events that precipitated her breakdown. It deals with personal material – injury to her knee, drug treatment and abuse, betrayal, loss of a baby, and love affairs – in a way that is designed to explain and sometimes perhaps even exonerate her from the judgment of her doctor and the severe judgments of the time. This '1934 Autobiography' has also been described by Hyde scholar Alison Hunt as a 'therapeutic text', because it was prescribed by the doctor as part of her treatment.* Its broken and abrupt ending suggests it did indeed have a cathartic effect, altering Hyde's way of looking at the world.

---

* Hunt, 'Cage', 148–9.

[text of '1934 Autobiography' begins]

"the Mob,")* but locally & when banded together, they seem to be all mouth and no courage. Shelley gave them the entire and simple outline of a plan of action, and they haven't music enough in them to have read it, nor guts enough to use it if by chance they did.†

Apologies: there were, anyhow, frantic telegrams of recall from N.Z. My Father, having quarrelled with "Robin Hood's" landlord, moved on and got himself into what I suspect to have been a rather amusing scrape, with a lady who indeed wasn't one.‡ She quartered herself on him, and brought a girl friend. I believe that she was an early edition of the cold-gold-digger sort of thing. Beyond his income, but disconcertingly Platonic. God help her, if she met my Mother! I don't quite know whether our family fought or ran away, but we started life in a new household.

Only a little more of this – and indeed, there has been too much. (By the way, I know all the sticky patches in our history, because mentioning the unmentionable – or rather, shouting it at the very top of one's voice – has almost forever been a custom.)

But I like to remember that my Father found or purchased a queer old flute, and that unsuitably garlanded with wild corn-flowers and scarlet poppies, we used

---

* Hyde refers to an emerging group in the New Zealand literary scene. Hyde's 'Mob' would have included young writers R.A.K. Mason, A.R.D. Fairburn, Denis Glover, Ian Milner, and Frank Sargeson. She had an ambivalent relationship with this group: while she praised Denis Glover for fighting the 'pretty-pretty' in New Zealand writing, she found their 'faults' to be 'endless, verbose political argument, and, like the erstwhile Spender–Auden–Lewis combination in England, on which its members have patterned themselves, not a little literary gang warfare.' 'The Singers of Loneliness', 1938. Reprinted in *Disputed Ground*, 357.

† Shelley's *A Defence of Poetry* often informed Hyde's thoughts on poetics, valuing as she did the true poet's excess of 'the faulty of approximation to the beautiful' and language that is 'vitally metaphorical' and 'marks' the previously 'unapprehended relation of things'. Shelley's prescription also stood for her against modernist self-preoccupation: 'All things exist as they are perceived: at least in relation to the percipient …. But poetry defeats the curse which binds us to be subjected to the accident of surrounding impressions. And whether it spreads its own figured curtain, or withdraws life's dark veil from before the scene of things, it equally creates for us a being within our being.'(Percy Bysshe Shelley, *A Defence of Poetry Itself*. www.poetryfoundation.org/learning/essay/237844? Retrieved 4 May 2011.

‡ The Robin Hood cottage was the family name for the Wilkinsons' house in Waripori Street, Newtown, Wellington. 'It was called "Robin Hood Cottage"'. See '1935 Journal', p. 258.

to execute formal dances in the evenings, with a clothes-prop for a maypole: and mushroom-hunting in the high hills, grey with a little pungent-scented shrub: sacrifices, moreover, on the huge Druid's Stone, which remains in my memory bathed always in ominous blood-red light –

There in the hills, that music came which you tell me has a perfectly natural explanation. There was a little ringed-in, rather frightening place of sunlight and wax-like pink flowers. (Once we were scared away from here by a man, enough to scatter us like a covey of birds.) The music just began, unearthly, vibrant, trembling, terrible in its sweetness – We all heard it, and stared and stared at one another's queer faces. It seemed to me to shake the heart of the hills. Oh, it was what I have always imagined a windharp's music to be, a shudder of chords too deep and wise for the mere pattern of tune.

You say it was nothing. The others all forgot it quite, I've sounded them. But it has stayed in me. And this is a rather laughable sequel – At one of those Helena Blavatsky affairs (you know, Theosophy pulling solemn faces at imaginary Masters, and hoping for the worst in the shape of a little <u>very</u> mild magic,) what they call an Astral Bell rang –[*]

Minimised and almost defeated by a stuffy room, it was my music, my swaying, shaken music again. Perhaps it was human trickery then, Nature's trickery before. But it has certainly lived in me, and I rather wish you could have heard it in those clean hills. But blessed is he that forgets, for to him shall everything be forgiven —

The very last time we were all happy together (except Mother, who just kept away, provided meals and manners, or sewed little frocks of brown tobralco[†] was at

---

[*] Helena Blavatsky, an important figure in theosophy and spiritualism in the 1880s, was said to conjure up an astral bell that chimed in gatherings wherever she attended, and was evidence of her psychic powers. Spiritualism was very popular after WWI, as people tried to contact their lost ones. Hyde attended séances when she wrote an exposing article: 'Psychic Piffle of Fortune-Telling Fakers' (*New Zealand Truth,* 11 October 1928; *Iris,* 120). Later, with her friends the Veitches in Wanganui, when she was preoccupied with thoughts of the losses of her baby son Robin and her friend Harry Sweetman, she took it more seriously. In Auckland, too, she apparently practised spirit contact but threw away her ouija board because she became very disturbed by the results (*Iris,* 141–5).

[†] Tobralco was advertised on 18 September 1914 as a cheap new washable fabric for children and women's clothing. Queree and Bros. in Willis Street called itself The 'Tobralco' Shop. http://paperspast.natlib.govt.nz/cgi-bin/paperspast?a=d&d=EP19140918.2.42.1 Retrieved 10 June 2011.

a picnic (just ourselves, of course,) in a gold-green place among the trees. I could, if I chose to be so wearisome, tell you our menu – all the funny things my Father bought. He was in khaki already, and looked astonishingly brown and nice.

Poor mother! She must have had an intolerably bitter birth with her war-baby, which arrived, red and appallingly ugly, a few months before my Father left. So debonair, to whistle "Loved I not honour more!" At any rate it snapped the very frail cord of decent family restraint –

She was so hard up, during the war – and once, we were burgled and she lost £14. Oh dear! The vicar wanted to take up a parish subscription for us, but at the last moment, she backed out. It was "no, and no, and no," with her mouth set. Only her very long, very dark auburn hair, which I used to brush for hours, was at all charming then. She was a stern, thin, unprepossessing woman. And I rather fancy our clothes were a bit nonchalant, for I started to have a bad time at school, and my elder sister too, I believe.

Yet how you'd have admired her! <u>She</u> didn't know that in the eyes of this generation Kitchener* would become no hero, but a man who "just couldn't get on with his colleagues." (Incidentally, I believe that he couldn't stand cats, either: much the same thing, very possibly.) I don't think she knows it or admits it yet, for his portrait is still in our house. When he was drowned, I remember seeing her cry, with her head on the kitchen table. "Oh God! My poor country! What <u>has</u> she done to deserve it?" England might remember that, of Colonials –

Why didn't her family pull us out of the soup? Reason (a) They were all very busy with the war. And her Mother and Father, and Aunt Louise, all died – reason (b) and the real one, I should think – She was in disgrace – or rather, just out of things for good – because she never returned to New Zealand at all. At least, not one of them has ever sent her a birthday or Christmas present.

She was V. A. R.† during the 'flu epidemic, and I believe it did her good. I went

---

* Kitchener, Field Marshall Horatio Herbert Kitchener, 1st Earl Kitchener, Secretary of State for War during WWI. He organised volunteer armies on an unprecedented scale, and was known for the recruitment poster that bore his face and pointing hand over the slogan, 'Your country needs you', which became a symbol of national stamina. The reference here is to his loss of reputation after his death in 1916; based on his poor delegation skills and secretive habits, he was branded, perhaps unjustifiably, as a poor administrator. http://en.wikipedia.org/wiki/Herbert_Kitchener,1st_Earl_Kitchener Retrieved 3 May 2011. Also see *Iris*, 69.

† Volunteer Auxiliary Reserve.

down with influenza and a spinning, throbbing head on the sham Armistice Day, when all the bells were ringing. I would, of course. But mine wasn't the very bad brand of influenza. She went into death-houses, laid out bodies, heard delirious Catholic babies rave about angels. (We lived in a strongly pro-Roman Catholic district.) We heard about these things at secondhand, and casually, because "little pitchers have long ears," and the women at the rooms where we were sprayed with that sickly stuff afterwards so often condemned, would have their daily bread of gossip –

I think she felt her feet again, after ages in a quicksand –

Then "the boys came back." We were ready, we children, to be most enthusiastic – I believe I once told you that our weekly "war lessons" used to tear me to bits – But my Father was stand-offish. I remember that he scolded me in the car going home –

But, we were to have our own house at last. It was hastily chosen, in a most unsuburban suburb near bush, hills, graveyard. We were all delighted, and there really was a flowering passion-vine, very pink of blossom, all over the back of the house – It's old and creaky and inconvenient to an unheard-of degree, yet I like its looks and its oldness and badness.

We all chanted in chorus, "Buy Laloma! Buy Laloma!"

Which was the former name of the place, and means "The House of Love."*

Chapter 3. Innocence.

I'd like to go wandering on and on among Solomon's seal and passion-flower (though the Smiths, damn their impudence, removed the lilies of the valley before we "took over." What would you expect of Christian Scientists?

But I suppose – know – tintacks are tintacks. Yet it's so hard to tell you the mixture; that I was utterly ignorant, that my anatomical knowledge would have made any cat grin, that we were nice children and strictly carried out stricter instructions not to talk about sex. We were even respected for our "innocence". (Haroun† whom

---

* This older suburb was Northland, a bush-clad hillside above Wellington's city centre. The word 'Laloma' is Samoan.

† 'Haroun' was the name Hyde gave in much of her autobiographical writing and poetry to her first love and friend Harry Sweetman. Timothy in *Godwits* is also modelled on him. Harry

I loved years later, used the phrase, "filthy innocence" in one of his very bad verses.) Yet with it all, I had an innate knowledge or awakening, as early as a native child's, as old as the first stony damnations of the Bible –

Hard to describe: a fitful flickering possession by this very old knowledge of the senses. I did keep away, utterly, from the hole-in-the-corner sexualities, verbal and otherwise, which seem to be rather like bad drainage at most schools. Perhaps if I'd just once been un-mothered enough to join in that, I'd have been shocked or frightened out of – oh, you would know its scientific name: an impulse to utter surrender, a fascination that men – not schoolboys, had for me, and I for them – a knowledge, that's the only word I can come back to. Don't hurt me over this. Even the Biblical condemnations – and there were times when I believed them word for word, and begged God, as one might beg a Devil possibly amenable to reason, to let me off – went away from me at times – .

I who hadn't done anything, had thought and felt and known and been, by the time I was seven – Queer – Rather like Danae's torrent of gold and her harsh stone tower rolled into one.* As I grew older, the gold became less and the tower pressed into my inmost thoughts, and every inch of it was carved or painted as might be at Pompeii –

But always – and here, and I think with your help – that has gone away and left me quite free, more free than normal people are, I think – I mean, there's a strange remote and absolute cleanliness in long periods of time, perhaps years, perhaps

---

died in England on 13 May 1926, but Hyde did not know this until 19 December 1927, when she received a letter from his brother Hardy in response to a telegram she had sent to Harry. In Chapter 16 of this autobiography, however, she claims to have heard news of his death in May 1927 before she was admitted to Queen Mary Hospital at Hanmer (*Iris*, 99 n†, and Hunt, 'Cage', 133).

* Danae was the only daughter of Acrisius of Argos and Eurydice. She was confined in a bronze tower by her father, who had been warned by an oracle that one day his daughter would give birth to a son by whose hands he would die. However, Zeus in the form of a shower of gold found his way into the tower and frequently visited her there. From his embraces, Danae had a son, Perseus, with whom she was exposed on the sea by her father (Dr J. Lemprière, *A Classical Dictionary* (London: Routledge, 1788, 1963), 191). Hyde often refers to this story. Her contrast of 'the gold torrent' with the tower that 'pressed into my inmost thoughts' (despite or even because of its phallic connotation as the rule of the father) seems to convey her fear of being punished for sexual knowledge or desire and a generalised shame about female sexuality.

months – And I call that region Hy-Brasil, who call the other Venusberg,* and know every inch of it, because I have eyes that must see and a memory that must retain – I woke up once, with the first line of a poem about Venusberg in my mind. It was

"Out of that slimy Hell he burst at last."

Make just what you wish of that –

I told you there were two men who wanted me, while I was still very young. About the second I may just conceivably have been wrong, though I don't think so. His secretive desire to have me alone, to pet me, make me little gifts, may, it is possible, have been a rather maudlin fatherliness. But I don't think so – or I wouldn't remember. I liked him, for the funniest of reasons. He taught me to play hockey passably, and I was already shame-faced about not being able to play games –

The first (you may have thought it diseased imagination,) was no mistake, though it was such a little thing, one single incident – and I was seven –

Picnic on the sand-dunes. This shining light of a Sunday School world led me away, quite casually, from the rest – I remember the little hollow of the sand, the hot sun beating.

He leaned over –

"Well, give us a kiss, Kiddie."

I did – rather shyly – perhaps Danae's shower wasn't known to me then. But I remember his thin face and ravening eyes –

He laughed, rather confusedly. I don't think anything much more happened, though it's all afar. We went back to the picnic –

He was prosecuted and imprisoned for interference with children, not much later. Don't think that made prodigious my own little, unclean experience – I had already been queerly frightened about it – Woke up one night, and told my mother –

---

* These two mythical locales were frequently juxtaposed by Hyde as two kinds of escape. Hy-Brasil (or Breasil) is the Irish earthly paradise, a mythical wooded place that was considered to lie in the furthest west of Ireland. (Later, Spanish adventurers who knew the myth applied it to the land they discovered – Brazil.) Hy-Brasil for Hyde is a wild sanctuary, while she would have known of Venusberg from Wagner's *Tannhäuser* as a place of destructive sensual pleasure and indulgence. Historically, Venusberg is the cavernous court of Venus in late medieval German legend, supposedly visited by the knight Tannhäuser, who then sought absolution. In *Young Knowledge*, Michele Leggott orders a group of poems around the title 'Hy-Brasil', Section Two, 124.

She only said, very soberly, "I'm glad you told me."

My clever Aunt Louise was probably the first to detect "the monstrous changeling." But as Dom Byrne* once very truly said, there's a psychic path. I don't know that I mind so very much now. I am freer sometimes – now! – than most women will ever know how to be. But it did bring me, when I was seventeen, this.

Flattery from an "artistic" Christchurch business man, who should be keeping a "maison de tolerance." An invitation to view his sketches at his flat … well that <u>was</u> obvious enough, God knows, and I did know a bit about myself by then, though still a ridiculous nothing of clear fact. (Poor Mother! <u>Her</u> idea was to leave a book that would have sickened anyone in my room. It wasn't explicit, just dramatic and ugly. For many months, before I left College, I drew myself into the smallest possible section of air, and shrank from every touch, because I believed that a disease which blinded and scarred could be caught – from any human contact. I must have mentioned it to her, for she hurriedly retracted: I'd only read half the book, anyhow. But like Balaam's ass,† I would no further go, and just shrieked to her to be quiet if she ever mentioned sex.)

I <u>was</u> abnormally conceited about my artistic judgment – That's my only poor and cheap excuse for visiting my good fox in his lair. You can guess what happened. Certainly no dignity nor decency in it, and a "virginity" (can you be a virgin when you mentally aren't?) precariously maintained by a fishwife's threat of screaming – I hate marble fireplaces like Hell, and I hate worse the scent of Three Flowers talc (for hot telltale cheeks, quite unsuitable when one's guests depart.)

The quaint thing is, that the men at the newspaper office where I then worked

---

* Possibly a reference to Dom Ambrose Byrne, a Benedictine chaplin who served in WWI and ministered to many men – not all of them Roman Catholic. James H. Hagerty, *Benedictine Military Chaplains in the First World War* (1998) 6. http://www.plantata.org.uk/papers/ebch/1998hagerty.pdf. Byrne would have been known to the returned servicemen Hyde spoke to in the writing of her war novel *Passport to Hell* (1936). However, the 'psychic path' sounds more like the Christian occultism associated with 1920s versions of yoga teachings for Westerners.

† Balaam was a prophet who was commanded by Balak, King of Moab, to curse the Children of Israel. His refusal to do so was followed by a similar act of disobedience by his own ass, who saw a vision of an angel and refused to carry his master, and when struck called out in protest (*The Holy Bible,* King James (London: Collins, 1975) Numbers 22:15–39). Hyde's behaviour towards her mother is similarly impassioned and wilful – like Balaam's ass, she believes she knows better.

had known exactly what was going to happen, and one of them, a fatherly being, solemnly congratulated me because I snubbed my fox very much in public, when next he called. (He was more amused than alarmed, I think, once I'd used his filthy "Three Flowers" and had given evidence of keeping quiet.)

No innocence anymore. But I did at least have some shred of myself left, (that is, if it wasn't all lost when I first became, in instinct, "a citizen of no mean city.") This (though the idea may amuse you,) was perhaps because a boy was marked out to die in his early twenties, and wanted me "as an ideal," and badly needed a dream I couldn't have given him, if things had happened otherwise –

For what is culpable (and there were doomed cities in the Bible, weren't there, though children still played in them?) let me steal a little Church thunder –

"Thou that takest away the sins of the world,
have mercy upon us … Forgive us all that is past."[*]

But no: I think I can manage without God. Like Olive Schreiner, I love Christ but I hate God.[†] So you can judge, who do not bother with superstitions, how much chance I have – you and the gardening shears and the phloxes – I told you I nearly ran to Mother Church, when away from here. Not quite – It was here, instead –

Chapter 4.
    Voices in the Night.

Oh dear! As usual, after reading over a page and a paragraph of this, I wonder if I should have cut it down to half a dozen facts, naked as they came into the world. But how can I? Incident means little or nothing, except a possibly neglected chance for new perception, new development. I've left out hundreds of millions of things, so that you shan't be quite overwhelmed by bindweed in these childish paths.

Yet because you fish a fly out of a milk-jug, that doesn't necessarily mean that

---

[*] *The Shorter Prayer Book* (London: Oxford University Press, 1946). http://justus.anglican.org/resources/bcp/Shorter/shorter.htm Retrieved 11 May 2011.

[†] Olive Schreiner, South African novelist 1855–1920. These are the words of a young shepherd boy wretched and lonely, with an overdeveloped idea of sinfulness, in Schreiner's *The Story of an African Farm* (London: Chapman and Hall, 1883), 23.

you want to hear every detail of its infernal history. I do it because sloppy wings and aimless buzzing annoy me, also because I like my milk without flies –

I have twice (once purely by accident, once against my will,) saved a life. One was my sister Edna's.[*] We could neither of us swim for toffee, and she hardly at all – I encouraged her to leave the shallows, because only in deep waters is swimming the heavenly cool sensation that it is. Suddenly she went under, gulped, came up with eyes tightly shut, and flung her sticks of arms (she was very thin,) around my neck. She wouldn't open her eyes or do any of the accepted things. I remember how I disliked that poor little screwed-up obstinate face, and wondered if I could decently or otherwise scramble away and let her drown. Somehow we did get in though, and I was very cross and appallingly rude. Well, to cut a long metaphor a little shorter, perhaps you will feel like that. But I'll make quite sure whether you want to see this long, lost narrative, before you ever do see it –

There was a blessing on the wildness of our new home and its surroundings. At first people were inclined to be friendly, but my Father had definitely improved since the war, and he made such a deal of noise when quarrelling. That's catching. I'm inclined to believe that we all shouted. I used to be chilly and quiet at first, then hysterical … then Mother Earth –

I told you that myth of the earth-giant whose strength increased tenfold whenever his wounded body touched his mother. – I used to run outside and lie face down in the wet grass – and oh, the dark sweet shadowy whisper of it! Not so much just flowers, which can be staring nincompoops at times, but the steady heart beating beneath. An amoral and very amusing woman I know laughs at my alleged desire to be At One (her phrase!) with "the birds, the bugs and the beetles." But I do love the earth physically, than which I can no further go. (I loathe touching or being close to many things and most people.)

I used to "run away" often, and be fished back in disgrace, a silly melodramatic red-eyed little fool. I couldn't stand the voices in the night. My Father was still, not in love with, but in need of my mother: she had begun to hate him. Half-heard arguments over a half-understood thing! It was like that idiotic book I half read: just ugliness, so close, whispering so often. And one can't tell one's progenitors "Do shut up." As far as that goes, if they had, the pity that lay beneath my horror would have gone on working –

---

[*] Edna was the name of Hyde's younger sister – the third daughter in the family.

I have known, since, so many returned soldiers whose self-control seemed to have been smashed to pieces. Pity the dead, because they are very peaceful and we have written hymns about them! But these <u>despoiled</u>, what about them? I know as well as you do how useless pity is. It's too late – undoubtedly though, my Father's already odd code of morals had become genuinely perverted –

He and I returned in a tramcar, with a soldier friend of his, from some show in town. The soldier friend was still in khaki, and I'm afraid I was one of the many sloppy little idiots who gave to that grim uniform the unthinking hero-worship which may have helped all modern men to despise all modern women. (I mean, hero-worship without understanding or genuine sympathy.) I chattered, preened my feathers, left the poor hero laughing and cheered up – My Father was very silent and morose as he climbed with me up the steep road to our house. Then, when the family were all gathered together in the name of supper,

"Iris," said he solemnly "I'm sorry to have to say it, but you looked at that man with the eyes of a harlot!"

"Bolingbroke, as low as to thy heart
Through the black passage of thy throat,
 thou liest."*

Only I didn't know that answer then. But I make it now, and it is true.

He was jealous of me, in a funny way – I remember – balloons, Christmas Eve, a lit laughing street, and a huge bearded Afghan who <u>did</u> look at me with some insolence. My Father turned and kicked him off the pavement – I only just heard his muttered words, which were, "Get back to your sewer, you rat."

But that I rather admired. I have no objection at all to a blundering attempt at chivalry. Still, no denying it, he <u>did</u> upholster me with the Scarlet Woman's trappings at a very early age. And right he may have been, but his way of making things conspicuous made them a little more real. Also – we do prize dignity, who are young: damned or otherwise.

---

* William Shakespeare, *The Tragedy of King Richard the Second*, IArden Edition, 1.1.124–5. Thomas Mowbray to Henry Bolingbroke. Hyde has substituted 'black' for 'false' passage.

Chapter 5.
    The Pool.

Only a word of this. We lived within five miles of bush, wild and very old. The first way to it was by stile, through an ancient neglected garden left by a now extinct Judge to the people of the city, who don't seem to know what to do with it. This became Haroun's garden and mine. The second was by stream. Such a dear way, past the little farmhouse that is completely ringed in by great firs, over stepping-stones, by deep amber pools where there are <u>said</u> to be trout. Wild purple-flowered mint grew here, and there were blackberries, possessed of the devil in their clinging propensities, but of precious few and <u>very</u> small berries.

    But there was the lost path that led to my pool – six feet deep, I'll swear, and with an enormous rounded stone, smoothed by the flying spray of a waterfall which leapt like a white spirit from broom-bushes above. The broom bushes hid it, and the St John's wort – you know, that fiery crimson-leafed stuff that you like. To get there at all, you had to crawl under great bent bushes of broom – and nobody did, thank God, but me. The very last of Wellington's wood-pigeons gorged themselves on fallen karaka berries, and others of a purple hue. The infinite delicacy of skeleton leaves and tiny lace-like ferns was there to enchant me, and I believe I <u>was</u> enchanted, sitting bare-legged on the great stone in the pool.

    I told Haroun about it, no other. He wanted me to take him there, but for some reason I never did. He knew it only by letter. Now it doesn't exist, for they have extended the great yellow-soiled graveyard, and shovelled tons of earth over the little flying waterfall. In a way I'm glad, but I wish I were so deeply hid as those two. When I was ill before – I mean, seven years ago – I sickened for that place. For a little while, I was at home. A grizzled old friend of mine, brown-faced and caustic-tongued, heard that I raved about the bush. He used to walk miles, in order to bring me great bundles of redgum and tree-arbutus and just the cool shapely leaves. That was almost as good as my pool, the one place where I have ever been quite my own possession. And this old friend was a darling. "Anything she wants" he said superbly "barring a roast peacock, she shall have." Once it was onions, to weep with, and tiny hankies, to dry the tears.

    And <u>he</u> died, in just the way that I have twice almost died. He wouldn't eat, would do nothing but grieve. I went to see him, and his family looked as if Lazarus had risen, when he walked out, a shiny-eyed ghost, to see me. He said something about his early sins and punishments, and asked me to speak of him kindly, when he was gone. I, blind fool, went away in tears. What do you think it was all about? Just that some investments had gone wrong, and he was no longer successful or prosperous, but, saddled with a big house and, I suppose, with the family ghosts of his own derision of weaklings, wasn't going to admit it to anyone. Oh, as if that mattered! Or as if my tinpot sexualities matter, I suppose! Why can't both be buried deep, like the pool that made its rainbow in solitude, and then died without the knowledge of people who would not have cared about it in the least?

> You shall go stooping low, the gold of broom
> Brushing against your hair, blinding your eyes:
> Scarlet of John's Wort seeking for your lips
> Till you shall think, "Were there perhaps a Queen
> Today, whose mouth burned so, she had made flame
> Of other towns, of other little ships.
> Another horse had tricked a greater Troy."
> Seven times your lips must drink of shadowed pool
> Seven times your body feel the flying spray
> Till every evil shall be gone from you.
> Then you shall see the spirit of the pool
> Sit, rainbow-haired, and watch the gold of broom
> And gold of sunlight mingle with the spray –
> Things of the bush shall come so near, so near,
> To peck at purple berries, or to go
> With a quick whirr of tiny frightened wings –
> You shall be bush-enchanted. All the trees
> Shall reach long hands to touch you, brother-wise,
> And you shall see the tree-fern's carven bark
> Rot in the amber stream. More than all these
> Shall gold of sunshine soak into your soul,
> Until it seem a rainbow-tinted thing
> Like his whose feet upon the mountain-tops
> Made a wild sunset for the little towns.*

---

* Hyde's own poem, this is a version of 'Bush-Enchanted', *Young Knowledge* 52–3.

Chapter 6.
Jezebel – Also the Monkey.

Now I'm damned if I know why I call her Jezebel.* She did me no wrong, the reverse rather, she is persistently friendly even now, she has faithfully followed all the laws of Nature & Convention, and she was beautiful, I think. Yet concerning her, I have one of the crazy unjust visions to which I am subject. I see her golden-haired and finely clad by her lattice, looking down anxiously, anxiously into the street below: and a splendour rides by, and flings her body down to be eaten by the dogs of a respectable boredom –

Poor Jezebel! She is bored, with her husband, and was before she married him. Most intimately bored, she told me so. And really he presents no reason why she shouldn't be –

But oh, she was lovely at College, in her eccentric way! You asked me if I'd had any "little love affairs" there. I didn't mention that I was far too busy at the time, making Jezebel love me against her better judgment and inclination. (She never had much time for anything but matrimony – but I did make her love me, and now it's she who runs after me.)

How many women do you know, whose hair is really golden? Not flaxen, or pallid, or reddish or brassy. Hers was gilt and perfectly straight. She had the green absent-minded eyes of a leopard, and bad clothes and a certain trimness of figure, and always a tongue that could say ugly things with lightning speed – Perhaps it was partly self-defence, her father shouted like Jehovah.

It was an ugly thing, the first she ever said – a mean impossible little accusation of theft, of all things. Nobody believed her, least of all herself. I was a hedgehog then as now, curled up, prickly and nervous –

---

* 'Jezebel' was the name Hyde used for her oldest friend Gwen Hawthorn, also 'Simone' in *Godwits*. Jezebel was the daughter of Ethbaal, the King of the Sidonians, and the wife of King Ahab of Israel (Kings 1:16–31). Jezebel worshipped Baal – a heathen idol – and persuaded her husband to build a temple in his honour. She and her husband both came to gruesome ends – her body was thrown into the street and the bones licked by dogs. Biblical commentators describe the story as illustrating the folly of marriages between Israelites and the people of the land, where the indigenous wife led her husband into pagan worship – Hyde seems to see Jezebel's punishment as marriage and family, betraying female friendship and dreams of independence. The popular 1950s song 'Jezebel', sung by Frankie Laine, originated from a 1938 musical of the same name, perhaps suggesting the biblical epithet was popular then.

But in some game or other, I saw her with wild-rose cheeks, her green eyes filled with tears because she'd just torn the entire knee out of a black woollen stocking. (We <u>were</u> frights in uniform. I believe they do you better at the Borstal.)

From that second, gold hair and green eyes were supremely important. I bided my time – She made a fool of herself in class, started to weep and was advised not to be a baby – I stood up: stamped, and declaimed "She's <u>not</u> a baby. She's got the most frightful headache."

Isn't it funny how sympathetic women are over headaches, when almost always it's an imaginary complaint?

She was curious, was Jezebel: a little annoyed, for I was younger than her – I <u>made</u> opportunities of championing the poor lass, of flinging off porcupine-quills at her (I didn't need any telling that she wasn't interested in other people's tears.) We drifted into partnership: she pretended to be unwilling, but – a sharp-eyed form mistress of ours used to accuse us of "undercurrents of understanding."

There was a funny old library, and I was part of its committee. Museum, ditto.[*] In the library I found books like Rostand's "Chanticleer,"[†] and lured Jezebel to it. We had a sharp attack of Alfred Noyes. And we both loved the watching, waiting face of the Mona Lisa, and the Laughing Cavalier, who watches in so different a way. Both prints hung over the stairs, worn quite hollow by the feet of girls now dead or old. I remember dusk there, and the wide green sweep of lawns, lunch with Jezebel in a cool corner under great English trees –

Just like my clever Aunt Louise, the headmistress always mistrusted me. She wore dangling earrings, recently became an OBE, made it a strict law that to be seen talking to anything male (of course we all <u>had</u> to argue with the caretaker, but he was at least ninety and just like a lamp-post) was a breach of rules that might have Grave Consequences.

There was the little flock of dusky sheep, of course – not a bit interesting, sniggering and commonplace. For other Jezebel, whose family blessedly moved from an old house near the College into green meadows and a ring of trees, in the Hutt district. She became an excellent rider.

We had our secret places – high in the tea-tree, where Life seemed spun of tiny

---

[*] At Wellington Girls' College in Thorndon.

[†] *The Story of Chanticleer* by Edmond Rostand, published in 1913; this and Alfred Noyes's 'The Highwayman' and his other poems, as well as the reproduction of *The Laughing Cavalier* by Frans Hals would have been popular cultural pieces to introduce to young people in the 1920s.

grey and green spider-threads, but the mosses were deeply golden. How she enjoyed the fact that I was Afraid of Cows – until with the perfect bravado that casteth out funk, I had my photograph taken, sitting on one of 'em in my bathing dress –

Dear lost lonely Jezebel! I don't sentimentalize about her much, because against crowds (and the enormous crowd who would vote for her marriage can't be missed,) I'm no use, except when in a temper. I don't even know quite what she betrayed, if anything. Art? Of one of her little paintings, a nymph held by a moonstruck faun, a friend of mine who really is a critic said "It's so nearly good that it's disappointing." Or was it love? And how can I possibly talk? Yet she knew herself that she was a traitress. Oh Lord, she's not thirty yet, and may do some fine thing, advertised or not, which will make me look pretty small –

What use to you are fleeting moon and pinewood, a gold-haired girl who stood straight as a shaft of sunshine, and drew devils male and female, and improvised dances in costumes that would have startled you? What use, the pearl fan of foam spreading wide under dark cliffs at Waverley?*

"They are gone from us, grown little and less
Than water under the wind's white knees."†

We got lost once: almost on purpose, in the huge black-clad hills behind her home – Very wet the manuka was, and bright gold the moss. I knew quite well that we were getting lost – and went on – I don't know where I wanted to end up. Dreamland? It was far enough and dark enough, when she grew nervous – not of the hills, but of Father – Jehovah! – and insisted on our turning back. Too late. It was black night when we saw the search party's lanterns, and my Jezebel was more frightened of Jehovah than ever I had been of the cows. I did the gallant (not from any gallantry, only because it was she, and I did love her.) I let myself fall "Plonk!" from an enormous fallen tree-stump, and had to be carried home, not quite unconscious enough to avoid a great deal of discomfort. Ridiculous! And, if you please, it got the solemn morning newspaper as a Rescue, and I have never quite lived it down at home. But I remember also the silky pleasure of the hot bath wherein Jezebel and I were unceremoniously dumped together –

---

* May be a reference to the greywacke cliffs near a town north of Wanganui: Hyde lived and worked in Wanganui 1929–30. Less likely to refer to Walter Scott's Waverley novels.

† Probably Hyde, but not found elsewhere.

I introduced her later to Haroun – and wondered if my leopard would go a-hunting, for there's no denying it, unless I were excited she beat me hollow for looks. But <u>he</u> didn't re-act, which was odd, for he made no secret at all of his love affairs, past, present and to come: and of other things, before he went away to die, that I believe men don't mention to women. I'm tremendously glad that he did to me. There's no cursed question of <u>forgiving</u> now between us –

And if my two, who by every law of nature should have fallen in love with one another, had done so, I'd have been lonelier than I am now. But they didn't –

When I was in hospital, she told me one thing, as if afraid to tell it and afraid not to tell it.

"A man ruined Olga."

Olga was her lovely, half-wild, dark-haired elder sister, who spent her time avoiding people and drawing exquisite child-faces. (She was the true artist of that family.)

The very first holiday that she spent away from home, there was a man, nameless – "a clod!" Jezebel said contemptuously – and there was to be a baby –

Their poor tired mother wept, and one of the two men who had formerly owned their place, and had remained family friends, found her. He questioned or coaxed her – I don't know! He was elderly, married and divorced before, a lonely, decent sort. <u>He</u> married Olga.

She rose to the occasion, that betrayed forest child, at one of the desperate little wedding feasts inevitable in a family with so many relatives – flies around the honey-jar! I believe she made a gay, polished little speech – she who at normal times could scarcely be persuaded to speak at all –

And she was the girl who went mad, when her baby was born out in the country – She's still hopelessly insane. "She was terrible!" whispered poor Jezebel – But now, she is very docile, and sings to her baby.

He died before he was a year old, of diphtheria. His father by proxy keeps snapshots of him – I know! And the father, at least I mean the imitation father, is dying now of cancer, has been since before I was ill and came here – I saw him once in hospital – horribly white face and huge eyes. There were others there. He murmured to me wearily,

"If I could only have died at Christmas!"

His suffering woke Jezebel up. (He had taught her to ride, and perhaps she loved Olga, though, as I've told you, she's a Family Skeleton whom one just doesn't mention.) For a little while, she was the girl I had known at College, but finer, more gentle, sweeter.

[heavily crossed out over three lines]

I wouldn't have told about Olga, but that secret's no secret at all in the district.

An elder sister confided in a little white toad of a girl friend, who, being annoyed, acted after the manner of toads one day. I suppose she – I mean the Toad – will live in peace and prosperity forever. It's a sad tale, this – But I have always felt I should somehow have helped Olga, later have helped George (who was my friend and a gentle one.) As for Jezebel – lost, lost, for ever lost, that's what I feel – She has two babies – The girl is rather a quaint Thumbelina elf, but the elder, a boy, I think absolutely distressing. "The dogs shall eat the flesh of Jezebel,"* that's that – I only hope she gets lost utterly in maternity – her family do – and forgets whatever dream of individuality there was to forget – The husband's a most efficient provider.

Well: poetry, and the monkey – of course. Writing trash that rhymed was sheer Hell at first, at college. (Mother started me on that downward path, some time during the war.) At College, it very naturally made me a foolish sort of freak, and it certainly didn't justify itself – But the others were so very bad, that I scooped the pool of really good monetary prizes, bestowed by an obliging Literary Club, one good feature in a bad school. You had to spend the money on books, but it was Heaven going into Whitcombe's and buying smooth new desirables – Spenser, Omar, Keats – one of the white-headed company, Shakespeare, is with me here and now, and the line beneath the frontispiece might be significant:

(Iris: "I met Her Deity
Cutting the clouds towards Paphos.")†

Don't know why I dragged in the monkey, except that I liked him. He was a skeleton in our museum. For some insane reason, skeletons and the bare bones of things seem very likeable to me.

Jezebel, being older, left College a year before I did. I patched up a secondhand

---

* Implicitly, the dogs of respectable boredom.
† These lines from *The Tempest,* 4.1.93 form the caption below the frontispiece illustration of Hyde's edition of Shakespeare. Hyde often employed the classical significance of her own name: Iris, messenger to the Gods.

sort of interest and acquaintance (never friendship,) with a girl whom she had liked, a dainty-handed but spotty-faced little wiseacre, a very Fact of Life in herself. She loved – Truly, purely, nobly and a' that – a youth at a college for boys. (It was a different tale she told me years later, at a house in this very road.) Well, Boys' Sports were on, and she <u>had</u> to see her Ted triumph in flannels, there <u>had</u> to be a companion, and it was I. (I was bored, don't make a good chaperone at all.)

There also had to be, later, a very stormy interview with the Headmistress. How her earrings flashed!

She really absorbed that "True, pure and noble" love story. I suppose that's why she now likewise wears an OBE – or is it just a sort of certificate thing, to be tucked inside the corsets? But she and I did not get on. Either the earrings rattled me or I rattled them. She asked me to take the self-satisfied look off my face. I've seldom if ever been really pleased with myself – nor had the chance! – and I suppose I retorted with savagery. I know that, whilst not being expelled, I was Publicly Disgraced – read out at Prayers or something, and stripped stark of <u>my</u> little badge of merit. Wasn't it funny, really? I didn't snivel then, but ran upstairs to the monkey, of all people, and did – bitterly. Then retreated to Jezebel's home, and her mother (who is an angel, in a listless sort of beaten way,) tucked me up in bed. I was retrieved by my Father, who, after next day interviewing the earrings, agreed with every word their possessor said. Oh, of course, if one's daughter has the eyes of a harlot (though I suppose in <u>her</u> company he was a little less scriptural!) Fact remains, I <u>was</u> bored and a chaperone on the silly expedition –

And I'm not really too deeply woebegone about my wrongs! I mean, it was funny, and Jezebel and her mother were darlings, and there can be no earthly doubt that I was a fool to take on such a worthless fag-end of adventure. If you like, I'll join in chorus with Miss M and my Father, and that will be funnier still –

Anyhow before I left that College, I'd written about half a dozen lines and suddenly felt, "That's not so bad!"

"For Cytherea's* shadowed face,
Faint amber of her wandering hair,
Purple vine shadows, that enwreathe
Her marble forehead, queerly fair,
And carven lips that seem to breathe …"

Lord knows what it was all in aid of.

Miss M had the last word – I had to be a prize winner at the last breaking-up ceremony, and in addition to Tennyson she bestowed on me the Book of Job.[†]

If I didn't know it for certain that motherly bosom is stuffed with horsehair, I'd think she had a sense of humour.

Chapter 7.

Song.

I am disconsolate over two things.

The first is that I realize too well, I should have painted in perhaps a quarter inch of this chronicle, with the care of a Japanese brushwork artist. Isn't it from <u>little</u> things that the discerning eye learns its all? Instead of which I am presenting you with an O. S. S.[‡] daub in mingled water-colours and oils.

Also – all your work is "le sacrifice inutile," I am afraid. That's it exactly. I <u>am</u> afraid, after all these hard years. Just some silly little incident, contact with one of the others, and I shiver, and feel sick and run away to cry – "Gone to earth," to crib Mary Webb's title[§] – I do try: lie awake and think of the very worst that might happen, if

---

* Hyde's school-girl poem continues the previous theme: Cytheraea (or Cythera), a disguise of the goddess Aphrodite, was married to the lame and unattractive Hephaestus but was pursued and fell in love with the handsome Ares. The two were discovered – captured under an invisible net set by her husband on their couch. Aphrodite fled to the island of Paphos. Robert Graves, Introduction, *The New Larousse Encyclopedia of Mythology* (London: Paul Hamlyn, 1968), 125.

† The Book of Job, one of the books of the Old Testament in the Bible, concerns the sufferings of Job and his steadfast faith in God.

‡ Over out-size daub.

§ A dark reference: Mary Webb's *Gone to Earth* was published in 1917 and its 'integration of … universal death myths' reflected both the author's despair and the 'catastrophic' mood of the times. See Gladys Mary Coles – Heritage Website, West Midlands www3.shropshire-cc.gov. uk/intros/T000626.htm Retrieved 11 May 2011.

I should get into some corner whilst you are away. Striped pinafores, eating coarse food with spoons, privacy stripped naked, the last days of Pompeii. Don't think I do not <u>know</u>, every inch of it. Even in my solitude I can't avoid hearing things. Well, I think "Even that: and still I shall be myself." (Probably an error of judgment.) I hear the wise gentle voice saying

"Of our philosophy you make no use,
If you give place to accidental evils."*

But I can't get away from a prejudice against the futility of mindlessness. Of course mindlessness is to be found everywhere among the sane – in women's talk and men's love-making. But there, one is free to run away and be an outlaw. Here, with you absent – I wonder? I wonder if that might not be the ultimate test? I should certainly fail in it. <u>I am afraid.</u> It's all very well to talk of

"Lonely antagonists of Destiny
Who went down scornful under many spears,"†

but what if they live on, and can't get up? You know what your colleague says about my constitution – Sometimes it's more dangerous than all other things, to be physically strong – May you never have to know that. But no, I'm through with this complaining, and I'll tell you of Song.

By some marvellous chance it was my Father who brought Haroun home, before I had left College. But Haroun had us all enchanted, Miss M even. I remember what we talked of, on our stiff sitting-room – But it doesn't matter, except that I was insolent, and remarked that I liked men who worked on the roads much better than I did those who worked in ~~hospital~~ offices.

Well: the very next day, the College door-bell clanged, and a senior who had been there a hundred years or upwards, trying to pass matric.‡ came flying down

---

* Dr Gilbert Tothill's wise words. The whole passage suggests conversations that have taken place between them and his advice on how to resist despair.

† These lines are taken from an Irish ballad, possibly called, 'Fair-haired Donough', which Lady Gregory (well known as a compatriot of Irish poet William Butler Yeats) uses as an example of the 'sorrow that is never far from song in Ireland'. http://www.gutenberg.org/dirs/1/8/0/7/18070/18070-8.txt Retrieved 11 May 2011.

‡ Matriculation, a school leaving and university entrance examination gained in a range of subjects. Iris did very well in all subjects except mathematics and gained a scholarship to the

the corridor.

"There's a man to see you, Iris!" Then in a burst of enthusiasm," Such a <u>nice</u> man!"[†]

Miss M sanctioned it –

Rough tweed coat, dancing green eyes, and (I'm sorry to be Ethel M. Dellish,[*] but I can't alter facts,) a cleft chin. I never saw Haroun in any but the one coat, and never wanted to. I cannot remember any physical fault – and I had eyes. Nobody ever spoke of him as a boy, though he was then less than twenty-one – I never have met a more mature mind, "burning bright," cruel sometimes but always beautiful –

He had an enormous bundle of his own poems, which meant well and were very bad: and a copy of "Marpessa," and of Maurice Hewlett's "The Forest Lovers."[†] For me.

Also he pulled an official reprimand from his employers out of his pocket. It was on blue paper, and began a long, long screed with "Please note." He had answered it by writing on its back one word, "Noted."

"As a matter of fact," he said, I am going to become a linesman. I will work on the roads."

It took my Father three days to become jealous and order him out of the house. I remember how I longed for him to kiss me goodbye, but he wrote instead – a hurt snappy sort of letter. Then he went away into the backblocks, being a linesman, whatever on earth that is, in good earnest.

I was sick and weary – and ever so glad when I got sunstroke, posing for a little lady artist on a beach than which Hell can have been no hotter. In the exact middle of the sunstroke, an enormous letter from Haroun arrived.

I'm rather glad I haven't those letters with me. (Hundreds of them lie in an old cabin trunk at home, together with scented verbena leaves and lace my Grandmother

---

University of New Zealand. The failure in mathematics obliged her to stay at school for a year longer to complete the qualification but she did not go on to university (*Iris*, 31).

* Ethel M. Dell, romantic novelist (1881–1939).

† Maurice Hewlett (1861–1923), English historical novelist and poet. http://www.poetry-archive. com/h/hewlett_maurice.htm 11 May 2011. His 'Forest Lovers' is 'a romance of medieval England, full of rapid movement and passion' (published 1898). Stephen Phillips (1864–1915), poet and dramatist. en.wikipedia.org/wiki/Stephen_Phillips. Both Hewlett's 'Forest Lovers' and Phillips's long poem 'Marpessa' (1905) were extremely popular in their authors' lifetimes. It's unclear whether Hyde is criticising Haroun's romantic taste – though she does comment on his 'awful poetry'.

once sent me from India, and a yard of the softest red morocco, which was always about to be made into my Sunday-best shoon and never was.

He was sometimes destructive, but never obstructive. "Destroyer and preserver!" He railed at me because he thought I could write, and didn't. Then he got his fingers into clay, and realised the fascination of sculpture.

I used to walk up our path with a throat that hurt me horribly – Would there be a letter, or no? There usually was. He made me see the cutting of tea-tree, his little country amours, his old home in the Waikato, "with the bees marking summer in the macrocarpas."

Returned to Wellington just in time for his twenty-first birthday. Observe raw seventeen's triumph over black-haired, black-browed forty – Kit, who was his mistress but <u>not</u> his lady. He ran away from her, to spend his birthday night sleeping in our old house. Also, he wrote that he found her letters a little dull. ("Cad!" you'll say. No, just utterly and honestly truthful. He was much more insulting to me, at times. But he loved me. He thought me rather a little fool – when I was much too busy listening to him, to care to talk: but he disclosed "honourable intentions" that gave him an amazing freedom in our house, and we two were to wander, beggars and Kings, in Europe, and sleep out under pine-trees –

Danae's shower was gold indeed, at last – I am very rich in that love which was never to "change, and alter, and grow less."

Quite suddenly I became pretty – oh, there was a brown hat with an orange feather, and I could carry my head high wearing it –

Great crystal-green waves swept in, immense and eternal, by the Red Rocks. The moon sailed huge and silver among bluegum trees on the Wireless Hill, and a hedgehog came tumbling out of the grass, with its funny little cold nose. He held me too closely there – I wanted him to, indeed – and then stopped, frowning.

"I'll never do that again."

He told me of a schoolteacher girl, and of another. Neither mattered. The only mercy I have ever found at all, is that he cared for me most and last, and wrote to me his last letter, and then tried to come back to me in a dream-ship – I think it's because we were always to need one another so, both deserving nothing from any code or society.

Now at seventeen, I didn't care for anything whatsoever except my lord. We found our way over the hills, to the old neglected garden of which I have spoken, and the pink lilies – belladonnas – were in bloom. Among those old trees and their gold lances of sunlight, I let down my hair, which had been put up recently. We said nothing at all, but I can remember his look, which seemed as though it would never end –

And he who was so very self-possessed and free with forty-year-old mistresses, turned and ran from me. I wasn't hurt – The trees knew, and I did. I wish that this little may be counted unto him for virtue, since virtue is such negotiable coin –

I saw him next – I mean, for the next long period, and after the many letters that still peopled my loneliness – in Auckland –

I think he had changed a little, was a little sex-spoiled, or perhaps haunted by the shadow of death. For each of us said one fatal thing.

"Iris, I don't think I shall ever have a son." Then his eyes were bright again, and laughed at me. "He might be one of the world's great men!"

In a little hot stifling place of nikau palms, he did try to make love to me. But I – though he was still, and more than ever, all that I cared about – had changed, or developed a new wisdom.

We had planned a moonlight picnic, just for ourselves, on the top of Auckland's highest and most darkly-wooded hill. The sunset was red and sullen, and Haroun disappointed and hurt. (He could be more unpleasant than anyone else, when hurt.) We trailed up grimly to the circle of trees – ah, just a "virtuous" little office girl, and a boy who didn't want a demi-vierge.

It was decent of the moon to be so enormous, sheer pearl. Suddenly in the midst of his sulkiness, I had an inspiration – I called "wait," and hid myself behind the trees –

I told you I was well-proportioned once – (not after wearing and sleeping in a Thomas splint for three years, though.) I was quicker than a shadow, and made no sound in undressing myself. Then I walked out and stood on a high, flat rock –

I had guessed right. For a moment, not a word. Then "I'd have liked you brown, all over, like the back of your neck," he said seriously. "But not now. You must be white ..."

He began to plan.

"A pool in front of our house, and you swimming in it, silver." Oh, the sudden laughter! There are more gods and goddesses than Venus. I remember fruit – grapes – crushed against my throat. But no other touch. And when we went down the hill again, he drew a long, tired breath.

"Coming up here was Hell. But now it's Heaven."

Next day he showed me the little roughly-worked figurine of a naked-woman, her head thrown back. It was called "Song." I thought it beautiful – and I'd been critical enough of my lord's awful poetry.

I helped him to finish it, indoors this time. I had to say the fatal thing, though.

"It comes into my mind that I will pay a great price for your night's work."

And he too – were we clairvoyant, or just moonstruck fools in love? For he cried out desperately,

"Oh God, little sweetheart, don't say that!"

We were seen home by little scarlet swinging lanterns, like will o' the wisps or ladybirds. (They still use them here in Auckland for roads under repair.)

The very last thing he ever said was, (this was under a streetlamp,)
"Yes: you have a good face."

When he did get his chance to go to England and study, and I was studying the art of using crutches and making up the most ill-tempered lies I could think of for the strange people who would ask me, "How did it happen?" I wouldn't have minded so. Indeed, I'm very glad he missed the crutches and the splint, just as I should be for a man I loved to miss the final ugly stages of pregnancy in me. But his last poor letter, that stammered as badly as I do and began, "I suppose you'll hate me," exasperated me to the last stage, because of its promise to come back to me after his wanderings. I lit a cigarette, and then lit that sheet of paper – My name was not Ariadne or Penelope,* and the promise had been that we should travel together – (But you'll not be able to understand.)

And then all the months of silence – I did think, he had just forgotten – So I razed that splendid house to the ground, and strewed the site of it with salt –

But you cannot imagine the sadness of the place of the pink lilies. I was fool enough to tell Jezebel about it once, and she – took her future husband there. It frightened her away – I don't know if it forgives me or not, "sweet place desolate."

---

* Ariadne, daughter of Minos II, King of Crete by Pasiphae, fell in love with Theseus, who was shut up in the labyrinth to be devoured by the Minotaur, and gave him a ball of thread, by which he extricated himself from the difficult windings of his confinement. After he had conquered the Minotaur, he carried Ariadne away with him but abandoned her on the island of Naxos (Lemprière, 74). Penelope waited more than twenty years for her husband, Odysseus, to return to Ithaka from the Trojan Wars (Lemprière, 459–460).

Nor if he does –

> You who would have forgiven all, and not a word said
> Of burnished sins like peacocks, of the little scurrying things,
> Not of your lips is pardon earned. For long since, you are dead,
> And that which glows in you is lost like Egypt's vanished Kings. *

I had to leave a boarding-house here in Auckland quickly.† For a long time the snoring, snivelling old man who, being a wealthy bachelor, had the big room next door, had talked of the poor young man who had left all the books and a reading-lamp there ... who had gone to England and died in three months of pneumonia. Then, quite by accident, I heard the poor young man's name. It was Haroun's, and his little lamp shone in the room so old and dingy and forlorn. I wish I had kidnapped it!

As to what happened to "Song," I don't know. Haroun may even have been dissatisfied and broken it up – But I have not helped in the making of any other song.

Chapter 8. To Be Skipped.

If you had wanted a way to make the egocentric sick of egocentrism, you have surely found it. The mere posturing and grouping required for all this!

And I'm inclined to think all the others are as bad, or worse. Somebody's had fourpence filched from her locker, or believes she has. Dramatic discussion on the verandah! (Oh, oh, if you'd only give me sound proof windows, or the sort of earth-cell affected by the dirtiest of Tibetan saints!)

"If I knew who'd done it," cries one dark-eyed little sensitive plant, "I'd report it without hesitation! She deserves to be sent to the Main Building!"

I used to hold that there were three essential virtues (I lack two of 'em:) a sense of honour, a sense of humour, and a sense of beauty. Now I'm inclined to add another, and say "Be this, if you will be human at all." A sense of proportion.

And there are two sins: the sin of ignorance, and the sin of cruelty.

One desires so much, just darkness and utter quiet. Diogenes cries (or would, if

---

* Probably Hyde.
† The boarding house was known as 'Burwood' and was in Princes Street (*Iris*, 54).

it were any use,) "Stand out of my moonlight."*

People think Death has a purely negative value. No. It has its immense gravitational pull, just like Life, but the closer planet wins – nearly always. Yet quiet has its unassailable fortresses. I told you how I prayed to ancient sleeping forgotten Dis, in the Waitomo caves,† which are old enough for him. But it takes more than a fly to make a god turn over in his sleep.

If you are ever so tired that voices cut into your brain, and what they say into the inmost solitude you have won, go there, and let Charon ferry you down the Styx,‡ and see the millions of glow-worms burn blue in the utter darkness. Geologists can tell you that it is many thousands of years since the slightest movement of earth – in this angry country! – disturbed the blue lamps lit to the honour of the darkest god. Each lamp is a life, born and winged, fed and to die, for no other purpose than to light the quiet. It was years and years, before my visit there last year, since I had known anything to equal that dark forgetting.

The torment of many voices is one that the Inquisition really should have known _§

And I would I might drink to thee

---

* Ancient Greek philosopher Diogenes, a celebrated Cynic of Sinope known for his controversial actions. When visited by Alexander the Great, who asked if he could help him, Diogenes replied, 'I would have you stand out of my sun light'. http://www.thefamouspeople.com/profiles/diogenes-of-sinope-224.php Retrieved 10 June 2011.

† The Waitomo caves in the Waikato are underground limestone caverns famous for their stalactites and stalagmites; visitors take trips in rowboats to view the glowworms. Hyde travelled there as a journalist some time in 1933 (for possible dates see Hunt, 'Cage', 178–9). On the theme of 'black and healing silence' in Hyde's stories, see Alison Jeffreys' 'Other Pastures: Death, Fantasy and the Gothic in Robin Hyde's Short Stories', in *Lighted Windows*, 78, and Alison Hunt on suicidality in Hyde's texts and life ('Cage', 23–42). The '1935 Journal', 15 May, p. 249, also describes this trip to Waitomo.

‡ Charon is the ferryman of Hades or the Underworld, and the Styx is one of the rivers of the Underworld.

§ In the record of the only formal interview, on 3 February 1934, that Hyde had with doctors in the period of writing this autobiography, it was noted that she complained of hearing voices and these voices were ascribed by Dr Tothill to a projection of her own experience (Hunt, 'Cage', 155 and *Iris*, 233). The doctor's records are not available but were described and quoted from by Derek Challis in *Iris*.

In my dark bubbling wine,
On the slopes of the Mount divine
Under the myrtle tree
Whose roots strike hollow, hollow
Through the caverns none can follow
To the depths of the secret mine.

Would I might watch the stream
Black and sluggish gleam,
A daze of terrors for lingering shades that dare not
Kneel to their dreadful King
With the last proud offering
Of the life for which they care not.

And I would that my heart be weighed
Whilst I waited, undismayed,
And a harp be struck in the dark, to whisper the story –
How to the land of the dumb
A stranger was singing come
To tell of its fiery nights, and its long-veiled glory.[*]

Sounds like a terrible mixture of mythological observances, but I've always held that Osiris, Dis, Pluto[†] are obviously one and the same, and their customs might very well be swapped without damage.

Ah yes, back, back, back, today. For the first time in months, I only lay still in the garden, didn't work there.[‡] The bright flower-faces meant nothing. No cause, but voices and accidental contacts, and Fourpence=Hell to somebody, and <u>now</u> they're

---

[*] Hyde's poem 'Homage to Dis' (Pluto, etc.) *Young Knowledge*, 97.

[†] Osiris was an Egyptian god venerated as ruler of the afterlife (Lemprière, 431–2) while Dis, a god of the Gauls, is acknowledged as the same as the Roman Pluto, the god of hell (Lemprière, 212).

[‡] Hyde's comment here suggests she had had her own garden plot since early summer 1934.

talking Bill Bayly.* Have you read Lorna Rea's book, "The Happy Prisoner?"† It's about a deaf girl, who is horrified when she recovers her hearing, glad when it goes again.

Never mind: it's nearly nine o'clock, and soon they will all be quiet. (Actually, nobody snores on the verandah now, but you should have heard my Lady M., who said reflectively of me, "She must be going to have a child," because I don't like bathing in public.)

> "Hardly a sound …
> The birds are asleep in the wood.
> Soon, so soon,
> You shall sleep too."‡

That's Goethe. Isn't it a blessing in words – "tired eyelids, upon tired eyes?"§

Voici! Our pretty little pink night nurse has arrived. She's one of the nicest, young, friendly, sensible, not a bit hysterical about the damned polishing (but then, of course, she doesn't have to be.) She never asks questions, or repeats knowledge. I wish you'd make her Great high Panjandrum,¶ or something! Her brown hair and clear skin are soothing. Yes, I know I've several times figured on her charge-sheet for writing late (when I couldn't sleep, or Yasminé** was ill again,) but like Izaak Walton impaling

---

* Sheep farmer Bill Bayly's trial for double homicide in October 1933 of a neighbouring farming couple opened in Auckland on 21 May 1934. Protesting his innocence to the last, Bayly was hanged in Mount Eden prison, Auckland, on 20 July 1934. See *International Police Association NZ Section Journal* V15 3 September 1981: 57–9 on http://www.oocities.org/mhall_nz/bayly4.htm#_ftn18 Retrieved 12 May 2011.

† Lorna Rea's *The Happy Prisoner* was published in 1932.

‡ 'Wandrers Nachtlied' or 'Another Night Song'. Longfellow trans of title. 1780. http://www.homehighlight.org/humanities-and-science/academics/goethe-s-wandrers-nachtlied-in-longfellow-s-translation.htm

§ 'Music that gentlier on the spirit is/than tir'd eyelids upon tir'd eyes'. From Alfred Tennyson's 'The Lotos-Eaters', *Poems, Chiefly Lyrical* (London: Effingham Wilson, Royal Exchange, 1830), 50–1.

¶ An important, or self-important, person: from 'Grand Panjandrum', a nonsense phrase first used in a satirical mock lecture given by dramatist Samuel Foote in 1754.

** Gloria Rawlinson (1918–95) was a young poet who, with her mother Rosalie, first met Hyde on 1 October 1933 (*Iris*, 226), although they had sent flowers when Hyde was in the cells at Auckland Hospital (*Young Knowledge*, 11). Gloria contracted poliomyelitis at the age of six and had been in a wheel chair since. She had spells of sickness and Hyde clearly felt a special

his worm,* she does it "tenderly and as if she loved him."

I think I'll tell you now about the dream. I don't know when it started, but it has a sinister reputation in our family, because it always comes before very bad luck. It's almost worth luck of any sort.

Wistaria† pours in pale amethyst torrents down either side of wide, shallow steps of white stone. These are the only signs of cultivation in the place, though I should say that it's beautiful people are decidedly cultivated. I don't remember any objection to their voices! The two women – one dark and slight, one an "amber blonde" (Oliver Wendell Holmes has devoted good time and thought to the classification of blondes,)‡ – are both a little older than myself, but by no means middle-aged, and lovely as the very softest of mellow afternoon sunlight may be. It is long since I have seen their dear faces, and (superstitions considered,) may be that's as well, here: for what evil might they not portend? It's not a purely feminine world, for a boy has gone by in meadow-grass, playing a quaint butterfly waltz on his violin. One of them – my two ladies – told me, "The beautiful youth has passed."

It changes its exact locale sometimes – there have been beechwoods where the light quivers like a painted green wing. But there always seems to be wistaria about, and I nearly wept when I found that yours was over, when I came back here.§

I walk and talk, am very active – not, though, with the strained fantastic activity of the dreams which were my escape from lameness. It's the utter unearthliness of the

---

protectiveness towards her. Gloria was only fifteen years old when they met but was already something of a celebrity and known internationally (see Riemke Ensing, *Te Ara Dictionary of NZ Biography* http://www.teara.govt.nz/en/biographies/4r8/1. Retrieved 3 May 2011). Later, Gloria Rawlinson became an editor of, and commentator on, Hyde's work. When she died, she left an unfinished but extensive biography of Robin Hyde that was completed after her death by Hyde's son Derek Challis, and published in 2002 as *The Book of Iris: a life of Robin Hyde,* bearing both names as authors.

* Izaak Walton, an English writer best known for *The Compleat Angler* (1653), a celebration of fishing in prose and verse.

† She prefers the alternative spelling of wisteria.

‡ Oliver Wendell Holmes: Professor of Physiology, poet, and satirist, famous for his verse as well as sayings, including many on blondes: 'There are two kinds of poets just as there are two kinds of blondes.' *The Autocrat at the Breakfast Table,* 212. books.google.com/books?id=07s8 cardeGIC&pg=PA212&lpg=PA212&dq= Retrieved 12 May 2011.

§ Yours = the Lodge's, and the 'coming back' was in December when wisteria would have been over.

place, and its happiness, that I love so much. No, I have never met there any person I knew or know on earth, though when I was ill seven years ago, I could daydream a sort of replica of it, and by running very quickly, find Robin, who was dead. That was very different – a conscious effort, to be made when I was wide awake, and to be paid for by the horrible shadows which beset the still waking, but overtaxed mind. (These shadows were just beginning to return to me, when I came here for the second time.)

You'd think it easy enough to manage a projection of one's own image, over the tiniest of frail white criss-cross bridges. But it wasn't. The ground – there never seemed to be any stream – used to swirl up in brown waves, and run how I would, I could never escape its difficulties – but I used to find Robin, and hold him as they would not let me, even for one minute, on earth.

Yes, I know quite well that all that was "wish-fulfilment," and that the aftermath of terror, which has never quite gone away, was merely the effect of a mental strain self-imposed. But I was ready to do that.

The wistaria dream is different: never asked for, nor, so far as I can tell, having any particular association.

One of the nicest and sanest men I know has his periodical, inexplicable dream, always seeming tinged with the same unearthliness.

He is invariably sitting before a fire, whose smoke is a fragrant-smelling cloud. Down the chimney fly hundreds of tiny green birds, and their singing fills the room.

"I'm never in the least afraid for them," he told me, "I know that they are perfectly safe – and they make one most extraordinarily happy."

Connect that with sex, if you are able! He is associate editor of one of NZ's biggest dailies (and a good writer, for all that,) plays the 'cello, used to teach at a boys' college, was in the war, has never had a mental or nervous breakdown. (I think he's a bit fed up with me for so doing: though he sent me books at Christmas, and little handkerchiefs exquisitely embroidered with grave formal roses. He is the only man to whom I ever send gifts, because the only one I know who is never sentimental. I point out that I am, but "I love your sentiment," says he.* For which

---

* She is referring to her friend John Schroder, who was editor of the Christchurch *Sun's* literary pages when she first met him, then associate and later assistant editor of the Christchurch *Press*. He was her mentor and faithful correspondent from 1926. Lisa Docherty's '"Do I speak well?" A Selection of Letters by Robin Hyde 1927–1939' (PhD: University of Auckland, 2000)

and for a thousand things, I have to thank him. I like best the Holbein men,[*]

"They are the lords and owners of their faces!"[†]

And incidentally, this is the deuce of a long parenthesis. Hic jacet.[‡])

The dream about Haroun and the ship from which we can never quite land in our old city of bluegums isn't – or wasn't, it comes no more – a "wish fulfilment" either. But such meticulous detail it had – and the very last time I've touched his old shaggy tweed coat was in a dream. Remember, then I was walking a dark way alone, and I didn't know that he was dead.[§] No, for all you say, I still believe he tried to beat his way back to his lost and unfaithful fool, when she needed him most.

"No God, no Heaven, no earth, in the void world –
The void, grey, lampless, deep, unpeopled world,"[¶]

but somewhere a garden, and my wise sweet-mouthed ladies, and perhaps J. S.'s green birds in some high tree, and Haroun. Surely that's more real than these crazy human voices, their lost fourpence, their Main Building, their Bill Bayly! And,

"Si le ciel est vide, nous n'offendons personne."[**]

---

gives more information on this correspondence and reproduces Hyde's letters to Schroder.

[*] Hans Holbein, German painter (1497–1543), known for the naturalness, objectivity and precision of his portraits, and court painter in England for Henry VIII, has given us a way of seeing important men: 'We do not doubt for a moment that they are faithful records of what he saw, drawn without fear or favour' (E.H. Gombrich, *The Story of Art* (London: Phaidon, 1970), 278). Hyde equates his subjects with Schroder here.

[†] William Shakespeare, Sonnet 94.7. Helen Vendler, *The Art of Shakespeare's Sonnets* (Cambridge: Belknap Press of Harvard University Press, 1977), 402.

[‡] Let it stand.

[§] See the discussion of when Iris learnt of Harry Sweetman's death in *Iris*, 96–9, and in Leggott, 'Notes to *Young Knowledge*', Section One, 'Making the Ghost Walk'. www.nzepc.auckland. ac.nz/authors/hyde/yk/pdf . See also pp. 69–70 n† and p. 128.

[¶] 'No God, no Heaven, no earth, in the void World;/The wide, grey, lampless, unpeopled world!' are lines from Shelley's long poem *The Cenci, A Tragedy in Five Acts* http://www.english. upenn.edu/Projects/knarf/PShelley/cencitp.html Retrieved 12 May 2010.

[**] It is a wide world that offends nobody: a more philosophical observation.

Chapter 9.
  The Evil Hour.

More Bill Bayly this morning – I do wish they would either hang that man, or not hang him – But I've discovered overnight a reason for all these hard voices. He that hath ears to hear, <u>let</u> him hear – and he that has a tongue or a pen, or any instrument of correction, let him later remember what he has heard, and act accordingly –

It's appropriate, anyhow, that I should be beset by human voices just now: for I have been putting off the evil hour of remembrance, the ghost of a time when, being clamped to my bed by enormous iron weights that at first seemed to draw burning nails slowly through my foot, I certainly couldn't run away from them –

Nobody knows yet quite what caused my lameness[††] – I think, a bad crack on the knee incurred by being thrown from Jezebel's horse. (Don't laugh, or believe me quite a liar, but that horse was named The Doctor. In thinking I was a poor rider, it was absolutely correct.)

Well: my knee just doubled up agonizingly some days later. I can remember the solemnly-jogging old horse between the shafts of Wellington's one and only hansom cab, in which I was sent home from the office. One of Wellington's very worst doctors (I wonder if he's a friend of yours?) declared I had inflammatory rheumatism, must to bed for six weeks.

Six weeks! It seemed an eternity. And our house is <u>not</u> the place for repose. There's always somebody quarrelling – Perhaps we're all geniuses. Dit Melchior Bungholt, "Genius bursts into flames, not into tears." Well, don't we just?

Dr P became frightened, as my knee set at right angles couldn't bend – and the agony grew so much worse. Then he started to give me morphine, and I can remember hours when I could cry at last, and the wonderful golden throbbing began in my arms, and spread slowly. Morphine is like silk compared to all other drugs' cotton – And I still hope you'll somehow, in Germany or England or America, manage to cook up some version of it which won't injure.

Even morphine and plenty of it, couldn't stop sheer <u>agony</u> when Dr P became

†† This remains unclear. Although, as she goes on to suggest, the inflammation of the right knee may not have been the result of the accident but was a tubercular infection of the knee (not uncommon at that time); whatever its origin, the result was permanent lameness of her right leg (see *Iris*, 55–7).

definitely frightened, and had me moved to the hospital – I was put to sleep quickly. Then, at night, waking up to a glare of red light, and the sounds of violent retching from a woman slowly coming out of chloroform.

Surgical ward: they chloroformed me, next day, and set my crooked knee in a decent position and a Thomas splint. Ah, the nail through the foot began then! It must have lasted for a long time, for I can remember being terrified of any movement, even though the great iron cradle protected me to some extent.

The young Portuguese house-surgeon who for some weeks looked after me was very merciful, and I hope he has an enormous practice now. He gave me morphine (by injection,) every night. And I nearly got quite better. By itself, my knee began very slowly to bend again. I nursed it, but practised it. Sometimes I think that's the very worst thing of all. I could bend it again – but not until after my kindly house surgeon had been moved, was I fool enough to tell the new one, Dr S.

He slipped his hand underneath, forced the knee up and down. "Look at that, Sister," said he proudly. Sister did – at him. And the little bunch of them moved on, and left the bandages undone, the splint unstrapped all day. By night it was agony again: he prescribed some new kind of splint, I've forgotten its name. Soon there was more chloroform, more straightening – I think three times in all. But no more mild gymnastics. The last minor operation a specialist performed. As I wandered back out of chloroform, I heard two women speak. One of them said, "I heard the doctor say she has a TB knee." The other, "I'm sorry for her, if she has."

But I'm talking as if it were all myself. It wasn't by any means. As you know, the pain soon dies down in a well-splinted knee, and I never had the faintest idea that I was going to be crippled. Beyond a normally abnormally fast pulse, I had nothing to be excited about – in myself. I fancy I looked rather TB, with very pink cheeks and bright eyes. We even had fun, sometimes, and made up libellous rhymes about the house surgeons. We were proud of a very old lady, past eighty, who had a kidney operation and quite recovered. And when they moved me out to the tiny courtyard, four starlings splashed in the stone fountain, and the sparrows knew their mealtimes to a T. They would come right up on my bed, I suppose because the iron cradle seemed to them a safeguard.

But ... there was that woman with cancer, who shrieked for what seemed hours, every time she was moved. And she lived so long! Another with cancer wanted terribly to live, because of her children. A woman who had lived near us during the war, and who had been in an upstairs medical ward, jumped from the window, and was brought in with a broken leg, screaming mad. True, they moved her to a private room, but oh, how her screams tore the place. "The devils" were after her. They took her to Porirua,* and she died. You can verify this, her name was Mrs Warwick.

I had my first really deep draught of the feminine moral code. A girl was brought in, screaming at first, then moaning. I heard her long sob. "Oh, doctor, I can't stand this any longer." And he was merciful, thank God. He said quietly, "No, I don't suppose you can." I think he gave her something … but I heard a nurse scolding her, because the blood from her body had soaked through to the floor. She died.

"That's what you get for messing about with married men, my dear," said one of my bed-mates.

An old, thin voice cried for a drink of water. Then it was silent. She was dead, and she didn't get her drink. "I was a-thirsty and ye gave me not to drink."†

One girl who was up and about, after an operation, seemed to love me. She had gorgeous leonine bobbed hair, that's all I recall. But I was warned against her. Though ostensibly a waitress, she was really on the streets. Her name was Kathleen –

And, once, there was a dark little sullen girl brought in … plain, lifeless-haired; after lying inert, she sat up and glared at everyone.

It was a probationer nurse who told us her trouble, (and, look you, there were younger there than I, though perhaps none so receptive.) She had syphilis, and was very temporarily in the surgical ward, because of the necessity for an operation which prevented a baby from sharing that fate. It wasn't put so prettily. Nobody spoke to her, and she to nobody, and all things were kept apart. Only a few days. My bed was near hers – but if I only had spoken! "May the sight fade from mine eyes, may my right hand lose its cunning, if I forget thee, oh my Jerusalem."‡

Insomnia had long begun, and much worse: the roaring of caged beasts in the Zoo not far away, got into my dreams;§ at first I was frankly a coward with my lions and tigers. (One awful little door would open, and I'd think "safe!" but no, I was in another room, and another. I have never minded death in dreams – sometimes it's peculiarly desirable, just a great roaring of waters and the swoop of darkness, and

* Porirua Mental Hospital just north of Wellington (its name was changed from Asylum in 1911) was also referred to above as where Olga was sent.
† *The Holy Bible,* King James, Matthew 25:42: 'I was thirsty and ye gave me no drink'.
‡ A version of Psalm 137:5: 'If I forget thee, O Jerusalem, let my right hand forget her cunning'.
§ The Zoo – Wellington Zoological Gardens – opened in 1906 and is near to Wellington Public Hospital in Newtown.

then – but you know what happens later.) Then I used to conciliate them, to bait traps of friendship for them. After <u>years</u>, I was triumphant with them. And now your Main Building has got into my dreams instead, and God knows I have no more years or energy to waste on the bogey-man.

Going out of hospital on crutches and besplinted wasn't pleasant. It was the almost unbelievable curiosity of people that jarred one (never ride in a tram-car, if you're maimed.) For I had no great pain, my all-important "job" was waiting for me at my newspaper office (I haven't made half enough of the kindliness and amusing side of that staid old place, so much more prosperous and less fortunate nowadays.) And moreover, Dr D. S. stated that I'd be well – I mean, not crippled – in anything from six months' time. I was almost amicable about it, and there were pleasant, hard-working months, for it was suddenly decided that I was a "witty" scribe – if not Pharisee!* – and should have delightful work at the Parliamentary Buildings. Those childish articles amused everyone, their be-crutched writer most of all. And it does not entertain you, when you're only eighteen still, to have tea in state and in private with a Cabinet Minister, who loves to hear himself talk to the young and feminine! The salary is good – £4 a week – there are pretty frocks, and greatest triumph of all, no more living at home. Our M. P.'s snore so late, taxis are so dear and my crutches so unsuitable for a steep dark road, that for an outrageous figure I secure very bad, but roomy, diggings for myself.† Occasionally I am hauled over the coals for a Labour bias‡– several Labour members make a practice of taking me to tea and giving me the latest news, that's why. <u>I</u> a cripple! I am only a little tired sometimes – and snowed under by bad dreams and worse memories.

I take it that this is pure logic. Either you adapt towards "les miserables" the

---

* In common parlance 'a pedant', the term derives from the name given to members of an ancient Jewish sect, distinguished by strict observance of the traditional and written law, and commonly held to have pretensions to superior sanctity. *The New Oxford Dictionary of English* (Oxford: Clarendon, 1998), 1391.
† Hyde rented a flat in central Wellington from June 1925.
‡ As a lady parliamentary reporter, Hyde's amusing columns attracted a 'stern injunction' from the conservative-aligned newspaper, the *Dominion,* which was employing her to omit all mention of Labour members, a difficult challenge when the small number of Labour members gave 90 per cent of the speeches and provided most of the incidents; she responded 'one might as well ask for a snappy scenario about Adam and Eve leaving out any reference to the serpent'(*Iris*, 61–2). Also see Nikki Hessell on this period in Hyde's journalism career, 'Novitia the anti-novice: Robin Hyde's Parliamentary Reports', *Lighted Windows,* 151–61.

attitude clearly summarized by a fellow-countryman of mine, Roy Campbell:[*]

"I sing the people: shall the muse deny
The weak, the blind, the humble and the lame
Who have no purpose save to multiply,
Who have no will, save to be all the same.
I sing the people, as I watch, untamed
Its aimless pomps and generations roll –
A monster whom the drunken gods have maimed
And set upon a road that has no goal."

That's honest. Either that – or else, to your Aegean stables, boy Hercules! To your leak in the dyke, little Dutch infant,[†] and wait for the roaring fury of contemptuous waters to smother you!

But without hysteria, there have been dreaming quiet minds and hands that have builded – a little. For after the coral insect comes the atoll. Of course all the morality of any possible reform will be wrong, because it's bound to be emasculated. Men of any significance can stand most things, but not committees. C'est ça. And the organ cries

"Pass on to Calvary – oh son of God!"
And the weary human heart answers –
"There on the edge of the purple down
When the tender dreams begin,
Look – we may look – at the Merciful Town,
But we may not enter in:
But we – pity us! Ah, pity us!
We wakeful: pity us.
We must go back with Policeman Day,
Back from the City of Sleep."

---

* Roy Campbell, writer, poet and translator, lived from the 1920s in England and Europe, but like Hyde was born in South Africa. However, she was acerbic about Campbell's politics compared to those of her compatriot Douglas Stewart, see *Iris,* 433.

† Reference to 12 Labours of Hercules and a story (probably originating from nineteenth-century American author Mary Mapes Dodge's story for children *Hans Brinker or the Silver Skates*) about a Dutch boy who noticed a hole in a dyke on his way to school and used his finger to fill it, thus saving the city of Haarlem from deluge.

Chapter 10. January 31st, 1934.

A wind-torn place, the blossoms wakening only
To be despoiled by this fierce outlaw day.
I wait amid the grasses, still and lonely.
The trees know best what little I would say –
How vain my strife against the winds, how vain
The little hours of sun, the ghosts of glory:
This garden is a half-remembered story
Sung by the ragged minstrel of the rain.

Yet, were my hands as white as any hour
As now this laughing, cool, unfearing rose,
Beauty had gained a little, by the dower
That we who pass leave in her garden close.
Knew I one word as wise as these old trees,
Then I were worthy some should call me friend
Let the wind whet his sword! But here I tend
A momentary haven on my knees.*

Chapter 11.
        Thirty.

Oh dear, and oh dear! Ostensibly it's just the same January 31st, but actually it
isn't. I am devoured by the wolves of mortified pride, simultaneously gnawn (is that
a good word?) by the fox of a desire to be funny. One simply mustn't be funny here,
or there may be some astonishing sequel. Besides, what I desire to do is to try to be
funny at the expense of a prominent Auckland businessman whom I don't know.

        You see, all the years (2 1/2) I was on the Observer, I dealt with his drapery firm,
and paid my account with scrupulous attention to detail. But when I jumped off the

---

* Alison Hunt comments that this poem 'about her plot in the Lodge garden, ... described in
    Chapter 11 as "a bad poem"' was, however, 'published with only minor changes under the title
    "The Garden" in the *Auckland Star* in September 1934, and again in *Persephone in Winter* in
    1937 (58)' (Hunt, 'Cage', 154).

wharf, I very naturally owed him £5/10/- – I sent him four – fête galante!* – when here last. Received a sticky letter recently about the remaining thirty shillings – everybody forgets thirty shillings, even Judas Iscariot tried to[†] – and wrote back sweetly in return, to say that I'd pay him same the moment I had it. Today comes Letter No 2, suggesting I should without delay start small regular payments of the sum outstanding. Now what I'd like to do to and for Mr S. M. of M. and C.'s[‡] is this. I'd like to write to him,

> "To pay you off I'm more than willing,
> But thirty shilling is thirty shilling;
> One pound ten is one pound ten
> And sometimes bothers the best of men–
> I promise I won't Do The Dirty
> (In after years,) about your Thirty."

But supposing I did and he posted it back to your colleague? Bloody vengeance upon the Malekites and Philistines![§] Besides, I can hear you advise me not to be funny with my creditors. But I can tell you, both my Mother and I wish we had one or two good Business-is-Business boys in our family, the length of their noses only excelled by that of their purses. We did have somebody in business once, nearly a century ago. He was a dealer in used bottles, (empties!) which I think romantic. You see the odd thing is, he was one of the Barren Valleys, and due to him were yearly very considerable revenues from his very own property. Well almost in old age, he suddenly took to bottle-collecting, and made it not only his hobby but his lifework. His money meantime went on accumulating. There is some legal doubt as to whether he actually, whilst bottle-collecting, married and was father to a child, or merely

---

* A celebratory phrase: originally French eighteenth-century for an outdoor entertainment, or elegant festival.

† Judas Iscariot delivered Jesus into the hands of Pontius Pilate's soldiers for 30 pieces of silver.

‡ Milne and Choyce Department Store.

§ The Amalekites, a semi-nomadic tribe from Canaan known for their cruelty and cowardice, were overcome in battle by the Israelites (with Aaron helping Moses hold his rod aloft): thus Amelekites is a generic term for enemies (Exodus 17:11–14). The Philistines were a non-Semitic people of southern Palestine in ancient times, who came into conflict with the Israelites during the twelfth and thirteenth centuries BC (*The New Oxford Dictionary of English*, 1394). Hyde is using these terms to represent attitudes of ignorance and hostility towards culture and the arts.

lived with somebody and did ditto. (This is all absolutely true, my Mother told me, and she has a holy horror of romancing, even in the best of causes.) The net result, though I scarcely recall the full details, is that, like every second Colonial family, we may have money in Chancery, or it may belong to the child's issue, if any – he seems rather obscured. It's an enormous amount, enough for everybody, prolific though her side of the family has always been. It was taken with sufficient earnestness to be investigated a few years ago by some very nice and very wealthy cousins of hers, Charles and Violet Holmes, who live on the Rand and have just finished the sort of wandering I always dream about. (Little snob coming out! Picturesque pose! But none the less Charles was awfully decent to us when in N. Z., and used to buy us the most tremendous bags and boxes of chocolates. And our long-lost bottle-seller does amuse me. Evidently nothing ever came of the investigations, for the hot water service at our house is still appalling – you have to light a red-hot fire to get a bath. However, Violet still writes often to Mother, and is the only one whom I consider a sports-woman. – i.e., one willing to oblige without putting me under an obligation.)

No more rot: no more rambling reminiscences. But I thought you might have had enough of cankers for the meantime (I told you I was going to use every journalistic trick,) and don't you think my rhyme for Mr S. M. rather good, for tosh? Yet the odd thing is, same day I've been thinking that to betray Barabbas* for fourpence is as bad in principle as to betray Christ for a bit more: writing a bad poem about my garden, waking out of a half-dream with the words "vital spark" in my heart, and thinking, that, that is what was drowned in me. I wonder how you manage to keep a steadfast path? And how would you like to be an entire company of strolling players, an audience and the sniffiest of critics, all in one?

---

* It was customary on the Feast of the Passover to release one condemned man; the man Barabbas was chosen over Jesus and released by Pontius Pilate from Roman custody. Matthew 27:15–26.

Chapter 12.
  Red-Riding-Hood.

Being a man, you will never know the fascination of buying pretty clothes. Yet listen! Black marocain (dull crinkly sort of stuff,) with a long fringe, because then fringes weren't only worn by Shetland ponies: flowery cherry-coloured chino, and a back hat with dangling cherries on it. Little white morning rig-out – oh, well! But I did look nice, in spite of the crutches. My holiday, to be spent alone at a new and charming place.* Incidentally, there were rather good facilities for treatment of the knee which remained so persistently stiff, and I meant to use them, and go back again quite well.† For the first time I had a little money, some earned, some handed over by my mother as my share of the legacy which came to her from the bachelor brother who was killed on Gallipoli. (I forgot to mention that he left to her several hundred pounds, to each of us a smaller sum – but it looked huge then. I never met him, and he has never seemed real. Even his poor old photograph is stiff and wax-moustached.)

The train journey was for ever and a day, and I too tired to look at anything, when I stumbled up to my hotel bedroom, let down my hair, put on a dressing-gown. I was sound asleep...‡

Enter the villain, with afternoon tea. I thought he was the waiter. He wasn't, and liked my hair, then and there. (But that's pre-dated.)

I shouldn't joke about my poor dear. For I have seen him in Auckland not a year ago, and if ever a man looked thin and tortured and done for, it was he.§ And he was Robin's¶ father, and there was a time when I clung to him for that alone. But the truth is and was, though I had sent Haroun farther away, in my heart, than ever he had gone of his own wish, I never loved anyone else. And the truth is, too, I have always been

---

* Rotorua was the chosen destination, at this time in its hey-day as a fashionable tourist resort.

† The Rotorua Sanatorium (later Queen Elizabeth Hospital) and the Government Bath House, which was a medical facility until 1947, managed by the Department of Tourist and Health Resorts.

‡ Her hotel was probably the elegant Princes Gate Hotel. Originally built in 1897, in Waihi township on the Coromandel, it was relocated to Rotorua in the 1920s.

§ Frederick de Mulford Hyde was a pilot in the (British) Royal Air Force in WWI. Here she calls him 'Cedric'.

¶ This is the first time she names her unborn child, Christopher Robin Hyde, born Sydney 1926.

punished for loving too little, never for loving too much. So when you read of me in unfortunate circumstances, think of his weary blind coil of troubles and no love: and think that when he was seventeen, he was a pilot in the Air Force. I like to think of his gallantry before he was spoiled. As for charm, he had that, for almost no known reason. Very dark, very thin (they called him "The Indian Famine" at school,) square curious hands, crooked mouth, loved music. He seemed to have plenty of money. He undoubtedly had plenty of friends –

But what is then to say of Cedric? I remember too much to be said. I think, he was unfortunate, and more particularly unfortunate in being clever and far from kind. Picturesque too. Am I tired, that I write so very badly? It may be this: I was unfaithful to love itself, before he was more conspicuously so in a love affair. I don't think there was a penny to choose between us. He was unlucky, in hurting me so badly, because it is unlucky to hurt me badly. (Laugh.) But the not very deft juggler of love affairs may have been simply a bewildered and heartsick boy. He was twenty-seven then. There was always a fluttering crowd of older women, maiden and otherwise, in the offing. At first they were remarkably sweet to me, then not so sweet – Should have been enough of a "Trespassers Will Be Prosecuted" notice. Not that I would have needed it, if I hadn't wanted to.

Anyhow I was too busy enjoying the atmosphere of that odd place, which utterly defeats dullness against heavy odds. Flamingo-red sunsets, tourists, heavenly baths (if there's a disease in direct opposition to hydrophobia, I've got it, I adore water,) informal sleepy picnics among the lacebark trees … my knee started to feel and look almost well, so well that they all thought the stiffness was caused purely by "nerves". I didn't need the iron splint. My newspaper gave me an extension of leave. I was happy, and fit except at times.

Encounter No 2 with the poor villain – It was all the fault of the lions. A circus came to town. (Usually if one does, I quarter myself miles away, and but for the Main Building I'd never understand why the roaring of the lions here doesn't torment my dreams.)*

This was funny. I woke out of one of those terrified dreams, and actually something was shuffling in the garden outside. The very unwilling and unchristian martyr in me

---

* An aside about the possibility of hearing lions roaring from the Lodge, which was in the suburb of Point Chevalier, not far from the Auckland Zoo at Western Springs. She's implying the torment of the thought of the Main Building eclipses other terrors.

shrieked – in silence, I couldn't even have whispered for the beating of my heart. Nervous indigestion when the pulse races! I wonder if frightened animals suffer from it – yet you can feel their hearts thud if you handle them. The noise went on, and I simply wasn't brave enough to lie there and listen. I managed to get out of bed, into a dressing-gown, dragged myself down the corridor and into the garden. It's much better to be eaten than wait for it.

And there in the moonlight, an old horse was making hay and havoc with the garden plot. He looked as respectable as Old Bill, but of course he wasn't – the "hoary iniquity!"

A door opened very, very softly as I steered myself back to my room. Cedric looked a bit Oriental in his dressing-gown – I <u>was</u> shot to pieces – very quietly, because I do detest making a fool of myself –

"Oh," said he, with as much promptitude as the entire Royal Life-Saving Brigade swinging into action, "All <u>you</u> want is a spot."

I agreed with him. I remember the light in his room was shaded by a scarlet silk kerchief. Red Light District?

But <u>not</u> seduction of a dream-dazed girl – He was – bien gentil,* that night. Only just naturally and of itself, an intimacy that he had wanted for some time started to develop –

He left the hotel, to occupy a house – an old, dark house whose gate was smothered in white jessamine flowers. Sweet-peas seemed inexhaustible there, and the frail misty gypsophilas. Against the roof a willow tree scraped a bent arm.

I didn't live there, of course, but in the daytimes, whilst he was away, I used to go over always and "tidy up" the rooms, with their mother-of-pearl papers – yes, me with broom and duster and vases to be filled with flowers. For my own pleasure. I've a passion for houses, as for baths – but only for old dark whispering houses. Here the piano held a forest of slim green melodies, and I would idly try my fingers at the very few I had picked up – I took a peculiar pleasure in putting back everything that was his exactly where it had stood, even the crumpled copies of "La Vie Parisienne."†

---

* Very kind, perhaps here very gentlemanly or respectful.

† *La Vie Parisienne* was one of the best-known and most risqué illustrated magazines in the 1920s – although innocent and inoffensive by modern standards, it was then considered to be erotica for the sophisticated man. Published in Paris, it promoted a high-spirited and slightly hedonistic lifestyle in which women, wine and having a good time were considered to be of prime importance. It made a name for itself by printing numerous drawings and illustrations

Cedric liked to sing, he and a lanky lass named Kathleen: this is a quotation from his favourite –

"Has not the actor got a heart to feel?
We are but men like you,
For gladness or sorrow –
The same broad Heaven above us,
The same wide lonely world before us."*

And the girl's sweet soprano voice rose in "My cinnamon tree – my cinnamon tree!"† Poor Kathleen! She loved him, but she liked the usurper too, because this usurper is a good audience, and not unkind to the love that breaks its wings.

I don't think we two occasioned any gossip: though once, friends of his and nice ones called during the daytime – and behold me with a broom in my hands, wishing to heaven it were a witch's one, so that I could mount it and sail triumphantly away –

It's hard to speak of the evenings. Cigarettes, white roses, "La Vie Parisienne," a sudden gorgeousness of those peacock dressing-gowns. At first I (like you,) thought that love-making in itself was absolutely nothing. I changed my mind – of a sudden. The moment he wanted me to, I suppose. I never found it a tender thing, but I had the daytimes and the sweet-peas. An exultant and mysterious physical thing it did become – and it's the <u>ancientry</u> of love and love-making that has always impressed me –

You'd think me (if you do not, already,) the very cheapest of sentimentalists, if I told you how much I loved one lakeside day, when we found a deserted farmhouse and orchard, the lemon leaves sweet after rain – The day slept on, bright-skyed.

There was a ridiculously fat black cocker spaniel pup, who we saved from a watery

---

(no photographs) of lovely ladies in all stage of dress and undress. http://www.rare-posters.com/lavieparisienne.html

* From the prologue of *Pagliacci,* by nineteenth-century Italian composer Leoncavallo: the story of a jealous husband in a commedia dell'arte troupe. http://www.nzopera.com/operas/cavalleria/the-opera/

† A song from a now-forgotten musical play, *The Cingalee,* by James Monkton, with music by Lionel Monkton, written and performed in London circa 1905 and set on a tea plantation in Ceylon; continuing the tradition established by *The Mikado,* 1885, for setting stories in the exotic orient. http://www.guidetomusicaltheatre.com/shows_c/cingalee.html

grave, because he was Superfluous Population like the unemployed nowadays, and they were going to drown him. He became Cedric's mascot. There were deer among those lacebark trees. Cedric sang, driving home –

> "Muleteer of Malaga!
> Have a care, have a care!
> 'Twixt two loves 'twere well to ponder –
> Which the sweeter, which the fonder
> Choose you the dark, or choose you the fair,
> But, muleteer, have a care, have a care!"[*]

It's extraordinary how little necessary it has been for me to lie to you over this. I've left out a few hard words and a few sweet ones – That is all.

My knee was so very well that it was decided "nerves" must be the cause of the continued stiffness. They were going to put me under chloroform, and I'd wake up, in all probability, quite all right.

They did. A young doctor, I remember, carried me back to bed. I even remember his friendly, concerned words.

"Well, it wasn't your "nerves" after all, old girl."

A few days, I did try to walk. Then it was the iron splint again, and crutches, and then a wheeled chair and special treatment – C'est Ça. They would never admit that they caused it all – but what else? And anyhow, what use to argue?

Like Cleopatra (but not in looks,) I was "sick and sullen"[†] when I next went back to Cedric's old house – It happened to be my birthday –[‡]

I suppose he hadn't <u>noticed</u> those iron fetters (and I was not looking pretty,) when I first came, and was nothing but a long-haired sleeping doll to whom he brought afternoon tea. But he did now, and that stabbed me. There was a change, as far as from a sort of queer Turkish paradise to anyone's idea of Hell. Just in speech, in look, in gesture. I made up my mind to go away quickly – and made arrangements to do so. But first I asked him most directly about "symptoms" that had worried me for some time. And he said, "No, impossible." He may have thought so. If not, that and one

---

[*] 'Muleteer of Malaga': Spanish song, words by Francis Barron, music by H. Trotère http://catalogue.nla.gov.au/Record/2647090

[†] *Antony and Cleopatra*, 1.3.13.

[‡] 19 January 1926 was her twentieth birthday. Though compare the end of this chapter, 'I was nineteen.'

other and far worse thing were the only suggestions of "betrayal" in this love-affair which was so barren of love at all.

Chapter 13.
Exits and Entrances.

Now of this very little. There was a lacquered screen with funny little Chinese men in the doctor's room, and no nurse, God be praised. (You don't know how some women <u>hate</u> having another woman present, when they're to be hurt or shamed.) I gave a false name, but he had seen me at the House,* and asked "Aren't you Miss — ?"

There was no doubt. For between four and five months, Robin had been making his plans. Few doctors are really unkind, unless really annoyed. This one was gentle in his questions, and I think honestly worried when, "You're right up against it, then?" became all he could say.

I wonder if women accumulate the triviality of coincidence more readily than men? The fact that a boy was singing lugubriously "You gotta pay the price for everything you do," the sweet fair faces of two girl-children in blue sunbonnets, are in my mind forever. I speak to you now as one appealing to your own special knowledge. Isn't there any escape from these maddening littlenesses? It's all very fine for me to quote and poetise, but I never have taken any drug or anaesthetic for years, without praying that "Blackout" will stay "Blackout." To remember one thing should be little or nothing. But to fritter one's mind away on all these trifles, and worse trifles, the most haunting any experienced person could pray against! I'm tired of it indeed. Every day adds something new – "Pretty tales of men with their eyelids cut off, left out there in the glare of the desert to go mad and die!" That's a sentence <u>years</u> ago read in a trashy magazine – But isn't it exactly what has happened to me?

I don't <u>mean</u> to indulge in all this, it just happens. The truest thing about Robin's few months of dream-life was, I ran straight away from Cedric and his lack of love, to the memory of Haroun who did love. (Yes, and if he had been there, he'd have looked after me, and if you are wrong about what happens when we die, then he is

---

* The House of Representatives.

surely Robin's best friend. That's no sentimentality. I know my lord, that's all.)

I could have been retrieved for a damaged respectability all right. My mother had half guessed what anyone but a fool like me would have known long before. Half guessed, then, poor dear, thrust away the idea: for a break in the conventions has always been the fall of Troy to her – Yet she loves me

Dom Byrne's[*] psychic path … the very night after I had visited the doctor, she came into my room and bullied the admission out of me. She would never have got Cedric's name, but she used unfair means. It happened that at the time, a very nice, cheerful and generous man, one of the Hawke's Bay "squattocracy", had occasionally taken me out – he isn't mentioned, because he in no wise concerns this affair. She said, though,

"It's that Mr W. H. I know where he's staying, and I'll settle with him."

It was no vain threat. I knew my mother – So I had to tell: and more. She started to talk and talk about Cedric, until I could bear it no more. I cried out the first penny-novelette thing that came into my mind,

"He was drunk, and he didn't know what he was doing!"

She stopped and looked at me. Then she said coldly "You drunken harlot," and went away. So I've had that word from both of my parents, at times almost from myself, I get so sick of arguing about it. But it's not, technically, quite true, is it? Can a gift be cheap, and doesn't a harlot ply for gain? I suppose my fine distinctions must seem simply funny to you, the difference between the "Companion – help, refined," and the "General, all duties." Well – as you like it.

That idea of drink stayed with her. The one possible solution! And ah, how she struck me, before Robin was born, with that self-same idiocy of mine!

"A child of drink … I wonder what it will be like? I've never seen one."

But that's not the truest memory of her at this time. Because one sentence happens, it doesn't say that any other brave and loyal thing doesn't, and curiously enough, I think it was after I'd beaten down her marriage-at-any-price idea, that our real comradeship began. It has always lasted.

I wired desperately to Cedric to come down, lest a worse thing befall. He did, almost at once – I wonder if he's expected this, for I had never written to him? – and he was quite gentle, and took me to afternoon tea at some fearful crowded show. He

---

[*]   See p. 72 n*.

says he definitely invited me to marry him, then. If he did, I didn't hear the clatter of teacups. But all I really remember is, that I launched the attack. I said, "Of course, you don't want to marry me."

I meant, of course I don't want to marry you. I hadn't begun to think of Robin, not even for a moment. All I thought of was that I loved and wanted Haroun, that I'd probably die (the "flare-up" of my knee confirmed that old idea that I had TB, and it was still crutches and splints,) and that there wasn't going to be any forced prideless marriage. Never was Ariadne in Naxos so unwilling to join forces with Bacchus.* But the time very soon came, when I could say "I am paid for't now."† I daresay everybody paid. Yet I can't be sorry, only sorry that Cedric and I were not more honest friends or lovers.

It was I who, when he met Mother, suddenly smashed the marriage scheme by saying "I am going to Sydney, nobody will know, we can get married if we have to" (I meant if I didn't die,) "later on." Poor Robin ... poor Cedric .. and poor Mother. I think Cedric had a sort of last-minute reluctance to let me go to Australia (I was nineteen,)‡ but it just happened, and nobody did know. I was alone, of course, Mother couldn't have and wouldn't have come. There were bouquets on the wharf, a decent cabin – I told you Cedric had plenty of money, and everybody understood that a purely mythical benefactress was providing me with yet more "Treatment" at the hands of a Sydney specialist.§

I had told Jezebel, nobody else, that I was going to have a child. And it was she, of all people, who woke me up to the fact of Robin. Bright-eyed and smiling, on the wharf, she handed me a tiny package. "Open it in your cabin," she whispered, "Miniatures!" I did, before the ship sailed – I thought she had painted something for me, queer old gold-haired lost artist that she was. The "miniatures" were the tiniest of tiny blue shoes, broidered with cherry-blossom.

---

* Hyde finds this a fitting story, almost: 'On the isle of Naxos Dionysus [her Bacchus] one day perceived a young woman lying asleep on the shore. It was the daughter of Minos, Ariadne, whom Theseus had brought with him from Crete and just abandoned. When she awoke Ariadne realized that Theseus had left her and gave way to uncontrollable tears. The arrival of Dionysus [Bacchus] consoled her and shortly afterwards they were solemnly married.' *The New Larousse Encyclopedia of Mythology*, 159.
† *Antony and Cleopatra*, 2.5.1193.
‡ Actually twenty – though nineteen when she got pregnant.
§ She sailed for Sydney on the *Marama* on 28 May 1926.

As the ship drew out, I cried as I never have before or since. I'd have married Cedric then, or, for that matter, anybody else. A bit late in the day. All I did was to drop my posy of brown-eyed pansies over the edge of the boat, to blunder into an innocent bystander, to appear red-eyed at table –

There was a green Mexican parrot who, when offered sugar, called the gentle donors a word beginning with the blackest of B's. And the far waves quieted one, (I'm a sailor sans peur et sans rapproche) and at last one morning, Sydney rose up misty purple, a dark city of dreams.

Chapter 14.
    She Is Far From the Land.

The Lord only sometimes looks after fools. Cedric had given me some money before I left for Sydney. But its size and its rocketing <u>noise</u> dazed me. I chose a suburb with a pretty name. It chanced to be Redfern – just between Redfern and Surrey Hills,* to be exact. You probably don't know it. It was encouragingly cheap – 25/- a week – and at first, it seemed quaint and amusing that people should live in such ridiculous little square boxes. But not at last!

I wore a wedding ring, and called myself by an alias never yet known to the police or registrar in Sydney town. No use! Under such circumstances, one must produce a husband or apparent husband, or <u>look</u> married. My landlady, who wasn't a bad sort, though suspicious and watchful, made no bones whatever about "knowing what she knew."

You'd have liked Art, the husband, who looked and talked like the Sentimental Bloke. But he had an appalling old father, a one-legged <u>and</u> one-eyed enormity, who started by looking merely piratical, but concluded by using his tongue as the green Mexican parrot would never have done.

Art and Letty had babies – beautiful babies, Letty assured me – with regularity, and as regularly they died of digestive troubles. What I can't understand, considering the milk supply, is why all Sydney children don't do likewise. Survived four-year-old Molly – not so <u>very</u> beautiful, but I used to tell her about the Three Bears, and

---

*   Inner-city suburbs of Sydney.

she stood it patiently.

Also shared the ménage, a rosella parrot (comparatively prim,) Art's slinky, quivering kangaroo hounds, and an unexplained and quite inexplicable horse, whose name, despite its sex, was Ada.

I think that little house hypnotised me (as not so long since, did a particularly evil-smelling cell with a barred window, in which I really couldn't have spent five weeks, but for being afraid to move at all.) There's no sound reason under any feasible mental system, why any young woman not destitute should have lived in such a street. Moreover, simply because Letty made it plain that she knew, and Art's father was a horrible specimen to behold, I, though quite a sound investment as a boarder, drifted into becoming a general servant too … . made beds, swept, dusted, emptied slops. As in a dream, I think – The city was so enormous, everyone was so far away – though there were gay [sweet] little native roses, iceland poppies, bluegum tips, at the flower-stalls in Martin Place.*

I thrust Haroun away, and tried hard to establish some sort of real intimacy with Cedric. But his half-dozen stiff, pathetic letters! Only one of them in the least human … "I know what a cad you must think me." It's not an age of letters or candlelight or ill-assorted verses, is it? Haroun was the strange exception …

Robin and I came to know one another better, Once or twice, I went to one of Sydney's huge alarming department stores, and bought silken things and lacey things, a queer trousseau for the paying-general who only went to green trees and grass after the housework was done. They were never worn, most of them I left in Sydney. But I still have Jezebel's blue "miniatures."

Suddenly and luckily, something snapped. Art's old father insulted me and Robin, and in a single hour I had packed up and was ready for any city. Letty had begun to tell me, at length, about her own confinements. There was a very

---

* Then the centre of Sydney's business district, location of the General Post Office.

[At this point 1 or 2 pages are missing and there is a change of paper from blue-lined, 34-line foolscap* to poor quality note-paper or pad with no watermark. The account takes up with a description of the Sydney Public Library]

which is the best one could wish to meet. Books on everything – from old shadowy ones like "Mardi"[†] to good technical ones on every imaginable subject, from "the call of the alone to the alone" to a book of poems by Rachel Anne Taylor, in which I found this verse :

"Sleep, sweet, sleep –
The Gods of Beauty seek in Spring
From out of the world's white flowering
Some delicate thing to keep."[‡]

But I began to feel conspicuous, and retreated to a suburban lair again. Not so bad, this time! I had made friends with a nurse, a shoe-eyed, slim-bodied creature a few years older than myself, engaged in private nursing, and always having the most astonishing adventures.[§] Wasn't she, whilst attending a pneumonia case, proposed to by the seventy-year-old bachelor son of the same? And she at the top of a ladder, picking loquats! (I hasten to add, she wasn't on duty at the time.) In another home, whilst tending a poor downtrodden wifely worm, she had flat-irons hurled at her by the husband. She left – but concealed the flatirons before departure. Australia suntanned and sweet, Kay was: always either very much in funds, or a bankrupt. My money wore down to the slenderest margin, and I found myself living on Thorny Mauds. Bright green little mandarins, juicy and sweet, thirty for sixpence! But

---

* Alison Hunt identifies paper for Chapters 1–14 as 'resembling paper used for patient records and scrap at Auckland Mental Hospital', while the paper subsequently is poor quality note or pad paper ('Cage', 319).

† *Mardi* (1864) a south seas travel narrative by Herman Melville, 1819–91.

‡ These lines, from a poem, 'Four Crimson Violets' by Rachel Annand Taylor, about a baby taken by 'the gods of beauty' in springtime, are the same as those Hyde used as a dedication for her Little Saint Christopher manuscript book, used for her poems to late 1927. However, there she adds a title, 'To the Little Saint Christopher', and her own final line 'Sleep, child, sleep'. Taylor's lines also appear in *The Godwits Fly* (254) to describe protagonist Eliza's emotion when her baby dies (see 'Introduction', *Young Knowledge*, 7).

§ Kay Brownlie, her best friend and room mate in Sydney, was 'engaged in private nursing' (*Iris,* 76).

Brownie and I celebrated, on my first day at the new room in Stanmore. Freshly-ground coffee, we drank, and reveled in asparagus, strawberry jam. Heaven knows what. We were justified, for Cedric, out of the blue, sent another stiff letter and banknotes equally crisp.*

Today, for the first time, it occurred to me that this was a Business Transaction. It never seemed so. Not to be quite friendless was delightful, and Kay wore the daintiest and most scrupulously-laundered of underwear – An American youth, who had just made the acquaintance of redgum-tips, was quite right about my friend. "Say," quoth he "you just like those little leaves – not the green ones, the pink ones."

To be truthful about Sydney would be to drift into such a long, long tide of ugliness, noise, fear, – and the sudden peace of dreaming, crystallizing the whole mixture into the fantastic forms of little shops, old stucco houses, loquat trees, staring bright sunflowers. They are so very clear, and I walk there so often. But why should any other person? There are fairer and graver cities, where a million milk-carts don't rattle over ill-paved streets, and yahoo – my first and worst loudspeaker, owned by the people in whose house I dwelt – doesn't howl until midnight.

The hospital where Robin was born was neither sordid nor noisy.† I'd been saving up for it. Old and cool and huge-roomed, with the jacaranda trees making a purple

---

* 'Frederick was providing 30 shillings per week for Iris's living and hospital expenses.' (*Iris*, 76 n†)

† The hospital was probably in Stanmore, a suburb that overlooks the city. The date of birth of Christopher Robin Hyde is problematic: here she speaks of his being born when jacarandas were in bloom, usually November. The same detail occurs in *Godwits*. However, from other sources it seems more probable that he was born earlier – for example, her mother arrived after the death of the baby and is pictured with Hyde in the Blue Mountains in October (*Iris*, 77). There is also little information to corroborate any of the different versions Hyde gave of the length of the pregnancy (in differing accounts, the baby made its appearance somewhere between June and November) or to determine whether the baby was born prematurely or was full-term, although certainly it seems here that he died during birth. The obscurity about the length of the pregnancy – here she says she had symptoms by 19 January – means she must have arrived in Rotorua before Christmas, though she makes no mention of this. It's also possible, although it seems extremely unlikely, that she concealed a different paternity for Robin. In a letter Hyde wrote to John A. Lee in October 1937 she is at pains to stress the age she was when she gave birth to the baby: 'Robin died at birth when I was twenty *and six months*', the words in italics being added in Hyde's hand to a typescript letter (Docherty, 'Do I Speak Well?', 259). Certainly by late November 1926, Hyde was on board ship for Auckland, accompanied by her mother – another detail elided here.

mist of blossom outside, and ah, such a far, glittering sea of pale lights spreading into greater evening distances than one could dream of. I didn't mean to have anything "common or unclean*"' touch him or me then –

I cannot write of it, only such foolish details. The red lilac in the waiting-room, the long-faced night sister who talked about the Via Dolorosa.† Though certainly I've tried since to come to terms with a plaster Saint Anthony,‡ that night was the last time I've ever prayed to God. I prayed that he might take care of Robin –

It was a long, long time, a day and a night, before Robin finally showed that he had changed his mind about coming into the world – Chloroform, but only more pain – more chloroform, such a strange dreary regime. Then at last,

"No, it's not all right, Mrs —. The poor little chap …"

But they let me see him, though not to hold him, after he was dead. I wonder if death gave him his white sweetness (since you're quite right, new babies are ugly?) He was very dark, the little face I touched was warm, the mouth turned down, the hands were square, miniatures of Cedric's. I made them keep on his arm the little bejewelled bracelet I had bought him as a first gift, and because I'd been reading some silly magazine article about newborn babies getting mixed up in nursing homes. They wouldn't let me see him again, – morphine and sleep instead – and the next day "arrangements were made" –

Kay helps still. She calls the place "the daisy home," and multitudes of white defiant daisies lift their heads from that awful red soil, which is like an open wound. I went there once, and missed my last train, of course, and was rescued and driven back to a nearer station by an ancient man with a horse and trap. Ah, so many, so many, the people in that dead city! I don't mind little drowsy golden-lit graveyards – one feels that the dead are all friendly there together – but he seemed small to be left in so great a place – Yet

---

*   Acts 10.14.

†   Latin for the way of sadness or grief, also the road Jesus walked in Jerusalem carrying the cross to his crucifixion on the hill of Golgotha outside the city.

‡   St Anthony of Padua, thirteenth-century Franciscan friar, patron saint of lost things and often depicted holding the infant Jesus. http://americancatholic.org/Features/Anthony/default.asp

"The gods of Beauty seek in the Spring
From out of the world's white flowering
Some delicate thing to keep –"*

They have never kept anything more delicate or sweeter –
There is no more to say of Sydney, though, indeed so much happened there, more than I have told, that I feel as if I had half opened a closed door. I was ill - terribly - on the boat coming home.† And I wanted to see Cedric, because – oh just because I was lost. I saw Auckland, green and sweet and fragrant, after those parched Sydney gardens. Spent a day here in a courtyard whose white and golden lilies were brimmed with November rain – I had wired to Cedric and a reply telegram said that I was to wait there, he was coming. But I couldn't, I just wanted to reach the place I had once known again, and quickly – So go I did.

Chapter 15. No More of Me You Knew.

Now as once before, when a well-mannered Fox with artistic leanings chose to single me out, most people knew a great deal more than I did. They had known about Cedric and Alice.‡ So it was surely tactless of me to cry "But she's <u>old</u> – quite old," when that night I discovered that not only now, but for years before, these two had been admitted one another's property. Middle-aged she was – a big, stalwart, dark woman, not a bit prepossessing to the feminine eye. She was a widow, and I had met her casually before –

I suppose such things have been happening for ever and for ever, and that it was an absurd conceit of mine to think that twenty years' vantage in youth counted much, for a weary young man who had gone too early to a war, and who now wore gorgeous dressing-gowns – Very angry with me for having come down – as far as men are concerned, their anger is only ugly when it's on the defensive, when they are afraid.

---

* See p. 115, note on Rachel Annand Taylor.
† Mrs P.[sic] Wilkinson, aged 47 years, and Miss I. Wilkinson, aged 20 years, are listed as passengers on the *Ulimaroa* from Sydney to Auckland, arriving 30 November 1926. See the Social Security Archives (SS) passenger lists for inbound and outbound shipping in the 1920s.
‡ Alice Algie and Frederick had married on 17 November 1926. Alice was a widow and eleven years older than Frederick.

He needn't have worried, I broke easily enough. As to that, I suppose it wasn't really he that I wanted, but, as usual "the ghosts of what had never been."

But this was betrayal. That old house which I had tended really belonged to Alice. She wasn't living there, but in another, more modern. I think that much he might have told me – but oh, it's only obtuseness that makes men commit real crimes. I think of him as someone puzzled, lonely, deprived of his own youth.

It's as impossible to account for the next few weeks, as for the months as Letty's servant, or the other recent weeks in the cell. I didn't and didn't want to leave the town. Cedric and I never became lovers again – cela va sans dire – but I believe he was actually commanded to make me as happy as might be. In fact, I heard Alice say, "Oh, comfort her a little." Once she'd decided I was not a menace, she wished to be –of all things – motherly – I scarcely saw her, with my blinded eyes. But I saw this. Cedric was sternly discouraged from singing anymore. He did not sing very well, but he did love it, and it was in him. But she had taken him in hand now, once and for all (of course he'd owned up about his tiresome position, Robin and myself, months before.)

"Oh, you tamely died!
You should have clung to Fulvia's waist, and thrust
The dagger through her side!"*

I began to drug – in so indiscriminate a way that you'd have laughed at it. I didn't know the names of anything. But this is very simple arithmetic. One sleeping draught purchased from Chemist No A, + one ditto from Chemist No B, and so on, makes a fancy total. Every night, I thought, "I won't wake up tomorrow," and the tremendous roar of waters deafened me – Waking up was as bad – but I, who had grown so thin and whose drained white face began to frighten these two old friends, was so very strong!

---

* Alfred Tennyson, 'A Dream of Fair Women', from 'The Lotos Eaters'.
　　　O me, that I should ever see the light!
　　　Those dragon eyes of anger'd Eleanor
　　　　Do hunt me, day and night.'
　　　She ceased in tears, fallen from hope and trust:
　　　　To whom the Egyptian: 'O, you tamely died!
　　　You should have clung to Fulvia's waist, and thrust
　　　　The dagger thro' her side.'

I went at last, quite quietly and without fuss – without tears, as far as I remember – Velvet red geraniums grew in the hedge of that old house of betrayal, and I put some in my pocket.

A dusty drive through to Hamilton, and a car breakdown. (Alice had been so careful to rouge my cheeks. And the young man who drove the car thanked me warmly for being very patient during the two hours when he mended his car. Last year, when this room was just beginning to be as shadowy as the road was then, and my handwriting to run off the paper, your colleague said very softly, "I can't understand you! In hospital, you were sitting up and laughing!")[*]

So of Hamilton only a blur … I was robbed there, later it was found that I had only about three pounds, and I had started out with fifteen. I remember lying in the hot sun by a lakeside. I went (crazed idea,) to a doctor whose name I don't recall – told him that the death of a friend was troubling me, and begged him for a sleeping-draught. He gave me something or other, and was pleasant …

The chemists were more or less pleasant, I tried them all, and did learn several names – veronal, luminal[†]– from a sharp-faced little man who seemed to have a grievance against drug-selling restrictions. Eleven grains of luminol, ten of veronal, and (bathos!) some aspirin, all together. And I woke up! Well, I meant that night to go to Wellington, and did indeed get as far as the station – And I saw my train come in, but helplessly realized that I couldn't move, couldn't think. My own name vanished, and everyone's.

Then the more utter blackness, which you know. It was broken only twice. I can remember the wet grass of a steep slope beneath my body. It was dead night, and I must have walked out of the hospital ward. That was triumph, the first of a series of aimless, meaningless, cunning triumphs. Poor Mother Earth!

The second memory: waking up, to feel coarse canvas against my skin, and my

---

* 'Last year' (1933) she was in Auckland Hospital DT (*Delirium tremens*) cells; the colleague was Dr Buchanan, Superintendent of Auckland Mental Hospital at Avondale, who saw Hyde and suggested she move to the Lodge. (For more detail, see 'Introduction' to this book; Hunt, 'Angel-Guarded Liar', 143–50; Hunt, 'Cage', 43–67.)

† Virginia Woolf took two overdoses of veronal during 1913–15, sleeping off twenty-five grains in the second instance, and early reports in the *Lancet* indicated that doses up to 125 grains could be survived (Hermione Lee, *Virginia Woolf* (London: Vintage Books, 1999), 180–81). On the dangers of the drugs Hyde took, Hunt writes: 'It was warned in 1934 that the margin between safe and coma-producing overdose of Luminal was small, that doses of two to ten tablets could be toxic'. (Hunt, 'Cage', 232–3).

arms tight at my sides. A nurse sat there, in a lighted room. I worked one arm loose – oh, so stealthily! The nurse saw, too late, and I smiled at her,

"It's quite easy – you see?"

A doctor came in. He was young and dark, and spoke brusquely:

"You've been romancing, young woman. Well, where's the baby?"

Oh, even then I could be cold in mockery of these loveless fools who thought that my Robin was somewhere, deserted or murdered –

I said "My son is dead," and heard a queerly different note in his voice. Was it pity, or did his little mind still scrape about like a dog for buried bones, and think of the police? God knows. The uttermost blackness came again, and I do not know how long it lasted, nor what was said or done.

"Finish, good lady. The bright day is done,
And we are for the dark."*

But I woke up, weak yet quite clear of mind, to recognize my mother. From Cedric's card, the hospital authorities had put through one telephone call, discovered my home address, and sent a telegram. We were to go home by train that night, and did start –

In the train I remember, not the blackness, but babbling aloud, calling for Cedric. Was my mother a devil, to take me away? What else I said, God knows. At Palmerston North I wouldn't go farther – I wanted to go back to Cedric. My mother had the sense to insist on a doctor. He was rather a fool (though, by the way, an uncommonly handsome one, with extraordinary amber eyes.) I will not mention his name.

Mother did all the talking, whilst I sat with hanging head, a beaten fool. He was sympathetic at first, or so she thought. (I supposed I figured as the Wronged Child, which was a lie, but perhaps we had come to a place where lies were necessary.)

A private hospital in Palmerston North† … well, that was better far than another inch of this journey away from my ghosts – So I lay still in a white bed – still more morphine! – that night.

---

* *Antony and Cleopatra*, 5.2.193.

† The name of the hospital in Palmerston North is not known.

Pity.

Cry then to Lazarus, "Rise not ever again!"
Say to the poor and the maimed, "Yours is a heavy load!
Surely your sides learn well of the stinging goad,
As ye plod like oxen under this yoke of pain!"
Give them your meanest coin, but never your gold:
Never the lips of truth, nor the strong unsparing hand.
Dare not the Thunder that pealed to the cripple, "Stand!"
Not the Lightning that rent the blind, with its cry "Behold!"*

Robin Hyde
****

Chapter 16.
The Night-Born Scents.

We two who were never to have met again met very quickly in this quiet place.
For I had seemed well enough, in its little garden framed with creamy rambling roses
(it's strange how often gardens have brought me solace,) then suddenly collapsed.
By day I lay still and would eat nothing. By dusk, I could find Dreamland – oh, with
infinite effort, then! – and after that, always the waking nightmare shadows came.
My Mother was "that woman in black," Cedric the only person I called for.

Do you know what he said? He kissed me, crying, the first time I've ever seen a
man cry. He said "God damn you for sending that wire! She got hold of it."

The strangest thing to say. It baffles me even now. Did he mean that he had really
wanted me a little, and had not been brave enough to stand a scene? For the only
wire I ever sent him was the one from Sydney, which said that Robin was dead and
I coming back.

Or perhaps it was merely "God damn you for getting me into a scrape," and he
didn't think a half-crazed girl would hear – or didn't care whether she heard or not.
Yet he looks so tormented nowadays –

---

* Not the poem of same title in *Young Knowledge,* which is a section of the long poem *Nadath.*

I heard little, remembered little of what else he said. I only remember that he was gentle – But great fissures were opening in my memory and thought (some have never closed,) and he didn't stay for long, it was useless. I said goodbye to him, (only we were in Sydney, it seemed,) quite patiently: we could always join one another again quickly –

We never have, nor spoken a word. I have only had the trouble in his eyes, and gone by quickly without speaking.

Morphine twice a night, and no sleep. Scarcely any food. I know now that once, at that time, I was subject to "forcible feeding". I didn't know, until here I heard the details of various means by which this is done. (Never ask me about that, I cannot bear it – I only know it as a struggle with nurses and – oh you can't wonder that I hate most women, except little dark ones like my Yasminé, and brave ones like her mother, and pink-uniformed nurses here who don't look as though they want to bite!

Anyhow, their force was a mistake, as force always is with me. I was too ill. In two days, I was delirious as well as half-insane, with a temperature of 104. My doctor decided on appendicitis, had made all preparations for operating (and, incidentally, had warned my Mother that he didn't think my weakness could possibly let me live.) But it's very true that death flies the seeker. My temperature suddenly went down.

I started to walk at night – not sleeping, not waking: always about to go back to Cedric or to Robin. In any clothes I could find. Of course they always stopped me.

I heard the night nurse laugh once, and say,

"If she only knew what she looks like!"

My dear girl, I heard, in a sort of way I knew what I looked like: only it wasn't of the slightest importance, I had other business to attend to. But if such as you knew how often and how much one <u>does</u> hear, a night nurse's life would not be happy one.

That was real. But not so the incessant voices, which talked, talked, talked – and so reasonably, so plausibly. Once it was Cedric's parents at the door. (He had loved his mother, who lives in this city and has never known of her first grandchild's few hours of life. She's a well-known and rather artistic little lady, always at clubs and gardening circles. I shrank from the possibility of meeting her here in Auckland, whilst such social activities were in my province, but by some mysterious fluke, I never did.) She was grave and asked many questions of me, in that our one dream-conversation, but I don't remember her shadowy self as unkind. Is it a compliment to be thought kindly by a crazy girl you have never met?

There are other conversations I remember quite clearly, too: but for the most part, they are unpleasant. My doctor, finding his morphine no success and my babbling a nuisance, began to be angry – with the anger that lies deep in so many, against unreason. It's a very ancient fear, the fear of madness. Read Shakespeare's

"You deserve
The dark house and the whip, as madmen do,"*

and from your own knowledge, judge how far we have advanced.

At all events, he ordered Mother to take me away. Poor Mother! I wish somebody or something, even her Church of England God, could have given her the pity I didn't. I still could talk quite rationally at times, and (with that sick dread of being farther away from Cedric still in my heart) remember begging him to let me stay, to go to the Public Hospital – He was a little cruel – Thought it necessary, and besides, he wouldn't realize that I knew and would remember. He sent me away – to that place of darkness where Olga is.† And like Olga, I screamed all the way, in the car – and remember it – Next the thin face of Wellington's admitted specialist – I didn't know he was that, only that I hated him and was deadly afraid of him, and that my words wouldn't make sense. "The woman in black" was no help. And they had the papers ready.‡

I'd never have come out of there. Perhaps it's because of Olga. But I know, with absolute certainty, that if its shadow ever touches me, I shall be done – Perhaps Jezebel told me too much about Olga and about others there – But I mustn't write about it, or this will become a mere babble of fear, and I can't afford to be afraid of things – fear is such a wonderful magnet!

Anyhow, it was the doctor of the lacquered screen§ who rushed in where angels fear to tread. He was young then, and acting as locum for an older Wellington physician. I wish I could think that I brought him a little luck, for he did rescue me

---

* *As You Like It*, 3.2.391–3. Rosalind: 'Love is merely a madness, and, I tell you, deserves as well a dark house and a whip as madmen do: and the reason why they are not so punished and cured is, that the lunacy is so ordinary that the whippers are in love too'.
† Porirua Mental Hospital.
‡ Committal papers.
§ This is the doctor who had confirmed her pregnancy with Robin, and who was kindly. See Chapter 13, p. 110.

from Olga's City of Dreadful Night. By some miracle I remembered his name, and asked for him – demanded him. He came, and it must have been because he was decent to me on that hideous shadowy day of the past, I recognised him – What I said I don't remember. I only know that concerning every obstacle and delusion, he said, "It doesn't matter." Also, he commanded that my Father, who was away, should stay away and leave the house free for a daughter with a "nervous breakdown." And it was so. He cut out the morphine at once – didn't substitute anything, so far as I know, except an ancient Highland night nurse who used to snore in the next room, whilst I was awake and in Dreamland. He made me eat something – anything – and for sheer sickroom spite, I'd touch nothing whatsoever but onions! I think you'll agree he was rather heroic. Rambling, physical or verbal, didn't seem to interest him – though one night whilst the Highlander slept, I walked in that dream-state quietly out of our door, and down the long dark road, a new-metalled one which cut my bare feet – Of course I knew vaguely that I was an escapee, but not really, until I walked crash into a lamp-post, and saw its swimming light – tiger-eyes. From the moment of real knowledge, I couldn't move and sank down in the grasses, aware of cut feet – A deep glen separated me from the nearest houses – I tried to call, but my voice was so weak – the resolution that rushed me through Dreamland was iron, like my body – but that lost, I was lost too – I crouched there in my night-dress (and you should hear our winds whistle, they're the keenest and fiercest in all Wellington).

A little black dog found me. Don't tell me animals don't recognize the hurt, even your old True Thomas does. Instead of assailing the stranger, he stuck to his guns and did the sensible thing, howled mournfully – He made night unbearable, until at last, just before dawn, the people in the house below came up and found me – So I woke up in my bed –

I told my doctor it was sleepwalking, because I was afraid of him. It wasn't, it was dream-walking. How far are they different? I've been terrified lest that should come back here, but it hasn't, nor in all the years that have intervened – That night and the swimming lights somehow finished it –

"Anyone else," said my doctor, mollified, "would have got pneumonia."

We kept on my night-nurse, because she was middle-aged, and it might have gone hard with her. But how she must have hated me, (and indeed, I suppose to a warder any escapee is naturally hateful) – I'm very glad now, for her sake and for my doctor's and several other reasons, that I didn't catch pneumonia on that queer night – She used to sit in my room, to stare at me with screwed-up face, to try the effect of ghost stories. Our stairs were very old, and creaked dismally in the wind. "Eh," she would say, "They're takin' a walk agen!"

But poor old dear, what good reason she had for hatred! My doctor of the screen can be nasty when annoyed: and she only snored because she was bored stiff, with pneumonia-jackets or dressings she may have been a marvel, but what is there to do, all night, with a girl who runs into Dreamland in her thoughts, and with that ugly cunning which you know a little too well, edges towards the actuality when the coast is clear? I've no excuse except one which I don't want to make, here: and there was this too.

"All night long I lie awake, and know
That you are lying waking, even so,
And all the day you tread a lonely road
And come at sunset to a dark abode."

Why should I tell you all these past things, which almost must make you doubt me and watch me and distrust me – when the touch of a hand, or a look a little more observant than usual, sends me now into hiding? You have only one reason for trusting me, the fact that I have an absolutely clear faith in yourself. I don't think anything could make me play traitor to that, except the blackness: you know best, will know better from these notes, whether that will come again, "that dolent city."* If it does, I hope the resolution in me wakes again, and kills me. But I do know, before now I have had liking or gratitude for people, or a hope of pity. I don't want pity now. With you, I am absolutely sure. I believe that's a rock in all this sea. There is certainly no other, and if I am wrong I cannot ask for or hope for even the mercy of death – Cleanliness is merciful, to the soiled and weary. Not death's most infinite processes with the body seem to me in the least fearful, but I do fear indeed the shadow of all the forced, coarse intimacies, the self-revelation and the self-parody, that the blackness would be. Sometimes I've thought the Schön Rosmarin† is wise, who tosses the golden head here in this old garden, and cries "Give me liberty or give me death."

---

* A phrase from Dante Alighieri's *Inferno,* 3.1–3. Indiana Critical Edition (Mark Musa Bloomington: Indiana University Press, c. 1995), 1265–1321.

† The name Hyde uses for Rosalie Rawlinson, mother of poet Gloria. 'Schön Rosmarin' (Lovely Rosemary) is one of three short pieces for violin and piano by pianist and composer Fritz Kreisler, 1875–1972.

Yet I do trust: a perhaps hopeless hope for strength – I've been hurt too much, and I have no use for the mentally maimed – Where's the valid reason why the weak should inherit the earth, and make it squalid? No, either I'm strong when I go away from here, perhaps in some quite imperceptible way, or else I fall "the thousand parasangs to Hell."* I am sick of half measures.

I want to finish, and now, with the queer little story of my Wellington doctor, who really was a hero, after his fashion. When I went away from here, and saw him again, the thin, worn-out, hopeless shred I had become wearied him.† Eight years, since he saved the child. Of the woman's moralities and complexities, he was hyper-critical and nervous. He had abandoned all "nerve" cases, really, and had built himself a very real success in general practice.

There was no foundation, no building – He hated even my loved and lovely print of Correggio's‡ "Io and Jupiter," and was excessively rude to Io because she had no clothes on. I call that picture "The Body in the Embrace of the Soul." It was given to me, with Holbein's "Man in The Biretta§," by J. S.¶ … whose dream of the little green birds I have mentioned. Oh, all that was I, in that green room which was mine for so many years, he hated – I don't blame him, I did look ghastly, and one hates to see one's old work undone. "The dark house and the whip!" Yet I'm sorry it was so, for once on a day he was reckless enough to save me from a place I dread: and he was gentle, over Robin. I hope his practice exceeds all reasonable bounds, and that all his patients are ladies who like abdominal operations. I hope, too, that I never see him again. He asked me to come back, when I last visited his consulting rooms, and there was a sort of horror of disappointment in me as I said, "No." But I'd have you know, he's an excellent doctor, likes detective stories and keeps a ridiculous little

---

* Parasang: an ancient Persian unit for measuring travelling distance, used in Old Testament.
† This same doctor must have visited her at her family home in Northland, a suburb of Wellington, sometime in October when she spent a fortnight there before returning to Auckland, between her self-discharge from the Lodge on 28 September and her return there on 5 December 1933 (*Iris,* 226, 227).
‡ Antonio Allegri da Correggio, (1494–1594), Italian late-Renaissance painter. The scene of *Jupiter and Io* shows a very fleshly Io in the embrace of a grey, smoke-like Jupiter (Zeus in Greek) – the style of the nude anticipates that of Bernini and Rubens.
§ Probably a print of one of the several paintings by Holbein of his friend Erasmus, the Dutch Renaissance humanist and Roman Catholic priest, in which he wears a biretta – a cap with three flat projections worn by Roman Catholic clergy.
¶ John Schroder.

scrap of a Sydney Silky terrier, Hobbs by name. He's right enough, to turn from the dark places of "nerves" or mind. I am glad that there was still some broken dream to turn to of the two things I have always wanted most, beauty and pride.

I almost forgot. With the exception of my Mother, the others remained and have always remained in complete ignorance of the cause of all this [*this written above the line*] breakdown – Don't think I wouldn't have known. The youngest, the war-baby,* was until two years ago absolutely hysterical, and dozens of times I've had "Lunatic asylum!" flung at me. (Mother's wholesomeness has developed in her, she is pink-cheeked and very proud of her "job", a girl guide lieutenant – of all quaint things for our family – and, best of all, alone among us can sing, in a contralto voice which I find charming. I didn't think she'd ever be salvaged, but once on her feet, she has, like the other two, become Church of England to a degree, and moral to a still farther degree. At one time, I thought she was going to have all my disadvantages, plus.)

And the nightborn scents. My old grizzled friend, who died later in so unhappy and unnecessary a way, used to bring me the bush, lots of it – and at last, from something I let slip, pink belladonna lilies. My love for flowers close to me at night began then, and has never gone away. And I thought of Haroun, as the sweet pink lilies pressed close to my face. I was prideless enough suddenly to send him – or rather, to dictate for him – a wire. Just "Are you back from your wanderings yet," no word of illness or misadventure –

A letter came very soon, and the handwriting on the envelope was Haroun's exactly – But the letter inside was from his brother Hardy, to say that he had died, and how long ago.† Just "He cared for you so much more than he would admit even to himself –"

I don't remember any great sorrow, only bewilderment. But I must have grown worse, for my doctor said that I was to go to Hanmer Springs,‡ and quickly – I believe

---

* Ruth Saxon Louvain Wilkinson, born August 1914.
† See earlier notes on pp. 69 and 96. In fact, Iris did not learn of Haroun's (Harry Sweetman's) death until some months later in December 1927, after her discharge from Hanmer. Why she writes this in error is not clear – perhaps to make her 'breakdown' more justified or in order to promote the importance of this relationship in her story (see also *Iris*, 99 n†).
‡ Queen Mary Hospital at Hanmer Springs was originally a military hospital for the treatment of shell-shocked soldiers but became in the 1920s a civilian hospital for the treatment of nervous disorders. The medical superintendent Dr Chisholm's dream project, the 'beautifully designed and appointed Women's Hospital' where Hyde was admitted on 7 May 1927 had opened the previous year (*Iris*, 86 n*).

he'd have made it the House of Shadows, he must have been frayed and tired – but he had his pride too.

I haven't told you one half of the little kindly courageous things he did for me then. It's too late a day, and as you say, hero-worship is a rather sickly emotion, especially when a new criterion of success is built up, and a second experiment proves too much of a trial. But kindly and courageous they were.

The hills around Hanmer seemed at first like threatening giants – but not later! Dr Chisholm* is perhaps a little more than middle-aged, sympathetic in a faintly absent-minded but absolutely agreeable sort of way – and he let me alone, and left me free – I must have been a pretty bad patient, for I was on paraldehyde for months – and I have only just learned that you don't give that for insomnia only.[†] I think my mind wandered, but harmlessly. I had a little blue room to myself, established no real intimacy of any kind with doctor, nurse or patient. But the freedom was a cure in itself. I only abused it once, climbed a mountain – a diminutive mountain named Isobel. Poor Dr Chisholm, what excellent reason he had for being cross! Yet I don't think he was, in particular, though I vaguely remember a very tearful and argumentative self doing battle with all the world – I think, he sees no particular use in being annoyed or disappointed – But I can only remember that he kept Scotch terriers, that I once took a very nice snapshot of him and have been pestered ever since for prints by adoring lady patients, and just two words, far from significant ones: a patient, "Well, Iris!"

But the sheer beauty of that place saved my mind. Do you know it? The hospital is a white slate-roofed crescent. In the grounds, daffodil and crocus burst up, a thousand flames, from the soil. The evening light on the mountains was that incredible Eastern blue that I saw here, from this room's wide windows, last winter. Ah, but I love the winter twilights! I came in autumn, when the leaves flamed. In winter the snow lay ragged on tall Isobel, perfectly smooth on old Baldy. The sunset light was a clear terra-cotta. In the woods, when I could walk so far, were little patches of frozen snow

---

* Dr Chisholm had been medical superintendent at the hospital since its opening and in the NZ Medical Corps, but after WWI 'received training in the treatment of functional nervous disorders' (*Iris,* 86 n*) and in 1922 was appointed civil superintendent. His sympathetic comments on her state of mind attribute her 'hysteria' and insomnia to a history of events (*Iris,* 86).

† Paraldehyde is a colourless but strong-smelling liquid (a cyclic trimer of acetaldehyde), used in making dye and as a sedative; it was widely used in mental hospitals. See also p. 193.

mingled with brown leaves – I wonder if you know what that feels like underfoot? The great boughs of fir trees were weighted to the ground with millions of little sighing white snowbirds. I think I learned to talk quite rationally again, except when I cried or was under paraldehyde. (Funny: I remember thinking how disgustingly sodden a certain Miss C. who had the same drug, always looked and smelt in the mornings, as she crawled past in her dirty dressing-gown. It never occurred to me that probably I looked and smelt just the same, until I was writing this.)

There were a few sad patches. A girl screamed incessantly and horribly for a little while. A little nun knitted the most beautiful baby garments. She was consumptive, and a tiny open room facing the silver birch trees was hers. Most of all I hate to remember Reedy, a tall, frizzy-haired, glassy-eyed woman who looked as though she could peck like an ostrich. She had been in Seacliff,* because she imagined that she had been the victim of a rape. And she would talk, talk, talk about it. (Actually, I now guess that she was the victim of the exact reverse to her fancied outrage. And I suppose she's in Seacliff again.)

But it was heavenly to wander lonely, where the winter sun loosed its bright tresses among the close-set firs. The smell and touch of it all, the feel of ice from frozen rushes rubbed on my face, is still quite near.

I must have been hard to get indoors, for I remember, one dusk, the impatient

[Missing page or pages, including the end of Chapter 16 and beginning of Chapter 17. Text below is probably Chapter 17. Zimmerman series C follows]

did my utmost to put away altogether, though I did dream over Haroun's old letters, and once, at a most uncleanly little spiritualistic séance, blasphemed the past by hunting for him – I may tell you that ugly story later, I don't know. At least it ended in a flare of anger, not in tears – It may have helped to drive my most intimate memories of him far away.†

Jezebel got married at last, and I was her bridesmaid: which was funny – But she gave her tamed artistry a run, in designing the frocks for her own wedding group. She looked like something between a goosegirl and a princess, in rose and silver with laced-up peasant blouse.

* Seacliff Mental Hospital near Dunedin.
† Another indication of Hyde's ambivalent attitude towards the spiritualism she was introduced to in Wanganui. For more on this, see *Iris*, 142–5.

I must stop for now. A girl has just come back after running away to see her mother, and there's nothing but talk of it. "She came in as happy as anything!" "She wants to go away with her mother!" "Oh, isn't she silly, she'll have to stay so much longer now!" "I hope they won't move her, but I suppose they will." "They always take it out of you for that – they think you're not quite sensible or you'd wait!" "She was going home so soon! I'm sorry for her!" They're not sorry, they're getting [*handwriting becomes loose, distressed*] a kick out of it, the mindless gloating liars – And that accursed word "They." Perhaps she'll be all right, but I know she won't, I know she won't. [*indecipherable struck out sentence*] Quote, quote, quote, and cry, remember scraps of books never written for "us." A parrot could do as well. Afternoon tea now. Then I'm going to my garden to count the phloxes again.* You told me once not to be Joan of Arc. If the burning of my maimed body and mind could only help, I'd be Joan of Anywhere, if I went to Hell for it.

Later.

Mindless myself, and futile – I deserve that for just this idiocy, you should throw this and me into the nearest wastepaper basket – but I'm letting the most foolish passages stand, for they are true. Schön Rosmarin has a theory about truth as the sole essential. Spinoza was kicked out of the synagogue for it I believe.†

I did go down, torn to bits with the tears I loathe: and planted the crimson flowers Mother sent me today (they'll smell sweet if they bloom,) and some gowan slips.‡

---

* Hyde had her own garden plot from probably soon after her readmission in December (see Chapter 8). In a letter to John Schroder, she wrote that she loved her 'own little garden which nobody else is allowed to touch'. And that 'It is utterly lonely and very sweet and was Doctor Tothill's idea' (Docherty, 'Do I Speak Well?', 143). Hunt sees the garden as giving Hyde a special relationship ('bond') with Buchanan, as he had lived in the house prior to its conversion into a voluntary ward ('Cage', 190). However, gardening was part of his policy; he 'showed particular concern for … female patients' in the main part of the hospital by 'converting their airing court into a garden [and he wrote]: "The patients thoroughly appreciate this change, and show active interest in the cultivation of flowers and shrubs"' (Hunt, 'Cage', 54).

† A reference to Baruch (or Benedictus) Spinoza, 1632–77. Born a Jew, he developed radical ideas/ unorthodox views, partly in discussion with Protestant 'free-thinkers'. Arguing for Nature (rather than God) as an infinite, necessary, and fully deterministic system of which humans are a part, and that humans find happiness only through a rational understanding of this system and their place within it, strained his relationship with his community: he was excommunicated and reviled by the elders of the synagogue of Amsterdam. http://www.iep. utm.edu/spinoza/ Retrieved 15 June 2011.

‡ A yellow or white wildflower, often a daisy or common marigold.

Thrushes' wings close, and the first pink aster out.

That girl who ran away walked smiling to herself through the garden – I tried to smile at her, to speak to her – I don't think she even saw me – <u>Some</u> Joan of Somewhere! Her poor face has never seen nor known even as much as a garden: and from him that hath not, shall be taken away even what he has.[*]

This should be forbidden ground. But I don't see why "we" – she also – haven't as much right to this as Emperor Mark Anthony, whom I love as the world's best and most princely loser, to this:

"Tend me tonight.
Haply it is the period of your duty;
Haply, you shall not see me more; or if,
A mangled shadow. Perchance tomorrow
You'll serve another. I must look on you
As one that takes his leave. Mine honest friends,
I turn you not away;
Tend me tonight two hours, I ask no more,
And the gods yield you for't."[†]

That was the last time when "the wounded chance of Antony" ever strove, before it bled to death – Is it too childish, to see the shadows and nights of the legendary great, in the face of somebody who looks sub-normal? Only, if God and Heaven are unjustifiable and indefensible because of such catastrophes as the war, man and the prouder earthly Kingdom are equally so, whilst the scapegoat still stumbles into the wilderness. Oh, badly expressed! But it seems to me that the real defence and protection of mankind lies for ever with science, the man-made and man-persecuted thing. <u>Against all odds</u>, it's with science to give us clean birth, clean love, clean death. What else can vision the fair and foul of body and mind, and be utterly impartial in

---

[*] Matthew 13:12, Parable of the Talents. Hyde concurs with the interpretation of Methodist biblical scholar Adam Clarke (1760/2–1832) 'Whosoever hath not, from him shall be taken away even that he hath – That is, the poor man: he that has little may be easily made a prey of, and so lose his little'. http://clarke.biblecommenter.com/matthew/13.htm Retrieved 16 June 2011.

[†] *Antony and Cleopatra*, 4.2.24–32: when Antony is taking leave of Cleopatra, Enobarbus, Charmian, Iras, Alexas and others.

working to that one good end? For that thing came ye into the world –[*]

Sorry: yet not sorry, and anyhow, I've been having a hellish time – The phantasmagoria of voices, and more this time. The car that drove up to take her away – The charge nurse calling to another to help – Her silly bleating cry – none of it happened. So far she is still here, and what I heard was purely a reflex of my own experience[†] – I understand and believe your explanation of these haunting voices. Perhaps, as she was so nearly due to leave, and returned of her own accord, she'll be allowed to trot off to her mother – poor smiling green-frocked scapegoat –

> These we can help no more. They have slipped from our hands
> Like the shining sands
> Of the castles we builded in childhood. The wind and the tide
> May not be denied –
> Not though a King cry "Halt!" to the hurrying waters,
> To the streaming manes that are grasped by the nereid daughters.
>
> These we must leave for the kites, in the secret strife
> Of a quarrelling life.
> Spent is their golden laughter. Haggard and poor
> They shall pass by our door.
> And it may be that out of their breaking, some music is wrung –

[rearranged following Zimmerman: end of series C, start of series F]

> But never to us has the cold blind wanderer sung.

Of course, something damnable <u>would</u> have to happen, the first day of your leave – Do you know Kenneth Grahame's "Wind in the Willows?" If you do, I wish you'd drop this chronicle of a black day – if you haven't already – and read instead about the purple loose stripe and the island where Ratty and Moly found the baby otter, safe in Pan's keeping – I'm going to close my eyes and try to remember the thrush and nothing whatsoever else.

x x x x x x x x x x x x x

---

[*] Matthew 28:19–20.

[†] Close to her experience of being removed to the Main Hospital in July 1933.

Poor Spinoza! The only grains of his essential truth that he could have gleaned from yesterday's bother are these. "That young woman's doctor is right, she is indeed a welter of emotional instability." "It's true that people do enjoy the misfortunes of others, but that's their misfortune." "The scapegoat theory is right in a dim, dumb sort of way, but God pity science when it's beleaguered with women's talk." "The essential viciousness of "Thegn"* is largely exaggerated." For that lass is strolling about free and sound, reading a book, this morning, in brilliant sweet sunshine. Oh, and one more truth. Late nights and early mornings don't agree with my complexion – Four o'clock, and never a thrush's wing, before I dragged into a sort of sleep –

I don't care – Nurse M. doesn't mind if I wallow in hot baths in the morning – I dress slowly and peaceably, and I may look slightly more than twice my age, but Anna Fitzherbert's new bath salts and lavender water have improved my soul the faintest shade –

There's no doubt, my own experience, more as a mental than an actual thing, has warped my judgment completely – I don't pretend to write from a normal mind. I'd love to be responsible for just one thing as "clear and cool" as Charles Morgan's book, "The Fountain."†

I was talking, years and years ago, about Venusberg.

There's a sort of little deep-sea creature, I believe, which periodically loses its own shell by growing out of it, and creeps about soft-bodied, until it calmly confiscates, pro tem,‡ the shell of another animal. Perhaps that is I, perhaps not –

I only know that from the shadowy green depths of Hanmer, until four years later, when I began to dream about Gerard,§ I was utterly different, no creature of myth or legend – but cold and hard and curious, with an amused deadly curiosity – My best poems were written at Hanmer, and during the few later months before home atmosphere and city atmosphere seeped into me. No more gardens!

---

* 'Thegn', or Thane, is an Anglo-Saxon word for ruler, nobleman or citizen. Here Hyde seems to be using the term for a doctor, perhaps the superintendent, or possibly the matron.

† *The Fountain* (1932). Charles Morgan, novelist, playwright and critic extremely popular in the 1930s and 40s, was known for his romance, mysticism, and serious themes. The character interestingly called Gerard Challis in Stella Gibbon's *Westwood* is thought to be a caricature of him. (Entry on novelist Stella Gibbons, M. Drabble (ed.), *The Oxford Companion to English Literature*, 5th ed. (Oxford: Oxford University Press, 1985), 668–9.)

‡ For the time being – from the Latin *pro tempere*.

§ Dream about having another baby – Gerard is her son Derek Arden Challis born Picton, 29 October 1930.The name was her own invention.

I have no excuse to make for, and no patience with, that lost self, a phantom in a crowd of secret phallic worshippers. (At one time, it seemed to me all men were such.) I was amused, and very deliberate. I watched their furtiveness, their utter lack of love and loyalty, their meanness. "Sans loi, sans poy [?], sans joi." I did not join – actually – in their promiscuities, I was too heedful of my own interests for that. But I did watch, and laugh. And I have heard many of the strangest stories, from beings drawn to reveal themselves to one in whom they sensed "broad-mindedness." Never was a woman less broad-minded – a gutter isn't either. I was merely amused.

[page break: order of pages uncertain]

It began, I think, when I took work in a little office whose true history (it's rather an old place, and was founded under curious circumstances and auspices,) would make a book, but a banned one, in itself –*

Its gates high-spiked and strewn with broken glass, and its windows protected (for they say that its original grew rather tired of being horsewhipped, but whether that's literally true I can't tell you) it hides its darkness in an alley – the reek of one little cafe, mixed with still another savour from a lead foundry, drifted up all day long – Huge rats rustled and peered amongst old files. I was doing my own work, writing: first only the most unexceptional fashion-cum-social stuff, quite well written, I believe, then a few more sensational screeds about fortune-tellers and faith-healers.† (I never, thank god, had even a finger in the Morality Pie. If I had ever done that, created splendid half-columns about the misdoings of shoplifters and divorcees, I simply couldn't go on now – but there's your nice "companion-help-refined," "general servant" distinction coming out again. Indeed, that word refined" was used of me, for the first time and last, in those months – Because it so happens that I don't drop my H's, the little crowd of black sheep were delighted with me.)

"Rare indeed must his composure be
Whom these soils cannot blemish."‡

---

* This is the office of the newspaper *New Zealand Truth,* where Hyde worked briefly from 13 September to December 1928 (*Iris,* 118–27).

† See note, p. 67.

‡ *Antony and Cleopatra,* 1.4.25–6. Octavius: 'As his composure must be rare indeed/ Whom these things cannot blemish'.

I was still young, had at first a faintly chivalric intention towards a soft-faced, soft-haired, uneducated little office girl of eighteen. There were two other women in the office, both older by far than this soft-looking little Phyllis and myself. One was a morally respectable beast, who sent confidential reports about her employer to his directors, who were stationed in another city. The other was perhaps less of a beast, in love with the handsome but exceedingly unpleasant (also married,) accountant, married in a semi-detached way herself, and since then convicted for some petty theft. They didn't take a week to tell me that baby-faced Phyllis was going to have a baby, per favour of the second in command at that place. A young Englishman, both clever and cultured, but more depraved, in a sleepy way, than anyone else I have ever met – Eighteen and with child! My own experience was a bit too close. Her misty blue eyes and round face seemed suddenly quite pitiable – more so, her lack of any intelligence, in her partnership with an older man who most certainly didn't want for that.

(That office pays high. It has to. He was comparatively rich, – if £20 a week seems wealth to you? Since then, I've heard, "Johnno" – that was Phyllis's characteristic name for the man – has held brilliant positions, has thrown them away, and has worked, more or less, on the wharves.)

But these two older women! "Where the body is, there also will the vultures be gathered together."* I hated their speech of her, their waiting for her downfall –

As a matter of fact, little Babyface had beaten them to it. Their suspicions had been perfectly correct, but the affluent John had "fixed things up," by medium of an illegal operation – Poor little thing! She told me later how much and how dangerously this had hurt her. I wish I could write of it all with more fellowship, even with the old "one of the boys" feeling. But time has so blurred the glass. I think she was generous and had a loving heart, and I'm sure about the soft hurt face. I helped her to choose, from her tiny salary, a very expensive birthday present for this devastating Englishman. And the last thing she ever said to me, very tearfully, was "I'll never have another friend like you."

Indeed I was no friend to anyone at the time, and she was the better of the two of us –

I started in, by being very nice to her and very rude to the two lady vultures. This

---

* Luke, 17:37, Matthew 24:28: And they said to him, "'Where, Lord?" He said to them, "Where the body is, there the eagles [also translated vultures] will be gathered together.'"

delighted and surprised "the boys." And her poor little friendship was easy game, like her poor little love – But championing her made me completely free of Venusberg and its secrets.

I think it's the completely matter-of-fact way in which every possible twig on the tree of knowledge was taken, that made the clearest impression of me. The mere action of vice is so often hurried, trivial, mistaken. But here there was genuine background. Everybody was so well used to everything! Ancientry again, nothing could have been more ancient than the tired acceptance of every rottenness that lay in Phyllis's John. Sodom and Gomorrah knew it. I went once, the only time in my life, to the Supreme Court, and listened to a frightened little rabbit of a man being chivvied through a divorce by lawyers. Could two people sleep on a couch of such a length? They argued about that. Then "Would you ever put your arm around her?" Oh no, the poor indignant little man panted, of course he wouldn't. Ah, but the clever private detectives had followed him to a sunny beach one day, and there he was, photographed with his arm about his charmer's waist! Bustle of feigned disapproval among the vultures. I disapproved of them, intensely, as I do of quacks (I could have given you a quite interesting chapter on the different brands of "healer" who battened on me whilst I was still be-splinted,) and of the really soapy brands of religion –

Each member of that staff – with perhaps three exceptions, one man who merely drank a great deal of gin, one who had a steady temperament and some talent, one who was old – had a curious and tragic personal history. But I believe that the business on which the office was based was really, for once, "begotten in sin." I am told that since then, it has changed greatly for the better, and all this may be unfair by several years. But concerning its birth and its atmosphere at that time, I am right. It was fathered by drunkenness, a warped brilliant mind, a cunning old knave of a lawyer steering the brilliance over many shoals. A thousand thousand curses have been naturally piled on it, but their effect seems problematical even to me. Anyhow – it stained.

I wasn't afraid of anyone or anything. I first settled on the hash of the charming John, who strolled in one night, drunk, to complain that I thought he and "little Phyllis" were in love. I told him it was a matter of complete indifference to me, if he were the lover of every woman on the staff, provided he left me quite alone. He grew respectful: the fool was half in love with me, after his fashion, in a short time – Well, I have never wanted quite that. He was "little Phyllis's" by virtue of an illegal operation that had hurt, and it was part of my cold amusement to contrive that as often as possible, he was thrust into her company. I might have thought more of her, she was very young and grew fond of me, and I did recognize his inner corruption: but she was lost in love for him, she had no brain to appeal to – and I was in the mood for leaving the child with its precious matches. They eloped in the long run – John having quarrelled with his employer, a fat smiling swarthy person who didn't look as though he saw much, but did – nearly enough to save his own skin, but not quite, for he was lazy as well as dishonest – I amused him immensely. So did everyone. How many people who talk about cynicism have even the vaguest idea what it implies – clever, camouflaged, or otherwise? He discovered I had ability, sent me off to fortune-telling lairs and the faith-healers.[*] All that I enjoyed too, except one single thing. Stephen Jeffreys, "evangelist," was holding spectacular demonstrations.[†] At one of them, a little boy of perhaps seven turned to me smiling, and had held out his hands, their fingers joined together by an accident of birth.

"God's going to tell the man to make my hands better," said he, with perfect self-confidence. I remember.

What a Brass Jack I'd become in looks! A friend of Jezebel's, an Assyrian artist's model, fine-browed, rather beautiful, and to my astonishment, "virtuous," took something of a fancy to me, and designed for me one or two of the queerest dresses. I found them fascinating, too, but was always about a submerged-tenth ashamed to be seen in them. I did manage to dodge the expensive London hats she'd have bestowed on me. They were quaint, and so and would have so definitely have classified me that I imagine your diagnosis might have been short and sharp. Yet morally and mentally clean as white linen she was – so much so, that when I took her graceful, dark-browed self to one or two parties, she was considered dull.

I remained for a few months only in that queer place. Then I departed with the company some £18 in my debt, for my swarthy employer was as lazy about parting with money as about all other matters. I extracted it from their little old lizard of a lawyer. He eyed my Assyrian-designed frock and cheap furs with interest. "I wish you had come to see me before you left!" said he.

I have left out a good deal in this episode, as in others: and I have added nothing

---

[*] Her article 'Cunning Witches Weave Wily Spells …' was published anonymously in the *New Zealand Truth*, 11 October 1928. See note, p. 67, also *Iris*, 120.

[†] 1876–1943, Welsh pastor, formerly coal miner, who saw visions and performed miracles. He toured New Zealand in 1928, when the Pentecostal Christian revival movement was strong. http://www.teara.govt.nz/en/nga-hahi-maori-and-christian-denominations/8

– I can only half understand it, I don't find it amusing now, and sometimes I think we
should all be born with ink-erasers attached. But you say it's well to face facts – The
effect those few months had on me is as nothing, compared to the slowly-working
tragic effects which I <u>know</u> that place to have had on others there. I haven't told
you of L. and his hideous prison sentence, of Roy and his tragic little betrayed wisp
of a wife, who stumbled fainting into my arms one day, and to whom, for her own
peace, I lied more resourcefully and fluently than ever since. Phyllis was abandoned
by John, to go on the streets in Melbourne. I had a pathetic little scrawled postcard
from her – she was ill – I answered it quickly, but have never heard from her again
– And for all this alone, I do deserve a Jehovah on the warpath; don't I? But I do not
know how it happened, nor why –

     Sodom today
       Has grown select,
With a borough council
       circumspect,

And your lust's clear image
       You shall not see
Save chastely covered
       'Twixt neck and knee

(That's until
       The star-flecked brown
Torrent of dusk
       Comes whirring down.)

God Pan cuts only
       Such modified capers
As shall not startle
       The daily papers –

Yet still, in fine
    Grey cinders, the wrath
Of God is sifted
    On Ashtaroth.*

Still there rings
    In her moon-blanched grove,
The dread commandment
    "Thou shalt not love!"

And the young sharp lips
    And the hands that cling
Freeze into senseless
    Posturing,

And a satyr bells
    In the flower-gilt meadow
Where poor lost shadow
    Lies bedded with shadow

Stay not too long
    In Sodom town
When the amber owl
    Of the dusk swoops down,

Choosing his prey
    In the little street
Grown blind and bland,
    And for ever, discreet –

---

* Ashtaroth was a Canaanite goddess of fertility, love and war (1 Kings 11:5, 11:33; 2 Kings 23:13). Hebrew scholars replaced the vowels of the original name Ashtart or Ashteret with vowels from the Hebrew word for shame 'boshtet', in order to bring dishonour on the memory of the goddess. Michele Leggott comments on this poem and theme: 'The sequence *Trilogy* (written 1942–44), written by the American poet HD (Hilda Doolittle), explores the same debasement of divine female power in the modern Western world and its apocalypse in the events of 1939–45'. 'Notes to *Young Knowledge*'.

Stay not too long!
    For with gaze grown chiller
The basilisk stares
    At each shadowy villa.

Still with her out-stretched
    Poignant hands
On the brink of sunset
    Lot's lady stands;

Spies in the welter
    Of bleak offence
The blossoms of childhood's
    Innocence,

And shrieks to the grim
    Swift marchers to halt,
Till her own tears freeze
    To the coffin of salt.

Girt with the roses
    Lord Youth hath made
Courtesan life
    Goes plying her trade.

Echoes her cry
    Through the hearts of men –
"Give me the grail
    Of my ~~heart~~ dreams again!"

Out of our darkness
    The curse of pity
On Him who spares not
    The desolate city.

But still in fine
    Grey cinders, the wrath
Of God is sifted
    On Ashtaroth –

[end of Zimmerman series F, start of series A]

And her wounded glory
    Of breast and limb
Sullied forever
    Are sweet to Him.

And Sodom today
    Is a plain yet good
Growing suburban
    Neighbour hood –*

Chapter 18.
    City of Trees.

It is the night of February 3rd – I am sick and afraid. I have, I confess, been playing the fool to some extent. Yesterday's episode, and one or two tragedies in a very minor key, made me see too clearly the meaning of what Schön Rosmarin says: "Everything here looks all right, beautiful even, but it's not. It gives me the creeps."†
I have been tilting against featherbeds, not windmills: against the arch enemy of us all, self-pity – Said "Let us be gay," or words to that effect, to one or two or three.

---

* *Young Knowledge,* 95–7.

† Perhaps because of this attitude, there is a record in Dr Tothill's files of one of Rosalie Rawlinson's visits 'seriously upset[ting]' Iris, an upset that prompted a letter of inquiry from Dr Tothill to Rosalie and later (24 March) a request that she not visit (*Iris,* 233). Hunt suggests that the fact this incident is not mentioned means that the 'Autobiography' must have been finished before 24 March ('Cage', 310). Rawlinson's suspicious attitude is also reminiscent of Frame's protagonist Istina in *Faces in the Water* and her attitude to the newly modernised wards.

And just fooled about – But fooling about doesn't suit me (it certainly isn't your prescription!) I'm tired now and lost in unreality. Indeed "Haply you shall not see me more: or if, a mangled shadow."* Serve me right; and my attempts to make a tiny crowd (whose real troubles I don't understand) cheerful instead of tearful are probably so unavailing as to be simply interference.

Indeed, if there were any friendship in the world, I wish it were hard by. The Schön Rosmarin says she loves me – she might as well love a veiled picture! – and my little dark Yasminé <u>does</u> love me, but, thank God, does not have to pay for that –

Well: at least, if this is to be unfinished (and I'm so dazed!) it shan't end in that filthy little alley.

I discovered for myself, this afternoon, a scientific ~~fact~~ truth. It's this. All facts are, as all men ought to be, equal in the sight of Me. There can't be any class distinction among them, except that given by duration of time. That, it is true, can weight with lead such a triviality as my lameness. Otherwise, the fact that mosses in the woods were

[missing page? lost order?]

of Boer ladies were found in a heretofore unknown cavern, hidden away for safety. But I gave the story a rather melodramatic ending – killed my poor Father off. "Wish-fulfilment?"

A red hawk's wing dips … no more of beautiful tree-guarded Hanmer, though I loved it well.

Why didn't I go back there, after leaving you?† I will tell you, in case you don't already know.

In "the secret places of the heart," there may be a creature wounded and trapped, suffering just as certainly from various compound fractures as though its body lay on the pavement.

Very few know those places, or dare to go there – for I am right, people, even doctors, <u>are</u> usually afraid of unreason and all the ancient shadows behind it. Now when you tried to open that door, I simply abused you – and so would the trapped animal, after its own fashion – But you were very patient, a host of phrases and

---

*　*Antony and Cleopatra,* 4.2.255. Antony: 'Haply you shall not see me more, or if, /A mangled shadow'.

†　After her self-discharge in September 1933.

sentences build that up into certain reality. Unknown to me, you must at the time have healed some wound a little. I know, I wouldn't go back even to Hanmer and freedom and beauty, because of eyes that might have been blank with fear or boredom. Or let me use the chosen words of one doctor who has been in this story; but which, I will not say. "Nothing you ever said before has disgusted me as much as this." (This, was a hysterical cry that at times I preferred the idea of murder to the idea of suicide: untrue, stupid – mad if you like. Murder doesn't interest me at all. But the self-revelation of that long furtive disgust disgusted me too, and frightened me – I don't know that I quite meant to try to see you again, when I came back ill and weary to Auckland – to sit until 10 o'clock outside the locked door of Mrs H's house,* she was away with Gerard at her beloved "bach." I did try to see the beauty of the north country where I travelled and wrote.† But when the glorious still Bay of Islands was just a blur, and people stopped me to ask if I were ill, and the voices wouldn't go away (it's extraordinary that I wasn't caught out over that before I left here, they

[page(s) missing]

had begun, and I gave myself away hopelessly one morning to one little nurse,) then I wanted help. And more, I was far more deeply disgusted with myself, with the depths of me, than the most exacting young man could be over a moment's hysteria. The priest who found me crying by poor plaster Saint Anthony knows that much! I thought, you might help. I knew nobody else could or would. Mother Church is easy on "the desires of the flesh," but she doesn't stop them – perhaps it's all unending. I know, after seeing you yesterday,‡ that you aren't sure whether I shall ultimately be a mental cripple or not. You wouldn't answer my question about the weak and the strong – But I do say, what I said to you once before, that I desire to be my own possession – to be given to a beggar if I like, but never from weakness. Love, physical contact, should always be from strength, never from weakness. So also the given dreams of the heart – You don't know if I shall be crippled or not – Well,

---

* Mrs Hutson. The Hutson family fostered her son Derek Challis.

† Following her self-discharge from the Lodge in July 1933, Hyde stayed with the Hutsons, spent two weeks in Wellington and went to Northland on an assignment.

‡ 'The first formal assessment of her condition by Dr Tothill in the New Year was made on the 3 February' (*Iris*, 233).

I know that I will not endure another day of that sick dreaming. But as a matter of fact, I believe I'm going

[page(s) missing? Following Zimmerman, sequence C moved from here to ch 17]

probable that I'll sleep now, and wake feeling perfectly well – If not, I must ask you to forgive me, and the "mangled shadow," as I ask the trees. I've rambled on and on, but in a loved place. It's only by sheer effort that I have written at all tonight but I did want to get away from that place of evil knowledge –

Yasminé would very wisely say to me, "Allez fe [fair] dodo." which means, she declares, go to bye-bye. Hope that's correct, my French is not even reliable Fourth Form –

Les feuilles tombent maintenant – Pourquoi dit-on, "C'est triste, Ha?" Encore sont les ~~arbe~~ arbres hauts et fiers, encore chantent les branches qui attenda[e]nt ~~silencious~~ leur rossignol, qui ne croient pas jamais que ~~ce~~ le chanson gai et vif est blessJ sans espoir. Les etoiles ne craignent pas les n[u]iages, n'oublient pas leurs amis qui semblent desolees. Fourth Form – bottom of the class – Something in me likes to write in stumbling French – My grandmother, the one in India, is of a French family – I wonder if she likes trees too – or only caged birds? Elle ne sait pas que deux fois, la fille de son fils a cherche[] dans les yeux d'un petit pour l'ombre lointair[n] ~~d'on visage~~ de son visage. C'est ~~tr~~ bon, Ha, qu'on ne sait jamais la tristesse de la fille qui serait toujours une inconnue –

"Allez fe[fais]dodo," is right.*

---

* A translation of Hyde's 'stumbling French':
'Yasminé would very wisely say to me, "Go to bye-byes" which means, she declares, go to bye-bye. Hope that's correct, my French is not even reliable Fourth Form –
The leaves are falling now – Why does one say that, "It's sad, huh?" The trees are still tall and proud, the branches are still singing as they wait for their nightingale; they will never believe that the gay, lively song is wounded, hopelessly. The stars don't fear the clouds, nor forget their seemingly sorrowful friends. Fourth form – bottom of the class – Something in me likes to write in stumbling French – My grandmother, the one in India, is of a French family – I wonder if she likes trees too – or only caged birds. She doesn't know that twice the daughter of her son has sought in the eyes of a baby the distant shadow of her face. That's fine, Ha, that she should never know the sadness of the daughter who will ever remain a stranger.'
Fais dodo: a traditional French lullaby with nonsense words and a gentle rocking (6/8) time signature.

Chapter 19.
   The Secret Child.

I'm tired and that's all –
Christchurch and its friends and trees I left for the silliest of reasons. My family bothered me into accepting a "more lucrative position" in a country town which is, by numerical strength, a city: but oh, very much still a country town!*

Now if it's difficult to remember realities, how much more so to remember ghosts? And that place was full of them. Only one reality – the great steel-grey sweep of river broad beneath my windows, bowing the stems of toi-toi bushes.

The first night in my new lodgings, I sat in a heap on the floor, and wept "tears as big as marrowfat peas."† I had rented it, spacious and unfurnished and complete with view, and my landlady had promised to furnish it nicely. Oh, the desolation fronting me! And the hiss and bubble and squeak of the evil-minded little gas fire! Nor was my room the worst. I saw those of the "gentlemen". Their curtains were exactly like starched and frilled white drawers.

Yet it was an interesting house, this: tenanted now by stark poverty, my landlady's husband was a vintage wine among the unemployed. Once, long before, it had been a private school, and boys, including a dusky prince of the Pacific, had told dormitory tales, perhaps held secret feasts, by the sooty flames of the lamps that then had lit my big room. (I once met an elderly ex-pupil of the school, that is how I know.)

Once, by accident, I opened the wrong door downstairs. There was a little step, and like Bluebeard's Fatima, I couldn't resist. Down stepped I, into the aged quiet of a dim room furnished in brocade – It had gone to sleep many a year ago, its gentle placidity had never re-awakened – Of course it was disused – I was sorry for its bits of porcelain, its books, its faded curtains. I believe it kept me in that dishevelled house, where there were noisy children and a noisier lodger who was always drunk, and always trying to make love to me.

This drunken and rather ugly individual, (he was quarrelsome, as well as much

---

* This is in Wanganui, where Hyde accepted a position as Lady Editor from May 1929.
† 'And the Duchess shed tears large as marrow-fat peas': a line from *The Ingoldsby Legends* by Richard Harris Barham, novelist, and humorous poet known better by his nom de plume, Thomas Ingoldsby. http://ebooks.adelaide.edu.au/i/ingoldsby/thomas/ingoldsby_legends/chapter17.html

too affectionate,) once started to ramble on about poetry. Said he, out of a clear sky,

"Let us alone. We have had enough of sorrow,
For ever climbing up the climbing wave."*

Finding "The Lotus-Eaters" in such a place was as odd as finding that dignified, faded room. I don't mind a bit about the "so much good in the worst of us," (pays to be good, usually,) but this yet living perception of beauty, stifled in a fat drunken body? Oh, of course, I did try a little priggish reclamation work, but I am no success as a reclaimer: because I have never been able to say

"I, Galahad, also saw the grail
Descending as a flame upon the shrine.
I saw the fiery face as of a child
That smote itself into the bread, and went."†

All the time now, it was Robin. The faces of living children began to hurt me, there seemed to play about them a mysterious sunbeam of happiness which I would never be able to hold, never.

I met Ishbel and Douglas and their fat two-year old Jock, who really was an adorable baby.‡ And those two constituted the best attempt at marriage that I had ever seen at close quarters. She was several years older than I in years, about twenty years younger in life and thought: a little Welsh girl, slender, with curious blue-grey eyes under dark brows. She was at once a psychic, and the cleanest woman I have ever known. (This is more than odd, for in New Zealand, the grubbiness of mediums and their followers is only surpassed by the mawkish tawdriness of their alleged "results.")

I entered as quietly into an intimacy with these two, as into any of my life. They accepted me completely, though there was a strong variance in their types.

Ishbel was no cheap sensationalist of the spiritualistic world, indeed I have

---

*   From Tennyson, 'The Lotos Eaters'.
†   From Tennyson, 'The Holy Grail'.
‡   Ishbel and Douglas Veitch were good friends of Hyde, and they liked and admired her as
    much as she them. Ishbel commented that Hyde was the first woman she met for whom 'work
    came first'. Later, Ishbel was very concerned that they had introduced her to spiritualism (*Iris*,
    139–45).

seldom known anyone less public. I think that perhaps Jock was their second child, the first dead and remembered. For once, there seemed a restlessness and unease between them, as they waited for that strange answer out of the darkness in which both believed. Then poor Ishbel cried passionately,

"Oh, he can't, he can't! He's too little!"

That struck indeed at my own heart. It hadn't seemed at all unclear, to sit with these two before a screened fire, to observe the funny mechanical rites – gymnastics! – of the séance. Sometimes the "messages" were extraordinarily clear and coherent, interesting to a degree not often found in books on the subject –

But Robin: buried, and for my safety and the family comfort more deeply buried still, in silence and secrecy. I never talked of him to my mother, and in time she forgot well enough to join with the sisterly chorus of disapproval, shock, horror – and curiosity – that had arisen whenever a girl of our district was "in trouble." (This was by no means infrequent, it seemed the popular way of getting married.) Sometimes I used to envy those publicised women, handed over to our modern council of virtuous matrons: envy them not their cheap marriage-rings, but the fact that living or dead, their children could not be so lost to them as Robin to me.

The secret child, of whom only Kay ever wrote, and she no more than a friendly, tactful word, seemed closer to me now: and at last an urgency and a longing in the dark –

Yes, I'm imaginative: but not so easily cheated, nor a very good bedfellow for the sensationalist or the liar – It was others who first heard the whispering voices that cried "Iris!" out of the dark. I heard little, but the darkness moved and spun with living sheets of deep sapphire flame – such an exquisite tender colour, not quite in our spectrum.

At least at home, or rather in that queer lonely room, I used to sit for hours, and watch with curious indifference a pencil that walked like a queer living beast under my fingers, and wrote and wrote.* At first, so sensible, very nearly "the voice of the Beloved." Different handwriting cutting querulously across a word, beginning a sentence that might or might not be finished –

By day I walked in a dream: yet I wrote "most satisfactorily," and amused those who wanted to be amused.

---

* Automatic writing was popular at this time both as a release of creativity and as part of the fashion for spiritualism. See '1935 Journal', p. 180.

At last, in this solitude, the final insistent scrawl, repeated and repeated.

"Put out the light!" "Put out the light!" I did just once. Almost at once the darkness overwhelmed me, and dragged me down through glaucous shadows into unconsciousness – It was an unbearable horror, I would not repeat it –

Still for a while I was sufficiently obsessed to use that little lethal pencil – Its scrawls were now quite meaningless. I chucked it away, and saved my reason, or perhaps some of it.

I never told Ishbel of this solitary experiment, she would have hated it, and like more than one other, she thought the old room where I lived evil. (An elderly and cantankerous man had died there before I rented it, perhaps he overshadowed the laughter and school-tales of the boys who slept there first.)

It was very rarely that I ever again went to a séance at Ishbel's home, and then in a cold and unquesting spirit: yet it was at one such that I first came to know Gerard's father –*

I have tried to speak for many people in this long wilderness, but he shall be allowed to speak for himself. He once wrote me, in early days of friendship, some verses.

"Robin has a trireme, with its lines of gold and blue,
It's ranks of stalwart rowers, and its fearless fighting crew.
Robin has a bright sword, too.

Robin has a galley with a crescent at the prow,
A light for nights of gladness, when we drink to Here and Now;
Robin calls a toast, "Here's how!"

Robin has a clipper that cleaves the sparkling sea
As it hastens down the eastings, with gems for you and me.
Robin has a pearl for you.

Robin sails a dark ship, by a flat and misty shore.
The gleaming through the lantern is a light on far En-Dor.
Robin at the helms steers true."

---

* Henry (Harry) Lawson Smith (1895–1982) was a fellow journalist; he worked on the daily newspaper in the nearby small town, Marton, and was married.

As it chances, the original of that is with me here.

Only this of him, that he was, Ishbel said in her funny little way, the most attractive person who ever came into her house. He certainly had the most beautiful of hands, long, white, carved out in old Greece. Timeo Danaos!*

And long after we'd known disillusion, and I had come to understand what it is to be hurt by subtlety and wit, we met in Christchurch. I had come to do battle really, for I didn't see why any man who had some share in Gerard, shouldn't at least take enough pride in it to visit him. We met on the banks of the Avon. There was an old tree rustled behind, and I looked round at it, and by the strangest coincidence, there was carved on its rough trunk the one word "Peace." Therefore peace it was, or a long truce, and I'd have been more sensible to have kept that quiet commandment. For the trees of Christchurch are my good friends, and wise.

You'll wonder how I could, in writing poems and in the talk of my friends, let myself be called "Robin." Don't you see, it was because he was so utterly denied and forgotten, buried so deep – for my safety! I wanted that lost name to have its significance, after all. At first, it cut me when people used a pen-name, or rather a nomme de guerre, in speaking to me. Then it seemed a little unconscious friendliness to him, something given without knowledge. I saw to it that only people whom I liked very much ever used it – Sentiment! But Robin's name was on the cover of the book of verses which Jessie Mackay and others wrote laudatory columns about, and of which J. S. who loved it, said that he "would write a few yards of justice."†

I think it was good – not so good, by a long way, as last year's verses, when dream and reality were both sharpened.‡

It may seem utterly ridiculous to you, this forcing into life of a lost name and

* Beware of Greeks bearing gifts! Literally, *Timeo Danaos! Et dona ferentes.*

† This is her first collection of poetry, *The Desolate Star and Other Poems*, published in November 1929 (Christchurch: Whitcombe & Tombs), and her first book under the name Robin Hyde. She had worked on the volume with John Schroder's advice from May 1928 ('Chronology', *Young Knowledge*, 385). Jessie Mackay's review appeared in the Christchurch *Press*, 23 November 1929, 13. Mackay was an eminent, older, woman poet and editor whom Hyde respected (see *Iris*, 150–1).

‡ The poems she was writing at the time of her breakdown in 1933; she 'began sending poems to the *Auckland Star* at precisely the moment of her removal into voluntary institutional care on 20 June 1933 ('She' appeared in the *Star* on 24 June; 'Seaborn' on 8 July)' (*Young Knowledge*, 10).

giving it such childish tributes. And now indeed, I have no cause to be glad that I did it, have I? I wish that I had left him to the care of the earth. And yet at times, when I think all's going to be quite well, I take for Robin Haroun's words: "He might be one of the world's great men."

At all events, he was the direct cause of Gerard's birth, and some day Gerard may take leave to blame me. I can scarcely identify the two as I wished, when Gerard was born with hair as red as a new sovereign, and is now a nordic blonde, not the least like my quiet child.

It's enough. Except that because nature seems always to humour me, the wisteria poured its amethyst over the houses where the children whose faces had hurt me played, when I let Gerard's father have his temporary wish, which was myself – I am glad, because that old garden of the wisteria is exactly the reverse of all the shadows, "the great black wings descending," that spiritualism is. It's a natural thing – It's benison I would like for Gerard, but I'm glad he looks so much too sturdy and blue-eyed ever to listen for the voices that used to call my name in the dark – Offal of the dead past they are, nothing more –

Chapter 20.
The Black Birch Trees.

Forests of them grow there, and through their little leaves the light sifts delicately green. The tiniest of grey birds hardly enough to fill the lifted palms of creamy blossom on the great bluegum trees, seem to love the black birch trees best of all, and the air is always astir with wings and with singing –

I am alone now, more alone than anyone else in the world, and happy in it. My brief stay at the Island,* solitary and lovely though it was, was not a happy thing. The people with whom I stayed there were surly and suspicious.

They, too, wanted a husband produced on demand. But here in this tiny, sleep-steeped town, with its unending golden sunlight which pays no attention to winter, I am quite safe: and Gerard is introduced to Mother Earth, with only so unimportant a thing as a woman's body to intervene between close-curled bracken, and just-stirring child.

---

* D'Urville Island in the Marlborough Sounds where, when pregnant with Derek, she spent June 1930, before moving to Picton where baby Derek was born on 29 October.

A very fatherly old pine is there, and one bluegum tree as straight and soaring as a ship's mast. I learn the elfin beauty of fish: tiny silvery ones, that go past in a great hurry, thousands at a time: blue cod, with their glorious gleaming scales: "Maori chief's," which are handsome, fierce -looking warriors of a tawny gold, and such sillies! They are no good whatever for breakfast, so I throw them back over the sides of the dinghy. Instantly they rush at the bait again. I've learned to row well and fearlessly, I who am so bad at sports. Well, I can betake myself five miles, over green water so very clear that one can see everything on the sea-floor, starfish, great fat sausage-like sea-slugs, golden-brown seaweed tresses.

I am almost afraid of the islet, where the sunlight plays like a quiet golden child. Is it the swish of seaweeds, in waters so deep, so hidden by contrast with the bay's clear jade? Island lilies grow here and nowhere else in New Zealand. Also, there is an enormous coterie of starlings, whose wings literally darken the sunset, as they return to their trees in a vast black cloud at night. What do they say of the trespasser, who lies so still in the sunlight, trying to drink up the earth's most secret essences into her body? Would they kill me, if I were to push the dinghy gently away, and stay in their haunts after night fall?

The Maori girls here hold it sacrilegious to cut their hair whilst they are with child – I decide to follow their example – economy, I'm only getting 25/- a week for the work I send my paper whilst "on sick leave." I don't care if I do look like curly Samson: my hair has, defiantly, begun to curl, and for a long while I look quite nice, though it's true there are often fish-scales on the one woollen suit which covers me all my days. (I never thought I could kill anything without horror, but fish like being killed, they are all suicidal maniacs.) Sometimes a smiling Maori wanders by, with yards of conger eel draped round his neck. I will speak to him (or her,) but not to the white people. Even the old librarian (female,) whose tiny library has a door hidden by a tumbling mass of roses, is so easily shocked. The Countess of Oxford and Asquith shocks her.* Now who could reasonably be shocked by such a funny old individual?

I read hundreds of books, all the same, for I can't sleep at nights, and the two local

---

* Herbert Henry Asquith was a British statesman. His second wife, Margot (Tennant) Asquith, Countess of Oxford and Asquith, 1864–1945, whom he married in 1894, was prominent in London society and noted for her wit. Her frank autobiography created a minor sensation, but as Hyde's comment suggests, was not very shocking. Colin Clifford, *The Asquiths* (London: John Murray, 2002).

chemists refuse me any sleeping-draughts, and an amiable if plump young doctor also advises exercise only. (Me with my hands blistered from the oars!) The days are blown past like garden blossoms. I sew Gerard's trousseau myself this time, and discover that I can embroider snowdrops quite passably –

Once or twice, longer expeditions, by launch. Ah, that's fine, the little boat digging her nose into the spray pretending she means to overturn us at the corner, righting herself with a superb gesture of defiance. I wish I could climb the misty bush-clad mountains, not far away, but I grow tired when walking. Once or twice I do get as far as Shakespeare's Bay: even more lonely and lost in the very heart of beauty.

Even religion seems momentarily more sweet. The little red church, with its vertical lines and its giant elm, is old – built in 1872 – and I like its sundial and its quiet. The door's always open, and I secure some polish, and slip in sometimes of a morning to give the brass an extra shine. The library is indebted to me too. Its file-room is a disgrace, and shocks the soul of a newspaper woman. I try to keep it in order, but I believe that the librarian must use the papers for blankets, or for lining cake-tins.

My landlady, who is elderly, becomes querulous. She wants a visible, audible, tangible husband too, it's no use, I don't look married and besides, I'm such a spasmodic and unconvincing liar. A post office box helps a little, with letters addressed to Miss –, (I can't prevent all letters!) but I suppose in as tiny and dreamy a town this is an open secret. She has daughters. One night, she simply declares with the honest conviction only to be found in those who like Jehovah and his thunderbolts, "You're a wicked woman, Miss –." Well! She bursts into tears and I can't help sympathizing, but you can't tactfully pet an elderly lady who has just cleared her fingers of the first stone. So I tell her not to be stupid, order my dinner to be served upstairs by a great sea-log fire (I feel rather like one in quarantine!) and next day move on to a fat and blessed Jersey Islander, whose cooking is divine. I don't think she cares whether I'm married, a bigamist, or living in sin – she just likes the 25/-, and is jolly about it – Jersey must be an amiable place –

From her verandah I watch the peachtrees come into flower, their frail pink blossoms seeming as though blown by across a fan by the skilled brush of a Japanese artist.

It's a fortnight before Gerard's birth that I get the news of an eruption of Vesuvius. I won't have my lucrative job to go back to … I suppose somebody guessed or gossiped, or else they just grew tired of my long illness. No tiny home for Gerard and me, no elderly kind soul to mother him in the daytimes whilst I work! Just enough I've got to scrape through "estimated expenses" until he <u>is</u> born, and then –

Green caravans and white horses, sudden love where least expected, becoming a beggar-woman (only could I carry myself and a probably squalling baby too?) I contemplate them all, and still none seems quite feasible –

And I've been so finally and definitely independent! <u>You</u> say men like pride. History's all against you. They like a show of it, that's all. The damsel of the Dark Ages used to pretend to run away, when marriage by capture was in vogue, but if she'd really sprinted, would her suitor have liked it? He'd have danced with rage and probably maltreated a sabre- toothed tiger. Well, independence, which apart from reticence is the only honest ingredient of pride that I know about, is sprinting. I had written that I wouldn't need financial assistance, then or now. At first, vehement annoyance: and then, I suppose, a gentle acclimatization to the idea of me as not a nuisance. I didn't quite think how unfair that might be to Gerard. Once more the sorry "I am paid for't now!" To persuade a man who is accustomed to you as not a nuisance that it's suddenly and acutely necessary for you to be one, is about the most unpleasant task one could find. (Yes, not if there's love. There never was, nor on my part even desire, only liking, and a ghostly memory of beautiful hands, and a mad longing for my lost child, that soaked in rough every day and night. On his part, interest and a great desire – I could have made that warmer, but I hadn't spared the time.)

I did think of the green waters then – But I wanted to live, I wanted the lost too much. If both of us had gone to sleep in that little sunlit graveyard, I wouldn't have minded very much – But life was sweet enough then. I still didn't quite believe my bad news; I never do, until it has filled my veins with poison –

A little more of the "happy golden land." That strange sweet kinship with earth's simpler forms of life seemed so very real to me, during those months. Almost at the very last, in a grassgrown sweet place where late daffodils bloomed, I found a newly-born lamb crying all by himself – dogs had frightened the mother off. He could just stagger, on his absurd legs. He wasn't afraid of me at all. I carried [him] down the hill to a friendly grocer, who didn't mind being turned into a Rescue Home for lambs, and in due course, I suppose, he became fat and solemn as are all pet lambs. I love to think of his little body in my arms: I suppose because I haven't been a very helpful person.

Gerard was born in a little green room – but oh, wasn't he objectionable about it!

Three days, and a process called induction – then some talk of a Caesarian operation – Fourth day, and I simply grew weary and screamed like a seagull – Reproachful, "But Mrs. C., you've been so splendid till now!" I didn't care whether I'd been splendid as Aldebaran.* Morphine for a while, then sinking in and out of chloroform. And this is most important, it puts Gerard on an equal footing with some of the Caesars, I forget which, and Owen Glendower,† who "could call spirits from the vasty deep." There was an earthquake just as he was born, enough to bring me back, for one weary sighing moment, from under the chloroform. There, no more worry of any kind whatsoever, until the doctor informed me with quite unnecessary emphasis that it was a boy. As if I didn't know that!

His little red-gold head! It was really rather pretty, that hair – should I have named him William Rufus? – and after critical inspection, said I weakly "He's quite a nice little baby." "He's a very nice little baby," remarked the doctor, like an indignant parent.

No more Gerard for some days. He was very good, (they said he didn't cry enough, as though every baby doesn't cry far too much,) and he and I at last came to stare at one another on my bed. I administered his bottles. The odd creature could be rolled over, without even uttering a squeak, like the unfortunate one in "Alice in Wonderland."‡ "Plays with him like a doll!" indignantly remarked my fair-haired little nurse. And by the way, Gerard was most polite when introduced to Lady Bledisloe,§ who visited the tiny town and its hospital –

He looked like a doll, sleeping and so very small in his clean little white cot, a parasol protecting his youthful complexion from the garden's sunshine –

And slowly I began to drag myself down the tiny street, where lilac and laburnum flaunted such gay banners of blossom – I had to go on – somewhere, anywhere –

He was a fortnight and three days old, when we left that place, and all its sunlit dreaming. Perhaps it remains in him, I begged the earth very hard for a share of

---

* Aldebaran – the brightest star of the constellation of Taurus and 'the follower' of the Pleiades.

† Several of the Caesars and *Owain Glyndwr* (1359?–1416, a Welsh national leader who led a revolt against the English) were said to have been born in earthquakes. Hyde would have known of Glyndwr from his portrayal as Owen Glendower in Shakespeare's *Henry IV, Part One.*

‡ Perhaps the Duchess's baby in Lewis Carroll's *Alice in Wonderland,* who was thrown to Alice, 'snorting like a steam engine' (London: Heinemann, 1960), 72.

§ Wife of Lord Bledisloe, Governor-General of New Zealand, 1930–5.

her kindliness as I lay among the bracken. But in me it has quite died, except as a memory that was sweet. I have blotted out all that wasn't, from this page. For once, like the wise old sundial, "Horas non numero, nisi serenas."*

[page missing?]

A voice in a morning, a woman's voice. "Miss –, you're to come down to the home." Into the heart of my safety.†

Ghost of another voice, heard not so long before. "I understand – but it's right up on the hill, away from the other place –" And the laugh that had reassured me so completely. "I won't put you down among a lot of loonies."‡

C'est ça. But I did offer to walk to the car, wish to – a last semblance of pride. It wasn't permitted. There were nurses to carry me, instead. Force is the easy way for one to kill me, for the touch of an unfriendly hand means shame, always. There's a woman here talks loudly and publicly of her unblemished virtue. Well, I have none. But I wonder which of us could be shamed the more easily and completely?

And fear too, of course. "The great black wings descending," again and again – But you'll admit, I didn't parade that.

I did try to explain, not to you but to your colleague.§ A hopeless tearful effort, that was. And it only served to puzzle, perhaps to hurt. I couldn't get the comedy into sensible shape, any more than I could my last muddle of a play. So just, "I see – you wanted to frighten us," was all that was said – And after all, how could one possibly say to any person "Well, you happened to be God, I didn't like Judgment Day so much, I wanted to get it out of the way, and I couldn't think of any other sound method?" Didn't hang together – It was funny, and I laugh at that perturbed self that lay so tearfully abed for half a day, then resolved to cry no more. I only broke my resolution once –

Why remember the ghosts of that place? The loss of privacy is the loss of everything to me – It might have been otherwise, had we been happy at home, or if

---

* 'I count only the hours that are bright.' American writer Bishop William Croswell Doane uses the line to begin his poem 'Sundial', *Rhymes from Time to Time* (London: Riggs Print, 1901), 80.
† This is the incident when she is transferred summarily to the Wolfe Home – the Main Hospital.
‡ Dr Buchanan's promise when she saw him at Auckland Hospital (in the DT cells) after her suicide attempt.
§ Dr Buchanan – later, on p. 172ff., Dr B. is also called 'you'.

I'd told ghost-stories once on a day in a good boarding-school. (Funny: that could have happened, if we hadn't lived in a city. I found when I was last at home the certificate of an old scholarship which granted to country holders, £40 boarding allowance a year. But there 'twas.) Your little room at the Home* seemed crowded with strangers, with fear, with dazed wonder as to how it all happened and what would happen next, soon with the quite real and throbbing agony of a daily headache that only your powders quieted.

It wasn't that, mere peace for physical pain, that began to build up this tiny atoll of confidence. After all, physically I have been hurt enough before. But – to begin with, you weren't exactly pleased. I had evidently said something or other pretty unforgivable about you – I still stumbled badly enough, in trying to explain I had been too sick to know or care what I said about anyone.

"I'm sorry. I should have known you were sick."

What ever else in this long wandering tale you find contemptible, there's at least those words of your own – a possibility of understanding, to one too tired to make anything clear, any more, and a belief that I didn't deliberately lie all the time –

Many and many more things – all trifles, "all in the day's work." I don't know of anything trivial, except for the trivial people, and even when I hated you, I could not have called you that. You cannot know how to the very sick, every word has its long dwelling significance, every look its message of good or harm or indifference – I believe such things change the very contours of the mind.

Not that I wasn't bleeding to death, in brain and love and pride. I've said no word of what I thought concerning Gerard, all this while: nor shall I. And pride …

"Never refuse a meal, in a Lunatic Asylum." Those words fastened like iron claws in my mind. A nurse at the public hospital, impatient, had told me something about forcible feeding. Data is not so very hard to collect –

The worst pain can do isn't the worst indignity can do – Except for two days, I always ate – a little. But I was so very glad, when I happened to find the scales in the bathroom one night, and found I had edged my way a little nearer to death –

Days were calm enough, on the surface – thanks to your powders. My nurse even tried to teach me to play chess, but I, who am usually quick, couldn't grasp the first principles. It slipped away – Ordeal by water, in the bathroom. You minimised that – screens ordered, and a quiet hour chosen – It must have seemed funny to you, a

---

* The Wolfe Home, perhaps consultation room.

157

ridiculous whim. Never to me, in all my life –

The nights were far worse – But "far" is the better word. Far away, and long ago, and what I remember of them is of no more importance than a very long nightmare –

Eternity's a funny sort of proposition – It can be exactly half an hour , and still rest eternal – My "wonderful self-command" slipped a bit at nights. Not quite enough for the last and deadliest thing, that waited for me just as I waited for it –

Mother came, and I could have gone quite away from all this – I wouldn't. I wanted one of two things – death, or else the impossible forgiveness for all I couldn't explain: forgiveness for being myself, I suppose. And that equally impossible shining armour of safety –

No way back to that. I know every danger, both here and elsewhere. "I know them: yea, and what they weigh, to the veriest jot or scruple."

Day after day, "I want to go back to where I was before." To a room, privacy, somewhat more of comfort? Ah! nothing so simple!

Chapter 21.
<u>Christmas Lilies</u>.

Gerard travelled to Wellington in an antique dress-basket. I was a little nervous of the solemn blue-eyed thing, and filled with an absolute passion of gratitude to him when he merely accepted his bottle at my hands, and slept the sleep of the unjust. He was so <u>good</u>! But then, he always is with me, when we're alone, and when I've enough quiet of heart to let me be alone with anyone or anything. There is what I can only, and very clumsily, describe as a bond-love between us. He hadn't seen me for months, once: one of his several proprietresses had been feeding him on condensed milk – I brought the two of them up to Auckland, and lo, no supply – Gerard and I both wept about it, he because he was thinking of his manly stomach, I because he hadn't "turned up his nose and laughed aloud" at such diet. In the midst of his grievances, he stopped, unfed, and stared at me with drenched Mediterranean blue eyes. (Gerard weeps like a budding film star.) He smiled … he was quite quiet when she came back.

So little of him at all. He had to be smuggled to Wellington. I spent the last of my money with the calm of desperation, enthroning him in a private maternity hospital. I was so weary. And I spent just three desperate weeks at home, where my family were all convinced that I'd thrown away Wealth Untold, and then, like curses and chickens, come home for ever to roost, merely for the pleasure of a prolonged holiday. I never survive a week at poor old "Laloma," without wondering just when the holocaust is due to take place. Yes, a joke: but it'll probably fill pages of New Zealand's grubbiest rag, before it is quite over –

A week at Jezebel's place. Her lord prefers them legitimate, which is passing correct of him – There were great white Christmas lilies there, and my lad slept among them – At night, in my room. Only those few nights – I was weary and strained and beginning to be just the little more than ordinarily afraid: but I can't pretend he wasn't a very nice and chivalrous baby, and I like to think of his small cheek pressed against the pillow, whilst the big moths fluttered around our candle and I lay and thought and thought of possibilities that just weren't possible –

"How little she cared!" Ah, even then, I was done. Jezebel's husband spoke of the Home of Compassion. It was only the beginning of the soiling and spoiling of those months that had been golden as the laburnum. I had enough to pay for a month of his life in advance, when I left him in Palmerston North with an old Irish woman – (He flourished like a wild flower with her, and I still like her better than the others, despite the condensed milk.)

Word of miracles – job! And by telegram, and with an Auckland paper I had never seen nor heard of, but promptly went forth into the wilderness to buy.

A little earlier or a little later, it might have been almost in the image of that crazy dream which had carried me through so long a while. Earlier, before I was afraid and bitterly hurt, open-eyed to every ugly possibility confronting this small dream brought into actual life. Later, after my physical weariness had gone a little. I'd started to limp again, in the old painful accursed fashion, and months of electrical treatment, after I came to Auckland, were needed to put that right.

Death: I don't suppose there has been a day I haven't wanted it more or less, since the day I received his father's first letter, not a week after he was born. Nothing much in it: but lack of everything, which, after all is exactly what I had earned and even asked for. But the death-wish hung then, and has ever since, between my son and me. Once or twice I have seen his blue eyes through it, and loved his little solemn important ways. I am sure I could have loved him very dearly, if I hadn't at an early stage become a fairy mother, living on ill-spelt letters or snatched interviews. Perhaps I do love him as I should, in a hidden way. I'm afraid not now. I said "Goodbye," before I went into the water, and the thing said makes itself inevitably true.

Chapter 22.
Poppy and Mandragora.*

There was he in Palmerston North (I hadn't dared to uproot him, whilst scarce knowing if that precious thing "the job" would or wouldn't last.) There was I in Auckland, and a little office of great age and grimness received me pleasantly, and I hadn't yet learned to hate Queen Street, from neon lighting to rattling cars and safety zones, to stammer, to dread telephones, to hate other people' s company only a little more than my own. But why catalogue such dreariness? I' d been mortally wounded in a rather crazy self-confidence a few days after Gerard was born, that is all. And he was afar, and I a fairy mother, dazed beyond the commonsense of bringing him straight to Auckland, of learning all that I had wanted so from his own very sweet little body and soul –

If there had been even one friend, man or woman, it would have helped. I knew exactly nobody, and hadn't the whole armour of God or of the devil, that I might come to meet and like someone, among the hundreds of charming people who litter the parks and pavements, and other resorts.

That's what my young and keen and clever editor never did, nor ever need, understand. The little "social work" I had done before was of a slapdash sort, in which I could be heard without being seen. Here – Government House,† and shabby gloves: race meetings and, "Oh, <u>would</u> you mind letting me have your name for our paper?" Telephone calls, and my voice sticky with sweetness, as I beseeched some strange far-off buzzing voice for the latest unconventionalities appertaining to its household. It was all funny, really funny, and normally I'd have laughed as I did it, and made friends if I chose to make them – why ever not? But then, the bright dream was clouded, and the little realities were a very nest of wasps. And now – I pretend and pretend, to everyone but you, and perhaps to Schön Rosmarin and Yasminé, who are waifs of dream as am I. Oh God, I'd like never to be seen, touched, spoken

---

* Mandragora: aka mandrake or satan's apple.
† In 1933, Government House (the official residence of the Governor-General) in Auckland was situated in the city above Albert Park. It is now part of the University of Auckland campus.

Penman
House

Centre for International Analysis

55

Previous page
Front view and entrance to the
Lodge, showing Robin Hyde's attic
at the top.

Opposite
Top: Hyde scholars Pat Sandbrook
and Mary Edmond-Paul in Hyde's
room at the Lodge. Balcony seen
through the window is shown at
bottom left. Bottom right: The main
stairwell in the Lodge.

This page
View from the attic window and
Mary Edmond-Paul standing in the
attic, where Robin Hyde wrote.

but the sparrow still beats the window pane
when it flies indoors by accident. There was
none to "Get me out of this." So I suppose,
though I can not remember, that a ghost of
that Palmerston North doctor, his morphine
and his later anxiety to be rid of me,
slid into my mind. Madness indeed, not
to realise that this was no little private
hospital, but - except here in "Solomben" -
the very twin of the place he'd have sent
me to.

I remember writing to Father Time, and
of that letter only that I asked for morphine.
Not for sleep, not for pleasure, not for
madness: except the madness of "Get me out
of here." I swear that is the absolute Truth -

Then, in my sick mind, I was safe
again and quite happy -
Was it one day or two, or longer? All that
time I had no fear, no worry. I'd settled
the question, brilliantly, I was to get
morphine and take it, you were to be
frightened and angry and send me away;
The wilderness is wide enough. I wonder
if you see, or if you believe me? It seems
so urgent to write this,

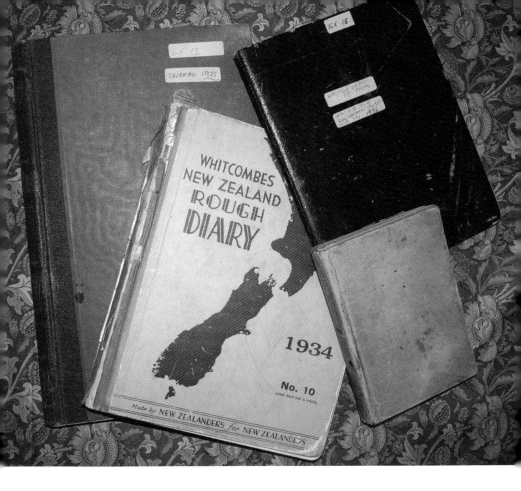

Opposite
A page from the '1934 Autobiography'.

Above
The manuscripts, left to right: '1935 Journal', '1934–35 Journal Fragments', '1936 Journal Fragment', '1935–36 Journal Fragment' (China Notebook).

Next pages
Front page of the '1935 Journal'.

A ladybird as blue as a chip of lapis lazuli arising out of the undergrowth of yellow grasses has just stalked contemptuously over this white page as if to show me how little the brink of it. Likewise the branch of a rhododendron with its grouped leaves bends down and sets the delicate shadows moving on the whiteness, together with little clear mirror-spaces of sunshine. And an ant arrives and stops, faintly worried with quivering antennae as to what black markings on a piece of paper almost conveyed something curious and doubtful to her. To complete the world, here is an old magnolia, its thick creamy blossoms dropping down a perfume as heavy as a sort of scent-manna: a broken arch of sky, fabulously blue, nine pine trees, which even now are black and which in the dusk can become formidable. To the right a little patch of sea like a piece of wrinkled silk is drawn back from a yellow foam-marsh and I can see a stranded boat sticking its improbable mast up, a perch for the seagulls, who often make the three miles from Point Chevalier to this inland place a part of their day's work —

That's all — I sat down wondering what to write like and the ladybird and the magnolia presented themselves — This morning on the other hand, when wondering the same thing I looked out of the bathroom window the answer was different — There were five white doves motionless like snowy odalisques, and near them drooping and in a hopeless minority one of the pigeons — I like, the grey, ruby-eyed, rainbow-breasted creatures — Poor dear, she had no idea she was to be left stranded with the odalisques. But the grey pigeons are more daring — The white stay at home and confidently expect they will be fed out of the bread-box. The grey ones circle and explore. So they picked up fair and west, and returned home to die sadly, one after another falling plump from the steep grey gabled roof. I saw the eighth to perish, there on the lawn with a little ruby of blood when its head had struck the ground — and is anything more difficult to connect up to an life and death? A second's difference, and the feathers still

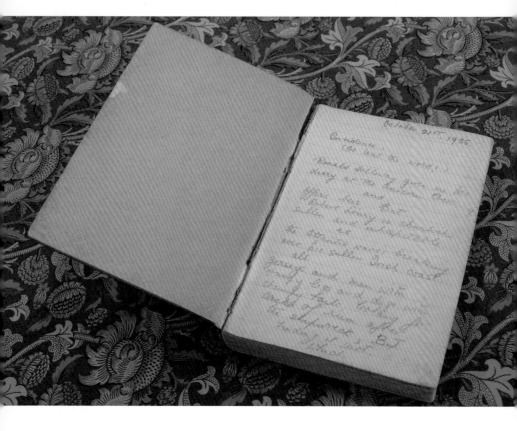

Front page of the '1935–36 Journal Fragments' (China Notebook), which was a handmade book gifted to Robin Hyde by printer Ron Holloway.

to ever again.

"Presently, when the stir
Dries in the little street
When I no longer hear
Clatter of passing feet,

When I have learned to rule
Ivy and bat and mouse,
Presently – I shall be
Master in my own house.

Too much disorder now,
Too great a discontent –
Too many voices heard –
Servants grown insolent."

I don't know where I read that, nor who wrote it. It was years ago, I think. But it is utterly true.

I needn't drag through the details of cheap boarding-house,[*] commonplace reading and entertainment, the stale food of a mind that was dazed more than diseased –

I worked well, because I always do. Said my late employer,[†] three months before I left his services, "Well, you've given me pages that are admired, feared, hated, read." And said he again when I last saw him, "You can do many things as nobody else can do them." A little poor conceit, salvaged from wreckage. But I am glad I worked well for him, and I wish that we had been friends. What did we know of one another's secret battlefields?

---

[*] Hyde's first Auckland boarding house, 'Burwood', was in Princes Street near Auckland University, within walking distance of the *Observer* newspaper offices at 12 Wyndham St (*Iris*, 204); she also lived in another boarding house, Hotel Rossville in Eden Terrace (conversation with Derek Challis, referring to information in her Mental Health Medical Record).

[†] John Gordon McLean (Mac), editor of the *New Zealand Observer*.

"The fourth sun saw the great black wings descending
Where crashed in blood and spume the charger lay:
From the snapped cords a shapeless bundle falls.
Scarce human now, like a spent thing he crawls,
Still with a shattered arm his face defending
As inch by inch he drags himself away."

Not so far away, as yet. Eh bien –

My friend the keeper of the gates of sleep* didn't really get his innings (he lived at the same boarding-house, a rather squalid place, as I had dragged myself into and couldn't be bothered to leave,) until a chance accident of pain arose. Not that he didn't try – he with his endless producing of his "emergency ration," ten grains of great usefulness. But I had no particular interest in that, and a great deal less in him. In one sense, he has always failed completely of his object, which was, I suppose, myself. I don't know that that matters much – except that a long scarce-conscious distaste is much more conscious, now. The drugs = immorality theory is all wrong, as far as I'm concerned. Drugs, for me, mean oblivion, and my bedroom has always been my own place: or else a cold north wind of contempt for the very hand that I watch at its quiet work of poisoning: or else, what a tortured broken child once wrote to me – "Dear Robin, have you ever had morphine, it's such a wonderful happy feeling." But not a happiness requiring sexual intercourse.

I told you I was never a drug addict, which I take to mean one controlled by a craving for some drug. That is perfectly true, though only because there's iron resistance in me somewhere, a protest against all proffered slaveries – sex, drugs, insanity, even unhappiness.

This accident of pain: I spent a night with a high temperature and a side torn by periodical spasms of agony. It was worse next morning. They telephoned, from my boarding-house, for a very kindly little doctor. Not appendicitis, said he, but merely a severe attack of some much less dignified little trouble. He gave me an injection of morphine. In the evening he returned, to find a revivified me. But he didn't let well alone! Just to be sure on the appendicitis question, he did all the many stern and unpleasant things a doctor of questioning mind can do to one's anatomy. Yes, and

---

* This was 'Joe', who ran a chemist shop in Queen Street and supplied Hyde with drugs, including smuggling morphia tablets in a box of chocolates sent to her at the Lodge. She also calls him 'Father Time'.

162

when he'd gone on his way in satisfaction, I began to feel again the throbbing of a pain that your most imaginative patient could envy. And Father Time was announced, plus a large and charming bouquet. (I do miss his flowers. They, much more than any drug, lead me to what you'd call unfortunate associations. I think if the Devil brought me blue lotus lilies, pink ixias, copper-coloured roses, I'd be just a little suave with the devil. Ask the charming Rattray girls, whose equally charming florist's shop used to be a vice with me. I don't see why one shouldn't be a little mad about zinnias, as about postage stamps or British Israelism.)

I was crying. I'm afraid I do, if badly hurt, unless simultaneously <u>more</u> hurt in pride or in love. And Father Time had his emergency ration, which was nice of him.

C'est ça. Twice, I think, in the better part of two years and a half, I took morphine every night for a month – never by day, I respected my funny nerve-wracking job, which might have been such real fun if I hadn't come to it so weary, and if two "temperamentals" (beastly word!) hadn't clashed a bit, as the creatures will. Mac had small mercy on my nerves, nor on his own. I don't honestly think I would have cared for myself much either, "shapeless bundles" are apt to be very exasperating.

We did fight, we two, against the heaviest journalistic, financial and social odds that you can imagine. And we won. I am more than ordinarily glad – if that ill-financed, once unwanted and curiously gallant little paper were to come to grief, you'd have a very sick woman on your hands. But it won't, and he won't. He presented me with a stammer – but we were forced into an <u>unfriendly</u> closeness of association and knowledge. Before I departed, I was completely careless of what he thought – I wish I hadn't been: it's not a good brand of loyalty.

I give you his side only of the picture, because I like to: and I think that in those days, my crest should have been a snob, couchant, on a field gules.*

Poppy and mandragora! Well, never the latter, I'm afraid. The former I only suspect, I don't know for certain. "You're looking so tired today, Iris." Oh yes: I allowed myself to be Christian-named, trotted about, be-flowered. (But <u>no</u> "hundreds of pounds" expended, sad as it seems.) Why?

"Too tired for love or mirth,
Stung as I was, and sickened by the truth."

---

* Gules: a tincture for the colour red in heraldry, here used as a ground or background. Oxford Dictionaries <http://oxforddictionaries.com>. Retrieved April 2010. Perhaps also a reference to the last line of Nathaniel Hawthorne's *The Scarlet Letter*: 'On a field, sable, the letter A, gules'.

I didn't care at all: but I was rude and unpardonably so, not once but a hundred times, to this little man, who perhaps was lost in the wilderness too, looking for the ghosts of his own youth. Typical programme: a restaurant meal, in complete silence. Then he, poor dear, would tactfully comment on the evening paper's news. Some chance word, of European squabbles, unemployment, currency, would light me up. He was well-informed. Then, "You're looking so tired today!" or, "You simply can't manage without sleep!" And that obliging readiness of his – and, I suppose, always a long fumbling desire that worked its way towards hatred. For the most patient little man does get weary of silence, currency lectures, and severely restrained "Good-nights."

But he doesn't, in the very least, matter. As so many things do, the two distant months of morphine-craving (I remember now that the second started after a train journey just long and uncomfortable enough to make me ready for any drug,) went away from me abruptly and entirely – I have never definitely known the nature of the large capsules which he gave me, in the nights before I finished that ill-scrawled chapter of life. I opened one, on one occasion, a dark powder, heavy-smelling. It made me sleep without dreams. The mornings were a cross, weary time, but the afternoons blazed up with a kindling light. I could write poetry again, and any form of prose had always seemed to me mechanical, compared with the clear, untroubled completeness of poetry – the Pallas Athene of the arts, it is. Some of the poems were queer dream-stuff: others good.

But ever since, that flower has stayed with me, my last companion. I am convinced that those who believe drugs = poetry, or art of any kind, are as wrong as those who believe drugs = immorality. No: a dormant thing may be wakened and fished up to the surface, that is all. With the more powerful drugs, it's at a cost that you understand much better than I. Coleridge, De Quincey and the rest would have been greater writers, not lesser ones, had they trusted their own inspiration, and, like John the Baptist, made ready the way for the lord of beauty.

A lesser drug, veronal, has a far more obvious and dangerous effect on me than its deadlier sisters. Ten to fifteen grains. One drops like a pole-axed ox. A week, and a crying, shivering wreck sits where a human being should. I had to stop that, for no temperament under sun or moon could have excused my white face – not even our undeniable piles of overwork. (Pharoah's whip never cracked more savagely when the Pyramids were being built, than that little old paper's when it was becoming neither so little nor so very old. But it always cracked around the editor's own shoulders, as well as mine, that's but the commonest justice. Well! Our diminutive Pyramid was built.

"My name is Ozymandias, King of Kings.
Look on my works, ye mighty, and despair!"
Nothing beside remains. But on all sides
The desert stretches, silent, stony, bare. *

Poor Gerard! "He is very happy and keeps laughing all day long!"† Well, by the time he was a year old, I did at least muster up enough energy to retrieve him.

I don't want to go into the details of house-hunting and mother-hunting for him. You believe, don't you, in Child Welfare Societies, rule, rote and regulation? The abuse of them you naturally do not see: the shoddy women who, disappointed in the prospect of still another weekly dole from their baby-farms, can scream, "£50 fine, if yer <u>don't</u> put it in a registered home."

Gerard and I took two or three days off from all this. From Christchurch came a long-legged, brown-eyed girlfriend whom I could trust.‡ She minded him whilst I worked – and after, we were all very frivolous together in a big room that looks over harbour and little golden-lighted ferry boats. I believe that from a scientific point of view, we were very wrong in feeding a one year old on tomatoes and grapes, but we decided that after the condensed milk, what the child secretly wanted was Vitamins. <u>He</u> made no fuss. Nor did I take any drug then. No sleep at all, but it was rather sweet to lie in the big room, and watch the golden-eyed boats and think. It couldn't last. Beula (that was my long-legged lass's name,) got into financial difficulties – (And wasn't she an example of unholy pride!) Would you believe that an artistic and gently brought up child could and would live for months on 10/- a week – 7/6' for a deplorable little room in Symonds Street, 2/6' for food, nothing for "incidentals?" That is exactly what she did, and wouldn't go home to her gentle but poverty-stricken mother, until she had developed some form of anaemia. She has a most gallant and loving heart, and a child's sense of humour: and a huge and threatening slab of Christmas cake, which arrived here for me, was her own patent.)

It was Mrs H at last: a decent enough little home, a green lawn for Gerard to roll

---

*   Percy Bysshe Shelley.
†   Perhaps a quote from a letter from his foster mother in Palmerston North.
‡   This was Beulah Jenkin, who later took her mother's maiden name Hay.

on (the infant prodigy could already turn somersaults,) cleanliness, and the sheer relief of knowing him safe. Until a few months ago, there existed a sort of surface friendliness between us. None now. What more I wanted then, just in unease and tired unhappiness, for Gerard, I want too clearly and savagely today.

I know how poor was the fight. I was beaten.
　　　What else to say?
Only this: that my heart had bled away
Long since, under my armour. Yet not as the driven cattle
Go to the pen, but steadily as into battle
I walked to that place, and stood for a moment so,
With my head held high as his who should bring it low.

What do I want for Gerard? You spoke once of people who want "big houses". Did you mean large establishments, complete with cutlery, napery, and what our Bolshie friends would refer to as "flunkeys?" Ah, that's a cheap and commonplace desire, indeed, an artificiality –

But tell me: how many dream about, day dream about, starve for old houses – houses that won't stare with bright new-painted faces? Old gentle houses that I love so, I wish you could speak for me and for Gerard –

I like soft light that falls graciously, and speech of the same order – I like the far, far shadow of music, a patient ghost in distant rooms: I like to think of doors never opened at all, of rooms left to the quiet and to the scent of pot-pourri. In Christchurch I learned a very little about old china, from a venerable collector named Seager.* You may have known him, perhaps. And here, Kohu the jeweller says I've a singular appreciation of some stones – only some, water-worn jade from Thibet, peridots, garnets.

But these are women's wants. For my son, I want certain things as odd. That he should ride: that he should learn how to fence, in an age which roars its appreciation – or otherwise – at more popular sports. I want Clio, History's muse, to be a friend to him, and dearly I should love that when he's seven or so, a great closely-lettered globe should spin before his eyes, as it did before the eyes of English boys so long

---

* Samuel Hurst Seager, a Christchurch architect 'committed to the social role of architecture and the importance of urban design'. http://www.teara.govt.nz/en/biographies/3s8/1 Retrieved 16 June 2011.

dead, who made England great.

More than anything else I want that he should be loyal in friendship and gentle in love. And for his own life, bitter or sweet as it may be, the greatest gift I ask is courage, not a desperate spasmodic thing, but a virtue very quiet and inflexible.

I have spoken of four necessary virtues, and of three clear rights to life. This is an age when men are said to have lost their power and pride, and in many cases it is true. Sauve qui peut! But I tell you, man never had but one authority over woman, and that is unbreakable. The authority of wisdom. I have met perhaps two or three who had it. They wear King's crowns.

Is that too much and too didactic a wanting, from a woman who also wants such very little things as to take a child out, alone?

I think he will be brave. You know that room at the museum, lined with great staring Maori idols? They <u>are</u> a grim folk! I took him there, and at first he wouldn't go near them. But <u>I</u> patted them and talked about their friendliness, and soon, his little hand grew bold, and he made very free with them – It's an important trifle – I who will probably die of fear, know it for what it is – I wish I could say, like Deirdre, "I have put away Sorrow from me like a shoe that is muddy, and Fear like a cloak that is grown old." But it would be a lie. Half my life is nightmare, half dream. I want neither for him, his mother has done enough dreaming for our family.

So if you say of us "Lop off the rotten branch," – and that is I – there won't be any tears or protests. But he must have at least a chance of what I promised him, long before he was born. And if there's no chance, without some desperate shift of mine, then be sure I will invent one. I am not drugged now, and like Kipling's sailor lad, I am a person of "infinite resource": not of infinite sagacity.* That's all, of Gerard.

<u>Many Waters</u>. Chapter 23.

I shall make this chapter the last, though nearly three years would perhaps like to have their quarrelsome say. "Servants grown insolent!" They were far from uninteresting. In addition to being an unpopular success, "feared, hated, read," in my journalistic work (how very uneasy these Aucklanders are, in their social consciences!) I, who made not a friend at all, seemed always to magnetize the

---

* 'the Mariner was a man of infinite resource', from 'How the Whale Got His Throat', *Just So Stories for Little Children* (Toronto: George S. Morang & Co., 1902), 4–7.

queerest scraps of hidden knowledge. I grew to hate it in the end. Was I a sort of human pitcher-plant?* I know – where a doctor who died not so very long ago really wanted to be buried, and why, and with whom – Not a month before his death he told me – for no possible reason. He got none of his wishes. "Ils ont des grands doleurs, les pauvres morts."

I know that another man, one of wealth and buried beneath a gigantic hecatomb of respectability, went to France a few years ago, to visit a mistress who had comforted him when he left England as a lonely boy. She had been over forty then, was now more than seventy, a tiny, frail, woman living in an immaculate Normandy cottage. But I liked that story, it seemed to me to have the faint scent of clove-pinks about it – Not always an episode, the mistress!

"Parmi le haut bois coudyrai mon amour."† Find out which pair of bright, restless eyes that motto lawfully belongs to, and you will know one who I really thought to be my friend. So of her, nothing. But it was pleasant enough to drink tea and smoke cigarettes, I very sumptuous in a purple gown that I bought because its slashed and puffed sleeves reminded me of Sir Walter Raleigh's doublet, and Sir Walter I liked. But it was under the sea, not over it, that I took his sleeves.

Oh, no more of this! If I could paint you one still grey day, the little seagulls with their extraordinarily neat colour design, the sliding of faintly opalescent water, it would be something! One "social" evening, the vague faces and well-fitting gown sliding by in a daze of sulphurous blue cabaret light, to the sound of music that was sounding brass and clanging cymbals! Or even the curious deep velvety purple of gladiolus in the tiny, uncomfortable flat that was my fortress for a year! Its shadows fell across my lithe crouching fawn, one of my few beautiful things. I cried in a weak stupid fashion here one evening, because I wanted those purple gladioli as one wants water or love.

Well: it was all over, quite suddenly, quite unexpectedly, and I stood on the pavement and thought of my insurance policies. I had been horribly ill for days, with influenza, one of the least friendly of complaints. Remedies, no time to spare, more remedies, a bad-tempered unimportant quarrel, what do they matter? There was more important business in hand.

---

* A plant with a deep pitcher-shaped pouch that contains fluid into which insects are attracted and drowned.

† 'I shall sow my love in the deep woods'.

Having had to wait until two boys had left the wharf, I spent quite five cold struggling minutes wishing them back. Then I had a little more courage, went deeply down once and again, and breathed in water as if it were life, not death – It really wasn't so hard. Semi-conscious, I felt my body turn slowly over in the water, go down again with its face turned away from the sky – That was peace: no green fields, but just a green colour and the sound of the waters, and suddenly they were dumb.

But then they were hurting my wrists, most horribly. After that a rushing moment in some sort of vehicle, with Policeman Day's sad dark troubled young face. (There really was a policeman.)

"Radiant heat" – and morphine – no, brandy first, morphine next. Oh the peace, the utter listless peace. Why can't one die when there is peace at last, fought for and won?

Poor M! Said he, with his usual conscientiousness,

"I ought to thrash you."

Ladies first, my dear Sir! She wouldn't let me see a lawyer, nor the kindly little doctor whom I have mentioned, nor yet would she say what was to happen. And M had told me that three notes I had written were in the hands of the police.

Well, two can play at the "Can't, won't, shan't, don't," game. And I really think I had the honours, even if she did have the four husky porters. I suggested that we should continue our discussion in the corridor, or in a private room where we would disturb nobody else. She should have thought of that for herself. She did think of the porters, though, and they won with superb ease, grinning like faintly embarrassed bears. (I suppose I should have been embarrassed, I was dressed in hospital night attire which exactly resembled a parachute: but honestly, it did seem that patience had ceased to be a virtue.)

Began the cell. I asked her if it were for maniacs or for V. D. patients – it really was smelly, the high small window was grated, and there were only men patients outside. Until they brought a screen, one of these men stared at me through the doorslit. I "didn't scream nor make a fuss," nor shed a solitary tear, as I remember it.

She-who-must-never-be-obeyed had snapped that the patients outside were not what I suggested. As a matter of fact, they were convicts, and my cell was used for delirium tremens cases in the female of the species.

But the nurses were nice – unquestioning, cheerful, even friendly. I clung to that. And the solemn young house surgeon who arrived didn't look a fool, or talk like one, or expect me to behave like one.

Father Time came, with flowers. Oh, he was deadly frightened![*] But he lied and said there wasn't going to be a court case. M[†] soon corrected that, poor harassed lad. "There is going to be a case, I can tell you," he said, "You seem to be going from bad to worse. I can't see anything for you but a cell in Mount Eden."[‡] Just exactly that, and I cried, yes, and tried to get him to promise that all would be well hereafter. The nurses weren't very pleased with him. For some unknown reason, (perhaps their last lady patient had thrown things or tried to climb up the wall,) they all championed me. They agreed that it was ridiculous to expect anyone who had influenza – or "a slight pneumonia", as the police sergeant civilly expressed it, – to deliberate on questions like suicide; we found very bad bruises on my ankles, and they were certain that I had fainted and fallen. "Not guilty of anything, nonsense to say so," was their kindly verdict. I don't forget it –

Police matron ... taxi ... now, she was nice too. I said something bitter about an old friend. She looked at me, wise and weather-beaten. "If you think things, don't say them just now, dear," she said.

Solicitor's room and M. The nurses had half convinced me that I was "not guilty," and I meant to say so.

I was told of what the police would then do and say ... the drug question arose, (I believe M's as melodramatic as I am at my worst!) and the notes he had given to the police. Columns and columns of sensation! Then that most pitiable, "Don't drag me down with you, Iris." Well, indeed I didn't. Neither cried nor argued, but merely asked his worship to let me go back to hospital for a day or two.

Though I was earnestly convinced otherwise at the time, I'm very glad there was no "dragging down." As I have said, there was a gallantry about that little paper, though JS, who never swears except in this instance, calls it "that cursed rag." He's wrong. Its age, its enfant terrible tactics, its very grime and poverty, and the fact that it does understand the use of the semi-colon, all make it – to me – lovable. There was much in the work that I loathed from my soul: the paper itself, (and that doesn't mean its weekly pink covers, but its whole history,) I rather love. Jeu d'esprit, that's what it is.

But I did pay rather dearly. Stop at the Police Station. Only a few civil questions.

---

* Hunt, 'Cage', 24, enlarges on the implication that he was frightened because he had been supplying drugs.
† McLean, her employer.
‡ New Zealand's oldest prison, located in Auckland city.

"Her height?" I've never felt free, not for one moment, since then. Perhaps I may, but freedom is of the spirit. When that funny little fat man got back in triumph from Elba, do you think <u>he</u> didn't know? Touch of authoritative hand, sound of authoritative voice! Authority is a myth and a legend, just like the Medusa: and God help all who come to find it true. Or, as General Seeley has better expressed it, "Fear, and be slain."[*]

Still I really needn't have stayed so long in the cell.[†] I liked Dr. C. (I think I like all middle-aged men who look as though they had been fathers for so long that they have got over their first natural rage and disgust.) A fearsome Hospital Board deputation wanted me moved straightway. They were very French, I thought, in their frank and open discussion of sanitary conveniences! I wept and begged Dr. C. <u>not</u> to move me. I didn't mind the rough burring voices outside, but the little shrill questioning ones – I still can't stand those. Poor Dr. C! He patted my hand and told me I should stay right there. "If Outsiders," said he, bitterly "would only leave the man who knows his job to do it!"

They say he is hard. I never found him anything but kindly to a degree that I like to remember.

I began to find funny reasons for wishing to stay in the cell.

Someone had sent me a huge sheaf of irises.[‡] It seemed to me high time that this place came into contact with the beauty of flowers. "You're looking at things from a most superficial viewpoint," I argued, in long, long imaginary conversations which never happened. And I saw those desperate hands clinging, many of them … and slowly trampled, one by one.

> The irises stand tall and blue
> and golden
> Like the great banners borne by
> warrior kings;
> But I am bowed like a reed, whose
> sheaf is holden

---

[*] British soldier and politician, Secretary of State prior to WWI.
[†] She was there from 2 to 20 June 1933 (*Iris,* 213–18), although she claims longer.
[‡] Irises sent by the Rawlinsons (*Young Knowledge*, 11). She also had visitors and received letters, one from Gloria Rawlinson (*Iris,* 216).

Deep beneath the waters of troublous
    things .. . . .

Hands that meet in the darkness. The desperate
    clasping of fingers.
"Hold but an instant, Beloved, the light is
    won."
But she who had sung like a child in the
    dappled Thessalian meadows
Answers no word. And the limp hands loosen,
    are gone.*

Now for the first time I felt a little less than desperate, when your colleague came. Being told his name, "Ah, you're the man I have to be careful with, aren't you?" asked I. And he laughed, taken aback. But oh, Cassandra,[†] it _is_ a damnably bad habit, and will it ever gain you profit or popularity? Never, never.

Now for a long time I thought rather unjustly concerning your colleague: a sequence of trivialities, mainly supplied by outsiders, built up a completely wrong picture. But that it _is_ wrong, I know from a tiny thing: cold watchfulness doesn't remember or take pride in the beauty of a pink-flowering tree in an old wild shrubbery. People _are_ inconsistent, but Peter Bell is Peter Bell for ever. I was the fool, and there's a really funny side to that little climax of a tale of woe.

Drowning men aren't half so unjust to straws as are drowning women! Just because I felt safe, suddenly, because of a cheery laugh and a few words as cheery, I created in nobody's image an angel of light and beauty: and there it stood in my cell, and invited me to this place which I call "Columben," for a reason that will keep. Oh dear! It's painful to be a Bourbon[‡] without the lineage – I mean, forever learning nothing, forgetting nothing. I didn't play fair from the start. I didn't tell about those trampled clinging fingers, nor about the scraps of verse, far more morbid than any I've shown you, that I'd already begun to write and to hide. Nor how one night, when the lights fused and left me in my locked, barred cell, I had clung half-fainting, crying to the doorslit, and with steady voice and steady hand, one of those convicted men outside

---

* One of 'Three Poems', _Young Knowledge_, 11.
† Cassandra, daughter of the Trojan King Priam, whose prophesies are true but not believed.
‡ A branch of the royal families of France and Spain.

had tried to soothe me. (An hour or more, before the lights went on again: it's a small annexe to a big ward, and the nurse never came during that time.) Most vital of all, I never told about my secret child. About Gerard, yes, as very occasionally, in bravado or when in a corner, I told some other, but not about Robin. In fact, I told nothing and came here to a pleasant, quiet room, a smiling, re-assured, angel-guarded liar. I forgot to tell you: I still thought in a vague way that death was close, they had x-rayed my chest twice and had seemed interested in it – I mean, as a medical specimen. Their very vagueness in speaking to one another had given me this comfort.

Oh dear! The locked cupboards, and that which I wouldn't and couldn't put into words. You may have guessed worse of me, or better. "Promiscuity is death." But it was so very pleasant to lie here, to type my first plays (all bad, but only the last of four a chaotic stumbling mass of suicide, begun in typescript, continued in a slithering illegible handwriting not my own.) The room grew dark and strange, but it was still pleasant – yes! I was quite safe, without reasoning why.

I am not, thank God, accustomed to expect the very few angels or archangels, either sex, whom I have encountered, suddenly to "fall the thousand parasangs"* to a weakly sentiment. No word or laugh, and this room, with its sliding floor, glowed with that ridiculous assured safety.

Only, like Cassandra, but incredibly and, at the moment, most inconveniently more so, you <u>could</u> read the cipher of heart and mind –

More clumsily than any silent lips have ever told their secret, the secret which was essential me, I did blurt out some parody of the truth at last. I who can remember so clearly, remember not at all what I said. Just, probably that Gerard was a second child, there's been another – But I <u>do</u> remember the soft monosyllable, "oh!" the tone like the drawing away of a steady hand. And the question of my own mind came to me to dwell there, "Am I mad, or merely unclean?"

I think somewhere among my belongings, there's a note scrawled, in that odd hand which wasn't mine, to Mac,† of all people. Just "Get me out of this," no more. It was at your Head Office for a while, and came back when my other possessions were returned. It was all I wanted – to get away anywhere at all, to hide –

We all (or nearly all,) exaggerate our crimes to such splendid proportions. Read

---

* An idiom meaning 'to give-up', as a parasang is a measure of distance, used of angels falling back from the word of God or a prophet.

† John Gordon McLean, editor at *New Zealand Observer*. Not to be confused with Henry McDonald Vincent, the editor at the Christchurch *Sun*.

Walt Whitman's poem in praise of animals: "They do not lie awake at nights, and weep because of their sins!"* My real crime, I know now, was against Robin. I should have been silent or been lucid, even until death or through the byways of madness. At the time, a word my Father used once, and once my mother, was in my ears. Kindliness still, great kindliness, but there are some things can't be allayed by that. I'd lost any coherence of thought – so easy to walk out, but the sparrow still beats the window pane when it flies indoors by accident. There was none to "Get me out of this." So I suppose, though I cannot remember, that a ghost of that Palmerston North doctor, his morphine and his later anxiety to be rid of me, slid into my mind. Madness indeed, not to realise that this was no little private hospital, but – except here in "Columben" – the very twin of the place he'd have sent me to.†

I remember writing to Father Time,‡ and of that letter only that I asked for morphine. Not for sleep, not for pleasure, not for madness: except the madness of "Get me out of here." I swear that is the absolute truth –

Then, in my sick mind, I was safe again and quite happy –

Was it one day or two, or longer? All that time I had no fear, no worry. I'd settled the question, brilliantly, I was to get morphine and take it, you were to be frightened and angry and send me away. The wilderness is wide enough. I wonder if you see, or if you believe me? It seems so urgent to write this.

---

* Walt Whitman, *Song of Myself*, Section 32, 1–10. Also quoted in *A Home*, 29.
† Avondale Hospital, the twin of Porirua.
‡ This letter and his reply survive in Hyde's hospital file (*Iris,* 221).

174

II

1934–1935 Journal Fragments

MSX-8216 Alexander Turnbull Library. Acquired by the Library in 2009. Handwriting at the front and towards the back of a book entitled 'Whitcombes New Zealand ROUGH DIARY 1934' ('Exercise Book 12' in a sticker on the cover in Gloria Rawlinson's sequence: Derek Challis uses this name, Michele Leggott uses 'Rough Diary').

DESCRIPTION: The Rough Diary is a thick quarto diary with a grey board cover with an illustration map of New Zealand in red. It includes advertisements and calendars for 1934 and 1935, pages of postal regulations, stamp duties, etc., and sections on taxes, labour legislation, local government and social items, as well as lists of banks and bank holidays.

PROVENANCE: The Rough Diary was probably sent with papers to Wellington or left at the Lodge when Hyde departed from New Zealand in 1938, and then sent to Edge and the Rawlinsons in 1945 after the deaths of Hyde's parents.

The entries are mostly but not entirely on the recto pages, with occasional unrelated notes on the verso pages. The journal entries are not made on the printed dates: the first date is 'September 24th' (1934), and the only other date is 'January 11th 1935'. Also included is the draft beginning of a story, 'My Countrymen'. It is possible that Hyde bought the Diary cheap in the middle of the year and started writing at the very beginning of the book. It is also possible that the 11 January entry, written at the back of the book, immediately precedes the first entry in the '1935 Journal' (pp. 182–3, 190). The sequence is interrupted by manuscripts of poems, two lines of another story and, in two places, torn-out pages.

As indicated in the following text, the entries include a poem written in pencil, which is illegible, and after that a half page of automatic writing. The Rough Diary was also used as a workbook for handwritten notes and drafts of twenty-five poems written between 1934 and 1935.*

---

* *Young Knowledge*, xvi.

No dates. I usually know when it's Friday, because then is served for dinner something which in its natural state would have been called fish. Poor fish!

I've discovered, after reading through an anthology of the verse of living writers, what abstraction in poetry should and must be, if it's ever to be at all. It's the distillation of one's most inward and secret self. This ~~essence~~ fluid, once released, is the correct colour-basis of poetic landscape, sky-scape, dream-scape. Most of the moderns, in a revulsion of feeling from the late Victorian verse which was simply music & anatomy, don't know this, and write then abstractions – or attempted abstractions – <u>outwardly</u>. Elizabeth Barrett Browning wrote with a stethoscope: these moderns with a microscope – as Walter De La Mare, Barrie* – a telescope, or a gyroscope. The results are startling but not convincing. I wonder if Epstein's "Rima"† is the distillation of inward and secret Epstein, applied to the green house of leaves, a fairy wood, and a fairy love? If so, what a splendidly savage thing it must be!

They – the moderns concentrate too much on technique. "Let us be abstract, let us renounce eyes and lips for the greater picturesquerie of a more delicate thing, delicately touched." Ah, the nice gourmets, one needs only the flamingo's feather, used in the ancient Roman style, to make the feasts complete. But Bach and Shelley went to Heaven for <u>their</u> abstractions – and the Kingdom of heaven is within.

I myself write botched attempts at poetry still from a starved strange body. I have not distilled my abstract, maybe never shall. But I'll not be fool enough to <u>renounce</u> my body, as they do, to shove it aside and say "out of the way, you, and let me contemplate that cow!" Why, how <u>can</u> I contemplate a cow, to its satisfaction or to mine or the world's, without the use of the senses which are rooted in my body? I believe what applies to poetry applies to every art. For me, I need to practise poetic five-finger exercises, hours a day, until the thin fingers of my soul ache and would

---

* Hyde sets herself with the heart register of Elisabeth Barrett Browning and apart from rather a broad group of 'moderns' in a complex argument that involves a critique of the problems of 'objectivity' and the curse of being bound by accident to the 'surrounding impressions' that poetic vision can release. For more of her thoughts on poetics, see the opening of the '1934 Autobiography', p. 66. .

† Jacob Epstein (1880–1929), US-born British pioneer of modern sculpture. His nude relief work Rima (1923–5) is situated in Hyde Park near the Serpentine, and like other examples of his work challenged cnotemporary expectations about art and public art. http://en.wikipedia.org/wiki/Jacob_Epstein Retrieved 8 July 2011.

do murder; but they, how can they practise the emotion which they have thrown on the dust heap? Poor swine – no abstraction, only an external, each one of them – go root for your pearl. Rooting may cause you pain or weariness, either an emotion. There's your pearl, mellow in gleaming, if you only know it when you see it. Your clever subtle fingers will understand then how it should be set. But I've a suspicion that your mechanics, your technicalities, will thrust it aside. (Ah, America, you have mechanised even poetry.) "That my pearl! Why it's only a tear! What use have I for tears? Let me go stare at that silvery sewer, instead!" My friend, even sewers demand a little give-and-take, something more of disgust and loneliness than you have in your wan heart! You'll get nothing there, only one more five-finger exercise. But if I ever write, I shall write from every nerve and tissue of this body: ~~did~~ and from all its long experiences, all these distilled and cooled and an essence.

I've a feeling the Chinese understood and practised all this, centuries ago. But this understanding was never put into words, and it's time somebody did that, if only whilst talking to herself in solitude. That loosed bird-song, who shall ever cage it again? Not any of you, who know so little of the art of mastering freedom. Perhaps some of the moderns think that their little outwardly-seen, and outwardly-drawn poems are Chinese.* No. Like the first porcelain to be manufactured in England, after Cathay's little dim flower-faces had proved so successful an adjunct to the gatherings of the West, they are merely, God help them, a quaint imitation, collector's pieces. But what wisdom, what passion, what shrewd observance and sense of humour, lay behind the virginal flower-faces – all these distilled, distilled, again distilled, trebly fragrant and potent for that.

I believe our own Elizabethans come closest to what I want. "Cover her face. Mine eyes dazzle. She died young." Who could write that today – or throw into space just one of the thousand thousand splintered stars in Shakespeare? Not one of them but burned first in his own heart. What a cold and blackened heart it must have grown at last to be! But for the human prey of wisdom and beauty to be tended in his dying by the angel of a phrase he himself created, long ago; that must be a rare ministration.

No other word: but to discover suddenly what has not been thought before, is

---

* On her critique of 'outwardly-drawn' imitations of Chinese poetry, a critique that Diana Bridge thinks may be particularly directed at Ezra Pound, see Bridge 'China, Imagined and Actual, in Robin Hyde's *The Godwits Fly*, Two Journal Entries and the "China" Poems', *Lighted Windows*, 96–7.

good indeed: as it was to discover Neptune flaming in the wastes. Of course there's no such thing as the <u>creation</u> of new truth. It burns there for ever, perceived or unperceived. But to realise it is something.

And for my part, it gives me an escape from this ghostly modern-verse violin shop, where all the fiddles would a-playing go, and never a hand to touch them nor a heart to be poured into them.

There was a verse came to me yesterday – It seems rather a weakling thing, but there's music in it, so I'll set it down.

The Kinsman

Somewhere there lived one noble, long ago,
Whose quiet slender hands acquainted were
With all the ancient things I hold most dear:
Shiver of cool arpeggios, in a dusk
That bore the satin scents of money – musk:
Swift answer of the sword: but best, the slow
Wakening of passion, 'neath that steady hand,
Of the true love his heart could understand.
(Haply the gods of beauty wove their mesh
Of flames and flowers and starlight o'er her flesh.)

Oh ghostly hands, seek for your sword again!
When did a woman plead with thee in vain?
How shall you rest, knowing <u>her</u> kin must cry
"Come to me now, or Love and Honour die?"

Robin Hyde.

Gloria my dear,
I'm going to write out bits and scraps of poems for you from now on – in the hope that you may one day like them a little and know that Robin hasn't forgotten you – Sweet day to you, child –

Iris.

178

The Farewell

Cold lips, cold heart, that once had been the donor
of all life's flowers, for her slim feet spread –
No praise of yours shall rise to do her honour.
Your singing love lies quieter than the dead.

For she was strange, forever, a goddess only
To dreamers, boys and fools that stray forlorn:
And you are man! (Say is your faring lovely,
Now you no more are fettered by her thorn?)

Nor you nor any man could dull the metal
Of her quick pride, the spear of Britomart.
But time shall wreak your will. Petal by petal
The rose of youth must flutter from her heart.

And she will wither – but what dies in you
This day by your own hand, oh you who spare not?
And an unpitying stern dusk burns blue, –
A chalice for the life of loves that care not.*

[Following this poem, the Rough Diary is used for poems – 'The Farewell', 'Blondel', 'The Dying Priest', 'Gates of Sleep', 'The Child', 'Poppies', 'Mountain Grass', 'Wilma Thule', 'Song', 'When the M were Ended', 'Singing', 'The Wanderer', 'Taking Counsel Like the Grasses', 'Lo One held Secret', 'Chrysanthemum' (see *Young Knowledge*) – then many pages are torn out and there are thirteen pages of notes for *Journalese,* followed by more missing pages, notes for *Check to Your King*, two lines of a short story 'Mrs Cowie's Children', some other notes on verso and untitled poems followed by the poem 'Prayer of a Poet' published in *Persephone* as 'Prayer of a Woman']

---

* Poem not found elsewhere.

September 24th –

What's the use of saying "I will write, I will write," when I just can't? This dead tiredness of mind has been on me for weeks. I go to sleep now easily, exhausted. I can pick up facts and memories but there's nothing creative in me. My body seems asleep too – For which relief no thanks at all, I don't care now for any peace, it's only the ability to scribble matters – I have chosen –

I've looked through this scrapbook: bits of it artificial. The work of a poseur[?], the rest mostly futile. A lot of claptrap about insanity and illegitimacy, of course what I really want is to turn out the glorified exception to all the little rules about both: which is funny and a bit like Adolf Hitler, that man knows he's a fool and he knows other people know it too, but his eyes say "Please be nice to me." Poor brute –

Still I think there's something constant behind all the unfinished things. Like all the poor little "love affairs" of the sex-slaved women here – They seem to be paltry and changeable but behind them is the great and constant fact of changeless love, unsatisfied. Get a leader who is not terrified of that force and Christ will come again. That is the psychologist's real function – to find the constant face behind the mutabilities. Only none of 'em dare.

> "Street of all Souls, have in thy
>   moonless keeping
> These weary souls – "*

[followed by half page of automatic writing]

---

*   Lines from a classical song.

Walk on the high hills and down the druid groves of the dark
Oh wind that knew my youth,
Walk with the mist in thy cloudy hair and a bird lulled at thy breast,
And a star's crystal white as the sudden doorway of Truth –
Touch the lit and lifted gold of the gorse-petals, passing by
On the heights where my feet shall come not again;
There shall be silence and sunrise yellow as gorse across the seas …
Walk with thy face cold, with thy feet bare to the summer rain –

Say to the guests in that hall of the country of God,
"Ye are well met,
For the bread of beauty is broken, the sky-deep chalice brims
And the earth's table here for His welcoming set.
Yet here is one who thirsts in a far place, and turns back
To the memory of her fellows, to the earth's [face?] kindly things –
And the beating of grey birds southward brings a thought out of the skies,
Laggard among the red [?] clouds and the lifting wings –

She who will walk here no more greets you thus wise
Friends at your feasting, a boon,
(For I was a child of the tall hills, and walked with the white tossed wind
And watched the shuttle of grasses fly the spun lint of the moon.)
Be not changed with the years, and grow not old and estranged,
But keep ever your state? Of the bright gorse and the dusk a blue veil:
For a child may come again greeting[?], and young eyes grow wet,
And young lips find comfort pressed to your beauty's grail.*

[Pages torn out between 202 and 217 – the journal continues at the back of the book]

---

* 'Wellington Hills', *Young Knowledge,* 127.

Friday January 11ᵗʰ 1935. The Grey Lodge, Gladstone Road,*
Mount Albert, Auckland. New Zealand.

I have formed only one New Year's resolution, which had nothing to do with the keeping of diaries – It was that each day I should speak to a stranger – not necessarily more than a word, but just something to redeem me a little from this isolation – and perhaps some others too. Today I didn't have to do the speaking – As I went up Gladstone Road to the tram, an old man, grimy, unshaven, in a ragged shirt, stopped and stared at me – He broke into a queer chuckle of laughter – "Eh," he cried pointing at my feet, "She's got blue shoes on! Blue shoes!"

"Yes, they are blue." I answered politely and went on. I don't know how or why blue shoes were the passport to his cloud cuckoo land – for no doubt he came from the lunatic asylum down the road – but I liked him. And in town another ancient suddenly stopped and over his beard gave me the most amazing toothless, blue-eyed, button-nosed smile – Little man with a nose like a button, I wonder [where] in what hidey hole you are tucked up tonight and whether I reminded you of some delusion of the lights? No. I don't aim to be Mrs Methuselah. But just any spontaneous, friendly contact with humanity – especially if it is brief and then finished, I can't now endure many prolonged acquaintanceships – seems to me now wholly delightful – and always out of an unending weariness, that other quest which has become a dream –

In town Rosalie Rawlinson saw me unhappy over my skimpy little blue frock (I look attenuated since my illness) with that almost mad generosity of hers she instantly dragged me into Milne's sale and stood me like a clothes horse, trying on 17/6' frocks and 6/11' hats – I came out cool, near-youthful despite 29 wicked years in cream silk and Panama hat – nice. This craving after pretty clothes which now afflicts me isn't vanity, but lack of vanity and a horrible self-consciousness mixed up – I want something to counteract a certain beaten-dog look. Like dogs but not in the human race –

I showed "Haste Thee, Nymph" to Rosalie who is as yet the only one who has seen the series of fantasies which I am trying to make pompous by calling 'em psychological reconstructions – Theory: if one can reconstruct a dinosaur (or wasn't it a dinosaur?) from a tooth, a moa from a wish-bone, why not a human being or the divine idea evolved by a human being from the most fragmentary relic of speech or

---

* Now Carrington Rd.

thought [?]? If the stories are bad they are proving a very strong temptation. I seem to be *guided* to obscure lights on the folk I want to write about – as happened when a few [*pages torn out*] months ago I was writing "Check to Your King" the Baron de Thierry's tale – Then coincidence after coincidence dragged me along – access to manuscripts whose existence nobody seemed to guess at* – and the continual bearing out of those guesses with which I was forced to fill in the gaps – For instance, knowing the Baron musical I was forced to provide him with an instrument, and so placed a harp in the old gentleman's hands – What do I find, belatedly, but account of a concert with the harp at Pointe-a -Pino and incidentally claimed a miserable 400 francs at the same?

With the stories, I am writing only of people or myths who for one reason or another have dwelt long in my mind and so made a place there – And I am nearly fool enough to believe there's a queerness in the ease with which these dead come alive for me –

But oh, when one is so cut off from the living!

It is necessary if I am to use this as a record, to mention the past a little – It has brought me to odd straits –

Some eighteen months ago after an unutterably wretched three years – and these were only more pointedly so than the years before, since at eighteen I was very suddenly

[writing breaks off]

[holograph poem, in pencil and indecipherable, followed by 66 blank pages]

---

* Baron de Thierry was an early settler to the Hokianga region, north of Auckland. The manuscripts Hyde refers to may have been de Thierry's 'Narrative of an attempt to form a settlement in New Zealand', which is in the Grey Collection at the Auckland Central City Library (*Iris,* 255).

'My Countrymen'

"I wish I could see my countrymen just once – mythical creatures that they are! To look into eyes like my own – to feel the beating of a heart very much a kin to mine – I think I have deserved that if only because I have survived."

(Said the girl who would not die, but who lay on a wave crest of six white pillows in a lamplit room traversed by the trellised flowers on the wallpaper.)

"Well, why not?" Said the unicorn, suddenly appearing around the curved and carven darkness of high dressing-table executed in black oak. It was framed in the gigantic niche of seven window-frames, which was deeply colour-washed by a blue dusk.* His expression was patient yet inquiring, and he seemed just one shade whiter than anything else could be – than blossoms on the pear or foam sprinkling on the hollow curve of a beach, than starlight like dust on the grey moth wings of a cloud –

"I know" said the girl, when the unicorn became stationary at the end of her bed, "People invented you because they needed you so badly. It can't have been that there were not sufficient animals, nor that they weren't grotesque or fierce or beautiful enough – look at hippos and tigers now –"

"People could quite see hippos and Tigers, that's the trouble," nodded the unicorn. "You've only to think of a mud-crater with a pink smile on its face and you've got the whole idea of the hippo. Tigers are worse. Imagine a blood orange against the breast of an Ethiopian and you know all a tiger can tell you, provided you can also figure to yourself a thunderbolt in action. They're so <u>describable</u>."

"Yes, yes," whispered the girl "That's just it – describable, I get tired of describable things – and people. Dear God, I am so tired of people."

"So were the ancients," stated the unicorn "That's where we started my friend the phoenix, the gryphons with his scaled golden wings, the noc[?] with the diamond in his beak and the shadow of his wings vast as a church tower, myself, and when it comes to people the Ch[inese?] of Tartary's little amber daughter. You know, littler than <u>little</u> she was, and her voice like the sway of paper bells against a wind. People couldn't quite imagine how little and sweet she was, but it was good to turn to her when everything else seemed gross[?] – Saw within us – the monsters – the unimagined quest flashing deeper and deeper into the forest – Good Lord, how sick[such?]

---

* This description fits with the layout of Hyde's room at the Lodge.

[followed by chapter headings for *Check to Your King,* and drafts of the introduction and chapter one of *Check to Your King*]

~~Rosalie~~

So therefore, being not on confidential terms
With the old leisurely Hereford in the meadow,
Nor [*crossings out*] an intimate of the bee, that might have
        grumbled all
Between honey-sippings, save that the lack of shadow

Where the boy lay depressed him, and poppy flaunted
Petals dared him declare himself their lover –
The boy, then, was left alone sighing : as best he
        might
The systems of birth and dying to discover.

This is best done with eyes closed. Through the
        shut eyelids
Pour the two lights, one from the inner being,
And through pine-boughs and lashes, the arc of that
        startling sun,
Scarlet and white and topaz – demanding seeing

To be disbelieved … the whine [?] of the light rays pattern
Danced in the air, seeming to thrill the slow flowers
Into symphony. A bird mimed in tune. A cloud moved.
Earth turned beneath him; He, guessing now that
        these powers

Of dance and song were curtailed through some reserve
Between man and nature, or that a privacy
Lies in the heart of beauty, pictured her petals
        unfurl
Into full movement: widening stealthily

Like great rose wings, in a light nor day
        nor dusk.
"All kings", he felt "thus some how, when alone
And not shocked by the failures of talk, expand best
        without doubt

A movement sleeps in the heart of his stone,
And warmed in the sun like a lizard, I too might
        clatter
Under the saxifrage, on absurd little paws,
But that I scare it ... men though well clad
In knights and horses, are not exempt from such laws.

[followed by 36 blank pages, then outline of family tree.]

III

1935 Journal

MSX-8216, Alexander Turnbull Library, acquired 2009. The manuscript is entitled 'Exercise Book 13' in Gloria Rawlinson's sequence but is also called 'Journal 1935' on a sticker fixed to the front board, probably by Rawlinson.

DESCRIPTION: The text is handwritten in black ink in a foolscap exercise book bound in green fabric-covered boards. Its closely written pages have been numbered on recto pages in pencil in another hand. The exercise book ceases to be used strictly as a journal after an entry on 13 June that finishes with the lines, 'I am for peace against the gates of hell.' The writing following this (dated 29 July) consists of three pages and a verso, which are mostly quotations and a sequence and a list of chapters from Hyde's hitherto unpublished novel 'The Unbelievers', that she was then beginning to draft alongside *The Godwits Fly*. However, the journal sequence from 13 June is concluded (or continued and broken off) in an entry on 28 July (that must have been separated by several blank pages from the 13 June entry before she wrote in those blank pages on the 29th) and finishes with a dedication to her doctor. All of these pages are reproduced here in their original sequence. The final pages of the exercise book (pages 89–98 in the original numbering) are used as a rough draft book for poems, for lists and word counts of stories, and lists of chapters. These poems and lists are not reproduced here but the poems 'Tulips', 'The Young', 'The god of Fear (first line – untitled) and 'For the Lark' can be read in *Young Knowledge*. One poem draws on a sequence of events from her childhood, which becomes a prose account in a chapter of *The Godwits Fly*.

PROVENANCE: The manuscript is not listed amongst the papers Hyde took with her in 1938 and sent from China on to London.[*] Probably it was left in Wellington before it came into the possession of the Rawlinsons. A typescript copy was subsequently made by Gloria Rawlinson, a copy of which was deposited in the Auckland Central City Library in 1990 (NZ MS 0837) with a subtitle she had added: 'An Autobiographical Work'.

---

[*] See Challis, 'The Fate of the Iris Wilkinson Manuscripts'.

Like the '1934 Autobiography' and the '1934–1935 Journal Fragments', this '1935 Journal' was written at the Lodge at the Auckland Mental Hospital at Avondale. But Hyde had been busy while there. By mid-January 1935, when the journal begins, and with the encouragement of her doctors, particularly Dr Tothill, she had resumed her professional career. She had written and published (with a New Zealand publisher) a book on her experiences in journalism (*Journalese,* 1934), sent a book of poems ('Thine accursed') to Macmillan's Contemporay Poets Series (published later in 1935 as *The Conquerors*), and was working on the manuscript of the biographical novel 'Bronze Outlaw', published as *Passport to Hell* by Hurst & Blackett, London, in 1936. She was also beginning the first draft of her autobiographical novel *The Godwits Fly* and of 'The Unbelievers'. From December 1934, she was producing freelance articles, fashion pages and book reviews for the Auckland weekly newspaper the *New Zealand Observer,* where she worked full-time from 1932 until her collapse.[*] During 1935, she began to get commissions from the *New Zealand Railways Magazine.*

As discussed in the 'Introduction', this '1935 Journal' is a very different document from the '1934 Autobiography', which was written quickly and urgently as a prescribed diagnostic and therapeutic task when she was very unwell, and was her first long prose composition (although she was also at that time writing and publishing poems). In contrast, Hyde uses the '1935 Journal' to record day-to-day experiences at the Lodge, her ideas on writing, comments on Auckland and Aucklanders, and information about its artistic milieu. She also discusses the treatment of mental breakdown, and engages with the ideas of Sigmund Freud and Carl Gustav Jung. We know that another psychiatrist working with borderline patients at Avondale, Dr Kathleen Todd, gave a copy of a psychological text to one of her patients to read during his treatment;[†] we don't know if Hyde was also given such a book, but we do know that she felt a common task with her own Dr Gilbert Tothill, and that she read works of Freud and Jung's *Collected Papers in Analytical Psychology* (1916). From her letters, we know that with Tothill's encouragement she was considering publishing both her '1934 Autobiography' and her untitled essay (subsequently titled 'Essay on Mental Health', p. 295) in order to draw public attention to psychotherapy and the familial patterns and social attitudes (including child-rearing and discipline)

---

[*] *Iris*, 258.
[†] Hunt, 'Cage', 168–9.

that could precipitate or prolong mental breakdown.[*]

For this publication, as part of the Marsden funded project that produced *The Book of Iris* and *Young Knowledge*, the typesecript made by Gloria Rawlinson was retyped by Lisa Docherty and checked against the original handwritten manuscript in the Alexander Turnbull Library by research assistant Eleanor Fearn. Readers will notice that quite often Hyde uses dashes to intensify her meaning or to link statements. In her orginal handwritten manuscript there are many sweeps of the pen forming dashes that often come between sentences, after full-stops and before capitals, almost as if they are elongated full stops. In two previous typescripts (Gloria Rawlinson's and Lisa Docherty's), these have been recorded as full typed dashes. Here, however, I have considerd it more faithful to register some of these dashes as full stops in places where they are not clearly intended to convey a specific link between ideas, or a mood.

---

[*] Hunt, 'Cage', 177; Sandbrook, 'Robin', 10.

IRIS WILKINSON

JOURNAL 1935

[An Autobiographical Work]*

A ladybird as blue as a chip of lapis lazuli arising out of the undergrowth of yellow grasses has just stalked contemptuously over this white page as if to show me how little she thinks of it. Likewise the branch of rhododendron with its grouped leaves bends over and sets the delicate shadows moving on the whiteness, together with little clear mirror-spaces of sunshine. And an ant arrives and stops faintly worried with quivering antennae as though black markings on a piece of paper almost conveyed something curious and doubtful to her. To complete the world, there is an old magnolia, its thick creamy blossoms dropping down a perfume as heavy as a sort of scent-manna: a broken arch of sky, perilously blue, nine pine trees, which even now are black and which in the dusk can become formidable. To the right a little patch of sea like a piece of wrinkled silk is drawn back from a yellow tidemarsh and I can see a stranded boat sticking its importunate mast up, a perch for the seagulls, who often make the three miles from Point Chevalier to this inland place a part of their day's work.

That's all – I sat down wondering what to write, the ant and the ladybird and the magnolia presented themselves. This morning on the other hand, when wondering the same thing I looked out of the bathroom window the answer was different. There were five white doves motionless like snowy odalisques, and near them drooping and in a hopeless minority one of the pigeons I like, the grey, ruby-eyed, rainbow-breasted creatures. Poor dear, she had no idea she was to be left stranded with the odalisques. But the grey pigeons are more daring. The white stay at home and confidently expect they will be fed out of the bread-box – The grey ones circle and explore, so they picked up poisoned wheat, and returned home to die sadly, one after another falling Plump! from the grey steep gabled roof. I saw the eighth to perish, there on the lawn with a little ruby of blood where its head had struck the ground – and is anything more difficult to connect up than life and death? A second's

* Gloria Rawlinson added this subtitle to the original manuscript.

difference, and the feathers still bright. Grey pigeons used to haunt the balconies of the hospital at Stanmore in Sydney* and say plaintively with infinite reproach "The jacker-oo, too-oo," as though whatever the jackeroo did were the last straw and had broken their faith in human nature for ever. (It was a November, the jacarandas were a sea of blue blossoms, blue as a twilight, and from that big room Sydney was a million points of diamond-clear lights).† Here the grey pigeons nest in winter in my chimney, which being technically at least not their own property appeals to them more than their own dove-cot. But there she sits, the one left, and surveys the white odalisques with disgust and wonders if it were better to live on here in dignity and loneliness or to hunt through a thousand back-yards until she finds a mate.

A year and a day ago when the tulip trees bore flowers of wine-coloured silk in this shrubbery a very sick young woman sat making rhymes for the doves.‡

Today I heard the doves cry, in a cloud
Of dreaming voices … far away, yet loud
Enough for such as I to hazard guess
What glinting thoughts stirred in their loneliness –
One praised her brood: and one, the joy it brings
When sunlight startles rainbows on her wings –
One sang her mate, and one the yellow grain
Some kind white hand had strewed for her again
And not a wiser thought from flower or bird
Than the impassioned things any heart has heard
From men – For each was lessoned in the school
Where nature trains her fool to rest a fool –

---

* The hospital where Robin was born: 'I'd been saving up for it. Old and cool and huge-roomed, with the jacaranda trees making a purple mist of blossom …'. Chapter 13, '1934 Autobiography', p. 116.

† Here Hyde gives November rather than earlier as the month for being in the hospital at Stanmore. While she may perhaps have stayed on after the birth, it seems unlikely considering the documented visit to the Blue Mountains. See '1934 Autobiography', p. 116 n†.

‡ Hyde is recalling the time shortly before she began the therapeutic work of writing the '1934 Autobiography' and before her mental and physical health improved. The day she is recalling 'a year and a day ago' is probably 10 January 1934, during her first summer at the Lodge: we can extrapolate this because the '[u]ndated first entry appears to follow on from diary-like entry dated 11 January 1935 in Exercise Book 12' (Hunt, 'Cage', 311).

Yet sweet their dreaming was – And wise, ah, wise
The stately candles lit in evening skies*

It all seemed then, a mindless sort of dream, with only some creatures of a major importance, the moon and the wind, possessing a lonely and sad wisdom – a wisdom, or rather an understanding sweeping like a sword through the nights and days of our lives.† Then, nothing any person could have said remained significant. But this was significant, the deep blue twilight welling up, an unearthly sea of blue, in the windows of my room. The fields turned that deep colour and were sad and very far-stretching. – The windows looked taller than they were. I have tried to see that blue colour again, but I can't, except just on the borderline of a dream. It doesn't belong to the spectrum. It is wrapped round the visible world, deep and tender, the colour of forgetting.

It was a matter of infinite effort then, with whatever help, to get up and down from my room, or to move at all, to do anything but sit in a chair looking out from the window – for nothing, nothing real. The time had gone past when any real person would have counted. I hadn't any body, only heaviness. No hunger, nor desire to sleep – it isn't Paradise, the loss of the appetites, as so many cowards suggest. Just now, when I am more alive, so many small-sized creatures are delightful. Over there on a pile of brown fallen leaves (which are a great nuisance and litter my garden badly), is a thrush with his head on one side and the beadiest self-confident-est eye – He'd never have fitted into that sad scheme of things a year ago, yet I do assure you he's a jolly soul.
[4 spaces]

11.p.m.

This is the indoors of Cloud-Cuckoo-Land. I thought of that name for myself before Naomi Mitchison bagged it for a book, so she must just be content to share it.‡

---

* 'Today I heard the doves cry', 'The Wise', *Evening Post,* 22 December 1936, 15; *Houses,* 64–5. Hyde's comment suggests the poem was written a 'year and a day ago'.
† Compare below: 'For a little more than a year, I never saw the moon'.
‡ *Cloud Cuckoo Land* (1925) is a novel by left-wing British writer Naomi Mitchison. Hyde also called one of her own stories 'Cuckoo'.

I am stationary between a full dose of paraldehyde[*] and a Cup of Cocoa, which is even now advancing up the stairs supported by a pink-frocked nurse. The gentleman (or lady) who said that Cocoa is a vulgar beast was unacquainted with the lower nature of milk – "Not sleeping? I'll bring you a nice glass of milk, dear." Ugh! Elizabeth Barrett's prostration at the sight of porter[†] was nothing compared with the way in which my soul and innards stage a little revolution at the sight of it, hot and with a loathsome skin a-top. Cocoa by comparison is brown-skinned, sober, discreet, almost decent – Better than paraldehyde which tastes like decomposed methylated spirits, if methylated spirits can decompose.

Dr. Macky[‡] informed me that he had at Porirua Asylum a young lady patient who would do anything for paraldehyde.

Me (faintly moral) "Anything, Doctor?"

He (resolutely) "Anything." He adds that the medical history was she had Russian blood in her veins and the stuff reminded her of vodka.

However, apart from stomach afflictions, this place is queer at nights.

A two-storeyed building surmounted by an unfrequented attic:[§] downstairs, the

---

[*] Paraldehyde was given for sleeping and sedation and was a staple of institutions at that time. It is a colourless, sticky liquid (also used for a varnish) and apparently had a strong smell that permeated the wards. Paraldehyde is similar in action to alcohol, but was considerably cheaper in the 1930s, leading to a wave of addictions with disagreeable side-effects; a *Lancet* report in 1934 stated that: 'if a nightly dose of two drachms of paraldehyde is continued for several weeks the patient loses appetite and develops gastrointestinal irritation and flatulence; he becomes irritable, morose, and suspicious, and may be mentally confused and agitated, with muscular weakness and tremor of the hands. Tolerance is soon established and an increased dose is demanded. […] If the use of the drug is prolonged, hallucinations and delusions develop and the final picture is one of mental and physical deterioration.' 'The Paraldehyde Habit', *Lancet*, 233 1934), 408–9; Hunt, 'Cage', 230.

[†] Dark sweet ale brewed from black malt.

[‡] Dr John Macky, another doctor at the Lodge. Alison Hunt makes several references to Dr Macky's patient notes as being short and consisting of mainly physical observations and formulaic content (as against those of Tothill and Todd) and to his cases being taken over by Dr Tothill ('Cage', 166–7,187). In January 1937, when Dr Tothill transferred to be Medical Superintendent at Tokanui Hospital, Dr John Macky took charge. Hyde then spent most of February up North and discharged herself from the Lodge in early March. She wrote of that time that 'all the glow had gone out of the attic', and that there was a 'sudden clash of dream against a person incompetent to dream', *A Home,* 15.

[§] She is describing the Lodge. The attic became Hyde's study, probably later in this year.

Pink Dormitory, which is indeed very pink, I suppose pretty in a Pink sort of way. A kitchen, locked save to nurses after 7.p.m. A dining-room now in a hideous chaos with painters, so that the patients now meal in the kitchen, morally supported by the appearance of new green curtains appliquéd with fat fruits. (That doesn't abolish the fact that two fly-papers with their ghastly burdens dangle plumb over the table.) In a little cubbyhole there sleeps the charge nurse, an Irish girl named Massey: sometimes accompanied by the cat, an ingratiating beast with a spotless white underneath. Also, in a second cubbyhole, her bosom friend, name of King, by day a nurse in the worst of all – Park House,* a lean brick building, when† the maniacs are uncompromisingly so. There is a sitting or drawing room, handsomely upholstered and dominated 12 hours in the day by the stentorious bellowings of a radio – It is held that this encourages the patients – God knows! My little elusive dream-spinet, with your scanty melodies like a fairytale wood nearly leafless, where are you?

Upstairs (I do like the stairs, all except the shrieks of the damned who get up at 6.30 to polish them and are pre-occupied about it for the rest of the day) there are three dormitories, one bathroom, a horrible hole where Mops and Dusters are kept, a balcony accommodating four patients in amazingly squeaky galvanised iron beds; and My Room.‡

Just sometimes when there is nobody on the balcony, the little space of this room is joined to the prospect of wide tawny fields, sloping out towards the sea – It is like one of William Morris's dream landscapes –

"The year wears on, wears on apace,
Yet comes no reaper, to the corn –
The golden land is like a bride
When first she finds herself forlorn …"§

---

* One of the original buildings of the main hospital.

† Reads as 'when': 'where' would make more obvious sense but 'when' could be a way of expressing Hyde's sense of patients being moved to the bad wards when they become uncompromisingly maniacal: 'If they get home-sick or freedom-sick, the string jerks and they vanish to the Main Building, … I used to cry for hours over these disappearances, …' p. 203.

‡ From her first admission, Hyde had the only 'private room at the Lodge' (*Iris*, 219) and retained sole occupancy until her discharge in 1937 (Hunt, 'Cage', 186). Windows in the second-storey room looked west through the 'balcony' (or verandah) where a few other patients slept.

§ William Morris, 'Spell-Bound', *The Defence of Guenevere and Other Poems* (1858), 199:

Like that: haunted, perhaps by the scattered brick buildings standing lonely there in clumps of tree – one dark tinged with much ivy is where the most difficult of the male patients are kept. I remember reading in a book about Haiti of the zombies, the living dead – I see at times black patient little lines of men moving as if in a deep dream over these strange, yellow fields – and I wonder – yet one can wish to be a zombie – I have wished it myself – to be nothing but a shut-in shape, brushing its hair out before a mirror.

I am divorced from all consciousness except the consciousness of the earth, such as may be found in the wild shrubbery: and a little, and lessening longing for human love – Even physically that isn't so acute as it was.

This room: at times it has even seemed beautiful.* It is wide and light-coloured, with a flowery wallpaper on which sometimes the painted flowers seem to keep up the dryest little fragile whispering. There is a white mantel over the fireplace, which never harbours a fire, so that its chimney has room for nests and very early I hear the little thin whistle of the starling, or the dove's rounded voice. On the white mantel are four gaudy fourpenny Japanese birds, painted bone: a ghostly print named "Beyond", two great watching eyes in a pallid face: a sunset painting that is good and glows softly: photograph of Vicki Baum† wishing one good luck for the next book, which I need: a Malory print that the Ronald Holloway–Aroha Hardcastle menage‡ gave me when his parents broke up their living in sin by confiscating the little Panmure cottage which was the only place they had. So now they are starving in town, she in a cell of a simple room reached by climbing down a precipice, he I don't know where: but near her every moment he can contrive. Oh, Poor Aroha! I have just remembered

---

the Electric Book Company Ltd www.elecbook.com [date retro] 19.2.2012. Hyde misquotes slightly: 'The year wears round to autumn-tide/ Yet comes no reaper to the corn; The golden land is like a bride/ When first she knows herself forlorn …'.

* 'The Requisition list for the Lodge conversion included the following furnishings for the 'Small Dormitory', which would become Hyde's room: 2 wooden bedsteads, 2 mattresses, 4 kapoc pillows, 8 sheets, 8 blankets, 8 pillow cases, 6 hand towels, 3 counterpanes, 2 bedside rugs, 1 hearthrug, 3 pictures, 1 fender, 1 fireside companion, 1 small rimu table, 2 bedside chairs, 1 chest of drawers with mirror, 1 chair seagrass, 2 vases, [1 standard reading lamp]' (Hunt, 'Cage', 197).

† Vicki Baum, Austrian-born American novelist whom Hyde met when she visited Auckland. See p. 199.

‡ Ronald Holloway, Griffin Press. Aroha Hardcastle may have been related by marriage to the painter May Smith, whose married name was Hardcastle.

how proud she was of the forty-two bunches of grapes nearly ripe on the vine she had trained and pruned and coaxed into fruiting at Panmure.* Now she won't have any of them – and if her tawny-grey devil of a cat, Mog, who detests me, should die of town life, I believe it will almost break her heart – Women's hearts are easily broken – we have so little to depend on.

Footsteps outside on the creaky board by my door – The little pink night-nurse on another of her dutiful rounds. At first on coming to the Grey Lodge† I hated nurses en masse, but have modified that a little – I like 'em now if civil – but still hold firm by a theory that it is a sin to employ untrained girls in mental nursing –

"Your mariners are muleteers, reapers, people
Engrossed by forced impress"‡ –

Not always true – But the psychological demands of this sort of place seem to me too large for a raw-recruit battalion to be allowed even a part in the work – which doesn't mean that some of the lasses (they mount cautiously through the spectrum, pink to blue, blue to sedate lavender, lavender to dazzling white, the matron wears it and I abhor her,) are not charming and tactful and possessed of goodwill not only to all men but to some of their own poor harassed sex.

I have heard the passing footsteps at night for nearly two years: or not all the time – sometimes they were lost in distance – For a little while there was a close unbearable contact with supervision which fretted me to the very bones. I think I have learned more courtesy now – (I used to lie awake and plan how I could keep a fork back from the meat-trays I didn't want, and with it assault or assassinate the night "special" who sat on my irritable soul, all thirteen stone of her, for twelve hours in the day – not a knife: at these enterprising moments the supply of cutlery is limited – anyhow I'm glad, not only for my sake, that I didn't actually assail her. She is very likely a splendid sort – But I never, never want to see her again –)§

---

* A village to the southeast of Auckland, now a suburb.
† Hyde uses this unofficial name, as do some other records. The Grey may come from the name of the previous superintendent – though his name is spelt differently. Or, Alison Hunt suggests, it may connect with doves and Columben (French for dove-coloured, derived from Latin for dove), another name Hyde uses for the Lodge (Hunt, 'Cage', 242 n1).
‡ *Antony and Cleopatra*, 3.7.35. Enobarbus to Antony.
§ This may be at odds with Alison Hunt's 'there is no evidence that she was ever "specialled"' – i.e. had a nurse watching her overnight – except when she was a patient at the Wolfe

Coming home at nights now (I can by asking permission go to town, to libraries, to offices where I free-lance a little and rather ineffectually)* I usually find in the kitchen a very small nurse chasing very large crickets – the crickets in Auckland are formidable with scaly black wings and policies of blind hatred and falsetto voices. They wail like Chinese in the cupboards and my little nurse dashes after them and thrusts them outside and sees old Shot, the fat apologetic retriever attached to the Lodge, thump his tail in the hope that it's not too late for supper.

For a little more than a year, I never saw the moon. I can't from this room, and I wasn't allowed out. I don't suppose anyone could understand. Then one night I listened. There were young leaves on a peach tree which guards a pleasant untidy house of brick set back from this road and a house which has in its garden marguerites, and lavender-scented geranium. The moon came up behind those nine pine-trees. It was so utterly alone. I wanted to break that crystal goblet over my shoulder, so that no one else should drink from it again.

I used to lie then, rather secretly, in the shrubbery after dark: the black motionless fingers of the trees pointing straight down to earth. Lie still and enquire of it with all my body what peace it had for me. Perhaps the peace of death – if death is peace. Life even now doesn't seem a very elongated caterpillar to me.

There are three clocks in this place: they are all liars, but one after another they have declared midnight. I'm going to sleep – à demain.

———————————

10P.M. Wednesday February 20th / 35

Well-omened and fair-favoured February day – though I did get pinned in the awful clutch of a nightmare last night and had to fight free for about a hundred years – Dr. Tothill says its [sic] an inner sense of imprisonment – must be right because I

———————————

Home from late July to late August 1933. Hunt comments, though, that the generous-sized double room that Hyde occupied was probably designed for a patient who needed 'special' watching (and that this made 'her single occupancy even more remarkable'). The previous patient occupant was a medical doctor with a drug problem and suicidal tendencies, who was 'specialled' (Hunt, 'Cage', 187).

* This is a freedom ('parole') that few of the other patients, even those at the Lodge, had.

can write stories now about the shut-in and obscured – one called "Sweet William" about poor Lady Arabella Stuart who died mad in London Tower, being much in love with the young Seymour – I'm convinced from her symptoms (she grew shadowy-thin and wouldn't do aught but lie on her bed, and yet summoned out of nowhere enough energy to dress as a young gentleman in russet-topped boots and ride to save her lover,) that I know her state pretty well – and so described it for the tale. For another about an escaped convict who didn't really commit a murder, and ended up very happy with a dream-world contained in an old house and garden where he met not only a ghostly child named Drusilla, but a unicorn, the blessed Ronald Holloway helped me to hit upon exactly the right title, "Unicorn Pasture".* A unicorn pasture is <u>exactly</u> what I've been thinking of, groping after, a life long – It's as I suspected with Ronald – He lives in a Freeman's Bay hovel with Bob Lowry, another student printer, the one whom the fat magistrate F.K. Hunt sentenced to 3 years' curfew (in at 7 each night,) for making flamboyant speeches of a Communist sort from the roof of a public convenience in Victoria Street†– Besides Robert there are innumerable fleas and Ronald has to debag and de-flea himself before approaching town – he still likes unicorns – he runs the Griffin Press, Lowry and Mason the poet the Unicorn

---

* 'Unicorn Pasture' was also the putative title for a planned collection of short stories. This title story was thought to be lost until located by researcher Alison Jeffreys under another title ('Other Pastures', *Lighted Windows*, 191 n30). Also see *Iris*, 263–5, 717. Relatedly, Unicorn Press was the name of Bob Lowry's Press from mid-1934 until he sold his plant to Ron and Kay Holloway in July 1938. Peter Hughes email 11 May 2011.

† Robert Lowry was the printer of *Phoenix*, the magazine of the Literary Club of Auckland University College, 1932–3, a publication often seen as signalling the beginning of the new nationalist literary movement. 'Ronald' is Ronald Holloway who first worked with Robert ('Bob') Lowry on issues of *Phoenix*. Lowry was part of a group who were distributing pamphlets he had printed to protest the lack of free speech since the so-called 1932 Queen Street riot. Others were arrested on top of the Beresford Street public lavatory building, but Lowry was arrested atop a parked car – that he had climbed on to support his comrades. In her story, 'The Cage with the Open Door' (p. 288), Hyde elaborates this detail. Also see Rachel Barrowman, *Mason: The Life of R.A.K. Mason* (Wellington: Victoria University Press, 2003), 193. Lowry was convicted 'and admitted to probation for a period of two years. Special conditions: that he be not found out at night after 7pm except with the written consent of the Probation Officer'. The S.M. recorded was W. Wilson, not Hunt as Hyde asserts. (Magistrates Court, Auckland. Criminal Record Book, 198, quoted Peter Hughes email 11 May 2011). Hyde's 'Flaming youth and free speech', *New Zealand Observer*, 16 August 1934, 5, is also about this incident.

one – Poor babes in the mythological wood!*

Still I did like yon February day – G.M.T.† did talk in an advisory way this morning which I love. He always notices the flowers. Had a letter from Vicki Baum, at Suva, about my book "Journalese" which the Wellington papers cut dead as mutton, though I lived in their abominable city for 17 years.‡ Vicki said, "It is so human, so well written, that it goes straight to the heart". And much else – I met her here on the balcony of the Grand Hotel among massive shrubs just one up on the agile aspidistra.§ Portrait of a successful woman novelist: hair peroxide: heart gold, so obvious – no she <u>had</u> deep and perceptive slate-blue eyes, a voice with more than depth – gentleness, humility – Hands of an artist, and sure enough she played the harp as a professional in Vienna long ago – During the war when Germany nursed soldiers with enthusiasm Vicki stayed behind with a little fat Grand Duchess Leonora, and nursed illegitimate babies instead, which I appreciated rather. There is a <u>youth</u> underlying painted face and smartly-frocked body. She wants to laugh – to cry – to enjoy adventure in loneliness. She once took a caravan into the Sahara by accident – she meant to camp a few days for a private view of the sunsets but an entire native village on camels tagged hopefully after her mounted on camels and delicately suggesting backsheesh – "I must go back to Africa, if only to get another desert fox." She had one, it died very ripe in years in Hollywood. Her first book was "Early Shadows" the story of her childhood, and it sold 200 copies counting those bought by relatives. "It was a terrible book!" I'd like to read it though – more because

---

* Mason the poet is Ron (R.A.K.) Mason. 'In mid-1934 Lowry returned to Auckland from Christchurch to produce poetry under R.A.K. Mason's imprint, The Spearhead Publishers, with his new press name, the Unicorn Press. The first production was Mason's own *No new thing.*' Peter Hughes email, 11 May 2011.

† Gilbert Mortimer Tothill: Hyde seems to enjoy the coincidence of his initials with the acronym for Greenwich Mean Time – he was perhaps as reliable as GMT.

‡ *Journalese* (1934) is an account of Hyde's life in journalism. Vicki Baum was an Austrian popular novelist known for her portrayals of the New Woman. Her 1929 novel *People in a Hotel* was made into a successful movie starring Greta Garbo and Joan Crawford. She emigrated to the USA in 1932, where she was treated 'like a media star' and produced more novels and movies; it was from Hollywood that she made a visit to New Zealand. ('Miss Vicki Baum visiting New Zealand', *Evening Post,* 2 February 1935, 11.) Presumably her ship called at Suva.

§ The Grand Hotel at 9 Princes Street was Auckland's leading hotel from 1889 until 1966. Only its facade now remains.

her eyes were deep and soft than because she was friendly.

Added to G.M.T., Vicki, "Unicorn Pasture", I see a faint far glimmer of daylight in some difficult research I'm doing trying to get together material for a sort of sketch-biography of Sir George Grey,[*] another of New Zealand's jettisoned statesmen, who lived in the good bloody days of cannibals and land-sharks. I think I've got it – series of contemporary pictures, with Grey's personality and policies in the background. Title, "These Poor Old Hands!" taken from the fighting chieftain Te Rauparaha's cry "What do you think they will gain by putting manacles on these poor old hands?"[†] Grey <u>did</u> – manacles of silk – and broke Rauparaha's prestige and played chess better than the Maori race.[‡] I am convinced the man is worth writing about from two tiny things: he planted oranges at his island of Kawau[§] and got 3,000 oranges from one; where now we may go hang or pay enormous prices for citrus fruit; and he said this of a sambhur skin: "I noticed it had the delicate odour of mountain passes, the

---

[*] Governor Grey, New Zealand's colonial governor for two terms from 1845–53 and 1861–68, was a wilful but genuine man whose interest in Māori in his first term was practical and admired, but he encountered more and different difficulties when he returned for a second term, working with the elected General Assembly. Te Ara Encyclopedia http://www.teara.govt. nz/en/1966/grey-sir-george/5

[†] Te Rauparaha to the Ngātiawa: 'holding up his hands as if manacled in view of all, he said: "Why should they seek to fetter me? I am old and weak; I must soon pass away. What could they gain by enslaving me? – by fastening irons on these poor old hands? No; that is not what they seek. It is because through my person they hope to dishonour you. If they can enslave me they think they degrade the whole Maori race."' G.W. Rusden, *History of New Zealand, Vol. 1.* (Melbourne: Chapman and Hall, 1883), 340.

[‡] Te Rauparaha (Ngāti Toa) was 'a great tribal leader' who 'took his tribe from defeat at Kawhia to the conquest of new territories in central New Zealand. As a war leader, he enjoyed great success. The tribes he defeated attribute his success to Ngāti Toa's possession of muskets rather than to Te Rauparaha's military genius. Without his leadership, however, it is doubtful if Ngāti Toa would have attempted the great migration and seized the opportunities open to them. Having done so, they changed the tribal structure of New Zealand for ever'. http://www. teara.govt.nz/en/biographies/1t74/1 Following the '1843 Wairau Affair' (which resulted in the deaths of 22 European settlers and several Māori), and a series of clashes between Māori and Government troops in the Hutt Valley, ... Sir George Grey was 'prompted to arrest and illegally detain Te Rauparaha, in order to pacify the local Māori tribes': http://rangiatea.natlib. govt.nz/BuildingE.htm Retrieved 24 June 2011.

[§] Kawau Island in the Hauraki Gulf, not far north of Auckland. Grey owned the island from 1862 until 1888 and had a residence at Mansion House Bay (the house and island previously belonged to the owner of the island's copper mine).

hunter's smell by which the old blind-father knew Esau." He was an Esau himself* – one of the inevitable dispossessed – and I am convinced that what the world retains of greatness is vested in its Esaus: I dislike the Jacob tribe at their desks, with their soapy voices, their tallow faces, their impressionable waxen hearts, always to be melted to another image next day – "These Poor Old Hands" – grim, bloody, tragic hands – I must make them move again.[†]

And Derry's father[‡] wrote to me. He said "You have the dangerous gift of making people supremely happy or utterly miserable." There was a tree in Christchurch where we met years ago, carved with the one strange word "Peace". I would like that to be true for ever – sick and weary, and knowing I didn't love him and couldn't depend on him, and not knowing what in the world to do with the baby I had wanted, now I had got him, I grew to regard his father with a sort of horror. When he arrived in town unexpectedly the other day and telephoned this place asking me to come to meet him I stood waiting by the library with no sensation but panic. The memory of him was dim and distorted. A man with lo-comotor ataxia, a thin man, started to drag his way up the hill in terrible little mincing steps. I thought – "There he is – he has caught some horrible disease, and he is coming towards me now." That poor creature dragged by, I never saw his blurred face. Then Derry's father did come: and Oh Lord, what was there to be afraid of? But frightened and shaky I still was, and said little of any sense before he left. He had seen Derry for the first time since his birth, and was obviously rather proud of him. Once he had gone, I knew that it was all right: I wanted to be friends, I would have been glad to see him again, to talk and laugh. I don't love him, if I have any love at all it's all given to a person in a dream, my one clear face. But at least all that hateful stifling fog of misunderstanding and misliking has vanished for the present – I told him, I don't care if I've had fifty babies, I'd like to be friends.

Those who in Auckland never guessed about Derry (though he and I went to the zoo together and were nearly brave enough to ride on the elephant and much

---

*   Esau was the brother of Jacob who sold his birthright to his brother in return for a portion of food (Genesis 25:27–34), but in turn was betrayed by his mother and brother (Genesis 27:1 to 28:7). Esau was not the chosen one (Hebrews 12:15–17) but Hyde identifies with his predicament as an outsider and 'one of the dispossessed'.

†   'These Poor Old Hands' was also the name of a manuscript (never located) that she was working on.

‡   Derek Arden Challis's father: Henry (Harry) Lawson Smith.

admired the bears –) achieved a belated revenge by saying I departed so abruptly from the wharf because I was going to have a baby.* Such an inadequate reason – but enough for them. And they don't understand that the raw surfaces of a mind hurt worse than any pregnancy, however inconvenient. Derry's coming, in Picton's long golden sleepy months of late daffodils in the grass, fishing from a dinghy, trespassing in the Convent gardens, walking too far, reading endless books from a tin disorderly library smothered in cream rambling roses, was almost pleasant.† And though I don't deny the atrocity of actual child-bearing, I shall always remember, always re-vision the Himalayan rhododendrons that an old author named Treloar rowed over to bring me – enormous faint-perfumed white flowers, tinged with rose at their beautiful hearts.

A pregnant woman is such an ugly thing. Yet one loved me for it. A day-old lamb, strayed and weeping bitterly in the Convent gardens. It had blue eyes and eyelashes, which seems incredible, and such a wobbly tail. It lay in my arms thanking Heaven for companionship and I'm certain that was because my own baby was to be born in about a month –

Brief gold: after Picton, nearly always strain, financial worry, horrible dissensions: and so an old sickness ripened again slowly, and there was a moment when I could really go into the sea and not call for help and even curse it when I knew it would come. Then, that retreat, cut off, the mind's other way, an exit into silence and despair – Does it ever end? I don't quite know, I am very often happy now, I work hard at writing, yet the thought of returning to the normal world makes me cold and sick –

I'd like to establish the exact degree of insanity attaching to this Lodge: but it's not easy. It stands on a hill-crest, separated by a half a mile's walk from the main building of the Avondale Mental Hospital. Technically at least it is reckoned a ward, but patients aren't sent here from the other wards unless they are "well". The house, a private residence and a charming one some years ago, stands fronted with a stiff lawn, flanked by a far better, wild, dreaming old shrubbery. Tulip and magnolia trees, double purple hibiscus where I have seen the miracle of two bees asleep together in the house of a blossom, a wonderful tall tree covered with thousands of pastel-pink flowers, whose name none of us knows. My little private garden, with a rosemary

---

* She is referring to false and quite ironical (because she already had Derek) speculation about the reason for her attempted suicide in June 1933.

† Hyde spent most of her second pregnancy on D'Urville Island in the Marlborough Sounds and nearby Picton, the small town at the top of the South Island.

bush and a scented verbena, and precious little else just now.

Few of the patients are allowed out of the grounds alone. If they get home-sick or freedom-sick, the string jerks, and they vanish to the Main Building, and there the key turns in the lock. I used to cry for hours over those disappearances, and indeed they are not less tragic because they are inevitable, and taken stolidly as a rule.

This is not the only thing that qualifies the smoothness of life here. Many, a great many, get better and depart – one yesterday, brought in a cowed terrified beaten child, a little thrashed animal to crouch in the corner. She was actually conceited when she left, always exploring new possibilities with a frizzy mop of curl-papered hair and face-cream pots. And she left with a brother who liked her, not with a father who would torture her. As far as I have seen in two years, patients are <u>never</u> forced back into relationships which have proved disastrous.

The reverse side of the case of the patient "dumped" here – cut off from family associations – Little Eileen is. Sixteen, a plump, bright-eyed, bright-witted, hard-working, attractive kiddie, about as insane at anytime as – Oh damn, who <u>can</u> be cited as a pillar of sanity nowadays? Anyhow she is not mad. She has twice attempted suicide, once pretty seriously, with lysol, once by the more humorous means of swallowing coat-buttons – Allegedly she did it because illegitimate, and I was prepared to dislike her as a prig.

But from the first day she came into my room, her grey eyes wide and pathetic like a kitten's. I knew the illegitimacy theory was bosh. Probably she has declared war on that especial point but she has a sense of humour and wouldn't really care if her father were the Secretariat of the League of Nations. What is wrong with her is a craving for mother love. She tries to work it off with those confounded mops and pails. Her mother (who appeared respectably as an Aunt until the child was fifteen,) is pleased to be civil when they are alone. But she has achieved honesty via marriage and there's a twelve-year-old daughter with benefit of clergy. The moment that one comes in sight, the mother snubs her mistake – I don't think conventional women should have illegitimate children, preferably they shouldn't have any children at all, they are bound to be a nuisance at one time or another. Her mother's conventionality <u>not</u> her lapse is unquestionably the cause of little Eil's love-hunger and lysol –

Here in the Lodge, having for several week-ends in succession expected her mother without result, she looked at me with bright eyes –

"Well, they won't give me parole, so I'm going to take it."

And she committed the mortal sin of mooning about on the golf-links – and hung by the gate, crying, and wouldn't come in. Last seen, drooping between two stalwart nurses, and on her way to the Main Building. What else could they do? I hear she is well and happy – But she did that, not from any illness, mental or physical, but because she was determined at all costs to recover the mother-love that had failed her. If you call that mad, call the child that takes the milk from its mother's breast mad. I tell you, if people are deprived of love, they must be provided with a substitute if they are to keep the balance known as sanity – I know nothing of the physical causes of insanity, but among those cases here for psychological reasons, nine in every ten are simply deprived of love. Love (it doesn't matter dam-all if Freud prefers to call it libido,) is the whole motive power of being – Only the psychiatrist who isn't afraid of love is the remotest use – and for a man to come near the staff of a mental hospital without a thorough knowledge of the meaning of the word sublimation is a criminal action – That's why I like Jung better than any other psychologist. He understands not only the roots of human nature, as Freud does beyond rivalry, but the leaves and branches. He understands the Heaven of the neurotic – that passionate desire to make the world over and over again which is perceived in so many alienated from normal life – And isn't this a good desire? Is society really so sweet smelling that we can see no noticeable dunghills? Jung, if I have read him rightly, would use this wasted force of broken, aimless, thwarted love, instead of merely observing it in his notebook.* It was he whose book told me of Goethe's "fantastic flowers" and I was so glad, because I see them too at times – not in dream, in an almost complete awareness – Colours, shapes, undefined by nature: softly changing, and glowing, and delighting, on a bank that lies somewhere outside the world –

Goodnight – It's midnight again.

---

* From these mentions it is probable that Hyde read Jung's *Collected Papers in Analytical Psychology* (1916), the first English translation: 'A copy of the second edition of [*Collected papers*] 1920 was accessioned by the Auckland City Public Library in April 1922 and a 1917 imprint of the first edition was acquired in July 1924' (Hunt 'Cage', 127 n6). Alison Hunt argues that Hyde's 'themes and symbolism' as regards suicidality, death, grieving, and conceptions of an afterlife,' drew on 'the links between spiritualism and psychology she read in Jung's *Collected Papers*' (Hunt, Abstract, 'Cage', 1). Hunt also identifies the Goethe-connection in the *Collected Papers*: 'Jung wrote of visions occurring in exceptional cases during waking consciousness: "Goethe, for instance, states that when he sat down, lowered his head and vividly conjured up the image of a flower, he saw it undergoing changes of its own accord"' ('Cage', 315).

February 21st.

I very nearly fell in love today – with a girl, she has the good name of Herminie
O'Reilly – and so much besides. But this should be told differently –

There was once upon a time in Auckland a little man named Mr. Aaron E. Isaacs,*
who believed that horse-shoes were lucky. For a considerable time he was right. His
horse-shoes were lucky a merveille and from horse-racing he built up a fortune, I
mean a real fortune, but there is no occasion to curse the Jews, because he kept on
horse-racing and lost it again, dying penniless. However, he was good while it lasted.
He built the greater part of a house called "Grey Towers", making it an enormously
tall place of stone walls three feet thick, and with the great tower cresting it, reached
from within by the most dangerous little spiral staircase I have ever negotiated. I first
saw two sad drooping Grecian urns and a little group of plumbers – on calling there
today. Then two stone lions scowling through the whitewash, and then the door, on
which the lock, the bell-pull, the letter box, all took the form of bronze horse-shoes,
overlaid with the green patina of eighty years. Inside there was a design of Greek
keys, sea-horses, dolphins and everywhere perfectly carved various little heads,
bearded, or fatalistic and smooth. There was also Herminie O'Reilly who being the
niece of the old school-mistress who has just decided to let the first Ladies' College
in Auckland† as flats showed me everything, including the sword named Grey Lady,

---

* This house, 'a beautiful property in Remuera Rd' (on a curving driveway that became Garden
 Road in 1924) was the 'second home of Ladies College'. Aaron E. Isaacs added a stone front
 portion, modelled (as Hyde describes) on a medieval castle to an original imposing homestead;
 however, Isaacs had lost his fortune and the College did not purchase from him. See Winifred
 Macdonald 'The Ladies College Remuera 1880–1934', *Auckland Waikato Historical Journal*
 (April 1987) No. 50, 21.
† Perhaps she means the first private school for girls; the first sites of Ladies College in Auckland
 were in fact in Brighton Road (then Bassett), where it opened in 1880 and at Portland Road;
 the building she is describing, Cleveland House (here Grey Towers), was in use by the College
 from 1900 and was located in Remuera Road near Victoria Avenue. Mrs Sarah Ann Moore-
 Jones was the second owner of the school from 1894, a talented woman with ten children
 and an invalid husband. Her daughters Miss Amy and Miss Winnie Moore-Jones took over
 the exclusive girls' school from their mother and it remained open until 1934. Their brother,
 artist, soldier and art teacher Horace Millichamp Moore-Jones, 1867/1868–1922, was known
 particularly for his watercolours based on sketches he made at Gallipoli http://www.nzhistory.
 net.nz/people/horace-moore-jones Retrieved 23 June 2011. 'Misty portraiture' is probably
 Hyde's response to his watercolour technique. This passage reminds us how taste for the arts,

and queer black and white pigeons nesting on grey roofs where the rainwater cisterns are long as swimming baths, and the tower room whose door shrieked at us and tore a great cobweb in half when she opened it. There was a top hat box there and still reposing in it, the ancient silken chimney.* There stood the child, curly-haired, slim, courteous, with a dying beauty all around her – A ghost, but a gay one. The place had valour and wit. I liked its sudden paintings, the misty portraiture of a Mr. Horace Moore-Jones, brother to the school-mistress, who seemed to have the Burke-Jones grace without the limp vacuity. An old stables where Mr. Isaacs kept the most dashing horses and equipage in Auckland is converted into flats likewise – you can still see the pillars that propped up its loft. The vinery and the orchard are gone too. I love vines, their gnarled knotty strength, the dangle of wax-green and purple grapes. All this has become the site of small fashionable residences for small fashionable people – Oh, such people – I knew them when I was by occupation a journalist. They look exactly alike and are. Come to think of it they are in much the same case as the neurotics here – they have never been loved! Nothing memorable is written on their faces. And I haven't had love either, except in the irritated elusive way of men who always wanted me to be something I'm not – but at least I don't enamel my disposition. Poor little wretches – But Herminie isn't poor, except in cash – I hope she marries somebody very gallant and has an orchard of her own. She told me her dream is to have the place reclaimed and saved from its withering. There was only gas there till a year ago for lighting. If the bell-pull sounded at night, she had to run down the great stairs in darkness, and strike matches, until the orange gas jets hissed above the parquetry floor of cream and sienna – Blest child –

"All lovely things
  Are beautiful"

I shouldn't care so much for large old remembering retired houses. It's that infernal Lighted Windows game again† – a kink and rather sloppy one. Always there seemed

---

particularly the visual arts, had been very much associated with a certain moneyed class in Auckland up until the thirties. With the Depression, the once-prestigious old school (with its elegant earlier history) had to be divided into apartments. Hyde is visiting with a fellow patient and niece of the 'old-school mistress', presumably a Moore-Jones.

* Top hats were called 'chimneys'.

† In an unpublished story of the same name, Hyde writes about this game: 'Shelagh hadn't played at lighted windows since she came to Auckland first. But it's really a very good game,

to be <u>somewhere</u>, the light pale on the blinds, the music drifting and dreaming, the sweet faces, lives contained by their own steadfast regard for one another – Always, and yet never – The text in the Bible about many mansions is beautiful: but not so true as "From him that hath not, shall be taken away also … ."[*]

I'm so tired – the summer is dying at last in our gardens, the long blue scorching days suddenly lost in a grey rain. The patients look for the most part like moulting birds – one of them, a hypochondriac with the I-can't-sleep delusion, a self-obsessed middle-aged unattractive woman who talks about sleeplessness so much that (since she really does sleep) nobody is very sorry for her, shocked me this morning. She said with the queer apologetic persistent smile of the woman who's going to make a complaint if she waits a year for the chance "I often hear that typewriter of yours going all through the night." Of course she doesn't – I never work later than 8.30 – but she honestly thinks she does, and seeing that cringing look (of course she knows other people don't sympathize, probably sees them as an army leagued against her,) I was horrified with a sudden knowledge of the torture she is undergoing – a sound, heard, persists, echoing and re-echoing in the cells of her brain – when she is released or semi-released by sleep, she retains no consciousness of it. Everything must be a maddening jangle, a whispering gallery – Her eyes are glassy, afraid yet still <u>persistent</u>. She confides her woes almost without ceasing to a fat stolid silent English woman who looks as though she had been reared among flitches of bacon and mugs of cider. How the devil <u>she</u> came by a mental breakdown I can't conceive, but she's patient with the insomniac – and I'd like, having been jarred by a notion of that echo in her mind, to head her off from the hedge of suicide, which she is going to jump soon, exactly like a sheep. How, I can't conceive. Giving up work altogether

---

because you can play it when you're alone. In any street, in any town, on any long grimy train journey. Only wait until you are so tired that everything is hazy and a little unreal, like those wild lights that had seemed to wave goodbye from Auckland. You go up the street and choose your house. Any one won't do, though nearly all of them are very dear, you can think, "Father, and Mother, and at least one dog, and all the little sisters and brothers are there." You make up different things that they would be doing at the time … Like roasting chestnuts, or playing a prim little parlour piano, or gumming paper dolls ….'. 'Lighted Windows', Unpublished TS, Challis, Derek Arden, 1930–. Papers relating to Robin Hyde [ca 1910–2000]. MS-Group-1648, Alexander Turnbull Library, acquired 2009.

[*] 'In my father's house are many mansions' (John 14:2) but she prefers the 'truth' of the parable of the talents again: 'That unto everyone that hath shall be given, and from he that hath not, even that he hath shall be taken away from him' (Luke 19:26; Matthew 13:12).

(which I can't and won't anyhow,) wouldn't do it – She's at the awful stage where a tap dripping becomes a solid instrument screwed through the brain –*

I'm convinced that the word "sensitive" is given too sloppy an interpretation: and usually is applied to exhibitionists and poseurs, tough as whipcord. The really sensitive person is simply the one whose senses are more highly developed than is normal. Take a person who sees, hears, smells, tastes, feels a little more acutely than the rest. Here you have a man projected by entirely natural causes into a world of different dimensions from those generally experienced. If you treat him as a misunderstood soul you may flatter the poor brute, but you won't be of much practical use. If you can do something to stop the screaming of his outraged senses, c'est bien autre chose – And inevitably our senses are mal-adjusted for the modern world, the sense of hearing in particular. Why can't we take warning from Poe's story of the house that crumbled to ruins because somebody played the unknown note on a violin? But of course nobody reads the early Americans, those dark and yet lustrous beings – Hawthorn, Poe, Melville, Whyte, remind me of such houses as the ones I saw this afternoon – the light made curious with panes of stained glass, topaz, carmine, blue: yet somewhere you're bound to find a wonderful view from a tower, or a telescope in a hump-backed observatory, poking up at the stars –

23rd.

I was locked quite fast in the invisible nightmare arms that wouldn't let go. As always, it meant long, patient, wary struggle. I wonder if other people experience the same thinking-out of strategy to defeat enemies in a dream? I couldn't see who was holding me, and was determined to. A voice kept saying "Don't look round, don't look round," but I did, almost by brute force. And I saw that the thing holding me was my own body – I saw it quite plainly, long hair down, body leaning sideways, in its blue dress –

Also there was a voice that said "There is no such companionship". Not another word – a voice that has never before spoken in any dream of mine.

So tired – want to crumple up and lie still for a long, long time. Feel like the straw

---

* This problem of Hyde's typing at night may have been the precipitator for her gaining access to the attic as her study.

a drowning man has clutched at, just about to give one frantic kick and disappear – But I wrote a new tale – It's called "Six Pomegranate Seeds,"* and is about the reasons the little Persephone had for being very fond of Dis† – the nicest part is where a rabbit comes down to see her: and Dis comes with her to the burrow, and he can't look at the sunlight but he stretches out his hand, and the light rests on it like a white bird, while his Persephone talks to him about spring in Sicily.

I can't write: slightly tearful, wholly worn out – Sometimes it's as well to pull down the blinds – Tomorrow I shall spade or hoe or fork my little garden, which is in great want of blossoms through my laziness. But a dozen small green primrose plants have bestirred themselves. I have been happy there – Oh, God, don't let everything be taken away from me, not everything – I've got over all the rest but I can't move without some sort of hope –

Coward, coward, coward – I wish for once I were back in the Wellington College, which I hated but for its hollowed old wooden stairs, a few books – Rostand's beautiful "Chanticleer",‡ and a little sad grey museum of which I was a part-curator – It would be enough tonight – I want to lie somewhere where there has been fellowship, a growth together of friendly things. Oh, it never was so there, and I am only cheating myself. But I'll always remember the little hollows in the stairs, the smooth broad green of oak-leaves at the bottom of the garden.

---

* Unpublished story. Challis, Derek Arden, 1930–. Papers relating to Robin Hyde [ca 1910–2000]. MS-Group-1648, Alexander Turnbull Library, acquired 2009. 'This story was inspired by a visit to the Waitomo caves where Hyde was impressed by the 'utter, unthinkable, black and healing silence' of the caves, and where she considered 'toppling over into river to end her depression'. Alison Jeffreys, 'Other Pastures', *Lighted Windows*, 78.
† Persephone, after eating the fatal pomegranate seeds, considered the symbol of marriage, was condemned by Zeus to spend a third of each year in the Underworld with her husband Hades, or Pluto or Dis (Roman), as the God of the Underworld was also known. *New Larousse Encyclopedia of Mythology,* 155, 158.
‡ She is referring to Chantecler [sic], a play by the neo-romantic French poet and dramatist Edmond Rostand (1868–1918), in which all the characters are animals. Rostand is better known for his play *Cyrano de Bergerac.*

Feb 26th

After midnight. All blisters and mosquito bites, both from honest toil. I dug my little garden, clay even as I am and every bit as sticky, from end to end. Likewise I put in fifty freesias, fifty ranunculae, four dozen scarlet anemones, two dozen blue spraxias, and three Black-Eyed Susans, which I have never seen in the flesh, but which sound very comely – And it all did make one sweet green moment in a day –

And another nice moment, right now. Against all rules and regulations, by-laws and inhibitions, yester'en's pretty little dark-eyed night nurse popped up, in green and gold frock, to say goodbye to me before leaving on holidays – The building would probably fall if our snaky-locked stony-eyed medusa of a matron discovered that one of her pink slaves came here out of uniform – (one of the reasons why I can cleave to our motherly Irish charge nurse is because she hates cats and her stockings not infrequently hang down.) Anyhow Dark-Eyes crept hither and smiled and shook hands and reported her destination, and I do so like to be liked, for nearly always I am touchy enough to argue myself into grotesquerie – a species of porcupine but with ingrowing quills – I love the young – the lithe – the merry-eyed – It's over ten years that my own body has been a burden to me: crippled, quite suddenly, and, hanging between two crutches, so heavy – How I'd love to be invisible, inaudible, intangible – a creature with devil a dimension! I remember, just after the accident that started it, lying in the little white bay where I had come to convalesce: sand warm under my hands, seagulls white as salt and screaming like untamed shrews. The world, with its waves and its dipping wings, was such a graceful place, it seemed ill that anyone should go heavily.

I have been weary today: too much so to say one sensible word to G.M.T. when he appeared and if I can't do that, there is no polite conversation to be expected in the world –

One of my stories, "Lonely Street", has won Art in New Zealand's competition;[*] I'm glad, for it's the first of these fantasies I have sent anywhere – C. A. Marris,[†] the

---

[*] 'Lonely Street', *Art in New Zealand* 7.3 (1935), 128–33. See Jeffreys, 'Other Pastures', *Lighted Windows,* 74. *Art in New Zealand* was the national magazine of the arts in New Zealand from 1928 to 1946.

[†] Charles A. Marris, 1874–1947, journalist, literary editor and associate editor Christchurch

editor, and something of a friend of mine now, seems pleased –
Night Charge coming, must duck – Goodnight.

February 27th.

Sad day mitigated by the purchase of two green ixias (and the old man saw how doleful I was because I couldn't buy a dozen, so he slipped in an extra one,) and a theme supplied by Rosalie Rawlinson for my mythological zoo – a story about a salamander. When Benvenuto Cellini was five years old, his father suddenly knocked him down, not for any misdemeanour, but so that he should forever remember the Salamander disporting itself in his oak fire.* Think I can make a tale of it – I have one about a Centaur, one about a Unicorn, and the loveliest one about a Griffin and the effect it had on a Grand Inquisitor's Mistress –

I wish I weren't lame: then I could curl my legs into the right position and practise yogi breathing and om mani padme om – Do so need it – To be angry in a little way with little people, people mentally near-invisible, is so cheap – and I am – I can't bear a certain capacious body, ungainly, red-faced, with the triumphs of materialism in its little eyes and little mouth. It ought to be pitiful, not being a young body, nor having any large advantages or comforts flanking it, but it's not – it has the power to lay claws on me every now and again and then I wish it dead – it's undignified to wish a thing like death for a person you dislike. Death should be lovely – full and veiled and forbearing. I could cherish death for myself, and respect it, more easily than life – To aim it as a blow at the head of our enemy is defilement. Let her live on, in that state neither life nor death, the limbo inhabited by the materialists.

Yes, just nonsense. And these pages aren't at all what the lady meant. I intended a spruce record of life here – but the thread keeps catching on the thorn of a minute –

Sun (1914–25), editor *Art in New Zealand* (1927–42), editor *New Zealand's Best Poems,* was a member of the older establishment of 'bookmen', and an advocate and publisher of Hyde's work. She first met him in 1927.

* A parable related by the sixteenth-century Italian artist Benvenuto Cellini in his autobiography. The salamander is a species of lizard which has some resistance to fire. He was told by his father that he was witnessing the first sighting of such a creature. Thomas Bulfinch (1796–1867). *Age of Fable: Vols. I & II: Stories of Gods and Heroes*, 1913. http://www.bartleby.com/181/365.html Retrieved 23 June 2011.

Alison Grant,[*] as was, Mrs. Hugh Robinson, as now is, sat in this room last night sprawling long slim legs from my little cane chair – still, as seven years ago, her dark face is ugly until an animation makes it vivid, all but beautiful – dancing amber eyes – but I'd like her the deuce of a lot better if she didn't call people "glamorous". She was wed in London, honeymooned in Spain, lived in a cottage 400 years old somewhere in the deep English countryside – I'd like a house in the forest of Ys – Isn't that two-letter word, Ys, pure Malory? Names were so lovely then – Camelot, Benoye, Broceliande, the Joyous Gard[†] – strung together, not like jewels, like the more beautiful, waterworn pebbles out of any old sleeping river.

Alison's brother Ian is a mental patient here in Avondale – better, and trying with futile bitter effort to get back to the normal world. I have been introduced to him – perhaps thirty, bitter-mouthed, dark young man.

The amazing thing (to a novice) in a mental hospital is the absolute <u>difference</u> of types. The stuff about madness being to genius near allied wouldn't hold water for three minutes if the little enfant who wrote it passed through here. Far more than half the mental patients seem excessively physical. Given the things that really have taken up a sort of owl-in-the-hayloft existence in their minds are physical experiences. For instance, there was an intensely excitable, tearful, agitated woman, married and with children, at least fifty, comfortably off. Her one anxiety seemed to be to tell how when she was about eleven, a man on a railway station had attempted some mild form of indecent assault – not very successfully. What's that memory but unsatisfied desire – a hunger after something that the civilities of matrimony have evidently not supplied?

Yet some are dear and queer and funny: one or two splendid. If I can't quite face a continual intercourse with a crowd of them, I have really <u>known</u> and tried to help a few, at a few odd moments. Three successes, one utter failure. The failure was, I suppose, an imposter – yet I still wonder.

I met her first before ever I came here: brought out by her sister to visit her. She lay in bed at the Wolfe Home – a pretty enough dormitory superficially, but it has its horrors – for me, anyhow. There she was, helpless dark head, golden-brown eyes,

---

[*] Alison Grant, 1901–2001, New Zealand poet, journalist, artist and broadcaster, who lived for many years in London; she had a 'long and complicated relationship' with poet and translator Arthur Waley and married him 'just a month before his death'. She was also his biographer. Diana Bridge, 'China Imagined and Actual', *Lighted Windows*, 197 n34.

[†] These are all places in Arthurian legend. Brocéliande is a forest in Brittany.

soft voice. I promised to visit her again – Didn't – Not a month later my own career as an efficient citizen was ended.

I met her next when myself near oblivious of all surroundings that I have no recollection of the child. She had been "promoted" to the Lodge. I slept and lived in this room and was only an occasional ghost in the corridors. But I must have had some subterranean goodwill towards her for she says that after passing her scores of times without noticing her, I called her name one day and overwhelmed her with fruit. I don't remember –

When I came back, perfectly conscious,* I became her confidante at once. Not an occasional confidante, as other women here, suddenly desperate or sad or sentimental, have made me – She was twenty-three – Every evening a dark little creature in very pretty woolly things she made herself would be in my room, telling me how she had been here three years, stranded, how she was desperately anxious to go free … something about a home and babies too. Not a sign of insanity, or mental weakness, or mental slovenliness. She had had a mastoid operation some years before and having read Rutter's book "Chandu", telling the easy Hell a woman slipped into after that operation,† I didn't think it at all an incomplete reason for her breakdown. Her home was non-existent – the Father is an old parasite, the mother working elsewhere – so her long stay here seemed simple enough.

I got her a job, through Rosalie Rawlinson: 25/- a week as companion to the Rabbi's wife – no bacon, but nice old house and nice woman. At the last moment, she just couldn't. There was another "place" offering in an indefinite sort of way, hope but not certainty. Charming old lady, passionfruit wine, big garden – Patty rejected the Rabbi and clung (apparently) to my old lady. But darkly by dead of night she wrote to Rosalie and told her she didn't want a job after all, being greatly attached to someone here. (Our Nurse Massey). Then, acute regret overtook her. So she couldn't bear to blame herself, to have closed the gates on herself. It had to be me – I think, in the end, she convinced herself that I was responsible for her failure to take positions. Then began the suicides. Suicide A, walking with eyes shut and groping hands to the balcony window, which is quite fourteen feet above ground – I thought it was real – sat on her bed for hours, held her, coaxed her, slammed the window shut, pretended

---

* When she came back to the Lodge in December 1933.
† Edward Owen Rutter (1889–1944), English historian, novelist and travel writer. *Chandu* was published 1921.

when a nurse heard that the autumn night was bringing large ungainly moths in – Suicide B, in my room: "Robin, I feel just as I did ... before ... I took ... all those ... aspirins – Robin, where are you? Why has your face changed?" I couldn't bear to tell, to risk sending a child down to the Main Building – and I thought too that I had been an utter fool not to shut her up at once when she first mentioned the word "job". But twenty-three seemed to me, five years older, and a thousand years older in other things, so terribly, piteously young. I do believe in the right to love all young creatures – including that tortured Hell-fire-ridden little fool who was myself once. On the third night, I heard her crying on the balcony – went out and put my arm round her – she was soaking wet, had held her nightgown under the tap before going to bed. (The despair in that was nearly genuine suicide, anyhow.) That was the end – for the time – I told her that next time I'd tell the Doctor –

We didn't speak again for six months. She worked here like a little Trojan – baking, polishing, knitting, and fretting; fretting; as only the young and hopeless can do. Once shammed illness to such an extent that she was sent to the public hospital, and at once returned with thanks – vague talk of suicide to other patients, but never again to me. She hated me.

Then through some misunderstanding with the charge nurse she got into hot water and Holy Wars. Was carpetted by the Matron – Crept about, a tearful shade. Seized me at last and informed me she was in Hell (true) and would do anything, take anything, to get out.

It was madness to listen. But I can so easily understand a sudden complete loss of nerve – and then hating one's self, and hating far worse the others who knew about it.

I dug up a doctor's sister, Miss Knight – Nice, quiet, doggy woman. Took Patty to her home. The child behaved like a seraph – eyes bright, the daintiest quick manner, and so interested in the wide and wicked world.

Miss Knight did the deed – Patiently found Patty a series of jobs, one of which she accepted. She had moved down to the Neurotic Unit, and didn't come to see me before she left. I think she knew what she meant to do.

The night before her departure, a terribly sick shadow of a girl, Miss Harford, had to go into her room to pull the pillows off her face. She was choking – very loudly.

She did leave, though: after nearly four years.

She was back again next day, just crying. The place was too hard, she said.

The Doctor was good – and I think any human being would need mercy in such utter helplessness as that. I didn't see her at all, she was at Wolfe Home first, then at the Neurotic Unit, back in the same quiet little room. But it wasn't peace. Three weeks, and she was throwing herself down stairs – never hurt – and talking suicide again. So she went over to the Wolfe Home dormitory and lies there crying, as I first saw her. Silly little tale, of bathos and good intentions and melodrama. She is not really interested in suicide, only in scenes: But if only somehow one could save youth from its various sloughs of Despond and worse. It is true she is rather ridiculous as a person: apart from that, there she stands, with brown eyes and trim hair and a home-knitted jumper of scarlet and white, as surely crippled as though somebody had walked up behind her with a knife and hamstrung her –

And of course nobody remains really sorry for ever. Only impatient, anxious, not to be trapped into useless pity again – This is where a God of Love would have been so useful – But love is what they all need – me too –

March 1st.

Our Irish charge nurse really is rather funny. The place is at the moment haunted by a sad little painter, Mr. Whale. I remarked that he seemed rather small for a whale. "Ah," said she, "He's just another of those exaggerated fish stories."

March comes in cool, grey-eyed, placid. The world has a morning face. I've been explaining to Dr. G.M.T. about David Livingstone's unpublished letters to Sir George Grey, a romantic item in a collection of early N.Z. manuscripts out of which I am trying to knock some sense – On the slave-traffic areas of Portuguese Africa Livingstone came across some blind old women who repeated the Pater Noster just as the Jesuits had taught it to their grannies a hundred and fifty years ago.*

Evening

The only moral is, it's useless for me to cry in my bath –
I know now at least part of what the N.Z. public doesn't want – This includes me

---

* During his tenure as Governor of Cape Colony from 1854 to 1861, Sir George Grey was acquainted with Livingstone. There are several lengthy letters from Livingstone to Grey in Special Collections, Auckland Central City Library, describing expeditions into Central Africa.

in lighter vein on the sorrows of NZ journalists. Had today a letter from Mr. B.C. Jacobs saying that the way of author and publisher was strewn with blood and tears – he being the publisher of "Journalese". As far as I can gather, I have made £5 from my book and the publishers have lost about £200. I feel sorry for Mr. Jacobs –

But then, coming home, I felt sorry for me: because the London literary agents sent back my four short stories, with which I had so much hoped they'd be impressed.* Reading them over, I still think three of them are good – But I made a bad choice, perhaps, or else they weren't enough in themselves to make the agent people see the possibilities of a collection – My stories must be good – And I must succeed as a writer, because I have no other plausible reason for remaining alive – pauperised, stranded, tired. I don't want to live but people make such a fuss about sudden exits.

The second letter in the English mail (the first was my returned manuscript) was from Jim Bertram, a Rhodes scholar whom I have never met – and he loved "Journalese" and sent me a flower from Katherine Mansfield's grave near Fontainbleu. I have the awful habit of falling in love with my work – so I can't know, know with any discrimination, how it really stands. It's only myself – unbalanced, spasmodic, never running smoothly – I thank whatever Gods may or mayn't be for a poem, irrespective of whether it's a good poem or not. And the stories seem beautiful to me. The phrases, the faces, the strange people and their strange tastes, all appear so right that I don't alter them. I never re-polish work and none of it is imitation or affectation. This is due perhaps to the fact that my smattering of commonplace, visionless education wasn't enough to fill me with any great respect for the minds of others. I am learning more now – reading wiser stuff, seeing more deeply moulded beauty in the works of men. But I live so much alone that I can't follow anymore – wish I could – I should love to be a disciple and to feel a master's hand on my shoulder at times –

---

* The agent was AP Watt & Son, London.

Outlaw I go to my grave and masterless,
For there is no master worthy my loyalty
In all this dark quiet land, where tress on tress
The folds of the pinewood deepen towards the sea –
A cricket is singing, so high and shrill and self-
confident Oh nature, why did you give some of –
us thoughts? It's all such a pitiful effort,
and broken off – before our hands can reach

anything or anyone –[*]

March 2nd

Settled: I'm going to write a novel, a fairly autobiographical novel called "The Godwits Fly" … telling about the Colonial England-hunger, and they that depart, and they that stay at home Girl to be called Eliza Hannay, God knows why – But there she is – Like me but very much pleasanter and I think a sense of humour would be a help.[†]

March 7th

Our little grey and white kitten has just died – it crept away yesterday and today they found it stiffened and swollen with poison. It was the cleanest thing in the place, with its soft white throat and white paws! It has been in this room often, curled up under the rug purring – I don't know how people can torture and murder animals. People, it's easy enough to see reasons for murdering people – most of them are offensive – but animals are so small and soft and friendly, with their dainty ways and

---

[*] This fragment of poem does not match any other poem in the manuscripts.

[†] She worked on several drafts of this novel before its publication by Hurst & Blackett, London, in 1938. For information on the progress of *The Godwits Fly,* see *Iris,* 270–1, and Sandbrook, 'Robin Hyde: A Writer at Work', which includes a detailed chronology of Hyde's published and unpublished writing. See also Sandbrook's introduction to the latest edition of *The Godwits Fly* (Auckland: Auckland University Press, 2001).

the jokes their bright eyes tell you. The white and grey kitten isn't the first – There was old True Thomas, who used to sleep on my bed here for months when I was too ill to move – he was the only thing that comforted me on the worst day of all. Then there was a purring grey gamin who arrived in my room with a green ribbon round his neck, last Christmas Day – He just disappeared. But the place is in mourning over little grey-and-white – and through it all goes on the voice of that patient and persistent white elephant with the non-sleeping bug. "Nurse, I wonder what I'll do if I can't get my sleep back?" One kitten is worth millions of them – some of them are kind though – kind and fat and inquisitive.

March 8th morning

The utter weariness of listening – listening with my heart beating too hard, sitting by the window to watch – one's life becomes pent and heaped up into such a narrow space. Then there's no escape – now the car moves off slowly down the slope and that's all over for twenty four hours. I know what McLean* told me is true. I don't know anything about love, not sane fertile happy-ever-after love – just some sort of vision or longing about a person – it makes all the rest of the human race seem unreal, distorted. If I have to go away I shall die, or worse – as the old Zulus said "If we go backwards, we die – If we go forwards, we die – let us go forwards –" But oh, where to? If I could be the slightest use – crippled partly, unfinancial, nearly thirty, no longer even satisfactory as a desirable body (and besides I don't want to sleep with men any more), I'd go. – If I had Derry. There's only one chance I can see, only one thing that seems real at all besides this fantastic love – The cause of peace – Then I do believe – I have read the notebooks of Rainer Maria Rilke† – after that nothing could lead me to the applause of one nation's savaging another. If I have a chance to talk to any of these smug clubswomen, I'm going to drum one thing into them and one only, Goethe's "Light, more Light". At this moment, peace is betrayed among the nations – Britain's White Paper of two days' ago, signed by Ramsay MacDonald and announcing great increases in air armament expenditure, has meant the postponement of Sir John Simon's peace causerie with Hitler in Berlin.

---

* Probably her boss John Gordon McLean, editor at the *New Zealand Observer.*
† Poet Rainer Maria Rilke (1875–1926): she seems to be referring to his semi-autobiographical novel *Notebooks of Malte Laurids Brigge* (1910).

"Hitler caught cold between the sheets of the White Paper". We have on our hands a recent royal alliance with the deposed monarchy of Greece – and not six months later, Greece flares with revolt against a monarchist movement. Germany is ringed with steel. Sir Maurice Hankey has visited the Dominions in connection with their "defences" – a pitiable subterfuge, we have no defences worth the name, except the difficulty of complete access to our country even by air. The mountainous nature of the inner islands, both north and south, should act as an impregnable defence against any sort of air invasion. I don't mean of course that flying over the country is impracticable, but that a thorough and persistent combing of the land from the air would take too much time and involve too much risk – That's previous, though from the dear traitorous Judas newspapers we're supposed to be sitting up at night with our lamps all trimmed and burning, waiting for a Japanese invasion –*

"There is no such companionship". Occasionally he talks a little to me – but one word or just nearness is more than anyone else could give – Only I wish I were some use.

March 10th

Week-end involving two insane ladies, one very queer gentleman, a new kitten who weeps if not cosseted, a house in the Waitakere ranges, and the complications of having a mental hospital for an address.†

The insane ladies were diverse – One, very large and heavy and sad, just wept and wept on the kitchen table, and wouldn't be comforted. Theory: if ultra-tearful, likely to run away: if likely to run away, best be sent back to the Main Building. Q.E.D. She was a voluntary boarder like myself, didn't seem mad, but cried so because the Grey

---

* This fear of Japanese invasion increased after 'the fall of Singapore and Malaya' in 1942, and put an end to 'a phase of "moral foreign policy"' under the First Labour Government that was similar to Hyde's in its 'internationalism and idealism'. John B. MacDonald, 'Regionalism: New Zealand, Asia, the Pacific and Australia' in Robert Patman and Chris Rudd (eds), *Sovereignty Under Seige: Globalization and New Zealand* (Aldershot: Ashgate Publishing Ltd, 1988), 172. Retrieved 18 December 2011.

† Possibly she was staying at the same house in the Waitakeres (at Waiatarua) as in March 1937, when she drafted the autobiographical fragment later published (1984) as *A Home in This World*.

Lodge, not looking so much like an insane asylum as the rest, reminded her of home. Poor, forlorn old creature – I hope she comes back very soon. I can remember (and still occasionally experience) days and nights of crying that tear me to pieces – that start anywhere, in tram cars, in streets, in tea-rooms, and will not at all be amended. I haven't been so moist just lately, but I rather wish I <u>could</u> cry. There is a terrible dryness of the heart.

The second, and much more insane lady, very thin, grey-haired, but also seemingly quite rational, started by screaming very long and loud in the middle of a recent night, because she felt like screaming – was put to bed. Today screamed more, threatened to smash up her dormitory (a good idea) and offered violence, especially to the new kitten, a ridiculous lithe grey scrap from Dr. Buchanan's. It is just like a spoiled baby, in constant need of attention and applause – She didn't take to it at all and it departed in dudgeon – So did she later, for wanting to hit somebody – but she's only hysterical – how I feel that to have talked for an hour or two might have pulled her together.

The queer bird is Stark:* half redskin, half Spaniard – he grew tired of having officer's stripes taken away from him for misbehaviour in the war so he had them branded on his shoulders. I'm going to write about him – At the same time the Eliza Hannay book, "The Godwits Fly", is going rather well. I've finished Chapter the Fourth –

Must try to save: must dream of more travel – am I a cuttlefish, good only for squirting ink?

At the house in the Waitakeres I discovered they didn't know my circumstances – Problem: whether to be frank and risk sympathy I didn't want, or to delude them – Just drew a veil –

There were green wide depths outside the window, and quaintly shaped rooms within.

Goodnight –

---

* James Douglas Stark, or Starkie, was the returned soldier, reputed to have a Delaware Indian father and a Spanish mother, whose story formed the basis for two of her books, *Passport to Hell* (here referred to under its working title 'Bronze Outlaw'), 1936, and *Nor the Years Condemn*, 1938. Stark was known throughout the country for his bravery as well as for recklessness and general disrespect for authority. Hyde first met him through a Reverend Frank Moreton, who was chaplain at Mt Eden prison where Starkie was an inmate, and Eric Blomfield, the cartoonist on the *Observer*. His life as it figures in her novels is mostly drawn from his own account. See *Iris,* 274–7 and also Alex Calder, 'Violence and the Psychology of Recklessness: Robin Hyde's *Passport to Hell*', *Lighted Windows*, 67–72).

[no date given]

"The Godwits Fly" is utter tripe or faintly promising – it's at least honest but I'm no novelist. But if I can only keep Stark to the point for another fortnight or so, the book about him will be absolutely outstanding – unfortunately he drinks and wants money, and I haven't any. Told Dr. Tothill who amazed me by using the inelegant word "Bludgering". I never thought he knew it, but it is not at all uncommon for him to surprise me. I have got Stark in rough Egypt and if I can keep him going tomorrow over the Gallipoli campaign I'll be exultant – I have something about his French experiences already, nearly enough to vamp up the book with what I've got – but don't want to vamp it. "Courage and time", as Rosalie says – in spite of my crossness, God bless Rosalie – and my mother – and all the family and dog – and Gwen Mitcalfe – and Harry Sweetman's dear ghost – and Beulah – and Brownie – and Ronald and Aroha – and lost Frederick de M.H.– and John Schroder* if but not unless he is going to be decent and criticise my stories – and a sturdy Scot who once laughed with me in a delirium tremens cell – and Walter de la Mare, for writing books I can read when sick to death of everyone else – and Gloria and Derry my son. (Derry's father can't want any blessing or he wouldn't keep telling me how wonderful his wife is) and most of all, for ever and ever, bless G.M.T.

Goodnight –

"Amen – Jesu Christo." – as David Livingstone's old blind native women used to say.

[4 pages torn out, not known by whom]

---

* Her friends: Rosalie Rawlinson, mother of Gloria; Gwen (née Hawthorn) Mitcalfe, her old
school friend; Harry Sweetman, her first love who died in England in 1927; Beulah Hay, a
young journalist colleague from Christchurch who briefly shared a room with her and Derek
in Auckland; Brownie, Kay Brownlie, a nurse she met when pregnant with Robin in Sydney;
Frederick de Mulford Hyde, father of her son Robin; John Schroder, literary editor of the
Christchurch *Sun*; 'a sturdy Scot', Dr Buchanan Superintendent of the Auckland Mental
Hospital at Avondale; Gloria Rawlinson, the young poet; Derry, Derek Arden Challis her then
four-year-old son; and Gilbert Mortimer Tothill, her psychiatrist.

March 20th

I feel a beast about Stark. I got the stuff about the Gallipoli campaign all right – amazing, dreadful, vivid stuff – and was duly self-satisfied. Tonight, very belatedly, came a little letter he posted when slightly intoxicated, four days ago. It was the most pathetic scrawl of a love letter, about "my white Iris –" I don't really think it incongruous that he should try and touch me for love and money at the same time – the very poor lead such desperate lives of reaching out for things. I want to finish that book, and to put understanding into it – but I don't believe I shall ever have any more love affairs. Haven't been kissed (except in chilled-asparagus friendship) for two years, and it seems much longer – don't want to be – a youth whom I once knew pretty well, meeting me some months ago, was in gallant enough mood to put his hand on my breast – I felt as though he had attacked me with a knife, and looked it. Most embarrassing for the young man – which is odd, for once I used to class the masculine technique of love in four simple movements (a) lips (b) breast (c) knee (d) ... . Anyhow, back to poor Stark –

For a fortnight life is going to be very lost and uninteresting – nightingales, nightingales, sing to me again of my one clear face.

March 22nd

Have been weeping in really thorough-going cloudburst fashion because I want (a) love (b) money, and haven't even enough sense to go forth and get either. I did manage yesterday to browbeat Alan Mulgan into paying me £1 for an article he has kept for six months without using.* But then today weakly parted with it to Stark who alleged he hadn't been able to draw his sustenance money and kept telling his infants that they would have nought to eat. It was really rather funny but as I haven't comfortable shoes, a winter coat or any but somewhat superannuated chemises and knickers the joke is on me – Stark writes me pathetic love-letters in which he sees my face in the cigarette smoke (I give him the cigarettes, so he ought to see me, if

---

* Alan Edward Mulgan, journalist (father of John Mulgan, author of *Man Alone*); 1935 was his last year as literary editor of the *Auckland Star*. He was also at this time foundation lecturer in journalism at Auckland University College.

anyone,) and has variously asked me for a sewing-machine, shoes, trousers, a winter coat for his daughter Margaret, and a headstone for his wife's grave. On the other hand, his wartime material has, to my mind, really outstanding possibilities – But people are too complicated for me – However I shouldn't be so extravagant myself about green ixias and giant nerines, which are in their own sweet way just as bad as Starkie's serried phalanxes of beer bottles.

The love question is so much worse – Bill Edge, who seems to be a Scottish philanthropist, made my will for nowt this morning.* I left him my typewriter as an appreciation: Derek my insurance money, and the principal shares in manuscripts which may be worth something or nothing: Mother a share in manuscripts also, and Dr. G.M.T. the papers he has (my lame-duck autobiography,) a half-share in my spoils (if any) from "Bronze Outlaw", and a third share – Mother and Derry the other participants – in "The Godwits Fly", the short stories and later poems to Dr. Tothill, for his beloved psychological clinics.† I left Rosalie and Gloria the proceeds of the collection of poems now in London, also "Io and Jupiter," my Correggio print, my bronze fawn and my bronze rabbit. I left Dad all my books, except a souvenir for Gwen Mitcalfe: and the "personal effects" to my sisters three. Bill Edge offered to act as Derry's executor. He is a bachelor, and lonely I believe – it was rather wonderful of him.

Then it occurred to me how much, how stupidly much, I'd like to leave something to Dr. Buchanan as well. And I can't. He is superintendent here. It was he who fished me out of that hideous cell, and laughed, and lent me old French books, and broke all rules and regulations by coming to see me here everyday. Only the unexpected thing was that, sick and three-quarters mad as I was, I couldn't bear him to learn the truth about me. I wanted his regard as I didn't then want food or drink. That was

---

* Bill Edge, a lawyer friend of Rosalie Rawlinson, with whom she and Gloria later lived in Epsom, a suburb of Auckland; after Hyde's death he became, almost by accident of relationship with the Rawlinsons, her literary executor. See 'Introduction', pp. 43–4.

† Dr Tothill's psychological clinics must have needed funds – Alison Hunt finds evidence of psychiatrist Dr Kathleen Todd running a psychological clinic [for children?] in Auckland city ('Cage', 161) but not of Tothill being involved with this or with 'The Auckland Psychological Clinic [that] was established in 1929 by the Eugenics Board and housed in rooms in the Sunday School building next to the Children's Court (Gray, MHDR 1930 3)' Hunt, 'Cage', 162.
Notwithstanding, the division of monies indicates that Hyde believed in the efficacy of his talking therapy for herself and others, and her fellow-feeling for her doctor.

that. I wrote an insane letter to a chemist who was always trying to become my lover, begging him to send me enough morphine to end it – He did, it was intercepted, I was very properly chucked into the outer darkness of the extremely grim Wolfe Home.* Of course I couldn't explain, and anyhow it was such a lunatic explanation – I don't think he ever forgave me. Certainly never gave the old friendliness back again – and do I blame him. That loss all but killed me. I don't know why it didn't – and I gave away what I was suffering, but never after I'd regained even the beginnings of self-control. For more than a year now, on the very rare occasions when he puts in an appearance, I've been what Mr Dernford Yates calls "Good old 'ard and bright."† Of course the worst is all over – Dr Tothill built up a sort of trust and understanding that in the end became more than all the lost things in my life – more than Harry Sweetman, or Frederick, or – perhaps not more than Robin, who is my life – more than any silly desire to pose as a perfectly nice young woman before a cheery Scot. How women hoard their old griefs! Of course now that I'm no longer a wilted lily or an embarrassment or anything but a fool who chooses to live and work here, that scrawled chapter is closed – I made a fool of myself and it's forgotten – But if I could only do or give something to make up for disappointing a friend who didn't deserve it.

~~Forgive me for the unrequited debt of faith betrayed, or gratitude unmet~~ –

Oh this is purely maudlin – and if only Dr. Tothill were here‡ I wouldn't think of it. Goodnight.

March 26th

I rather thought something turbulent was going to happen, and so it did. I became engaged in mortal combat with a large unpleasant aggressive half-caste woman, name of Briggs, who insists on coming into the bathroom when I am undraped, and won't go away on demand. She considered me unduly favoured here and is inspired with a laudable desire to take me down a peg – or two pegs. I dislike excessively sharing intimate details of frame with any except possible paramour of artistic and

---

* This expands on the account she gives at the end of the '1934 Autobiography'.

† The pseudonym of the British novelist Cecil William Mercer (1885–1960), whose novels and short stories were bestsellers in the inter-war period.

‡ It seems Dr Tothill may have gone away for a fortnight – see end of previous entry.

sympathetic habit, hence in the end shrieked at half-caste lady to the effect that she was very vile. "Call yourself a lady!" retorted she, saturnine – a thing which by the way I never under any circumstances do call myself. On her continued refusal to go, simply screamed at her, and draping blue dressing-gown around dripping body fled to the landing there shrieking for the nurse to remove the very large Briggs body – Briggs, a little alarmed, subsided muttering. I wept for three hours, less in anger than in demoralised irritation. Read today with some surprise, in a paper named The Guardian, that Miss Iris Wilkinson is a very natural and level-headed author.* Query: if this is so, how many doctors and other experts due to be certified? Answer: I think the Guardian is perhaps deceived.

Something very strange has happened – I am giving Stark half the proceeds from book about him[†] – yesterday found that on the strength of this, maniac in the city (senior partner of Burns and Nash) had advanced to Stark £182 with promise of further advances. Saw maniac who admitted he realises publication of book at all was only a matter of luck, profits might be nil, Stark's share of 50% only – Saying which, he smiled politely and declared himself satisfied.

I cannot understand this.

On learning of Stark's success in gaining £182 for part-share in book of mine not yet written, went around to publishers of "Journalese", who have so far despite many flowery reviews of this book bestowed on me only £5. Hoped to ask for further payment or advance. Unable to secure admittance.

I can understand this.

If this world is sane, I am unquestionably mad – and vice versa – I have many symptoms of mental derangement. I lose things, and they aren't really lost – hunt in my bag again and again for papers, tickets etc. Understand Samuel Johnson got a very dirty bill of health for this. Sudden gaps appear in my memory. Also, am subject to extraordinary fits of hate, in which I tremble, usually weep, and wish to do murder with a good deal of blood – These are occasioned by ladies in the bathroom, too much noise from the radio, too much polish on the floor, or the merest glimpse of our Matron, for whom I feel the same unmitigated aversion that I had in my childhood for lentils. This disappeared at the age of 15 – I hope my feeling for the Matron doesn't do the same, it would be very disconcerting and alarming, as I have

---

*   Review of *Journalese*, *Guardian*, late 1934.
†   *Passport to Hell* (1936).

really been insulting to her. However, I feel it is an honest hate with some basis in actuality, and will probably last me out my time.

Enter upon the Grey Lodge scene, relieving for Dr. Tothill, Dr. Palmer, English newcomer, dark, slight, possibly 27, certainly not more than 31. Awful destiny for young man to have to be firm and fatherly with all these vast mountainous women who so regularly gave birth to mental mice. Dr. Palmer gave me a lift into town per taxi – appeared doubtful whether I would take this in spirit of mistaken levity, sat in back of car, read letters – I, statuesque, wished that I had not upon the back of my neck scar of the one and only, but very vile, carbuncle known to my health record – There was nothing at all wrong with my deportment, but did he notice about the carbuncle?

Received from my mother a box of plants, including orange lily, pink daisies, (large and nice), auriculas, gaillardias, pelargoniums (that word is so like a disease.) I have planned a blue bed for the scrubby patch under the trees where nothing will grow – border of forget-me-nots and blue primroses, rows of blue spraxias, blue Iris Lingitanis and centre-piece of blue cinerarias. The nearer bed already sprouts freesias, anemones, ranunculi, green ixias, black-eyed Susans, daphne, daffodils, boronia – I want Iceland poppies and pansies too.

Tonight wrote a story called "God Rest You, Merry Gentlemen". Am inclined to think it good – sent it to the Auckland Star, who will turn it down as too controversial, though to my amazement they converted a letter of mine about the needs of crippled children into an article, and actually paid for it.

'Tis midnight. The nurse says, go to bed. I go –

March 28th

Books for which I have no appetite. The better they are the more their dim sententious superficial cleverness bores me. The vile modern trick of giving an exact <u>surface</u> presentment of everything, including the surfaces and surface-contents of the brain cells, would make me still more exasperated if I weren't convinced that it is not only a libel on nature but a travesty of art, and therefore can't crawl into a slimy aeon-eating prolonged life. There's more colour, lucidity, truth, expressiveness in one book like The Cloister and the Hearth than in a million bloody Herghsheimers [*sic*],* Woolfs, Wests, O'Flahertys, Sitwells, all spilling their guts and sawdust, according to which their beings are stuffed with, over the pavements – But dieu soit loué,[†] they can't touch the pastures, which count for more. While there is the light friable brownness of garden soil between my fingers and the fingers of every child born like me we'll still have a way of escape, a means of growing both upwards and downwards in privacy. I wish I could be reincarnated as a Chinese woman, though it might be better not at all.

Stark continues a rather pathetic problem but at the moment I'm too cross and cold and bored to be bothered with the thought of him – Instead, useless and unanswered thoughts of others. I think I'm going to be ill – Head heavy, funny ache and mistiness when I stoop down, nightmares. Funny, the dangerousness in dream of perfectly normal things. Last night I was perfectly terrified of falling when running away (again, running away!) down a mountain road, quite a broad road, across a chasm of which I could see very clearly three singular chateaux, the middle one of an almost apricot stucco, and two others, rather taller, red-tiled, on either side. In actual fact I am not at all afraid of mountains, never have been since ages ago in childhood I got stuck halfway up a stone quarry with Gwen Hawthorn, who negotiated it a bit better than I did, and made fun of me until I howled. This she related with great gusto to several young damsels at college but for once they took my part and begged her not to tell tales. Resultant hypodermic jab to my self-confidence must have been some use, for never since have cliffs or bridges or crannies made me feel at all ill. I remembered all this nonsense on waking out of my dream, and thought indignantly what a beast Gwen was. And it's fifteen years ago, and she has three babies and

---

* Hyde was often cutting of these contemporaries who explored style to interpret mood and reveal the individual (at the expense of event). Her preference for *The Cloister and the Hearth* (1861) by Charles Reade is for a documentary, historical epic novel that drew on original documents, as a genre mix similar to *Check to Your King,* the book she was working on at this time. However, Reade can also be seen as having let 'his passion for realistic detail at times overwhelm ... his considerable narrative powers' (Margaret Drabble and Jenny Stringer. "Reade, Charles." The Concise Oxford Companion to English Literature. 2003. *Encyclopedia. com.* http://www.encyclopedia.com Retrieved 24 June 2011.) Hyde's impatience with the moderns was an emotional response to their combination of privilege and self-revelation. Her conservative stress on materiality and privacy was also part of an evolving self-debate and discussion (particularly in letters to John A. Lee).

† The Lord be praised.

probably more to come, and I love her much better than most people, but it's an ineffectual and thwarted variety of love. Also it hasn't a logical leg to stand on. She was a vain, hard, rather shrewd, and at bottom deadly respectable little worldling, who made use of me as an audience and became fond of me against her own will and judgment. But there was a sort of beauty about her, or about an idealised picture of her, that still haunts her body now she has the reality of loveliness no longer. Still I try, in writing to her, to be as eloquent as possible. Still I want her to see the other self behind appearances. For years I wrote all my best poems to her. I don't do that any longer, but the rest is sincere enough, mostly with the sincerity of an old habit.

Night –

I'm not living up to what I promised myself when I felt well enough to make any promises about this place – I took a sort of despairing vow to become "something to be proud of". That was more than a year ago, I am 29 now, and neither physically nor mentally have I succeeded. I <u>think</u> I've written a little that is good – short stories, poems, bits in two finished books and one unfinished one. Poetry, blessed, blessed, healing poetry hasn't touched me for months, except for two prose-poems when I was re-writing "Check to your King."* Both of those seemed good – a book called "Journalese" was published – good in a superficial way. "Check to your King" seems to me alternately beautiful, and rotted to the core with sentimentalism – though I camouflaged that a good bit in re-writing it. "The Godwits Fly" certainly isn't sentimental – nor will the Stark book be so – but oh, dear Lord, just to lie still, to let the waters of dreaming take me again, deep, deep, and swirling – I trust nothing but poetry.

April 2nd

Rather curiously, on top of having read one of the new books about Freud's new book, came home and dreamed a dream in which I can't see any sexual significance.† Romantic it certainly was, but I don't see how it can be reduced to the

---

* Published by Hurst & Blackett in 1936.

† This will be one of the 'first four volumes of Freud's *Collected Papers*, which were translated by the Stracheys (James and Alix), Joan Riviere, and others, often under the supervision of [Ernest] Jones, and were published in the 1920s and 1930s in London. All four volumes

basic sexual-symbolistic terms of the psychoanalyst – any more than I can discern a sexual significance in a recent dream in which a young Dutchman handed me a very beautiful blue diamond, saying "This is the Lilac Tear."

Last night there were diamonds in the dream again, but not mine – I was living in the house of a man – not at all definite in face or any association, but young and evidently a most beloved friend of mine – who had in some way fallen foul of the law, but was not at all worried about it. The place had a distinct Lorna Doone atmosphere about it, the house, which was very large and in which I can especially remember long cellars, a stairway and folding doors, being set in the midst of silvery, reedy patches of water. These we called "meres" in the dream, and my friend had a curious pastime of jumping the stretch of water between one island and another. An older woman told me disapproving that one day he would be drowned. My friend was more than ordinarily athletic, and I had one very clear picture of him standing some little way off, his body braced splendidly for running.

I seemed to know more than he did about the network of danger surrounding this place, and to be very anxious to warn him, but not able to set about it – I was afraid of spies. A little boy, a most pathetic, ragged, stoical little scrap about five years old strayed in, and I brought him food. He was lying on a pallet bed in the lower part of the house – He was afraid that <u>his</u> enemies would find him there. My friend said that he should be safe, and picked him up in his arms, carrying him to a hiding-place which was like a sort of giant cupboard, concealed behind folding doors. I was so sorry for the little boy that I was crying, yet at the same time it seemed to me dangerous that my friend should give away his hiding-place, and I tried to warn him – But his reckless and lovable nature was not to be thwarted. Then he became involved in some enterprise of getting back diamonds that had been stolen from another woman. She did not appear on the scene, but I tried to dissuade him, together with two other people in the house, one a fair beautiful woman in a long close-fitting gown of scarlet, and wearing a golden fillet about her head. I think the other person was her husband, but am not quite sure. They first said goodbye to my friend, and

---

of the *Collected Papers* were republished in the *Standard Edition*, with corrections and improvements' Riccardo Steiner http://www.enotes.com/psychoanalysis-encyclopedia/standard-edition-complete-psychological-works Retrieved 26 June 2011. The 1934 volume included essays on 'Repression' in Ernest Jones (ed.), *Collected Papers* (London: Hogarth, 1934a), Vol. IV, 84-97, and 'The Uncanny' in Ernest Jones (ed.), *Collected Papers* (London: Hogarth, 1934b) Vol. IV, 368–408.

went, leaving me alone with him. We walked out-of-doors, across green fields, and as we went I was convinced that he was going to his death. I said, "Isn't it a pity that women must always be a drag on you? Why don't you take that horse and go over the hill, to meet the woman you haven't loved before, and smell the peat-smoke fires?" The horse, some distance away, was a fine long-maned chestnut. My friend was nearly as much distressed as I was, but not to be turned aside. I was crying bitterly, and at last he hurried away from me towards the horse. It seemed then that something very precious was being wasted and I cried out in French, "Ah, not all that – not all that –" ("Pas toute ça –"). This is the last memory before awakening – and incidentally, not by any means the first time I have talked in French in my dreams, though I am far from being a scholar especially in point of conversation.

If this were a dream, this moment, I would say, "Il vient – Presque il est ici – Qu'il serait gentil ce matin – Qu'il parlerait un petit peu avec moi – Qu'il veut me voir heureux –"*

And now that's all over – And it's enough – It always was enough – though so little – Sentimental fool – mad, mad, mad.

April 5th

Dear Dr. Tothill,

I am writing this in case anything should happen to me – sudden death, departure, disgrace. If you ever see it you'll never see me again, so I can say what I like.

I think the only happiness I have ever really had and trusted has been in knowing you. I don't mind so much that it's a phantasmal happiness, and one-sided – "For so was it not with the old love …" Read Malory's Chapter about Queen Guenevere's may morning, and you will understand –†

---

* He's coming – he's almost here – if only he'd be kind this morning – if only he'd talk to me a bit – if only he wants to see me happy.

† This is a reference to Book 19 of Malory's 'Morte D'Arthur' when Queen Guinevere, a-Maying in the woods, is captured by a Round Table knight, Sir Meliagrance, and his men, and later rescued by her lover Sir Lancelot. Many of Hyde's poems at this time and earlier used Malorian motifs and stories. Megan Clayton's argument that there 'is in Hyde's thinking a conflation of the adulterous transgressions of Malory and the transgressive nature of her feelings for Tothill' but that '[w]ithin this transgressiveness is also a feeling for Hyde of immense safety and fulfilment, an emotional space in which, perhaps because the relationship can never be consummated, there is safety and nurture and the return of the lost innocent self'

I am afraid, and of such childish things. Of <u>seeming</u> to "let you down", in the classic phrase of the Avondale Mental Hospital: of showing myself as the cheap sentimental little fool I am – "for from him that hath not shall be taken away also even that little he hath –"

Starkie is worrying me terribly – not by wanting money, (he wants that a bit too, but that merely amuses me) but by wanting all the desperate faraway things people do seem to want, like children. He wants – what do we all want? To be good, to be loved, to be worth loving. Of course he's trying to attach himself to me. Equally of course I shan't let him do so in any vital sense. But to use stern measures seems so impossible – like kicking a stray dog that <u>wants</u> to be well-groomed and beautiful and always your faithful servant – do you understand? They're all such babies, the physical and earthbound type of men. You are the only one who gave instead of taking.

I'm not going to write any more tonight – but I'll finish this letter, if it is a letter. Starkie tried to kiss me tonight. I haven't been kissed for two years. But there has been peace.

April 6th

I don't have to finish so dismally after all. I told you nearly all that was worrying me this morning, and now I'm better again. You said I could go and take tea with Starkie on Monday, and write fraternal letters if any use: whilst mentioning that Greys Avenue is sordid and I mustn't get entangled – that helps. After Monday it will be difficult to break off, but not nearly so hard as if I'd gone underground. It's rather exasperating – and yet very sweet in a queer way – that nobody in the world but you can give me peace – and now I can stop being a forlorn sort of deathbed letter to you and go on in the natural sequence of a diary. I'm happier. Every word you say means something. Thank you: and goodnight.

---

can be seen as a variant of the idea of transference. See Clayton, 'Iris, Read and Written: A New Poetic of Robin Hyde' (PhD: University of Canterbury, 2001), 167, and 'Thoroughly Modern Malory', *Lighted Windows,* 107–18.

MacMillan and Company are printing a book of my poems in their series of Contemporary Poets, which is honour and glory and even an advance on royalties of £5. But I'm so proud about it – with a rather desolate sort of pride. The poems are fiery and bitter stuff, the main theme the humanity of Christ – Book's called "Thine Accursed."* All but four were written here, when I was blind and mute and deaf with illness – didn't care for any human creature, but read over and over again the pages of "Antony and Cleopatra". That play is like G.M.T. – it all <u>means</u> something – the significance dwelt on when all the rest faded – some were later and gentler poems – But the whole book was honest and I feel now that I've done something to justify an harassed existence –

And of Starkie's book have done the first 70 pages† – I think it's going well. Is a straightforward and action-laden tale, very pitiable in places.

I've been thinking and talking long about the problems of insanity – I learned last night that the massive and half-caste Mrs Briggs, with whom I had a furious quarrel because she would stare at me in the bath, was recently an extremely violent and dangerous person, who on one occasion was removed to Park House in a strait jacket. She tips nurses into baths: physically injures the Matron (three cheers for Mrs Briggs), rips the clothes from innocent bystanders, squeezes throttles and kicks shins. All this is rendered more interesting by the fact that she now sleeps in the dormitory just over the passage, with no locks on the doors and nobody to curb her pleasures. The little night-nurse is set to polishing brass downstairs and in any case is only a trifle larger than the enormous black saucy crickets she has to chase out of the kitchen. Presumably as Mrs Briggs is here unguarded she is regarded as an extinct volcano, but to me it appears that there is a very dirty look in her eye. Poor devil – she was shut up in a room down below. She rubbed the flesh raw on her hands, her throat, her breast. I wonder if I'd have had the nerve to defy her, had I known her record? I think so – violence is only a question of letting oneself go and I could do that too – Am horribly afraid of <u>ugly</u> physical punishments like vitriol and razor-slashings and syphilis, not much of the simpler for me. But I should much prefer Mrs Briggs unarmed with even the bluntest kitchen knife and still further I'd like to go away.

I was told with virtuous horror of the case in Park House, from which Mrs Briggs

---

*   Published in London in 1934 under the title, *The Conquerors.*

†   *Passport to Hell* was the story of Douglas Stark. See p. 220 n*.

proceeds. A Mrs Bramley there is what the nurse who told me describes as a sexual maniac, which is odd because Dr. Tothill, when I accused myself of being that, said that there aren't any. However Mrs Bramley's emotions are considerably more violent than mine. She tears off her clothes if approached by the doctors – Our new Englishman, Dr. Palmer, thought by the nurses to be very green about mental hospitals (but I'm not so sure of that,) doesn't in his Park House rounds avoid Mrs Bramley as the other doctors apparently do. Consequently she has to be held by a squad of nurses to restrain her from activities, and the sub-matron, an old tartar named Redman ("Auntie") grimly informed Dr. Palmer that Mrs Bramley would insult him if she got the chance, but the nurses wouldn't let her. Query: can one insult a psychiatrist? But the point about Mrs Bramley that interested me is this. She calls Dr. Palmer either "Daddy, dear", or "Dr. Bramley". Now clearly that is the clearest possible dual indication of that "transference" that the Freudian analyst goes a-hunting – the clue to the mental labyrinth. In the "Dr. Bramley" she gives sign of that identification with herself which Freud cites as the attempt of the weak or disordered mind to attract to itself the libido or life-force of the stable one. In "Daddy, dear", she gives the clearest possible indication that she wants this identification to date back to the love of her childhood. Dr. Palmer is now the psychological father of Mrs Bramley, and one for whom she has all the respect, fear and love of which a madwoman is capable. Query: in far-gone cases, can such transference be of any use? Further query: even if it could, will they give it a chance? Oh, I wish I understood instead of groping in this blind ignorance – But the case bears out my own theory, which I worked out independently of Freud or any other. The entire native power of these broken and disconnected lives is love – when love can be evoked in them the first step has been taken. The psychiatrist who is afraid of that leech-like love must fail. He has to work straight through its embarrassing physical and emotional presentments until the clay gives way to enduring marble. Worth doing? Yes – if only because it takes courage – it is what I should have done, but am too emotional and easily swayed to do, with Gloria Rawlinson, Starkie and others.

I met another queer Avondale case, directly, this time – Ian Grant, Alison Grant's brother. Five years ago he drank himself almost to death in Sydney, slept out in parks, came back to collapse and be dragged into the asylum. He is now a tall, dark-moustached, dark-eyed young man, courteous in his manner, hopelessly erratic. His mother knew mine long ago. I ran into her by accident at Point Chevalier and had tea with the two of them.

Conversation like this: "I went out to Alison's place, and the old bull-terrier there looked terribly worried about me, wrinkled up her old nose, she knew I was in difficulties, you see – Well, I asked her what to do and she told me and we parted great friends." Not only sane, but quite charming. Then suddenly he would begin to jabber under his breath, or make some pointless incoherent yet half-reasonable remark. But it was always possible by comment or question, to bring him back to himself. He suffers terribly from restlessness. I think it is obvious that in this case two states of consciousness, very thinly divided, are in existence side by side, or rather one on top of the other. Ian Grant's surface consciousness is quite all right, able to register impressions, remember facts, argue from points – its defect is that it is worn thin, almost over mastered by the continual breaking through of the secondary and dreamlike state of consciousness (it is so diluted with ordinary consciousness that I don't think it could correctly be called subconscious or unconscious,) in which all the reasoned disorder and illogical logic of a dream can be perceived. Is this blended frontier a result of the physical impairment of his brain by alcohol and other causes? And couldn't the normal consciousness be strengthened and thickened? I would attempt this is [in] two ways – Firstly, when he makes some semi-rational remark from his secondary consciousness, I would bring this to the surface of his primary consciousness by treating it in a serious and matter-of-fact way. In this way his conscious mind would gradually cease to lend assistance to his habit of secondary-conscious-thinking, coming in the end to despise the topics fished up from this state as absurd and unimportant. Secondly, I would set him to do a series of daily "Present Exercises", that is, essays or sketches describing as minutely as possible his immediate surroundings and the happenings of the moment. "A cricket is singing – the grass is green" – it wouldn't matter how childish these products were, the diversion of attention to what was actually happening around him would draw his faculties towards the fortress of the real. I have noticed that the majority of mental cases have some desire to express themselves – If they were carefully dealt with, mightn't such "Present Exercises" tend to externalise them and take them away from the subject of their endless imaginary woes?

"Physician, heal thyself."* Goodnight –

---

* Luke 4:23.

April 12th

I feel so sick, body and mind. Just deadly sickness in the pit of my stomach and a cold numb weight upon me – So little to be sick about –

April 17th

D.K. Richmond is dead[*] – "Aunt Dollar", they used to call her in Wellington. I remember her white-haired, stoop-shouldered, with ivory face and serene eyes, right back in my childhood, the tortured childhood that is softening now into such regret. She was an artist of little note, but none the less of a sure and cultivated talent – a painter of water-colours, very good still life, and her best work, which nobody mentions, little shadowy stockyard pictures, their beasts having something of the rough pathos of the pilus in Roper's paintings.[†] But in my infancy it wasn't her paintings I liked, only her old house.[‡] This once belonged to Sir Harry Atkinson, an early Premier of New Zealand,[§] of whom the Richmonds were connections. I had been sick – as usual – and for a heavenly month we rented this place, which stood between a little half-moon named York's Bay, and high-sloping bush, full of dark little ferns and wild myrtle. It was the first really bookish house I ever inhabited – shelves and shelves of books in almost every language, out of which I particularly remember the Koran, some exquisite verses of Oscar Wilde's, and a little book written by one of the Atkinson family to this same old lady, now dead. This was the dedication –

"Love me little but love me long,
Me, little book of dolorous song –
Had my life been gladdened by sunshine of thee
My songs had been writ in a major key."

---

[*] Dorothy Richmond (12.9.1861–16.4.1935). Watercolour painter of landscapes, plants and panoramic scenes, she was a close friend of better-known painter Frances Hodgkins.

[†] Richard Roper, 1730–75, portrait painter, but particularly known for his horse, dog and dead game paintings.

[‡] Richmond's house was at York's Bay near Day's Bay in Wellington; the family probably travelled there for their holiday by boat.

[§] 1831–92, Atkinson, a Taranaki farmer and military man, was Premier four times.

I remember well the bold, high stares of portraits of military gentlemen, all scarlet coats and prominent eyes: the gentle breasts of a painted girl with a bunch of violets in the white fichu of her crisp muslin frock. In the great panelled kitchen there was a Madonna after Raphael, the child leaping in the woman's arms. Here by lamplight my lovely brittle Gwen Hawthorn and I, Gwen who is buried, buried, buried in her marriage and brats, and with all the bright gold gone from her hair, used to act the Quarrel Scene,* and act it well, too, for I was always on edge with her. There were French windows, white rambling roses without, and a little lawn haunted by a lame seagull named Balthasar. I used to lie there in the dark (darkness didn't then reduce me to utter terror,) and write the first of my poems that were any good at all – Balthasar, Gwen, my Mother, the Madonna – "Oh, where? Oh, where?"

D.K. Richmond used to paint the red-headed Atkinson children. She was kind to me, she knew I was shy, so she never made me uncomfortable or awkwardly shy. She was a beautiful sunset. I am not sorry she has died – that is "night of stars and night of love" perhaps. She never married – like me. But she didn't beat herself against the transparent cool glass.

Easter Saturday

It's untrue to say that the insane haven't any sense of humour – or of beauty – the main building seems to be overflowing just now, and in consequence some very queer apparitions are up at the Lodge – briefly, for the most part, as the grounds are so large and open that there are no real facilities for keeping much of a watch upon the very restive – no bars, no stone walls, cells or strait jackets. Just the charge nurse, whom I like very well when she doesn't shout at patients or (as she occasionally does when in the sulks) assume the appearance of a mule with a constitutional grievance. She is not temperamentally a nurse, but she has all the same shrewd commonsense and wit of the Irish peasant: a lovely fresh skin, a passion for animals and flowers, a deft way with the sick, and at times a very real tactfulness with some of the patients, not with all. If she doesn't like them or loses patience she bawls at them, exasperates them, bosses them. And we must be infernally irritating and depressing at times. Well, I like her – she doesn't listen at

---

* The scene they are acting is probably *Julius Caesar,* 3.4: the quarrel between Brutus and Cassius.

the door when the doctor's talking to me, for one thing.

Enter upon the Lodge scene, for a little while, a Mrs Fielder – big, tall, stout, short-haired, coarse-skinned, dressed in one of the awful calico nightgowns of the asylum and eternally puffing hand-rolled gaspers. Mrs Fielder wandered about night and day, peering at people. She was perfectly cheerful, but very restless. Conversation between Mrs F. and me:

Mrs F: "What were you talking about to the doctor? Were you telling him about me?"

Me: "Don't be an ass. If I started telling the doctor about other people I'd pretty soon be told to dry up. He comes to see me because he wants to know what I've got to say about myself, not about you."

Mrs F: "Yes, I suppose so, but we're all like that down here, you know. We always think they're talking about us. I've been in and out of here for twenty two years. My mother died in the big building – she was 70 then, and Dr. Beatty said it cast a gloom over the whole place when she died. She was an Englishwoman. She knocked me down, once – then my father picked me up and put me out of the window, and for a fortnight he kept me hid away from Mother. That was her punishment – Not to know if she'd killed me or not. Poor Mother! It was cruel of him, yet in a way it wasn't. My father drew the plans for the building down there, and when he'd finished he said 'It's worse than a gaol, just a big brick box, I wouldn't like to be one of the poor devils living there.' Well, I'm incurable, you know. Me mentality's all right, it's just nervous debility – I'm going to get Park House all right this trip."

She used to scare seven devils out of fat, garrulous, worrisome old Mrs Money by attempting "the laying of hands" with her, and goggling at her awful black glasses. Old Mrs Money (now gone home,) really was a pest, and Mrs Fielder kept threatening her with Park House terrors. "When they get you down there, they'll knock you about and kick you. I've seen nurses jump up and down on patients like you." (There is one nurse who knocks the patients about in Park House. I know her name, I got a good few case histories out of a little nurse who likes talking to me. And by God I'm laying for her if she ever comes up here.)

But Mrs Fielder, when I remonstrated gently with her about singing all on one awful flat note, was quite nice. "Ah, yes, my dear, beyond these voices, eh? That's my favourite book, 'Beyond These Voices.'* I read it every now and again." I haven't

---

* A late work, 1910, by popular sensationalist novelist Mary Elizabeth Braddon (1835–1915).

read Mrs Fielder's book, but I do know the line "To where, beyond these voices, there is peace." And it has an extraordinary degree of application in a lunatic's noisy world.

About a week after she arrived here, Mrs Fielder strolled out into the upstairs corridor, stark naked, a large globular white belly proudly borne before her and singing lustily. I was present, and just shut my eyes and ran. I must have some very smutty Freudian kink, I just can't bear nakedness, male or female, unless beautiful. My own I'm just as shy about as other people's. The only people I haven't minded meeting with my clothes off were (once) Harry Sweetman: and I was pretty then; and it was moonlight, and he'd never seen a naked girl before – And later Mac V.* who loved me much more physically than anyone else has ever done, with a frank hard unashamed sort of love which communicated its unashamedness to me. You can't possibly detest the memory of a man who makes love to you in broad sunlight in the middle of a golden and honey-scented field of lupins: or in the spray of a waterfall at Arthur's Pass, lying on the brown rock-hollows so that my wrists and shoulders were cut with their little sharp edges. No, Mac did really love and respect my body, which was all the pleasanter of him seeing I had been for years a cripple when he met me.

Mrs Fielder was moved down to F. Seven (Female Admission Ward in the Main building.) Probably she'll get to Park House all right. At the present time the Lodge houses one woman whom everybody calls Kathleen (because she's foreign and no one can pronounce her name) and who returned to sanity after three years in Park House – three years as a raving lunatic. She is the kindest thing, but fat and thick-skinned, as so many of them are – My own skin was horrible for a while, and I have seen most unwholesome complexions and rashes come out of the Main Building. Kathleen lies curled up on a bench, fat, sleepy, kindly. It must be a queer world for her – she's frightened and doesn't want to go out – the doctor is trying to urge her into it probably fearing that if she stays here she'll slip back again. For three years she has lived on the sole diet of Park House – unsavoury minced meat dished up in a greasy stew, eaten with spoons. No knives or forks allowed. Those who believe in the mental stimulus of a careful diet would be greatly interested in the diet-sheets of

---

* Henry McDonald Vincent (known as 'Mac') 'was the last editor of the *Christchurch Sun* which ceased publication in 1935' (*Iris*, 130 n†). Hyde had a 'brief love affair' with him during the three happy months in early 1939 that she worked on the *Sun*. Challis suggests that her affair with Vincent prevented a proposal of a marriage from John Schroder, also working on the *Sun* (*Iris*, 133).

the really insane. At the Lodge it's not bad, though monotonous – But three years on that hash! No wonder her skin is coffee-coloured – Park House bed cases are full of scabies.

And locked up in one of the single rooms of "that dolent city"* is a fifteen year old girl, Mavis Skinner, who was up here, pink cheeked and quite cheerful, a few months ago. She went away from the asylum altogether. Hung about till they took her back. Was at the Lodge, rather rebellious but certainly not insane, till sent down to F. 7. for a quarrel in which she slapped the face of another child patient. I believe that in F.7. she behaved very well, and came back to the Lodge looking fit.

She was sent down again for hanging around a conceited youth named Richardson, who comes up from one of the men's wards to do some gardening here at times – Now, apparently out of sexual control, she's in Park House, locked up when the doctors pass through lest her sexuality take some outrageous form. She is wasting physically, less than six stone now. I can only know these things blindly, as facts, not as cause and effect sequence. But this I do know. Love is the psychopath's God and Devil. Love saves or destroys. I should

[The next page has been removed either by Iris herself, which seems unlikely, or by the Rawlinsons. A reason to support the latter view is that Hyde's references to problems of love and psychopathology more than once include the example of Rosalie. See above, p. 233, where Hyde seems to be suggesting that the Rawlinsons' love was 'leech like' and unhealthy and needed handling in the way a good psychiatrist would handle obsession and longing in a patient, converting it to a positive. A missing page in *A Home in this World* occurs at a similar juncture.]

But, my dear and useful Mr Freud, take the case of the little girls to whom this enlightenment either comes not at all, or is so driven into the wilderness by the ban upon talking, thinking, asking about sex that she never quite accepts it† – The little girl without brothers in a house where the presiding spirit, far from putting woman

---

* A reference to Dante's *Inferno* – she uses the phrase similarly in the '1934 Autobiography', see p. 126 n*.

† Hyde's example here draws on herself and her own family. She uses Freudian terminology to re-tell her family story and to *explain* her own 'single-ness' and 'aberrant' sexual life. Alison Hunt summarises the argument as being about a mother's class ambition serving to alienate her daughter from herself: 'When a working-class mother assumed a bourgeois sensibility, she denied her children the peer-disseminated sexual enlightenment, which amongst the true bourgeoisie found a substitute in professional sex education.' (Hunt, 'Cage', 216).

in a position of inferiority, is triumphantly female: a strong-willed Mother, weak-willed Father, sexual taboos. Very well: we now have the <u>active</u> stage of the girl's sexual life indefinitely prolonged – and I do indeed believe that in cases where no sort of sexual perversion takes place – I am most certainly not a lesbian – still that <u>active</u> attitude, when the little girl grows up, creates a certain amount of resentment in the male, who is accustomed to passivity in women, though in that very quality of passivity lies his almost invariable sexual disappointment.

In the course of her childhood and adolescence, the little girl who literally hasn't grown up suffers the tortures of the damned. She passes the period when minor sexual freedoms were commonplace among other children, as they are round about the age of four or five. Her modesty and shame, backed up by the taboos enforced upon her by her Mother, isolate her entirely from the world of youth. She sees herself as a criminal among normal people – always different, and always longing to be as they are! Actually she has a hundred times their innocence. The very perception of sexual differences which has reduced other girls to Freud's passive state of development has lowered sexuality in their eyes. They talk a great deal about the birth of babies, menstruation, and, make no mistake about it, the sexual act itself: all with pitiful ignorance and lack of vision. The little pariah who doesn't quite understand what they are talking about hangs on the fringes, catches a word here and there, runs away, frightened, if she hears too much. I suppose in better-class homes, physical and mental training help her, she is more constantly under medical or educational supervision. But I'm inclined to think the brotherless girl with a dominating and sexually narrow mother always has an appalling time.

Apart from her own hidden torture of passion, she has an infinite sense of loss. This is simple enough. She <u>has</u> lost something – the Father-love which Freud reckons as the basis of her psychological life. Perhaps in some cases she can transfer this to the Father-image of God. But here the sense of sin comes into sharp conflict with the longing for love. God, as taught to children, is pre-eminently the sin-chastiser, not the lover. She shrinks from him, sometimes hates Him –

The whole motive of her life is longing. When at last she comes in contact with men, she (unless she <u>is</u> a sexual pervert, and I'm inclined to think that the pervert's mechanism is quite different) seeks eagerly, too eagerly, for "that which was lost." You will find this type of girl looking for the society of older men, not of the boys who are her own age. Why? Isn't it because she wants the Father and the God she has never truly known? She is sentimental, subject to attacks of hero-worship: while the others, safe in their glass case of sexual passivity, tinkle with that cool and frosty laughter which men call "youth" – until they have been married to it for a few years. Meanwhile the outsider is only too ready in her physical surrender – once learning the possibilities of relationship with men (she, in her dissimilarity, has never been happy in relationships with other women) she is eager to give physically. But some part of her mental or spiritual make-up isn't "feminine". Men sense this without understanding it, and resent it. Not realising the "inferiority" of feminine sexuality, she has grown up, warped perhaps by suffering, the psychological equal of the male. It is because men are unused to this equality that they resent it. Their resentment is purely sexual, neither mental nor physical. Physically the love-chance of this type of girl is much the same as any other woman's – mentally, men find her stimulating, and are apt to reveal themselves freely to her. It's in the formation of an abiding sexual link that their distrust comes to the surface. They resent the passive woman for her passivity: they resent the active woman because she isn't passive. It must be understood that as far as relations with men are concerned, the word "active" is used in its psychological sense only – I should think that physically the woman always follows the lead of the man –

[2 further pages torn out]

April 25th

Tired to death again, and worried over money, or lack of it – being a spendthrift in a small way has its depressing features at times. However, I've finished the book about Starkie – I think I'll call it "Crime-Sheet" – and like the Lord on the Seventh day of Creation, I find it good, in spots, anyhow. I look an old woman. That's worry, lack of love, lack of sense, lack of care. Feel too spent to worry much about the little I could do to improve morale, but oh, dear Helen, Cleopatra, Elizabeth Arden and Lilly of Bloomsbury Street, how I should wallow in a long soothing course of massage, hair shampoo, manicures, Turkish baths – everything that makes the body feel and look alive –

"Now let the stricken deer go weep,
The hart ungalled play –"

I am one day going to write a venomous story about ungalled hearts. Meanwhile have reverted to "The Godwits Fly" and finished Chapter Nine tonight. I don't know if it will ever be published though.

April 26th

Still feeling very sick and dejected. Money didn't turn up, whereat I wept – foolishly, for I can and must contrive. Have written an article about D.K. Richmond as one way of restoring financial stability. * Oh, dearie me! The Matron also is now prowling about like a cooly of Midian showing somebody over the Lodge. She never comes in here and when we meet we cut one another as dead as sausages, like Smith and Brown upon their turtle and oyster island. I suppose when you dislike a person greatly, you become a sort of magnet for all the unpleasant things connected with the same. She probably considers me a lazy slut because I write instead of polishing the floors for her, and I consider her a fiend. There was a woman in Park House, a really nasty woman I believe, but since she's in the refractory ward of a Mental Hospital surely sick enough to be held irresponsible – This lady foully abused the Matron in Sergeant-Major terms some months ago. For weeks no nurse was allowed ever to speak to her, so that she got solitary confinement to an extent which wouldn't be permitted in any gaol. Source of information, one of the nurses who got blasted for passing the time of day with this unfortunate. Unfortunate is now on good-behaviour, solitary confinement thus permitted to be brightened up by an occasional "Howdy?" from a nurse.

Dreamed about home and Dr. Buchanan – sadly, vividly – Mother was doing something, I forget what, which would make it impossible for me ever to go home again – At first I was indignant. Then I made up my mind that she could go ahead and do it, I knew I wasn't wanted. Told Dr. Buchanan about it, crying. He very nice, told me I wasn't really in a lunatic asylum. Me, "Oh, but I've been in the Wolfe Home" – True, but a late date to weep about it in my dreams. Surely all this secret sorrow can't be just because 30/- hasn't turned up. I am very tired and sleep little. Like the widow of the Chinese gentleman "She wishes she were those two yellow birds, that fly across the house-tops."

---

* Hyde's only income over the years in the Lodge was from freelance journalism and other publications.

Haven't heard for long from Rosalie or Gloria Rawlinson. Still in Wellington. Would rather like to do so.

April 29th

I love you, with all the stupid useless love of which I am capable. I suppose you know it, but I'll never put it into words so it can't hurt you. But all the time I'm torn with the dread of losing the little I do see of you altogether – you might go elsewhere, or I be sent away. Five minutes in a day, sometimes less – But when I don't see you, all the rest is dust and ashes. Today I didn't think you'd be here so I went out, and you did come up with my manuscript and looked for me.* There you are, such nonsense to cry about it – I <u>know</u> you'll come tomorrow but I'm afraid in case you mightn't, mightn't ever come back at all. If I could only be a man, and your servant. You're my captain, which is more than any man has ever been – it's not only that I <u>will</u> do what you tell me, but that I <u>can</u> do what you tell me. There is nothing whatever servile about it, nor even very weak – You can't say I ever embarrass you – But there is a great and not very well understood power attached to obedience within freewill – one can be what one is not. I believe I could be physically brave for you, and I'm an awful coward about pain really – Only this fear – it is weakness – that I might not see you again. I ought to be able to survive on and for the idea of you, but oh, it's been only shadows for so many years – <u>You're</u> not shadowy to me – I call you my one clear face – you make all the rest recede and fade, even what I have loved very dearly.

Goodnight. I prayed that you may come tomorrow. Perhaps you won't, or perhaps you don't like my manuscript at all and are going to be cross with me for writing it, or perhaps you'll just look round the door and then go away again – But that would still be better than being with anyone else in the world – So perhaps at least I shall see you –

---

* She is probably referring to the manuscript of what was to be *The Godwits Fly*, as the manuscript of *Passport to Hell* was already with the publisher.

April 30th

Give way to restlessness, to an empty heart's disquiet –
Haply he will not come this way again
There are so many roads. What new thing shall you show him?
Curve of pine-bough, or the strung, separate drops of rain,
Or a frost-white sun in the clearing that else were dim?
There is a well in the shadows – none shall drink there but him.

What is your world, that narrows between two pine folds,
Strong hands cupping the breasts of a nameless sea?
Naught save the place of the lost and the hunted down,
Rustlers of leaves, the thralls of a wary destiny –
Shall he be held of the towers where no light sings?
There is a wounded bird. His hand shall gift it with wings.*

May 12th

I haven't written for many days – too weary except at intervals too sick of myself. Rosalie and Gloria back from Wellington, better at ease I think, and settled into a little flat in Princes street, where once I lived at an awful den called "Burwood".† They both look fresher and gayer. Gloria and I have arranged the verses for a little book of children's poems, which Beula Hay is to illustrate – I think we're going to try if Angus and Robertson will publish it for Christmas.‡ Gloria has the proofs of her English book of poems§ – I still think them very good indeed. They are a happy menage just now – but lack their large ginger cat Freddy who is out on loan or hire with relatives.

---

* 'The Well in the Forest', *Young Knowledge,* 167.

† 'Burwood' was one of the merchants' houses by then used as boarding houses, on the corner of Alfred and Princes Streets, now the site of the Auckland University library. The Rawlinsons' flat was opposite the Northern Club on the corner of Princes Street and Waterloo Quadrant – where a high-rise hotel has stood since the 1960s.

‡ This collection, called 'Littlest Moon' in her list on the next page, was never published.

§ Gloria Rawlinson, *The Perfume Vendor* (London: Hutchinson & Co, 1935).

I have just finished "The Godwits Fly" and am not a bit sure of it, except for the ending, which is rather lovely. But a plague on introspection. The wench in the book sort of talks her way through a no doubt admiring but long-suffering world. Yet there are good bits and true in it, and I think I shall risk being badly snubbed by sending it to Watt's.

My five years' or five months literary plan then is this :

"Thine Accursed", book of poems, accepted by MacMillan's –

"Check to Your King", biography of Baron de Thierry, entered for Atlantic Monthly's competition –

"Unicorn Pasture", collection of short stories, (good) publisher needed –

"Bronze Outlaw", biography of Starkie, entered for Houghton-Mifflin literary award –

"The Godwits Fly", novel, publisher needed – and I mayn't ever get one –

"The Littlest Moon", children's verses – to be sent to Angus and Robertson's –

"Bronze Outlaw"* is certainly the best, in prose – not uneven or rambling, as most of my stuff is. It is, however, sordid. Starkie asked me to marry him. I refused by letter, not without a certain amount of purely speculative regret. I mean, it might have been an adventure to marry Starkie. (He'd wring my neck inside a month – just as well for I hate to think what would certainly occur inside ten months if he didn't! However, I am not going to marry him.)

I want next to write two things. A novel of early New Zealand history called "These Poor Old Hands,"† and much more important, a history of the Maori Kings and the Mau Movement in Samoa. That should really count. I'm going to tackle the problem straight away – must try to get in touch with Father McKeefry again and also with George Graham the Maori interpreter. Oh the colour, the pride and the endeavour that are lost between the folded pages of history! Besides, the subject has a more vital importance than the historical one. How do the native races, in subjection, attempt to catch up with the white rulers? What are their independent or semi-independent movements towards a civilization of their own? In this lies a great deal of the probable fate of white dominance – but none of the fools can see it – I told Rosalie but she didn't even catch a glimpse of what I was getting at. Perhaps it

---

* This was an earlier title of *Passport to Hell*.

† This manuscript has never been located.

is madness to even dream of a possible progress and growth among the children of Ham. I'm going to try, anyhow. Am losing my old fear that other people can do these things better than myself, as I see more and more of their self-satisfied inertia – I know I'm an uneven unfinished and emotional sort of writer, but they –

"They use the snaffle and the curb, all right –
But where's the bloody horse?"*

I had a charming letter from an old Polish Professor of Philosophy, one Wincenty Lutoslawski.† How intricate and fascinating the jumble of unpronounceable letters on his envelope, and the blue stamp with the imperialistic-looking eagle! He sent me his portrait – white bearded kindly old gentleman – and that of his youngest daughter Tania who looks like one of Felix Salten's wild brown rabbits. Shall write to him often – His portrait now stands between Vicki Baum's and one of Russell Flint's illustrations to Malory Percival's sister cutting off her long blond hair. He should be comfortable enough there.

Nice child named Mary Smee‡ has presented me with a huge bundle of clippings and plants for my little garden – nerines, tiger-lilies, all sorts and conditions of things – must put them in this afternoon. I wish Dr. Tothill would come.

I read Upton Sinclair's "Journal of Arthur Stirling" with more liking and sympathy than I ever felt for any other book of his. Probably because of the subject. Arthur Stirling was an

[Page torn out]

---

* From 'On Some South African Novelists' (l. 3–4) by South African poet Roy Campbell (1902–57). Kingsley Amis (ed.), *The New Oxford Book of English Light Verse* (Oxford: Oxford University Press, 1978). http://quotes.dictionary.com/they_use_the_snaffle_and_the_curb_all Retrieved 8 July 2011.

† Polish philosopher (1863–1954). His *Pre-existence and Reincarnation* was published in 1928.

‡ Mary Smee, later Mary Dobbie (1913–2009) became a prominent Auckland social campaigner and advocate for women and children. 'As a young reporter on Auckland's weekly *Observer*, she managed to escape the fate of most woman journalists – being confined to the society columns – and was shown the basics of news gathering by Robin Hyde.' Christine Cole Catley, Obituary, *NZ Herald*, 20 June 2009 http://www.nzherald.co.nz/nz/news/article.cfm?c_id=1&objectid=10579592

And from her sandhills, tautly strung
As some great harp's unheeded chord,
Moans the harsh passion-music, wrung
In drops of blood to please my Lord

Where soon by dewfalls other soil
Knits under glass to kindly clod,
My every sand grain separate flames,
A burning-glass to draw down God

That I may feel His lean flames run
Beneath my breasts, between my flanks
And all the dark disturbed in me
Take life at last, to shout Him Thanks.

But great as clouds and kind as vale
Moves Hagar ever in my sight,
The dark unvext and simple loam
In which men build their race aright

Ploughman and harvester in turn
Have known her wealth since time began,
And from her breasts the rivers run
That comfort yet the child in man.

A curse on crying lambs, on foals
Like wind – thoughts sheathed in sorrel silk,
On the fresh hayfields nourishing
The deep old udders dropping milk

For shut within her, Abram's dream
Unfolds its limbs, grows fierce and tall
And of that passive flesh he moulds
His heir the individual

247

Ah, let Thy livid torrents slake
The land named Sarah! Let some wild
Eclipse of reason plant in me
The overthrow of Hagar's child!*

Robin Hyde[†]

May 15th

Three hours of crouching on stairway in draught, likewise in very thin, very shabby mauve silk pyjamas. Reason not positive dementia, but sudden inability to bear the noises of my fellow-creatures, as heard through doors and windows, even one minute longer without screaming. If I screamed I'd be reckoned mad and sent to the Main Building – but isn't it just slightly eccentric to keep the radio blaring from 9am to 9pm, every single day, in a home for the treatment of nervous disorders? The extraordinary theory is that it cheers patients up, and so it does, all except me and one or two others – les misérables – Further Eileen Nelas outside my window and Peggy Stewart ditto want to know in their flat hard voices if I've ever been lo-o-ownly, if I've ever been bloo-oo-oo – And that prodigious policeman's wife by name MacMullan, in a garment like an Axminster carpet, prowls up and down outside for hours like a bloody panther only not velvety as to paw. All this is accentuated by the fact that I've been sent to bed for a few days because I look exhausted and ought to rest – I am exhausted, but oh, dear Lord, their crackles and rumbles and maladjusted octaves exhaust me more. Therefore I adjourned to the stairs and held a little private prayer meeting or even commination service,[‡] at which I have caught a

---

* Sarah the wife of Abraham offered her handmaiden, Hagar, to her husband as a second wife; however, when Hagar became pregnant she treated Sarah with contempt. After consultation with her husband, Sarah banished Hagar, but Hagar was visited in the desert by an angel who told her to return to Sarah and Abraham's house, where she bore Abraham's first son Ishmael (Genesis 16:1–16).

† This is the poem titled 'Sarah' (*Persephone*, 26; *Young Knowledge*, 182) but missing its first two stanzas, perhaps because of a page torn out. Hunt's description ('Cage', 311) reads 'undated March'.

‡ Commination (Church of England): a recital of prayers including God's judgments against sinners.

cold. Seriously, I hope it develops into double pneumonia and kills me – I have done a good deal of work – And I am utterly unwanted, and very tired.

Seriously also, one day some psychologist will really concentrate on the problem of the nervous affection caused by sound. Considered as a bar between human beings, it's so much greater a disability than deafness. I can like these people and be passionately indignant for them, and even practically decent when they look woebegone – But when they're making and causing their usual lusty cheerful rows, the ends of my nerves are little twisted tatters and I don't want to live. That's why I so loved the Waitomo Caves, especially the glow-worm grottoes – the utter silence, the utter, unthinkable, black and healing silence. I felt there as if all the tendrils of my mind, having been crushed down with a weight of noise and vexation like some huge stone, began to lift themselves up in the darkness, tenuous as those pearly threads on which the glow-worms themselves hung suspended, gleams of fiery blue against the old, old blackness. I behaved absurdly, under cover of the dark. Cupped the brackish cave-water in my hands and drank it seven times in honour of Dis, Lord of Shadows. Considered toppling over into the river but knew they'd fish me out, and probably slay the glow-worms with flaring torches – So it lies behind – I have written a story called "Six Pomegranate Seeds"* which is really about the velvety peace of that place, but doesn't say so.

There's one great compensation in the last two days of bed and brain-fatigue – I am able to write poetry again. Have written two verses, "Sarah" and "Truce on the Ark", and am besieged by ideas for more – I might have known it. I lie here aching with loneliness and with that old incurable longing – the real cause I suppose of the vexatiousness of little things – and then can write a poem.

May 17th

Much better tonight, though still cross and, getting up after only three days in bed, peculiarly shaky. But I put in all my little rock-plants and herbs, though the garden looks like sticky wet porridge. I suppose that's about half a good deed for the day. My South African honey flower tree is blooming – two daphne trees on the very point of it, and I felt a queer thrill when on looking at the green sheath of

---

* An unpublished short story, see p. 209 n*.

plant I beheld, folded up, the buds of the first white narcissus. The tiny garden is abnormally slow, too shady and soil unspeakable, and in winter, being on a slope, just soggy with wetness. My cinerarias look all right, however, and I have planted scores of other things. The desperate part is that I'm not at all sure I haven't planted about a hundred chives in the middle of the first flower-bed. Little bulbs on one end, narrow green pipes on the other. But surely Mary Smee wouldn't give me a <u>hundred</u> chives? All the other little things were printed [*sic*] with great lack of discrimination, but perhaps they'll do – My pansies look very dwarfish and low, like Hermeia [?], and none of the latest batch of St. Brigid anemones have as yet come up – I can't get over a wretched feeling that I planted them upside down. However will know in time. Wallflowers, Canterbury bells, a few little gaillardias and Mother's orange lily have taken. I have discovered a filthy trick on the part of Macky's the nursery men. Having bought several flowering shrubs from them, the roots carefully done up in sacking, I was curious to know why they never flowered after the first show, nor put forth leaves. It is quite simple. The poor things never had any roots at all. They have been selling lusty flowering branches as trees. This was the case with a solandrum uniflora and a pink azalea I bought from them, and I think it is a really low and mean proceeding. Somehow one feels human dirtiness oughtn't to extend to plants and flowers.

Yesterday, having cried nearly all day because of the radio and general iniquities, was rewarded by a rather curious hallucination – waves and waves of light and colour, mostly pale gold, pouring across the room, and seeming to emanate from my own head – The waves started in a sort of jet, which seemed to occur at intervals of about five seconds – rather like a cuttlefish throwing out ink, to use an inelegant simile for something that wasn't forbidding to look at. However, after a time the passing of the colour-waves from my forehead and before my eyes started to cause me discomfort, so I fought against it, turned over, read a book, until it went away – now what's the <u>good</u> of mentioning anything like that to a doctor? Dr. Tothill told a visiting man, Dr. Marshall, that I had "a very true realisation of what <u>is</u> unreal", but I can't stop things from going on just because I know they can't possibly be really happening – And, especially with voices, it takes time and cautious enquiry to find out what was real and what wasn't, for as far as my own experience goes, things said are very seldom utterly fantastic or unconvincing – From Palmerston North* I can

---

* Hyde was in hospital in Palmerston North in 1926, following the loss of her baby Robin. See

recall long conversations which I know to have been unreal, and yet some of them were so much out of character with anything I would be likely to say, and so truly in character with the natures of the persons who seemed to say them that I just can't see how I could have imagined them. However – useless to reflect on this.

June 2nd

Too disheartened over stupid little things to write for a long while – But now I have several blessings for which to thank the Lord – or not the Lord. Getting on well with "These Poor Old Hands."* I'll have to rewrite some of "The Godwits Fly", I'm not quite sure how or why it dissatisfies me, but it just does, except the first book and the very small one which is at the end.† The ending is really good, I think, and the whole book mustn't be wasted. However, for the second time I have put it aside for further reflection and gone on with a simpler theme, and luckily, as to the simpler theme, ça marche –

Little things more promising too – The Railways magazine has ordered a series of articles, just travel, at the amazing figure of £2/10/- each, which sounds too good to be true.‡ I'd have done them for £1, and cheered. The story called "God Rest You, Merry Gentlemen" won the Auckland Star's competition, which is not much of a competition nor yet much of a prize, but they did print it very nicely and on reading the last paragraph I wept again as I did when writing it.§ Then discovered that by dint of being sent to bed for a week and feeling very haggard and sick, I could write poems again, two really good – As soon as I have finished "These Poor Old Hands," I'm going to try for a month in bed.

On the strictly personal side, it's an enormous relief that tonight the Matron has rescinded the order by which my little night nurse had to ring every half hour from the office, which is directly under this room, to tell the Main Building all is well. It started because she (the matron) saw or thought she saw a Mrs Kemp, who is

---

'1934 Autobiography' Chapter 15, p. 121.

* This manuscript has never been located.

† This was the first draft of the novel.

‡ These articles were probably a series on travelling north of Auckland published in the *New Zealand Railways Magazine* in May, June and August 1935.

§ Published in two parts, *Auckland Star,* 28 and 29 May 1935, 17 and 20.

supposed to be suicidal, standing by one of the windows. Just how ringing the Main Building every half hour from downstairs can safeguard Mrs Kemp, who sleeps upstairs, I cannot say. Indeed it would seem to give her more opportunity, the nurse being thus regularly out of the way. However – two nights and I was a wreck, so were most of the others. Last night nurse Lovell didn't do it till the night charge came up and told her she must. Then I burst into tears – unnecessary for now unless the Matron changes her mind again it's all over and done with.

Had delightful and interesting letter from Jimmie Bertram who is at Oxford, and whom I have never met in the flesh, which may be why he is so extremely nice to me.* I am going to write him something about the size of a young Bible as soon as I revive.

Dr. Tothill not up so much, but just the same when he is. I hope he does not imagine me to be as much of a fool as I really am. Probably he does. In any case, I don't think he resents it. Had a row with a wench who would run an alarm clock outside my window and asked him to move me down to the Main Building, very stammery but not mentioning why. He was gentle, which is more than I would have been in the same circumstances.

Met Ronald Holloway and Aroha Hardcastle last night. Proposed to them we should get up a procession to walk down Queen Street at a given date, rending our garments, beating our breasts, and crying "Yerps! Yerps! Yerps!" That being our view as a whole of the modern world and its peoples. They accepted, and we tried it out walking up by Grafton cemetery. It is surprising what a good street cry the word "Yerp" makes, if the constabulary had been about their business it is unthinkable that we shouldn't have been arrested. Ronald and Aroha have a friend, Terence Morgan, who makes outré masks – should like to meet him, there is something very satisfying about mask-making.

---

* James Bertram (1910–93) was a New Zealand journalist and academic, and author of *Crisis in China* (1937) and *North China Front* (1939). He later (1939 in London) became a friend of Hyde and she consulted him on his experience in China (where amongst other things he interviewed 'Mao Tse-tung in Yan'an' and 'travelled for five months with the Eighth Route Army in north China') when working on the final draft of her China book, *Dragon Rampant*. http://www.teara.govt.nz/en/biographies/4b27/1 Retrieved 8 July 2011.

June 13th

I can see – a poem to be called "Chariot Wheels",* all but the last of it in blank verse and rhyming verse. The theme, the age-long defence of the city named Melchek – slaves in the stable-yards –

"Where the innumerable armies
Sand-grain on sand-grain, locust on locust pour,
Where the ponies' hoofs are fire on the ringing sands,
And ever the marge† of the waste is blackened against the coming
Of the new, the far-born hosts –"

And an old man who leads his tattered little host into the courtyard. They ask him if he is friend or foe – he answers "I am for peace against the gates of Hell."

The same in the Middle Ages. The chariot wheels suddenly commanded to halt. Men stop – they hear nothing but the beating of the human heart and the song of a lark threading its way into the abyss – nothing, nothing. The water of the wheels closes above them in an iron sea – .

"I am for peace against the gates of Hell.

July 29th

[This entry, which appears to be mostly quotation,s is written at this stage in the book but it is dated after the final entry 'July 28th' below: Iris must have left blank pages that she came back to for this entry.]

There is a stage at which man is sexually a child. He takes and breaks, without any intelligence of appreciation, and with no knowledge of his own spiritual chemistry, by the reagents of which he might produce rare and beautiful qualities in another

---

* The lines quoted here also exist on a page of manuscript, untitled, which is the start and apparently all that survives of the poem first planned as 'Chariot Wheels' but which became a play in three acts – unpublished, two typescripts (MS-Group-1648, Alexander Turnbull Library). The play has 'a first act set in the ancient Near East that culminates in the arrival of the peace-bringer, an old man who momentarily stops the roar of war chariots getting ready to mount a last defence of the besieged city of Melchek'. See Leggott, *Victory Hymn*, www.nzepc.auckland.ac.nz/nzauthors/hyde; 'Introduction', *Young Knowledge,* 16; *Iris*, 288).

† Archaic – a margin.

person. He is at this time sexually destructive, and, like the child, lashes himself into a frenzy of boredom. It is only when he emerges into the constructive stage that he has any prospect of enduring as an entity neither purely mental nor purely physical, but both – For until that time comes, his desires are his own distaste.

The man who binds another person is himself a slave, in the only true sense of the word. For he exhibits fear and respect of bonds.*

The man is right who follows his vision, no matter where it may take him: for it has taken him onward. But that vision must be not what he wishes and not what he hopes – only what he knows from beyond himself.

Courtesy is the father of the virtues, and shall sit at the head of the wise man's table.

The man who has learned to be a courteous friend, that man has not learned to betray any human creature, man or woman.

I have two arguments against war: they are my two hands. While I can use them to build, I am pledged against destruction –

But though the hands be maimed and the eyes blinded, yet every woman has one argument against war, and it is deeper within her than words. For this is her womb. While she can bear a child into this world, how shall she say, "Slay on?"

That love is best which is grounded in friendliness: for friendliness is made out of patience, and of sharing things together: of listening with understanding, of speaking quietly.

[A list of chapters of 'The Unbelievers' follows, topics on recto and versos not reproduced here, and finally a passage from this novel (on verso).]

---

* Could be from Yogic scriptures – *Leaves of Morya's Garden – Book 2 – Illumination (1925):*
'One must manifest discipline of spirit; without it one cannot become free. To the slave discipline of spirit will be a prison; to the liberated one it will be a wondrous healing garden. So long as the discipline of spirit is as fetters the doors are closed, for in fetters one cannot ascend the steps.' http://www.agniyoga.org/ay_lomg2.html Retrieved 8 July 2011.

July
[verso p. 83]

Echo

Throughout her life, Echo found that as soon as she got to prison there was an immediate move on the part of the M.O.'s* to segregate her, put her to bed, and stand over her, arguing thickly (sometimes with the aid of cigarettes in red sevenpenny packets, which they offered her to make her feel at home.) This was not only because of Echo's rather willowy physical aspect and the pale green of her eyes (which lent colour to the idea that she might have a case of arrested development,) but because doctors, owing to their long association with unmitigated human bodies, are profoundly lonely creatures. Echo provided them with an emotional outlet.

It was not so much that Echo collected strange things, as that strange things collected her – temporarily, casually. One odd little incident after another took her to itself, elucidated itself in a moment of fear and wonder or startling beauty, then, with a brusque kiss between her eyes, released her – She often felt, a little resentfully, that the odd was simply making a convenience of her.

"This street", she thought, "Loneliness – the grey day – it's my tumbril,† the guillotine's at the end of it. It gives me a motive for keeping my chin up." The idea pleased her, and she swaggered a little, looking sideways to admire the panache of her orange feather in various shop windows.

Socialist Sunday Schools – old Russian interpreter – Galupchik – Downstairs in Little Grey Home – the glow-worms – Aroha's cherry orchard – Mick's nudist Negro wedding – England – passport diapers – frozen mutton – the Italians fling down their arms – will the Ethiopians let them? Life from a poached egg – The blind man and the Eastern dress – Samoa and Pacifism.

Roxanne and the sea-anemones – she thought, "They are not weak, they are strong – they yield, but they are strong with a mighty force of colour and reasoned movement, of taking what they want and rejecting what they do not like. I could do worse than be a sea-anemone."

Inanahi.

---

* Medical Officers.

† A farm cart for carrying dung, of the kind that tips back to off-load its cargo: a cart of this sort was used to carry prisoners to the guillotine during the French Revolution.

~~Airene~~ – Ronald had caught her as she fell over the cliffs of reality into madness. As she was now, she was not only a new person, but a new species of person.

The marriage in the cave on Aüe – Ronald in the air. The tow-headed bitch and bloody Mary. The sacrifice.

The great hollow sententious voice of the wireless – rumbling from the belly of civilisation – anyone, hearing it, could guess at once that America is dyspeptic right through to her soul.

The winnowing of wings in the dusk, under pine-trees – cockchafers, bronze-green, making a noise like little fierce scythes, and the lay of the lamplight falling before them as they crashed into Echo's shoulders. Contrary to the beliefs of scientists about women, Echo rather liked the electric tickling of the cockchafer's legs.*

Sunday Night
10 P M.
July 28th 1935

I haven't written in this as a diary or notebook for months and months. And did you ever see such a disconnected sentimental pack of nonsense? But tonight, and in fear of what the morrow may bring forth – (as usual!)

The other day you looked terribly tired: and you said you hated pettiness – So do I. "Take us the foxes, the little foxes, that spoil the grapes!" But one has to be afraid of the pettiness in one's self as well – or I do, anyhow. And now I am afraid my vineyard is all foxes, and the foxes of the neighbouring vineyards are fighting with them, and something must be done, or all will be spoilt –

Am idiotically and hatefully sensitive to ugly sounds. Now on the verandah an orchestra of one mouth organ, one harp, starts up in the early evenings – I can't work, think or settle against it – I have tried twice to walk it off. The first time, Saturday night, was rather lovely in a fantastic way. I walked along towards Avondale from the bottom of this road, bareheaded, and the rain simply streamed down, silvery-black, leaping, living rain. There are pine-needles and blue-gum leaves and I put some down in front of my dress as I once used to do to remind me I'd spend the evening

---

* This passage follows on from a list of chapters planned for 'The Unbelievers' and appears to be notes/draft about its protagonist and plotline. It suggests a parallel with Hyde's reception by her doctors following her initial collapse but not described elsewhere.

with Haroun, who is dead – "Grief goes over" – but what if it leaves nothing at all but emptiness, loneliness, longing?

At all events, you and nobody else at all have given me peace: for which I do thank you, living or dead. And "peace with honour" – since I came under your care, I haven't broken my word.

It seems so useless to talk. I feel that all these little things – little people – are driving me to take false steps, manoeuvring me into false positions. If I ignore them they have the weapon of their noises, they can ruin my work – If I don't, it means dragging you into it and perhaps you'll see me after that as one of a pack of quarrelsome women. God knows. Yet I've nothing to offer, in return for all you have done for me, except my work. It seems to me that has to be protected – so I have to take risks, to abandon the human discretion of not making a fuss. It's very queer to love anyone as much as I do you – and in so many different ways. Through my work, through the deepest possible sense of reserve and confidence, even through a kind of humour. I like you to laugh at me – to see the funny side – it makes me feel befriended. And yet the laughter of others can leave me raw – a ridiculous limping figure.

All poets and artists were, though – Think of Swift with the wen on his furious nose: and little mincing Pope: and Byron gone fat, and George Eliot achieving matrimony after all, and Charlotte Mew* committing suicide in a lunatic asylum: and Iris Wilkinson, or Robin Hyde, shrinking into a burrow because of a mouth-organ and a harp and a few cheap superficial judgments. Little queer poets as well as great ones. But I doubt that many of them had peace, as whatever the petty tempests outside, I have had from your unselfish kindness.

I shan't die (willingly) unless I lose that peace – unless the funny little figure obscures the other whose work you have helped. I couldn't bear that – to look at you, and know that you found me dull and tiresome, just another mosquito persecutor – couldn't and wouldn't bear it.

There is something of the work I wanted to do in "The Unbelievers". It is unfinished, but may be publishable if anything happens to me – I'd love you to read it, if you're not sick of reading my books. You're to come into a chapter that is not

---

* Charlotte Mew (1869–1928), English writer, who 'presses her private experiences of pain into the service of a wider empathy'. Jeredith Merrin, 'The Ballad of Charlotte Mew', *Modern Philology*, Vol. 95, No. 2, 1997, 200–17.

written yet – a chapter called "Echo on Aüe". There are creamy small ponies on Aue and living flowers with the power of movement, especially one blazing blue flower which grows in a white-sanded cave. That is where you live, in my book. You told me once to keep my fantasies, so I have made a home for you in fantasy – on Aüe – I hope you like the climate, and I am quite sure the creamy ponies would appeal to you. But that is not half what I would wish for you, if I could build like the old people of fairytale. And yet all I could make would be no more than subject to you, who are real and worth more than any mist.

Of the other work, I think "Bronze Outlaw" is all right; the Baron book, maybe; "Unicorn Pasture", yes; the poems, yes; "The Godwits Fly" is badly in need of first aid. I doubt if it's publishable: "These Poor Old Hands" should be, and there is also a play called "Chariot Wheels" finished – Ronald Holloway, Unicorn Press, Kitchener Street, has a copy of the Victory Hymn which should come at the end of it. And there's old "Journalese". And the papers you have. And any odd fragments – stories, sketches – you have some stories tucked away in your desk. After Derry is provided for, you and my Mother are the "residuary legatees". I love her too – all my family, in a funny exiled way. An old friend wrote the other day after a lapse of twenty years, calling us "The Little Wilkinsons of Waripori Street." You've no idea what delightful queer old memories that conjured up – little crystal ships, and having hot baths in the copper (we had no bath) and darkest red velvety "pin cushions" growing along the garden borders. It was called "Robin Hood Cottage".

If I do come to a not so untimely end, I'd like little Nurse P. Lovell to have the books in my room that belong to me (some are libraries). She has been so uniformly kind and decent to me that I'd like to make her some small present.

Am tired now. Strange, when there's so little said, and almost nothing done of all I should do. "If I love thee, what is that to thee?" I wish it might be a talisman for you, for ever – against loneliness, or fear, or failure – You have shut me away from the consciousness of these, and given me faith so that I could work again. Even aside from work – do you know, sometimes, when you have come in for a few moments, I have felt something like the woman I should have been – and never was with any man, for after all, I suppose fifteen, which was when I first met Haroun, is childhood. I was very much lacking in any way of expressing myself with him, anyhow, and not wise at all. But with you, I've felt at ease: and not without grace, or dignity, or an equal footing of minds on which I could speak to you.

Stilted, foolish wandering, all this – I have tried to be just as stilted always with you in some ways. I wish I could see you now for one moment. I never go past your house, or your car, without saying "God bless you and make you happy". You will be great, I think – nobody but a great doctor could have done as much for me as you have. Remember what I wrote to you once, long ago. "The quality of mercy" – that is what it's all built upon.

I hope I don't look ugly when I am dead. I would like to be fair then, for an hour or two – But may the living be the fairest of all for you, for ever and for ever.

Goodnight, G.M.T.
Iris.*

---

* A blank verso follows this last entry. The book is then used as a rough draft book for poems, with a short fragmentary plan for *The Godwits Fly* and two pages listing story titles at the very back of the book.

IV

1935–1936 Journal Fragments

MSX-8206, Alexander Turnbull Library, acquired 2009. Five handwritten diary entries in black ink and a poem in pencil on lined paper in a small handmade book (155 x 125 cm, bound in fawn paper on card, with green endpapers) gifted to Robin Hyde by the printer Ron Holloway in October 1935. Came to be known as the 'China Notebook' (Leggott, China N) as Hyde also used it for making detailed notes while travelling in Hong Kong and China in 1938.

DESCRIPTION: The first entry comprises a poem, followed by a few pages written at and after the time of Holloway's gift (October 1935 to Easter 1936). Hyde must then have put the book aside and not used it until she embarked in January 1938 for her voyage to Europe via Asia. That voyage unexpectedly became her experience of war-torn and occupied China. She used the notes she made in China to compose 'Accepting Summer' or *Dragon Rampant*, as it was published in 1939 in London. These and a few unrelated notes on some verso pages (also written later) have been omitted in this publication.

PROVENANCE: Sent to Hyde's family after her death in London (amongst papers brought home by Edge), the China Notebook subsequently came into the possession of the Rawlinsons before it became part of the Derek Challis Collection acquired by the Alexander Turnbull Library in 2009.

October 21st , 1935.

Incidence:
      (Is that the word?)

     Ronald Holloway gives me this
diary at the Unicorn Press,
     and
offers beer. But
Robert Lowry is churlish
sullen and inhospitable
     as
the Atlantic waves breaking
over his sullen Irish coast,
     all
jerseys and men with
stumpy legs and dogs with
stumpy tails, looking for
casks of rum after
 the shipwreck, But
finding it not.
Which
Brings me back to the beer;
      while
Ronald seeks it, I do sit in
the sun on a broad-based
 rock of
       volcanic origin But
imperturbable nature, Hard By
an ivy geranium, complete
     with
Pink stare and baby snail,
And
    There dream, watched by
Loafers, dogs with scabby

tails, sparrows, shiny car-
surfaces, hot-baked bricks
like
    Loaves crusty from
The giant's oven,
     And,
The Police who know no
     Better: Till
Ronald arrives with the
    beer and,
under the disapproving
    eye of Robert, We
Drink it out of a jug
Which has held nasturtiums,
    Brown
velvet nasturtiums, cinnamon
clear
 orange flowers, flowers
absorbent of too
    much sunshine, too
great a lucidity and
grasp of
    the sun's big idea,
too
    marked a comprehension
      of
    what it is all about, too
    little tolerance
      of
groundlings, nidderings; star-
squibs, the
trite and the obscure, the
    Rueful ones left out
    When
Colour was handed round.

From
the earthenware influenced
by these masterful
Flower-dragoons, I
Drink beer without visible
effect, but
not without comfort;
And
return to sitting on the
stone in
the sunshine,
Like
a lizard but not so
green;
Salve regina – that is to say
The
nasturtium: salve
Imperator, the
beer. Save all of us
except
Politicians: and Robert.

Amen.*

----

* *Young Knowledge*, 147–9.

October 28th 35

Concluding paragraph of a book called "Death of a God," to be written around the life of Woodrow Wilson:*

Thus Wilson fell. Unfortunately what was not realised at that time, either in America or in Europe, was that for international purposes, Wilson was America: and America, when she shall speak again to the nations, will still be Woodrow Wilson, however shyly and cautiously disguised. For the genius of America, whether expressed internationally among her own vast system of states, or outspoken before a world, is essentially a messianic one. The things that her alien and fusing people bring to the melting pot are far less their aptitudes and crafts, than their dreams, the dreams which are at once the fetters and the release of the fugitive, the painful but sincere demands of the enslaved, poor and oppressed yesterdays upon their free tomorrow. America is less the land of the free, than the land of freedom-seeking –and for generations yet, few good things shall come out of America that were not thought or done on impulse, the impulse natural to the idealist. There shall be a strangeness about her actions, terribly and rending cracks in her belief … such as that which opened beneath Woodrow Wilson's feet when America realised that the Old World was laughing at the New World's god. Terrible and violent will be America's disillusions, her sudden changes of emotional temperature. For she is not earth yet, but a slowly-cooling star: yet if she passes the period of this danger, which will be great and for the present more serious internally than from any other source, America may be of such value to the world, and of such an eminent dignity that she will even be regarded without envy. I do not say that it will be so; But remember Woodrow Wilson when America speaks again: Do not ask her for politicians, or

---

* Woodrow Wilson (United States President, 1913–21) was the foremost advocate for moral internationalism and US involvement in international relations to achieve democracy. Towards the end of WWI, Wilson led negotiations with Germany, including of the armistice. 'In 1918, he issued his Fourteen Points: his view of a post-war world that could avoid another terrible conflict. In 1919, he went to Paris to help create the League of Nations and shape the Treaty of Versailles with special attention on creating new nations out of defunct empires. In 1919, during the bitter fight with the Republican-controlled Senate over the U.S. joining the League of Nations, Wilson collapsed with a debilitating stroke. The League of Nations was established anyway, but the United States never joined'. http://en.wikipedia.org/wiki/Woodrow_Wilson Retrieved 21 May 2011.

treat her as the single entity of a state, which she is not, and cannot be for at least
another hundred years

Receive America's naïve generosity ungenerously, her sentiment with cynicism,
and white civilisation is lost. For she has no more self-possession than a schoolboy,
and, driven back upon herself, will be the victim of a sham materialism and an
emotional conflict that will utterly destroy her. There is no middle way for America
– it is lustre, or eclipse – But it would be cowardice, blind, bankrupt cowardice, to
reject her. There is a singing spirit still in Europe that shall flash out to greet the
prophecies which are her necessary form of speech.

October 29th 1935.

There is something one never gets used to: it is this – the very fact that one has
grown accustomed to pain, so well accustomed to it that instead of crying out one
only draws in one's breath: That one has learned to be patient is so strange. It is like
an alien ghost, it is like an old spectre in a house meant for the young.

November 26th .

Can't sleep. Worried unnecessarily about much nonsense. Denis Archer's have
accepted "Bronze Outlaw"* and it's on my mind that there's too much of sham
realism in it. Dunno. Also vague ephemeral dreams-are-master policy of some of
the other stuff annoys me like a curate's dog collar. What a fool I am when I know
that both varieties are good – better – na, but still not what I want – I am going to
write a series of short stories as hard and tight and cold as I can make them. Name
of one "Fear": name of another "Freedom" and a third "Answer to Payer": things
that happened, that are. The dreary exaggerated realism of the Yanks bores me stiff.
It's only French nineteenth century with the wrong hand mixing the salad. They do
not the Americans understand oils. They go in for dry feeding and dry frocking and
dry loving. Like Porthos:[†] "Too heavy."

---

* Published Hurst & Blackett, 1936, as *Passport to Hell*.

† One of the three musketeers in the Alexander Dumas' novel *The Three Musketeers*: a friendly
and sociable character, he over-eats and puts on weight, becoming a giant in size.

A week after Easter '36 – I am tired beyond belief, waiting for my book to come out – they have called it "Passport to Hell" which isn't very good – Here it is hell – the flat grey sort – I can't fit in now with all these women, the glancing angles of their minds – it's like a succession of distorting mirrors and my own shape the most distorted – I am more often to blame than they because of a neurotic hatred of noise, and dread of enemies – known in the vernacular as "looking for trouble." I write always now in the attic and even there am unquiet – still love GMT better than all else and stay here because of him not for want of enterprise – I don't know whether he loves me, shall never know, but we are starry-led – Have known D'Arcy Cresswell and Miss Stronach* late, with relief – he is a true poet a bit overburdened with craftmanship and an [breaks off]

---

* D'Arcy Cresswell was a South Island poet who returned from Europe in 1931 to live in Auckland. In 1935 he moved into a small bach in the garden of the family home of the elderly Jane Stronach and daughter Elsie Stronach, in Castor Bay on the North Shore. Elsie was the North Shore Plunket nurse and had been a hospital nurse at the same hospital in southern England where Starkie was a patient. Although Cresswell often irritated Hyde with his 'misogynistic dogma', it was through him that she met the Stronachs, who also extended their hospitality to her and other writers – she lived in the same bach for a brief period in 1937 (*Iris*, 315–16).

V

The Cage with the Open Door

MS-Papers 9110-009, Alexander Turnbull Library, acquired 2009.

DESCRIPTION: This story exists in Hyde's original draft typescript, with corrections and additions made in her handwriting. These have been incorporated here: the italicised square brackets indicate *Hyde's corrections and additions*. The story is set on 4 October 1935 and was probably written shortly after that, although Alison Hunt suggests early 1936.[*] It is published here for the first time.

PROVENANCE: Hyde took a manuscript of short stories with her when she left New Zealand in 1938. This was probably posted with other papers to London from Hong Kong, returned to her parents after her death, and then sent to Bill Edge and after his death into the possession of Derek Challis.[†]

'The Cage with the Open Door' has the form of a complete story and appears on a list Hyde made of more fiction-based short stories at the back of her '1935 Journal'. It has been considered as fiction by Alison Jeffreys in her essay 'Other Pastures: Death, Fantasy and the Gothic in Robin Hyde's Short Stories',[‡] but it is also clearly an autobiographical piece. It follows the thoughts and movements of its narrator who goes out on (implicitly) a day's parole from a voluntary mental hospital ward, recognisable as the Lodge, into Auckland city to visit her newspaper office and a series of friends. (Its 'topographical information' is, as Michele Leggott describes it, 'accurate'.)[§] Yet Hyde's merging of fact and fictional form place the story as simultaneously a creative and personal narrative (her sense of how life can make a story) in a way that matches her state of mind and thoughts in late 1935, when

---

[*] Hunt, 'Cage', 285.

[†] Jeffreys, 'Other Pastures', *Lighted Windows*, 75.

[‡] Ibid., 77. Hyde wrote over one hundred short stories, sixty-seven of them identified as published in newspapers and magazines. A group of stories, also written at the Lodge, were intended for a collection, putatively titled 'Unicorn Pasture', that remained unpublished. See also Alison Jeffreys, 'The Short Stories of Robin Hyde (Iris Wilkinson) 1906–1939' (MA:University of Auckland, 2001), 1.

[§] *Young Knowledge*, 15.

she was experiencing a growing peacefulness and globalising sense of common humanity: a feeling that 'we are all so much the same person'.

Hyde's new sense of her mission as a writer came precisely at the moment when threats of a new world conflict made this story a kind of requiem for peace (and supportive of the strong international pacifist movement): 'I think, "They are going to die because they do not know how to live. They want to die because they want to fill their empty bladders of minds with some sort of emotion, and death and glory comes cheapest"', she writes.

Alison Hunt links this story with Hyde's reading of Jung's *Collected Papers* and embracing of his recommendation that part of the process of recovery for a neurotic should be to 'adopt a "religious-philosophical attitude", ... a timeless sense of unity and totality, of belonging to a species'.* This sense certainly haunts the story, although Hunt also points out that Jung's endorsement and 'celebration of social consciousness in recovering neurotics', was in contrast to 'Hyde's [own] doctors' who worried about the negative effect of what they saw as her social campaigning 'tendencies'.†

The title 'The Cage with the Open Door' most obviously refers to the voluntary ward where Hyde was living, but the unrest within that house, as Alison Hunt reads, the 'skirmishes which rock the women's confined world' are 'echoed on a global scale by the Italian bombardment of Adowa in Abyssinia [former name of Ethipia]'.‡ By the end of the story, the cage is a way of thinking about the world: 'House a cage, street a cage, world cage, body a cage.' Yet this is a yielding rather than a claustrophobic understanding, that links suffering and littleness all over the world.

The story records (or fictionalises/dramatises) events that actually occurred on 4 October 1935. We know this because the morning paper headline announcing the invasion of Abyssinia, 'Italy Strikes at Adowa', which the narrator reads on the tram, matches the *New Zealand Herald* morning edition of Friday 4 October 1935: 'Italy Strikes: Attack on Adowa: Many Deaths Reported: Extensive Advance: Excitement in Europe'.§ Alison Hunt writes:

---

* 'This he declared to be the very basis of civilization, a fellow-feeling which inspired human beings "to do creative work for the benefit of a future age, and, if necessary, to sacrifice themselves for the welfare of the species"' (Hunt, 'Cage', 272).

† See Hunt,'Cage', 272, 277.

‡ Hunt, 'Cage', 284.

§ *New Zealand Herald,* 4 October 1935, 11.

For the previous four days, Adowa had been headline world news in the Herald, and on Saturday its entire world news front page was given over to dramatic reportage. The Auckland Star was similarly preoccupied; it ran a one-page photo-essay on Saturday, headed: 'Ethiopia – Where "the Greatest Massacre the World Has Ever Known is Well Under Way".'*

The story's mention of the narrator's poem also matches Hyde's own protest poem 'Italy, Old and New. Lines for an Unknown Poet' that had been published in the *Auckland Star* on 16 September.

Hyde wrote 'The Cage with the Open Door' at the same time as she was drafting 'The Unbelievers' and shortly before she began working on *Wednesday's Children* (and continued to revise her first draft of *The Godwits Fly*). All three novels attempt in some aspect to convey that timeless sense of unity with a whole species that we find sketched here. According to Hunt, two of them (*Godwits* and 'The Unbelievers') also portray a world similar to that in the story: 'The inner city environment and lifestyle, and the social circle cultivated by the narrator in "The Cage with the Open Door", are the same which Hyde wrote into "The Unbelievers" in late 1935'. And she further comments that *Wednesday's Children* 'shares the short story's internationalist and pacifist themes, and is also threaded through with references to Abyssinia. Wednesday, who vacillates between retreat into fantasy or engagement with the active world, takes on the role of healer to those she describes as caged birds.'†

---

* *Auckland Star*, 4 October 1935, 7; Hunt, 'Cage', 285.
† Hunt, 'Cage', 288.

The Cage With the Open Door.

The little orchestra starts to tune up, somewhat on the wrong side of four in the morning. They awaken me, but I don't object to that, because I know that in a moment I am going comfortably to sleep again. The room, filled with an unreal, deep and tender blue, smells of flowering currant and tobacco smoke. All the windows are shut, so that I won't hear the movements and voices of the women who sleep on the balcony outside, and … equally important … so that the pale wand of my reading-lamp, which burns all night, won't slip through the blinds and disturb them. xxx The voices of the birds become passionate, argumentative and loud. As a matter of fact, they are merely enjoying the conception that they are birds: their bodies are little grey funnels with feathers stuck on the outside, and through them pours song. If it didn't, something terrible would happen to the world. They must know that, and it gives them confidence to talk so much. Riro-riro, waxeye, tui, fat, mottled English thrush, common or garden sparrow, starlings and pigeons, the two last nesting together in the enormous unused chimney whose gulf opens into my room: they fiddle away in full blast, and I think, "In a moment, my good birds, I shall forget you and go to sleep again. The most interesting dreams always come on *[in]** this peculiarly absorpent [sic] fringe of time, when one isn't awake and isn't xxx asleep either. Like the jellyfish we used to find in the very shallow water at Lyall Bay, when the tide was spread out so flat and thin that the sea was almost land. They had fringes of tiny tentacles, said to be poisonous. Some of them were indigo blue, others looked as if they had been badly dyed with cochineal. Why do I remember little things so sharply of late? Last xxx night, I couldn't get out of my head the smell of that little bathroom and kitchenette in the flat at Symonds Street.† The gas and the sun which baked the tin walls and roof somehow fused together to make a smell like pear-drops. In memory it becomes disgusting. That must be five years ago. I will tell you now, my

---

* Hyde's corrections and additions are in italics; any editorial comment is in roman.

† Where Hyde lived probably in 1932 after leaving 'Burwood', the Princes Street boarding house that was her first accommodation in Auckland.

good birds, what your voices are. They are little blades of silver, beaten out flat on the anvil of the morning. When you have them shiny enough, then you can go prinking through your greenwoods and win battles. In the garden there is an enormous old tree with a horrid name ... it sounds like spittisporum,* but surely it can't be .... The fact remains that it is covered all over with thousands of pastel-pink blossoms, the size of half-crowns. That would be a good place to win a battle, especially since I have circled the roots with red bricks ... jam-tart effect ... and planted spraxias, which lean over them.

It's no good. Somewhere, passing an ~~xxxxx~~ inconspicuous ~~litthe~~ road-sign green with eld and hiding out of sight under a great bush covered with snowy flakes of blossom, I have missed the way. This is not the road back to sleep, and once you start looking for it you can never, never find it. All the things that insist on being known come and beat like snowflakes into your eyes and ears ... like dirty, cottonwool snowflakes. Now in a few moments it will begin. Life coming back to itself, and not wanting to come back. Life not knowing where it is, or why ... weary, aimless, and oh, so bleakly desolate. By slow degrees I have grown to hate it, though it seems impossible one should hate anything so pitiful. It's in self-defence, and yet, just as I know that I've missed the milestone back into sleep, I know that ~~xxxxxxxxxx~~ self-defence is the wrong policy.

"Curse the beggar in the street
That he is more poor than I,
Curse him~~x~~ for his withered limb ...."†

but more especially, curse him because nobody has enough to give away, because tears run dry, and hands lose the power even of stretching themselves out.

If I wake up when the first and full blast of the wireless is over, somehow it isn't so hard. When they turn it on first, at about half-past six, it trumpets so vehemently.

---

* *Pittosporum*, an evergreen New Zealand native tree or shrub. Perhaps her tree is the Norfolk Island Hibiscus, *Lagunaria patersonii*, a feature and street tree in Auckland, which has pale pink flowers and could be mistaken for a type of Pittosporum.

† A play on 'The Beggar', a poem by R.A.K. Mason and the title poem of his 1924 collection (Auckland: Whitcombe & Tombs). She echoes both Mason's opening lines: 'Curse the beggar in the street/ That he has less joy than I,' and the last verse: 'Curse the beggar in the street / Curse the beggar that he die:/ Curse him for his shrivelled feet/ And his cruel, sight-striving eye'.

It's like a great beast. It has brayed the walls of Jericho down, and now it stands with its foot planted in the ruins, making a noise like itself. When it has got that off its chest, it can relax a little. The announcer comes on and rumbles in a gentle voice, not more than ten times lifesize. Then it may even become sentimental, and convey the tender approaches of a violin. Poor harlot music! … I should think that being supported by ~~that~~ *[the]* business man in the wooden box would present its ~~xxxxxxxxx~~ difficulties.

On the balcony, in the hall, there's the sound of brooms, mops, pails and women. When the birds first awake, obviously their first ~~xxxxx~~ consciousness is, "I'm a bird, I'm a bird." Otherwise, they couldn't know that they're intended to sing. But when the women awake, they aren't conscious of being women. That belongs to a dead and beautiful past, a dream-past, when they were beloved. They are conscious now, helplessly, of chains … of a thousand little bitternesses and irritations, feuds, resentments, difficulties. ~~Thxxx~~ These are the devils that rush in and occupy the house where love is not. I can hear one of them sobbing, quite loudly. She is a woman of more than forty years of age, and undergoing the change of life. Do you know why she is sobbing? Because, downstairs in the lower hall, she polished a patch of floor to her own satisfaction, but the moment her back was turned, Miss Collie, who will not believe anyone can do anything well except herself, flung herself on the same patch and polished it all over again. Miss Collie, hearing the woman's sobs, remains on all fours, uncomfortable, satisfied, ~~xxxxx~~ vindictive. Somehow she has pleased a hard little core within herself, which demands that she shall make innumerable sacrifices to it. At times, the consciousness that it is there drives her almost frantic. She becomes a ~~littlexxxx~~ spectre with a pale face and haunted dark eyes, running up and down, or lurking in bedrooms, weeping. Then the mood passes and she is ~~xxxxxxxxxxxxxx~~ satisfied again. It is Miss Collie who always turns the wireless on so loud: that is another necessary sacrifice to her core.

I make up my mind, "This time, I won't go down and turn that thing off, I won't notice it." There is a book, half-read, but it's no good. If I start to cry, I'll work up sufficient indignation to be able to chuck away good resolutions. I go down the stairs and turn it off, talking loudly about instruments of torture, I know perfectly well, as I pass Miss Collie, that she is pleased, and that as soon as I go upstairs again she will turn it louder than ever. The walls of Jericho are down, down, down …. who-ever said we were human? What gives you the right to more humanity than anyone else? That's ~~xxxx~~ just it, you see. For months I was sorry for her: now, ~~xxxxxxxxxxxxxx~~ I still preserve the ghastly remains of that pity, like a dried head stuck on the ridge-pole of a Dyak's house.* But actually, she isn't human to me any more, she's just a noise. Hands get too tired even for stretching out. ~~I wish I hadn't been~~ born so xxxxxx ~~accursedly sensitive to sound.~~

In the kitchen, after breakfast, they are all excited and pleased, drawn together for a moment by a little thread of drama. Somebody who read the morning paper early walked in and announced, "War has been declared." Italy .... Abyssinia .... "Do you think Britain will be involved?" The usual commentary. However, they hope Britain will be involved, they hope there will be a war, a big war. I don't think they would even be frightened if an aeroplane appeared like a roc above the roof-tops and started laying bombs. Nature abhors a vacuum. And they haven't love. They guess they would be drawn together in peril. That would be better than nothing at all.†

I am going into town. First I smoke a cigarette in front of the mirror: the house is quiet now, the war news has made them so human that they have turned down the radio. I looked rouged and rueful, with fair eyebrows much too thick to paint. The smoke stays down in my mouth for a moment, then curls slowly out, a glossy little grey-blue dragon, but only newt size. Somehow that's soothing ... a wreath of incense for a fretful god. There is black lace on the edge of my hat. I'm glad I bought it. My vanity is to me like Miss Collie's cruelty unto Miss Collie. It xxx runs in the family. When my grandmother, whose name was Augusta and who had beautiful, narrow hands, departed this life, I remember perfectly what my mother said. Very xxx slowly ... "Poor, vain old thing!"

Spring comes smoothly to Auckland .... not in young xxxxxx winds and a tossing and ~~fortx~~ frothing of clouds and trees, but ~~lmost~~ in an added cleanliness. The world looks bright-eyed, deep-eyed. The shallow little streets, their asphalt broken with pepper trees, brim with sunshine. Outside the house I like, (~~who oh~~ *[it]* is on the

---

* Dyaks are the indigenous people of Borneo.

† Hyde shared the sentiments of many in England and Europe (and some in New Zealand) who abhorred the prospect of another war and supported the principles of collective security embodied in the League of Nations – an attitude evidenced in the results of a Peace Ballot in Britain in June 1935. This popular and left-wing opinion stood in opposition to war and to sanctioning invasion. British diplomatic desires to bargain Italy out of full-scale invasion, but not to oppose her, and thus avoid the failure of the League and Italy's 'volte-face into arms of Germany', were less principled but also ineffective. Andrew Crozier, *The Causes of the Second World War* (London: Blackwell, 1997), 108.

right hand side going up, and built of almost colourless bricks, which appear again in broken paths covered with shivery grass and white marguerites,) the little boy with the brown eyes is playing. He wears his cowboy suit …. sacking, with fringes on the trousers … but he's silent and doesn't look at me. We used to have quite a game in the mornings. I would say, "Hullo, Brown Eyes!" And he "Hullo, Blue Eyes!" smiling, a bit cheekily, as if he had done something rather daring and might be scolded. Now he doesn't talk; and I'm sure his mother has told him he mustn't speak to strangers. I never try to coax him out of it: childhood mustn't be invaded. Nevertheless, I feel it is rather arbitrary of her to decide that anyone is a stranger. We are all so much the same person. I pass a little girl of about fourteen, very slender and supple in a knitted suit of olive green, which shows her figure. She might be a little statue of some dark dawn. She has a shock of black hair, dark, musing eyes, and a look of bitter dejection. Either she is in love with somebody, or her father has taken the stick to her. It might be a little bit of both. She swings on into the morning, going the other way, and is gone.

I buy the morning paper at the top of the street, and mean to read it in the tramcar, but Mrs. McPhail gets in.[*] I like her, but I don't want to talk. I'm still raw from that wireless and the knowledge that I have made a fool of myself again. She, however, is determined to talk because she has just come back from an educational conference of women in Wellington. She has none of the smugness of the average social worker, and wants now and again to be reassured as to her usefulness. She has bright, grey eyes, the leather-coloured face and hand[s] that go with the gardening woman, and good cream lace at her breast … no, it's too flat to be called breast, just chest. When we can't get a double seat, she sits behind me and leans over. The newspaper has an enormous black headline, sprawling over its whole leader page. "ITALY STRIKES AT ADOWA." I want to read it, and hate myself for wanting to, so feel inclined to revenge myself on Mrs. McPhail. "Whyxdoxxxany of She is talking about [two] little girls who didn't get up to give her a seat, coming home in the tram the night before. "They both belonged to the Bible class," she says, "If they knew how they'd gone down in my estimation! …. It's not [just] that they didn't get up for me, but I felt they were letting our sex down." "Why don't any of the xxxxx women's societies make an election issue out of the fact that women still pay unemployment tax on their wages and incomes, and don't get a penny of relief when they're out of work themselves?"

---

* A Mrs J. McPhail was mayoress of Birkenhead in the 1930s.

I demand, folding the newspaper, "I was amazed to see that there had been a national conference of women, and the ~~thing~~ *[subject]* hadn't even been raised. They swung it on to us after the last election was over, so we had at least the excuse that we didn't know what we voted for. But we know now, and keep sweetly silent about it. Don't you call that letting down our own sex?" She looks distressed, and murmurs that she will bring the matter up herself. "But the ~~xxxxx~~ National Council of Women is non-political, my dear." "You mean that they are Tory, and subservient to people who despise them. Personally, I'd rather bite the hand that underfeeds me than lick it; as a matter of principle." "They <u>are</u> slow," she says, and gives various cases of poverty and prostitution over which we can be in ~~happy~~ agreement.[*] Just before getting out of the tram she taps my shoulder again. ~~"xxx,~~ "Look, isn't that beautiful?" An old woman has a great armful of double white flowering cherry, the creamy blossoms just touched with red where corona and calyx meet. Immediately I can see the Bride Tree at the foot of Orangi-Kaupapa, the impossibly steep hill we had to climb up and down every day going to school.[†] As this times of the year [sic], it leans out, white-veiled, opulent, innocent and splendid. We used to find four-leaved clovers in the long grass tangled about its roots. Although it grew almost on the cliff face, technically speaking it belonged to the garden of Alan Burney, a mild boy with pink-rimmed eyes and pink hair. He was very devout, and belonged to the choir, but later informed the clergyman that he was the prey of evil thoughts, and could not continue in his Sunday School duties. The clergyman, who was an old woman, told all the other old women, who scoffed at the idea of poor ~~xxxxx~~ mild-looking Alan possessing any evil worth mentioning. I think they respected evil and despised his lack of virility. Now I hope that what he had always cherished concerning them was a sentiment towards murder, not sexual offence: but at the time, I merely thought that he was not a very imposing overlord for the Bride Tree, which was spring's most beautiful gesture in those parts.

---

[*] The National Council of Women held conferences every second year from 1929. In the 1930s, its focus has been described as shifting 'from equal rights to moral issues', which fits with the sentiment expressed here. However, in '1931 the Auckland NCW Branch co-operated with its affiliate, the YWCA, to open a register of unemployed women, the first time they were ever recorded officially'. http://www.ncwnz.org.nz/1896-1965/ Retrieved 27 April 2011.

[†] A winding steep street off Glenmore Street in Wellington, near to Hyde's family home in the suburb of Northland.

I should go to the library and see if there's anything in the Maning letters …* but I can't, I won't, I don't want to work. Queen Street is exceptionally hideous, filled with large, narrow and rather ornate buildings, like public lavatories. Lilac is to be the colour worn this spring … lilac, and a blueish-green named after Princess Marina.[†] How indefatigably stupid they are! Dear William Makepeace,[‡] why don't you return from that bourne which you must have xxx explored well enough by now, and write a Book of Toadies as companion-piece to your Book of Snobs? We could give you some fine, fat toadlet specimens. The lilac dresses are of silk and linen, hanging limply on the shoulders of papier mache figures, gilt, steel-blue, black. Nevertheless, they make me think of Kensington Gardens, which I have never seen, and of women walking there in feather boas and large round pre-war hats like saucepans, with their skirts down to their ankles and silky dogs, like fawn-coloured muffs, towed behind them on leather leads. Lilac …. "The lilac bloomed at xxxxxxxxx Fontainbleau, when I was there with you."[§] Katherine Mansfield is buried at Fontainbleau, and France rang the bells on the morning she died … almost the only decent thing France has done since the war. Jimmie Barclay sent me a spray of flowers xxxx from her grave. On inspection they proved to be not xxxxxxxxx flowers in the respectable sense, but a little stalk of flowering weeds. After all, that was in keeping. Katherine was never cultivated, but the wild flowers took to her of themselves …. And how I hate symbolists! They are not writers at all, they are dressmakers. If I have been born in the Burne-Jones epoch,[¶] I would have been the worst of the pack of them.

The office first, for letters and messages. Wyndham Street is completely filled with the large matronly backsides of 'buses – people can ride in them free to the top of the hill, where they are expected to enter an emporium and make purchases, very inexpensive, in its many xxxxxxxxx *[departments]*. Usually they do this, obedient

---

* Frederick Maning, author and political figure (1812–83), best known for his work *Old New Zealand.* Seven of his letters are held in the Grey Collection at the Auckland Central City Library.

† Princess Marina of Greece, who became the Duchess of Kent.

‡ Thackeray's (1811–63) *The Book of Snobs* (1848) is a collection of satirical articles that had previously appeared in *Punch* (as 'The Snobs of England, by One of Themselves', 1846–7).

§ Katherine Mansfield died at Fontainebleau in 1923, where she was living at the spiritual healer George Ivanovich Gurdjieff's Institute for the Harmonious Development of Man.

¶ Edward Burne-Jones was a British artist and designer who worked with William Morris and was associated with the later phase of the Pre-Raphaelite movement and the Arts and Crafts Movement.

and sheep-like; but sometimes, instead, they get out, stare around, and merely look at the sea, or go into the near-by Catholic Church[*] to confess their sins. Apart from the free 'buses, Wyndham Street is pleasantly old and dirty. Its asphalt is hot under the sun, and over it pads a big black and white retriever dog. He thinks he is being silent, but as a matter of fact, his paws go "Phit-phit, phit-phit," at ~~xxxxxxxx~~ every lope. The Herald office, many storeys high, overshadows and dwarfs the grimy little building into which I now turn: there is another disadvantage.[†] The Herald, from their top floors, can look right into ~~our~~ *[the]* lower windows. They can see The Old Man drinking port wine out of a tumbler, and suspect (truly,) that the tumbler has not been washed. They know about the skull which is kept on top of a cupboard, and the rats, and the ~~xxxxx~~ linotype machine that limps with one foot, and the pornographic picture gallery of all Auckland's oldest citizens, wearing beards and frock-coats, but nothing else. What they are not sure is that their own directors and founders are included in the ~~xxxxx~~ gallery: but they need have no fear ....

Mr. Rukutai will talk about the native village at Orakei. 'Phone for an appointment. "In the lunch-hour, Monday or Tuesday," says the agreeable Maori voice. I hesitate. "Which would you prefer?" "Either would be convenient," says Mr. Rukutai.[‡] As a drowning man sees everything in his last second, I see that I really want it to be Tuesday, because on Tuesday I know for certain that Berry[§] isn't coming to see me. On Monday, he might, or might not, look in for a moment. "For five minutes! ... and you make all this fuss about it, you order your days so that you won't miss him. If he comes." "I'll come on Monday, then, Mr. Rukutai. At what time?" "Half past twelve," says the fatal voice: yes, and if Berry does come, you'll have left. Fool! Another unnecessary crisis created out of nothing. Crisis be damned. I'm free, white, and twenty-one. What's that expression one hears so often on their radio? "Sez you! ...."

---

[*] Probably St Patrick's Cathedral, also on Wyndham Street in Auckland city.

[†] The *New Zealand Herald* was, and still is, in Wyndham Street, adjacent to the street where the smaller and weekly *New Zealand Observer* was located.

[‡] Hyde wrote in support of 'the Ngati Whātua facing eviction from their land at Orakei in Auckland. She published an article about the controversy in the *Observer* in October 1935, and maintained her involvement after leaving the Lodge, writing a second *Observer* piece in July 1937, and an angry letter to parliamentarian John A. Lee that August' (Docherty, 'Do I Speak Well?', 249); Hunt, 'Cage', 277. Her articles on Orakei are reprinted in *Disputed Ground*, 334–44.

[§] This seems to refer to the narrator's doctor but, unlike elsewhere in this story, here she doesn't use a real name.

Mick's office is in Exchange Lane, two floors up, and at the very end of a black corridor. ~~Nobody els e l ives so obscurely in the building~~ Last, two lavatories, labelled, "Gents." and "Ladies." Beyond this edge of the world, Mick. It's daylight robbery to charge ten shillings for that office, but they know he sleeps and lives there as well as merely working … he sleeps and lives there a great deal more than he works, come to that … and sting him accordingly. Marie is there.* She wears rough green tweeds and a brown beret, and has a look of race, but tries to get over it by imitating Joan Crawford. Her legs are long and thin, in stockings of bronze silk. ~~They~~ *[Both]* are very silent, which means that they have been quarrelling. "I'll make you some tea, but there isn't any milk," says Mick, operating on the spirit stove, which is going to explode some day soon. Marie scrapes the silver paint off the coiffure of a dummy with a black face. The silver hair has come out somehow fat. It was meant to ~~look~~ look like a court wig, but instead, it's like curds and whey. The Morgan woman has a ballroom dancing studio in this same building … teaching the portly middle-aged to get another pleasure than the gastronomic one out of their stomachs … and her radio is far worse than the one I have to put up with. It simply howls: and you can't shut the window, because if you did you would perish of suffocation and spirit stove. At it is, Mick and Marie continuously inhale ~~xxxxxx~~ the frying of sausages from an eating-house, steam from a laundry and lead from a small foundry. "Don't notice the radio," says Marie, "If you became conscious of it ~~xxx~~ at all, you could never be conscious of anything else. I'm going into the Mater for an operation on Monday." Nobody receives this with excitement, because Marie is a pathological liar. Once she told me that she had V.D. It was only so that I would lecture her upon morality. It is very disconcerting for the young to find their morals taken so much as a matter of course. They have a sneaking feeling that their fathers did worse. ~~Xx If you ask me,~~ This is at the root of the so-called inferiority complex. "What will they cut out of you?" I ask, as a matter of form, and she says, "Just a lump … a little lump." Since she has already started to scale the lump down, I know she is almost ready to abandon the whole idea and talk about something else. Then, as Mick

---

* Marie is possibly poet, playwright and broadcaster Marie Conlan, 1912–42. Derek Challis comments: 'By mid-1935 Iris was socializing more freely … she often met friends at Blake's Inn in Vulcan Lane. The Rawlinsons' Princes St flat also became a meeting place for journalists, writers, students and other friends. Marie Conlan, Aroha Hardcastle, Ronald Holloway, Allan Irvine, Warwick Lawrence, Robert Lowry, Jane Mander and of course Iris were often amongst the guests' (*Iris,* 289–90).

turns round from the destructive spirit stove, I realise why they have quarrelled. He hasn't shaved for perhaps three days. A fair beard looks so silly. Mick wants to write and wants to ~~xxxxxx~~ draw. He does both very well, but by such miraculous leaps and bounds. The first chapter of his novel gave the best picture of a man shooting a dog in a mealie patch that I have ever read, but twenty pages on, there, without apparent reason, was the same man, although ~~without~~ *[minus]* his dog, in the middle of an Australian desert, collecting the Government bounty on wallaby ~~eyes~~ *[ears]*. Presumably he had ~~xxxxxx~~ secured a separation from his wife, who in the first chapter says, "Swine, swine, swine!" Mick's skin is becoming the unhealthy white consistent with not enough air and not enough food. They give him these horrible little heads and figures to paint for shop-window displays... two shillings each... but he insists on trying to make them really presentable, then flies into a passion and drops them out of the window into the courtyard below. I make him in a better temper, because I will criticise his novel, and he feels that while anyone will criticise it, there is hope. I know that feeling. If the brutes would only say, "This is wrong," or, "That bit is right," instead of the soft answers that, far from turning away artistic wrath, stimulate it to frenzy! Today, between Wyndham Street and this very office, I was stopped by old Mr. Murchison, the jackal of the Kelly Gang. He belongs to the Rotary Club, he is successful, he lives in the right suburb, yet somehow his reputation is faintly sinister. My own idea is that this is because he cannot resist laughing at the Kelly Gang. He is in bad odour, anyhow, and both looks and breathes it. He smiled at me, showing yellow teeth. "I read your long poem about Italy," he said, "The one in the Star." Then, when he saw that I had braced myself to receive the compliment, he grinned wolfishly, "But I couldn't understand a word of it," he said. I was more angry than I should have admitted. Why stop me, on a fine morning, to confess to something offensive? Why are people so proud of their demerits? "Lots of people can't understand poetry." I said, "It's nothing to be ashamed of. I suppose it's simply the lack of an extra sense." He continued to grin and ~~xxx~~ *[talk],* but I felt that he was hurt, as if a story he told at dinner had fallen flat. He hadn't got his laugh. Afterwards I was ashamed, because one should never let the stories of old people fall flat. Old people are the only ones in the world who have any chance of becoming ~~xxxxxx~~ dispassionate, and therefore their opinions arc *[sometimes]* worth ~~xxxx~~ while. But he went on, satisfied at least in the knowledge that he was rich and I was poor, which is compensation for a good many lost laughs.

Mick's uncle, whom I hadn't met before, has bought a new suit, chocolate-brown, and comes into the office to show it to Marie. The extraordinary thing about him, however, is not the chocolate-brown suit, but the way his white spikes of eyebrows project over eyelids that are almost domes, so round and full they lie over the grey eyes. I have a feeling somebody should paint that face, before it is lost and mingled with the dust... but the people who could paint faces are all dead, dead many centuries. He is full of the war news: not lacking in optimism. "A trained force of men with rifles in their hands … men smarting under military discipline, which is the most galling thing in the world to a man … are a very different proposition to the same fellows, hanging about outside their pubs, loafing, talking. You ask a man over his back-fence to revolt, and he'll laugh at you. Ask him after three months' fighting, and there's another story. I had four years, four weeks of the last war, and I know. Let me tell you one thing. They gave up singing "God Save the King" among the battalions long before the last war was over. I've seen whole divisions mutiny. Six months of Africa should see the end of ~~xxxxxx~~ Fascism, and thank God for that." "Yes, but how do you propose to limit the extent of destruction? If it gets loose in Europe, won't the cost, in property alone, shatter the world into ~~xxxxxx~~ bankruptcy? We're living in a world under blackmail, the blackmail of terror. What I would like to see would be a world-wide strike of the workers, beginning in the munition factories. My God! Surely someone can persuade them not to make the Lewisite for their own backs?" Marie says, "I wonder what it would be like to be the daughter of the man who invented mustard gas? When the S— crowd were here," (she mentions some armament manufacturers who had bought ~~xxxxxx~~ *[them]* a yacht, and thought to cleanse their systems in the Pacific,) "I met them. Their morals stank, and so did their minds." Something queer is happening behind the eyes of the old man in the chocolate-coloured suit. "I can't tell you," he says, almost absently, "What it does to a man, when a shell falls close to him. I can't tell you. A hole in the ground, ~~xxxxxx~~ ninety feet deep." There was a pale, pale gleam at the back of his eyes as he spoke. It made me think of a cautious, glimmering light, hiding itself far back in some dank tunnel. I thought of the returned soldiers, three hundred of them, still shut up in the Avondale Mental Hospital. Those of them who have any sanity at all are allowed as much ease and privilege as possible. They are kept apart, as far as ~~possible~~ *[is feasible],* from the others, and allowed such little comforts as newspapers. This morning *[some]* one of them would have read out, at the breakfast table, "War Declared. Italy Strikes at Adowa." One, ~~of them~~ whom I have met, talks at times most sanely and even delightfully ~~over~~ *[about]* a friend of his, a bull terrier pup. But I saw him one day under the purple cavern of an enormous rhododendron [sic] bush, its blossoms bells for the sleepy bees. He was shouting out prayers at the top of his voice, bellowing prayers, like some wounded animal which happens to use words instead of a scream. Besides his prayers, he had nothing to say but these words; ~~which I shall never forget, although they were the ravings of a lunatic.~~ "I've got to suffer, I've got to suffer, because it's taken him thirty years to smash Christ out of his soul."

Marie ~~xxxx~~ says, "Go down and buy a razor-blade." "But it's two flights. I can't be bothered." "Do go. We can't go out to lunch like that." A gesture of distaste towards Mick's chin. No, we can't go out to lunch like that. I get the razor-blades, Mick shaves, dropping white blobs of lather on the silver hair of his black model. "He wouldn't have done it for me." Probably because it's really serious to Marie that Mick should look human, and to me completely unimportant. At Long's they will lunch you for sixpence, Indian curry (with two sultanas each,) a dab of rice, all ~~xxxxxx~~ splodged together like dried trout-eggs or the verses of T.S. Eliot, and tea in ~~xxxx~~ cups like soup-bowls. They are arguing about the poor. "But you handle them as if they were bric-à-brac, and they're good, solid earthenware. You won't get far with them. What you will get is *[to be]* edged out of your own flock, the Jean ~~xxxxxx~~ Wallers~~x~~ and Co. They will think you odd. They do, already. You will never marry, and you will never be contented. All in tones of triumph. "Never mind him, Marie. You have beautiful ankles." She gets up a little before the lunch is finished, and saying, "I've got to take those blasted heads of yours up to Smithfield's, Mick," leaves her rice a conqueror on the edge of the plate. As she ~~xxxxxx~~ passes among the little red-clothed tables, her head, in the brown beret, held high, her shoulders stooped in the slouch that would have made my grandmother cry aloud for a backboard, she reminds me very clearly ~~xxxxxx~~ of the Bride Tree. She is beautiful, and young, and ready to love. Those are good reasons for assassination in modern society, but we slay slowly, ah, so slowly, my impulsive friends. What was it?

"These ~~are~~ *[were]* but as fire is, dust, or breath,
Or poisonous foam on the tender tongue
Of the little serpents that eat my heart."*

---

* From A.C. Swinburne's 'The Triumph of Time': she substitutes 'serpents' for Swinburne's 'snakes'. *The Poems of Algernon Charles Swinburne*, 6 volumes (London: Chatto & Windus, 1904). http://www.victorianweb.org/authors/swinburne/triumph.html Retrieved 2 May 2011.

"I'll have a car soon," says Mick, with the look of an idealist, "And then I'll take you for a drive." "Over the hills?" "Yes, Waiwera hill, perhaps. When all the pohutukawas are out." "What to drink? Cider?" I think, I should like to go, not with Mick in particular, but just somewhere where it's windy, hilly, and cool. I'd like to sit among the fern, and watch the sunset laid with long, flat strokes of red and amber against the grey sea, the grey Auckland sea, too tame, as a rule, for my liking: but not so bad from a hillcrest. The cattle swing their old, slow bells among the manuka, which has tiny leaves and a crisp, bitter smell. Its blossoms are little brown and white cups. Almost furtive, the flowers of New Zealand, drifts and waifs of colour, of half-colour, blazing nowhere save in reds, deep in the bush, or in impossible blues where the Alpine gentians storm the mountains in the South. I wonder if having Mick close at hand would make any particular difference, with or without cider. Don't think so. Who cares? I care … care for all the prolonged, disproportionate, publicised nonsense attached to the casual touches of word or hand, meant to last for a moment. On the whole, I'd rather have my hillside alone. Mick says, "You're the only one I like, because, to be honest, you are useful to me. You'll tell me about my novel." I think, "I'd have felt like that, if I'd been bullied horribly at school and there was one of the big boys who'd promised to teach me boxing: Only the xxxxxx worst of it is that I can't teach anyone anything." Still, we're happy for a moment, liking one another. Mick walks to the top of Princes Street with me. The English trees in Albert Park are in their first incredibly vivid and blithe green of spring leaf. Oak, elm, chestnut, lime, silver birch. In their own green and sedate English background, they are xxxxxx vivacious enough. Picture them here, among the dark xxxxxx perennials, the trees that never waver in their allegiance to their same xxx old Sunday suits, their same old garnishments of coral and orange berries, small, tricky-coloured flowers, shaped like old-fashioned powder-horns. The wind is clean. We shake hands under the fatherly shadow of the Northern Club. No women are allowed within, they just go on and on drinking beer and resisting trends. Somebody must. "Goodbye, Mick, I like you very much." "Goodbye, I like myself too."

Rosalie and Yasmini* are not only in, but want to see me. Sometimes their flat is surrounded with a sort of thorny hedge of dreams. It is invisible, xxxxxx impalpable, but it is there. They live very much to themselves. A little old lady, all bunched together in black taffetas, gets up as I come into the front room. At first glance, only

---

* 'Yasmini' is the name she uses for Gloria Rawlinson.

her diminutive stature, the three jet brooches nearly as large as a breast-plate over her front, and the very bright hazel eyes are noticeable. But as soon as she speaks or moves her little claws of hands, one notices that she is like a Queen. Her voice is very soft. She is ninety-two now, and has lived all her life in this country. She remembers ... she knows it is really a country, not a suburb of England, in which nobody who is anybody could conceivably want to live. Five years ago, when she was eighty-seven, everyone thought she was going to die: instead of making a will, she wrote a very long death-bed poem, ~~xxxxxxxxxxxx~~ a goodbye to the world she had loved. When she got better, it seemed to her a pity to waste it, and so she had it printed in a little booklet, of which she has given Yasmini a copy. To my surprise, it ~~was~~ *[is]* good poetry. One knows at once that the death-bed had clean sheets and a mountain view from ~~its~~ wide and airy windows. Adowa, Adowa .... There are reported casualties of seventeen hundred, including many women and children. People running, little black figures bunched together or scattering out ... but running isn't as swift as flying, you know, and man has learned again what the beautiful boy, Icarus, perished for after but an instant's knowing. This is our gift to you ... out of the skies ... for we are civilised, ~~you see~~ we have learned how to fly, and we never go too near the sun. But there was no time to air the death-bed, everyone must just tumble in together. Savages don't need clean beds, anyhow ... savages oil their skins ... savages smell .... "Peace I leave with you. My peace I give unto you." Betrayed again, poor Christ. A million times again to hang suffering over the battlefield. But you have this great advantage. You do not grow tired of stretching Your hands out to the world, because we have nailed them in position, firmly to pieces of wood. This must be a great consolation to You. As the ~~great~~ *[heavy]* drops splash down, and the sun is like ~~brass~~ *[brass]* over Your head, like a brazen shield and a war-gong in one, do You not become confused, and wonder, dazedly, if it is Your own blood that drips, or merely that of the disembowelled black woman, lying hunched up at a little distance away from Your Cross? Do You not strive, with dying anguish, to convince yourself that as You have suffered endlessly for the sins of the world, so, at least, the rest must be free from suffering, the innocent must be snatched out of the jaws of the beast? But do not concern Yourself too greatly. It is all one to us whose blood we hear falling. Yours or that of the squalid little black woman. We are an empty suit of khaki, surmounted by a gas-mask and bearing weapons. Who told us we were human? The walls of Jericho are down ....

The old voice, when it says my name, has a musing dignity, and sweetness. We have awaited long for some word, and it never came. But I think I will go to see her some day. I shouldn't be surprised if there are strawberry finches in her garden; the which are a very small kind of bird, with little creamy splashes on breasts of dull red. They lay eggs too, that are not so big as threepenny bits, in nests like ~~xxxxxx~~ crown pieces. They fly out of bushes with their shrill melancholy cries, like some very humble out-of-date ~~xxxxxx~~ stringed instrument, and sweetly confuse the world.

Rosalie says, "The Poetry Bookshop is closed down, and Winifred Holtby's dead.* They told her she had a fortnight to live, and so she finished two novels and then died. She was the only one who wrote a decent review of Stella Benson's last novel." Her eyes are bright with tears; ~~and~~ she knows perfectly well she is a sentimentalist. But there is worse to come. Yasmini has become seventeen. It happened on a Tuesday, and I wasn't there to see it. They drank the lees of the wine and ate the cake without me, except a small celluloid dog flanked in a large pink icing rose. This has been reserved. The room is full of bouquets for Yasmini, poppies, cornflowers, narcissi, mignonette, bouquets that are wilting; but they will *[somehow]* live for ever, ~~somehow~~ inside the thorn hedge of dreams. The canary sings very loud, like a little golden drill in one's ear, and the cat, Freddy, who is really an heraldic cat and assumes mad conventional poses, such as cat couchant, cat rampant, Cat Cheshire and Grinning, rolls over on his back, desirous of having his white belly tickled. Otherwhere he is a golden ginger, and with amber eyes. He is so over-civilised that he understands everything which goes on, and yet he cares only to have his belly tickled. But occasionally he tries to make an impression on Rosalie, for the same reason that Mick will shave to ~~xxxx~~ lunch with me ... his vanity, his vanity! He once brought a six-inch worm into the house, and with a profound obeisance laid it on the carpet, done up in a Figure Eight. When they laughed at him, he fled, and has never made any overtures since. We decided to write a story hinging upon a cat. The cat was to belong to a prostitute, and participate in three dramas. In the flat occupied by its mistress, first the prostitute interviews her old mother, who has

---

* Both items of news from abroad. The Poetry Bookshop in London, 1912–35, was a bookshop, a venue for readings, and a publisher. See Howard J. Woolmer, *The Poetry Bookshop: A Bibliography* (Winchester: Woolmer Botherson Ltd and St Paul's Bibliographies, 1988). Holtby was an English novelist, journalist, pacifist, feminist, and committed internationalist. Amongst her many activities, she lectured for the League of Nations; she died on 29 September 1935 at thirty-seven years – her best-known novel, *South Riding,* was published the following year. http://www.spartacus.schoolnet.co.uk/Jholtby.htm Retrieved 27 April 2011.

brought her a basket of Ribstone Pippin apples: then her lover, who has grown tired of her: then her landlady, who wants the rent. In all three acts, conversation turns on the beauty and majesty of the cat. At the end, the cat goes quietly outside and is rather ill under a lime tree.

It is a blow about the Poetry Bookshop, not for practical reasons, but because, while that existed, one felt there was still somewhere a place in the world where it was not actually discreditable to be a poet, and neither an Eliot nor a Sitwell. (Save the mark! I have often wondered what is the meaning of that expression.) "It is horrible. In the first place, the newspapers here pay seven and sixpence for a poem, and then they print in type like advertisements for Woods' Great Peppermint Cure. When I ~~xxx~~ saw my Italy poem in the Star, I could have wept to think how many copies would eventually ~~xxxx~~ line cake-tins or make curl-papers, or ~~xxx~~ worse than either." Yasmini has had three of her poems printed in a little book with a dark red cover. On the cover is a unicorn. One is a rondeau, one a poem about a fawn, and one about a reed. The printer was Ronald, who sat up half the night and came up perspiring and inky with the proofs before her birthday was over. Today she looks much more like fourteen than seventeen, owing to a frill around her neck. We are all to grow rich on poems, although the poets we know have gone on relief works, and, simultaneously, stopped being ~~poems~~ *[poets]*. Some might say that this was a healthy sign, but there is a good deal of superfluous ~~x~~ beef in the world, as witness Adowa. "It is the end of Abyssinia, whatever happens," says Rosalie "Poor ~~xxxx~~ devils! ... the monkey, the cats, and the piece of cheese." That fear of national dishonour is at the back of about half the pacifism in the world. I have just thought: the thorns that grow in a hedge around this strange room, with its flowers and its books of poetry, Yasmini lying on the couch which has been hers since, at ~~xxxx~~ seven years old, she fell victim to infantile paralysis, Rosalie making the tea …. they are the same thorns, really, as the one twisted around that other, lamentable Head. They both grow out of the brows of suffering.

At the Unicorn Robert* won't talk of anything except the behaviour of the Labour

---

* 'At the Unicorn' Press – this was Robert ('Bob') Lowry's Press until he sold it to Ronald Holloway in 1938. He and Holloway were both printers and Lowry's press had printed works by R.A.K. Mason, Allen Curnow and Hyde. In the second half of 1934, Holloway moved his Griffin Press to a shared printery with Lowry in Kitchener Street: 'The two presses, very different in character, continued for a number of years to use the same plant and premises'. (Kay Holloway, *Beta plus,* Griffin Press, 1992, 237) The printery in Kitchener Street, along

City Council, almost brand-new ... it was elected three months ago ... which has withdrawn all permits for the anti-war meetings ... and Ronald won't talk at all, but goes flying down the road and comes back with three chocolate ices, in little biscuit cones. Communist, pacifist, bourgeoisie ... Ronald is the bourgeois, his father is a ~~xxx~~ naval officer .... we eat the ices, and they are good, though in Sydney's ~~xxxxxx~~ Haymarkets you can get bright green ones from little Chinamen with faces yellow as doubloons, who will also slay and pluck for you chickens under your very eyes ... if you let them. Robert is going to help in arranging a meeting, City Council or no ~~Coun~~ City Council. We were all aware of the catch in the ~~Coun~~ City Council, anyhow. Hebreweries,[*] as an old lady of my acquaintance calls them. ~~He~~ *[Robert]* has been in prison once already, for making speeches from the roof of a motor-bus in a public place.[†] They put him in the condemned cell, which did not upset him, but meeting the hangman, whose hobby was knitting coloured waistcoats, did.

The printery is almost next to the Magistrates Court.[‡] Little lanes slide between it and the main thoroughfares, where one can experience all the pleasures of being a lame pedestrian in a motorists' world. In the lanes are flower-shops, filled with wall flowers and long branches of dark blue French forget-me-nots, the first tulips, for which they charge sixpence each, silly little pottery jars and vases: eating-houses, hat shops, frock-shops, all small and individualistic places, conducted by one or two girls, and selling their wares to a clientele they know by sight. The world here doesn't smell of mass production, but as soon as one gets to Queen Street, there's the straining shout of the little newsboys. "Extra!" they yell, "Read all about the air-raid! ... read all about the air-raid! ..." There was a perfectly good murder trial on this week, pages and pages of it. Either the man murdered his wife or he didn't, and there was another woman, who either was or wasn't ~~xxxx~~ his mistress: the titillations

---

with Blake's Inn and the Queen's Ferry in Vulcan Lane, became a gathering place for the literary set (Peter Hughes email, 11 May 2011).

[*] In spite of this comment, Hyde's friends were also concerned about anti-Semitism; in 1934, R.A.K. Mason planned a publication to be supported by the Auckland Jewish congregation to counter 'this rottenest of superstitions'. Barrowman, *Mason*, 189.

[†] Barrowman (*Mason*, 193) also describes this incident: Bob Lowry, distributing free-speech handbills (free speech had been curtailed following the unemployment demonstrations and Queen Street 'fracas' of 1932) at an illegal street meeting in Beresford Street, leapt on to the bonnet of a car to speak in support of his comrades who were being arrested.

[‡] The Magistrates Court building still stands on the corner of Courthouse Lane, below Albert Park.

of the public were equally delightful when she appeared in court.* The husband said, that the dead woman had drunk herself to death. Every shoddy fact of their lives, everything he could ×××××× do, say, look, everyone remotely connected with him, had suddenly become of enormous importance. But Mussolini had crowded him off the billboards, which looks like being the crowning glory of Mussolini's career. The Poetry Bookshop went out of action, and Winifred Holtby died, and they gave each a paragraph, as was their due. "Terence, when drunk the other night," said Ronald, "declared that he was a fairy, and that he meant to go up to the university and turn X," (a Professor of a solid sort,) "into a wart-hog. But when it came to the point, he bilked the matter, and said he couldn't do it, because X had always been a wart-hog, anyhow." The cars in the streets ×××× look like wart-hogs. One of the few things for which I do not dislike H.G. Wells is that he describes the ××××××× car of today as a sullen, aggressive-looking beast. Snort, on the horn; and legs, legs in artificial stockings, legs in shoddy trousers, scurry from patch of safety to patch of safety. The streams of people, the streams of cars, pass interminably up and down Queen Street, coagulating here and there, thick as flies, outside a shop with particularly bright lights. Fragments of glaring blue and scarlet Neon lettering are plastered on the heights of the buildings. Only the Power Board has lifted its queer little towered head into a deep haze of misty green, giving it a dignity which, compared with the rest, is almost ludicrous. The people, (it is a ×××× Friday night, and the shops are open late,) pass up and down, looking for the most part young, pretty, meaningless, shoddy, but not hungry. I think, "They are going to die, because they do not know how to live. They want to die, because they must fill their empty bladders of minds with some sort of emotion, and death-and-glory comes cheapest." It's not their fault, however: the reaching hands on the two beams of aspen wood know that. It is a good thing they were nailed into position, everyone else is tired. The shadow of Adowa's seventeen hundred dead … the dead we did not know, the dead we have somehow betrayed … fills the emptiness of this street. One wonders if they will prove too exacting.

The gardeners have planted a circular bed of night-scented stock in front of the

---

* The controversial trials of musician Eric Mareo for the murder of his actress wife, Thelma, included evidence from dancer Freda Stark and have since been well documented. The preliminary hearing at the Police Court took place between 29 September and 30 October 1935. See Charles Ferrall and Rebecca Ellis, *The Trials of Eric Mareo* (Wellington: Victoria University Press, 2002), 10. This also confirms the dating of Hyde's story.

house.* The night is perfectly clear, and heavy on it, sweet beyond words, lies the fragrance. House a cage, street a cage, world a cage, body a cage. The moon, half-crescent, floats in the indigo, attended by stars. Do you remember those old blue-painted watering-carts, always drawn by white horses, which ~~used to xxx lumber~~ *[lumbered]* solemnly along the hot little streets, laying the dust with jets of sparkling water? We used to run behind the carts and splash the water over our faces, our bare arms and legs. The old drivers cracked their whips at us, but they were not seriously offended. The streets were cool, the dust, it seemed, had fallen never to rise again. Now all the dust of the world is somehow swept out of the way, it is dark, and everything is miraculously clean and cool. Something has done this for us, I do not know what. I say to it, "Let me be yours ... let me belong to you, not to anything else at all," knowing in my heart that I belong to every littleness, like the rest of my kind. Only that is not little, perhaps tonight, among all those who sing and are triumphant, an Italian soldier is weeping at Adowa.

Robin Hyde

---

* The Lodge had a circular flowerbed, contained these days by a driveway.

VI

1936 Journal Fragment

MSX-8183, Alexander Turnbull Library, acquired 2009. Exercise book ('Exercise Book 15' in Gloria Rawlinson's sequence; Ex 15 Godwits, Leggott), largely used as a manuscript book for poems,* but also included notes for the second version of *The Godwits Fly*. One diary/journal entry appears three pages from the back.

DESCRIPTION: Lined exercise book cloth-bound in black with red edging on pages. The pages were numbered later, upside-down at bottom right-hand corner in pencil 112, 110, 108). The entry is handwritten in black pen on lined paper.

PROVENANCE: Probably left with other papers in Wellington before Hyde left New Zealand in 1938, conveyed to Bill Edge after her parents' death, listed by Gloria Rawlinson, thence to the Derek Challis Collection and finally the Alexander Turnbull Library in 2009.

The date of the entry (13 March) means that it is overlapped by the last of the entries in the 'China Notebook' (p. 267), which is named (though not titled) as being written in 'the week after Easter' 1936.† However, the entry stands alone as an indication of her mood and situation in March 1936. Written after a three-week visit to Northland, it ends with an address to her first love, whose letter she had been re-reading, and to her beloved doctor.

The notes in the manuscript (not published here) also indicate a mood of thoughtfulness about family and her own inheritance (particularly the possibility of being broken by circumstance), as well as politics. She writes: 'My mother remained herself by a constant process of rejection. My father was like a walnut smashed too hard by the clumsy hammer of fate. On the table only little bits of kernel and shell, all mashed together.' She also muses on the magical quality of words in relation to the word 'job':

There's something magical and uncanny about how words adapt themselves in sound and

---

* *Young Knowledge*, xv.
† Easter Sunday fell on 12 April in 1936.

291

association to their meaning – A word's image in the ear is like the image of a face in the mirror – And consider their rhyming associations – sporadic, I admit, – but still uncanny. Job – that word job rhyming with snob, yob, blob, nob, gob *[cross-out]*, mob, rob, sob, sob, sob – that's how it works out in my auro-image. A word with a faint ugly sound of snarling and sobbing – yet everyone wanted one. Haven't you got a job yet, Don't say you've lost your job. Not enough jobs to go round. Come along to the unemployment bureau jobs are being jobbed off .

March 13th 1936

I'm desperately tired – overwrought – saw a very large fortune teller today, and she at once visioned me walking into space and told me to keep away from water – Also prophesied great literary success – At the moment I can't care seriously for either possibility – watery grave or battle mead – I can only think of the two who I seem most closely and dearly to have loved – Haroun and Dr Tothill,[*] who is away leaving this place a desert.

I brought back with me from Northland[†] an old letter of Haroun's, almost the first – Twelve pages of it and tonight lying next to my heart! – If that seems childish, so was he – he had a curl of my hair, and says in the letter that to sleep without it gave him nightmarish dreams –

I dreamed of him twice in my little green room at Northland: oh, so sadly, and with fear overcast in the dream at last, as if I knew he were dead, and was afraid of the strangeness of that conclusion – And I dreamed also of Dr. Tothill and was reassured – He is my safety when I have any safety – but to read Haroun's letter is to realise how much I have lost, how much gold has gone out of the world – This literary success, he'd have enjoyed it so much more than I. But he had not my malleability, nor slapdash observance – and most of all, he didn't long enough, and was too busy just living, while he lasted, to turn into ink –

Reading his letter I can't believe but that he did love me: and it's all so confused, the retrospect that I can't even remember why it became clouded between us – I suppose I was too self conscious –

Goodnight, dear beloved dead boy – And goodnight to you, my living and understanding friend, with whom I can be at ease though you know all the worst and poorest sides of me – I wish I could do something to thank you – but can think of nothing more graceful than to die and leave you a literary fortune, and as nobody will buy my books, that doesn't seem feasible –

---

* Her old friend and first love Harry Sweetman who had died young, and Gilbert Mortimer Tothill, her psychiatrist, who seems to have been absent for a fortnight.

† Hyde 'left the Lodge on the weekend of 13 February for three weeks in the north' (*Iris*, 397). She had arranged through her friend Gwen Mitcalfe to rent a 'shack' on the Whangaroa Harbour, in an area above the old fish factory at Totara North, in order to work on the completion of *Godwits* (see *Iris*, 397–8). It seems likely she had left her old letters with Gwen – who now lived with her family at Totara North, where her husband was a primary school teacher.

I am so tired – so tired – It's as well you are away, or I might be a dead weight upon you – I can't get back vitality and strength, except in a few things written. But "schladfen gwhol," (is that authentic Welsh?)* and be blessed – And Haroun, I don't forget, I never forget – If one loneliness can be comforted by another, there it is –

---

* Not Welsh, but a joking German version using some Welsh letters.

VII

Essay on Mental Health

As explained in the Introduction (p. 42), this is the only piece of Robin Hyde's autobiographical writing not yet in a public collection. This essay exists as a typed copy, probably made by Gloria Rawlinson from Hyde's original typescript (which has not survived) and headed 'Untitled'. It has been referred to or recorded as 'Essay on Mental Health', the title adopted here, and has also been called '1936 Mental Health Essay' by Alison Hunt. A photocopy of Gloria Rawlinson's typescript of the essay is in the possession of Mary Edmond-Paul and will be lodged in the Alexander Turnbull Library following publication here.

DESCRIPTION: Patrick Sandbrook suggests the watermark of the Ariel Bond paper on which the essay is typed dates to 1936 or 1937.* The date of the essay's composition can be inferred to be 1936, from the reference to Inis Weed Jones's article in 'December issue of Scribner's' which was published in December 1935. However, given that Hyde would not have read this article when it was published, as magazines and papers sent by ship to New Zealand took some months to arrive, and that the story element of the essay is set in late spring, as the season warms to summer, a later date in 1936 is likely, perhaps November, the transition month seasonly in the Southern Hemisphere. Whatever its exact date,† this is the last or one of the two last compositions Hyde wrote at the Lodge about her experience there, before discharging herself in March 1937.‡

The Rawlinson typescript is of twelve pages, with the last line breaking off.

PROVENANCE: The original typescript of the essay may have been left in Wellington or at the Lodge before Hyde sailed for Sydney in 1938. Equally, it could have been amongst papers she took with her and posted to London from Hong Kong. After her death, it would have come into the possession of Rawlinson and Challis in the same way as most of the other papers.

---

*   Sandbrook, 'Robin', 394 n.46.

†   Alison Hunt ('Cage', 313) also discusses the dating of this essay.

‡   Hyde drafted *A Home in this World* (published in 1984) shortly after her discharge in March 1937, while she was living in a rented bach at Waiatarua in the Waitakere ranges, west of Auckland. (For more information on *A Home*, see its Preface, p. xx).

In this essay, Hyde takes a new approach to relating experiences and conditions at the Lodge. Writing in a vein closer to her journalism, she describes the 'house' and its environs in self-consciously objective detail, and evaluates treatment offered there with references to other writing, and comparison to other institutions – particularly in the United States. The essay is written in the present tense and from the perspective of someone who is inside the house – although not explicitly from the patient's perspective, its references to other asylum autobiographies suggest that its author is a patient. Hyde deliberately refrains from mentioning the name of the country in which the 'house' is situated: '[t]he institution is not in America – say that it is in Ruritania', perhaps because she feels its publication might embarrass local practitioners.[*] Notwithstanding, the tenor of the essay is mostly positive and focuses on 'the courageous modern attempt to treat mental patients as human beings', that she had experienced at the Lodge. It also emphasises what can be learnt from mental distress.

Alison Hunt suggests that Hyde's angle is typical of what has been characterised as 'a capitulation to psychiatric science', in that early to mid-twentieth century asylum narratives are 'more likely [than nineteenth-century accounts or more recent ones] to emphasise psychopathology and extol the virtues of psychiatric treatment'.[†] However (as the argument of my introduction suggests) we can balance Alison Hunt's twenty-first century description of changing discourses alongside the specificity of Hyde's experience. At this time there was a keen interest in patient narrative, and optimism about recovery, that Hyde was lucky enough to encounter when she arrived at the Lodge. As it turned out, this suited her and enabled her to gain new perspectives and to support an extraordinarily rich if brief writing career.

Of the authors mentioned in the essay, the one with whom Hyde seems to feel most affinity is Jane Hillyer, whose *Reluctantly Told* she mentions reviewing 'when it was first published' in 1926 (a year before she herself was a patient at Queen Mary Hospital at Hanmer). Then 'she did not guess she would ever have a personal interest in the subject' of 'how one mind could come back from the darkness and, like Persephone out of Hades, come laden with flowers'. Alison Hunt describes Hyde's 'Essay on Mental Health' as being 'like Hillyer's book' in being 'a witness statement, a critique of the mental health system and a tribute to enlightened psychiatry'. She

---

[*] For a discussion of this, see Alison Hunt, 'Cage', 181.

[†] Hunt, 'Cage', 182.

also finds a number of parallels between Hillyer's account of her experience and Hyde's versions, in the use of the imagery of Persephone and Dis, and in Hillyer's focus on her 'removal without notice from a private institution' to 'the worst of wards in a public mental hospital'.*

The essay reads as though it has been written for publication and it may have been designed for submission to the *Atlantic Monthly* – Hyde had submitted the first version of her historical work, *Check to your King,* there in 1934, and one of the authors she mentions in the essay, Charlotte Kellogg, had published her description of a visit to a model mental hospital and a call for similarly humane conditions to be adopted elsewhere, in that magazine in March 1935. Thus the essay can be seen as belonging to the genre of asylum autobiographies developed when early twentieth-century psychiatrists became interested in their patients' histories and in the 'wider dissemination of information about mental illness'.† The most famous example of this kind of writing from this period, at least in the United States, was Clifford Beer's 1908 account of illness, suicidality and recovery in *A Mind that Found Itself;* by the 1930s it was well known because Beer co-founded the Mental Hygiene Movement which spread internationally, to the degree that there was a branch in New Zealand in the 1930s.‡

---

* Hunt, 'Cage', 182.
† See Mary Wood, *The Writing on the Wall: Women's Autobiography and the Asylum, 1868–1932* (Urbana: University of Illinois, 1994) and her 'A Wizard Cultivator: Zelda Fitzgerald's *Save Me the Waltz* as Asylum Autobiography', *Tulsa Studies in Women's Literature* 11 (1992), 223; Susan J. Hubert, *Questions of Power: The Politics of Women's Madness Narratives* (Newark: University of Delaware-Associated UP, 2002); and Jeffrey L. Geller and Maxine Harris, *Women of the Asylum: Voices from Behind the Walls, 1840–1945* (New York: Anchor, c. 1994).
‡ Hunt, 'Cage', 177–8.

Untitled

This, except for the actual roof-peaks, is the highest point of the house – the attic, unfurnished except for a light-weight table, a bench and a typewriter. The little windows look out in one direction over a quiet, countrified road, its right-hand pavement plunged under heavy-seeded masses of yellow grass. Behind the grass fringes are three or four red-capped houses – the abodes of the staff doctors, and further down the road the nurses' home. And again, behind the green lawn-and-rockery patches tilled out for these houses, the fields, changing from green now to the ripened look of summer. A clay road cuts them in half, and along it trundles an old wagon, laden with great bundles of fresh-cut hay. If you met it lumbering up the road, you would probably think what a queer old gnome the driver looks, with his blackened, unshaven jowls and the jersey cap pulled down over his ears. But any of the people round about the district could explain his oddity in a phrase: he is one of 'the poor chaps from the Mental Hospital'.

The big farm, theoretically at least, is supposed to pay for itself. There are vegetable gardens, squawking poultry, demurely-patterned strawberry and white cows, like china cattle, even pigs. I remember in a book about Haiti, 'The Enchanted Island', that the author was once told a line of dead-and-alive-looking farm workers were 'zombies', corpses resurrected by witchcraft: and his spine prickled, until he realised that his zombies were a harmless gang of labourers from any asylum. Here, one sees the same gangs of little black-clad figures moving, slowly across the yellow fields. They don't really look like zombies, and if one sees them close up, sometimes their faces are far from dead-and-alive. All the same, the landscape has a curiously slow-moving, dreamlike quality about it. There isn't the stir and rattle of the energetic outer world. And behind the clumps of dotted willows and pines are big square buildings of creeper-covered stone or brick, houses of unreality, usually known by numbers – Male 9, Female 2, and so on. One of them is set aside for returned solders who lost their reason, either during the war or as a result of its after-effects.

Around this old house with the attic, doves circle like silver boomerangs. It is far more like a private home than the brick and stone buildings, and, indeed, that is exactly what it was, years ago. One doctor lived in it, then another, before it was decided to convert the place into a women's convalescent ward, and in some respects a show place, of the Mental Hospital.* One of the doctor tenants, as luck would have it, was a love[r] of trees. He planted a great shrubbery with native trees and exotics, purple double-flowering hibiscus check by jowl with rambling island jasmine, white cherry trees shaking their skirts at the mandarin formality of bamboos. The shrubbery is the most private part of the house. Patients with 'ground parole' can always find a nook to themselves among the trees –

There are two other small wards regarded by the inhabitants as on the hither side of real 'asylum', a little villa housing only seven, each with separate rooms, (these patients are mostly quiet old stagers, and the envy of their fellows;)† and a larger, more dubious home where there are observation dormitories and boxlike rooms, wherein doubtful cases are 'specialled'.‡ Of the twenty or so patients in this house, a very few are complete newcomers, women whose breakdown has not been so serious that the doctors in charge care to commit them to the main building. But nearly all are recovery cases, sent here from other wards and on their way back to the outer world. Some – perhaps a small percentage, but over the three years I have known this place, their numbers must amount to hundreds – will fail in this last lap, either now or in their own homes, and will return to the main building. Others have already been in the institution for the third or fourth time – I know one patient whose mother died in the main building, and who has herself spent almost all her life here. She is a married woman, with children. But the happiest, and they are the majority, recover, go back to normal like, and never come back. And even among those who are not quite so happy, or so easily returned to normality, there is often such courage and such humanity that they are by no means the stuff despair is made of.

Innis Weed Jones' article on the mental hospitals of America, published in the

---

* The Lodge was previously the home of superintendents, including Dr Buchanan, and was converted in 1931 to an independent ward to accommodate twenty-four female 'neuropathic' patients – 'advanced convalescent' or 'early-border-line cases'. (See Brunton, 'A Choice of Difficulties', 275; Hunt, 'Cage', 185).

† See Hunt on Director General of Health Theodore Gray's institution of 'the Neuropathic Hospitals and later the Lodge as front-of-house show wards, distinct from the insalubrious parts of the mental hospitals which housed the chronically ill' ('Cage', 59).

‡ Probably Wolfe Home – where Hyde herself was 'specialled' from late July to late August 1933. Warwick Brunton comments (275 n.90) that after 1931 Wolfe Home became a 'male unit' complementing the Lodge facility for women, but this cannot have been entirely so.

December issue of *Scribner's Magazine*,* was interesting and illuminating. So was another article written last year by an American Woman, Dr. Charlotte Kellogg, entitled 'An Institution for the Living'.† Both writers tried to stress the same thing – the old mental hospital inhumanity and hopelessness, born of the ignorance which is true product of fear, and the courageous modern attempt to treat mental patients as human beings. Innis Weed Jones mentioned the scarcity of books and articles on the subject. As far as one can gather, apart from exponents of the Viennese cult,‡ there are not many physicians who reap very great rewards from this field; the mental hospital doctor here, for instance, is probably considerably too busy to spend much time advertising either his work or his needs. 'Imagine a doctor with four hundred cases!' writes Innis Weed Jones. I know one who handles over six hundred cases, and who, moreover, contrives to take special and intelligent interest in them. In an institution with considerably over a thousand cases, not counting out-patients, there are in all five medical officers – the superintendent, three other staff doctors, one of whom attends only to male cases, and a woman physician whose time is taken up by the ridiculously inadequate little 'psychological clinic', a couple of dingy rooms in a city office, where the problems of childhood are expected to be unravelled and healed.§ Naturally, achievement is to some degree limited by facilities. But it is such workers as these, I think, who have some title to heroism and some claim to human gratitude, though, possessing only twenty-four hours in the day, they will probably never make any contribution to the literature of their science.

And, as far as mental patients are concerned, reticence is very natural. At the very best, when they rejoin the world outside, their experiences in a mental hospital are, for relatives and friends, an awkwardness to be slurred over in pitying silence. There are very few congratulations on recovery, nor much interest in the fate of others behind the brick walls. On the other hand, there is a considerable amount of morbid curiosity. I have come to the conclusion that a certain section of the public finds a release for its adventure-cravings in other people's chambers of horror ... but always, please, other people's. Never in the family!

---

* 'Man's Last Specter: The Challenge of Mental Disease', *Scribner's Magazine* (December 1935), 331–7.

† 'An Institute of Living', *Atlantic Monthly* (March 1935), 325–42.

‡ An unusually (for Hyde) off-hand reference to Freud and Freudianism; perhaps intended to win favour with a sceptical audience.

§ Possibly referring to Dr Kathleen Todd's clinic.

[page break]

Years ago, Jane Hillyer's 'Reluctantly Told',* (Innis Weed Jones refers to it in his article,) taught me how one mind could come back from the darkness.† At the time I did not guess that I would ever have a personal interest in the subject. Anything written by a mental patient on his experiences, or those of others around him, is still 'reluctantly told'. But those writers are right; it is very necessary that the public should know a little more of the human side of mental hospitals. And still far too close in memory is Shakespeare's

'You deserve
The dark house and the whip, as madmen do'.‡

This institution is not in America – say that it is in Ruritania. But I don't suppose that conditions are very far different from what they would be, at least in some parts of the United States. Conditions, building, staffing, equipment, are piteously behind America's models – there is little trace of Dr. Charlotte Kellogg's 'Institution for the Living'.§ On the other hand, the entire community receives a compulsory, though fairly cursory, education. This means that the real 'hill-billy' ignorance and cruelty concerning insane people does not exist, though there are dark enough corners in a sawmill and isolated farm. The population of the country has a high rate of insanity, but this, according to a doctor who specialises in mental cases, is partly because the public have a nervous horror of mental disease, and rush their cases into institutions, when sometimes there is little need for it. The medical profession need not be blamed for this; with the exception of a few very expensive private nursing-homes, there is only one large-scale institution in the entire country which receives patients suffering from nervous breakdown or exhaustion, but not in a condition to be committed to

---

* New York: Macmillan, 1926.

† The image of Persephone is 'a favourite trope, which in the title of Hyde's collection *Persephone in Winter* alluded obliquely to mental illness and institutionalization' (Hunt, 'Cage', 181).

‡ William Shakespeare, *As You Like It*, 3.2.391. Rosalind comparing love and madness. Hyde uses the same quotation in Chapter 16 of the '1934 Autobiography'.

§ Kellogg's essay 'An Institute of Living', published in *The Atlantic Monthly* in March 1935, described a visit to a model American institution and called for similar humane conditions to be adopted elsewhere' (Hunt, 'Cage', 182).

the mental hospitals.* This institution always has a waiting-list, and is only available for paying patients.

There is no separate home for defective children, and no really adequate clinic for the treatment of child patients. Here and there are a few plucky and ill-financed classes where children – from the 'backward' to the really defective – are given special lessons by trained instructors, sometimes with remarkably good results. But in the main building of this institution, there is a children's ward where more than a score of children live a life in which there seems very little hope. Again the cruel question of finance and facilities arises. Of course, this and that should be done: but how, without space, instructors or money? If I have read the articles of American writers correctly, the same problem arises even now in parts of the States. It will be solved, there and here, on the day when the public realises that a mental breakdown, or mental deficiency, is not more disgraceful or hopeless than a broken ankle in the one case, or a form of paralysis in the other. Of course, there are child-victims who will never be cured or even bettered. A doctor cannot recreate what was never there. But at the little schools for defective children, teachers tell how seemingly hopeless pupils were coaxed into an interest in music, colour, their own plots of garden …

Patients come here under two headings, 'voluntary' or 'committed'. The latter are usually certified insane. In theory, and very often in practice, the voluntary patient can leave if she wishes, by giving a short notice. But naturally if a voluntary patient's condition makes it dangerous for her to go out, she is dissuaded; and there have been cases when patients who insisted on giving notice when unfit were committed. There is no other distinction at all between voluntary and committed inmates. Being 'voluntary' would not save a patient who was dangerously or violently affected from being sent to the brick box of the main building, or to the ward which is a sort of unholy rumour throughout the rest of the institution, sometimes known by its number, sometimes by its name. Call it Scar House. It is for the worst female cases. Yet dozens of cases who have been there, and some who have spent years there, have passed through this convalescent ward, on their way back to the world, most of them permanently cured. The old horror-legend hangs around it. Patients and young

---

* She is referring to Queen Mary Hospital at Hanmer Springs, near Christchurch, where she was a patient in 1927. Having begun as a convalescent hospital for soldiers, it morphed into a facility for shell-shocked soldiers and by the end of WWI it expanded to treat civilians with nervous conditions. A women's hospital opened in 1926, shortly before Hyde went there (*Iris*, 86 n†).When it closed in 2003 amid public outcry, the hospital had a long and revered history.

attendants gossip about everlastingly-locked doors, bare cells where the only bedding is thick stitched quilts, so strong that patients can neither tear them up nor use them for purposes of suicide, the little exercise-yard. Yet, of the patients who came from this place, I can remember some who were far from being the pitiful wrecks one might imagine. One was a girl of about seventeen, with a beautiful singing voice. In this ward, at the same time as the daughter arrived, also stayed the mother – a tall, dignified-looking woman, her black hair coiled about her head. We heard – mental hospitals are even more hotbeds of gossip than ordinary ones – that the mother was so grieved over the daughter's insanity that she herself broke down: and that the two passed one another in the main building, without recognition. But both were discharged cured, and neither has come back again. That is not the only case of a relationship in this mental hospital. From the men's wards, every Sunday, a little old man with a white beard used to wander quietly up, to spend the afternoon sitting on a seat in the shrubbery with the woman patient who was his wife. Hour after hour, these two would sit together, hardly ever speaking, holding one another's hands: Darby and Joan transported into a world where freedom was, to say the best of it, comparative, and even recognition of one another almost a matter of pot-luck. There seems to be no halfway measure, as far as the attitude of relatives towards the insane (or mentally affected,) is concerned. Either parent, husband, wife or child shows an almost painful devotion, and turns up every visiting-day, month after month, or else the patient is abandoned like an unwanted umbrella. As to friends – it is often best to forget them. They are so enormously sensitive about one's possible sensitivities that very few of them count. On the other hand, people one meets after a breakdown, people not in a position to sentimentalize over the past and feel intense discomfort in the present, are often understanding, kindly and even humorous. But if one translated the French of 'alienée' simply as 'the alienated', one might be incorrect in letter, but not in spirit. There are no rules, however, for human loyalty. One of the most devoted husbands who ever came here on visiting-day was married to an enormous native woman, sullen at the best of times, and, in really serious attacks of illness, one of the most dangerous patients in the institution. Nurses were afraid of her, among the young and indiscreet, tales of her prowess when annoyed were many and various. Yet, when she showed signs of recovery, she was given every possible chance. She was sent from 'Scar House' to this convalescent ward – much to the terror of a tiny, round-eyed night nurse, a child in her 'teens, who had sole command of the ship at nights, save for interim visits from the 'Night Charge', and who had been fed on lurid tales of Mrs. S. Mrs. S., however, went home without violence – but in a few weeks' time returned again, and to Scar House. Sometimes, it seems that nobody can foretell how a patient who appears perfectly well and confident will re-act to the test of home surroundings. Perhaps this is partly sheer nervous irritation on the patient's part at the cautions with which she is received – and at the tendency of some relatives to order her about like a child. Others cannot get the 'disgrace' of the mental hospital background out of their minds. I know one such case at the present moment – a young girl, gentle and loveable, whom everybody likes. As far as rational conversation goes, there is nothing the matter with her. She works, never quarrels, keeps herself neat and clean – and spends all her time in tears. 'I feel so dreadfully cut off from my own mother and brother,' is her only explanation. She went home once, and came back – hazy, depressed, her confidence broken. 'It was the thought that I'd let my family down so badly'. Childish, perhaps, but the soft-hearted are childish, and until the stigma is removed from mental hospitals, there will always be patients whose recovery is retarded, or who will slip down into hopelessness again, through the mere memory of what has gone before.

Sometimes the dislocation between patient and community is almost incredible to another patient who has seen, day after day, a cheerful, self-possessed, coherent individuality. There is one woman for whom that description is no misfit. She is the kindest and most harmless creature imaginable, she looks and speaks like a lady, is immaculate in her care of herself, only occasionally talks rather fast and excitedly. For months she remains something balanced in the midst of the unbalanced, (for it's no use pretending that good temper and self-possession are not as rare as platinum here.) Then she goes home – and in a few weeks, returns, running up and down and quoting the Bible. Specialists probably know why: to the lay mind, it is simply mystery. Even in that periodic crisis, however, she retains her dignity. She demolished one young patient, who presumed to argue with her, with a sentence. 'Woman! – don't you know I'm a certified lunatic?'

Innis Weed Jones speaks of the unconscious humour in mental hospitals. It is cold fact, though perhaps less so in a convalescent ward. Humour queerly mixed up with other qualities. Once, from a very silent patient, I remember a flash of real wit. A wee man name Whale brought up our stores, she gazed at him. The, 'Ah, he's just another of these exaggerated fish stories!' she remarked. One shrewd old party, brown as a potato, could rattle off quotations from Shakespeare as though brought up by Irving. She had a fair amount of parole – freedom to go into the city – and used to attend cinemas, always for the better class of film. Peeling potatoes at the back of the house, she would give pertinent criticism of 'King Henry VIII', and Bergner in 'Catherine the Great'.* Small sums of money kept evaporating. Eventually she was suspected, searched, discovered to be in possession of a mysterious jackdaw fortune, and marched grimly off to the main building – a fate which she accepted quite stoically. I don't think we others need have grudged her her stolen sixpences. She was one of the forgotten-umbrella cases – and besides, it wasn't as though she had had a craving for Rudy Vallee.

Once a patient in one of the awful calico nightgowns of the main building came singing loudly and out of tune down the stairs. 'Oh, do stop it,' I begged her. She stopped it. 'Ah, yes, my dear! – 'To where beyond these voices, there is peace!'† Do you know the lines? Do you know, my father built this place?' She told me about her childhood. Her mother, an Italian woman, was at times violently insane, at times normal. Once she knocked the little girl unconscious. 'For a whole week, my Father pretended to my Mother that I was dead, and I could hear her calling for me. He wouldn't let me go near her. He was a hard man, but very just. That was to punish her.' Unfortunately, that, or like, punished the child as well. When the mother dies, insane, the daughter began to come into the mental hospital for periods ranging from a few months upwards …. Now she has children of her own. One wonders desperately what law, beyond blind desolation, operates there. But may it not be true that in some cases insanity, like tuberculosis, is not so much a matter of hereditary disease, as of childhood environment and upbringing? The child remembers violent

---

* Both *The Private Life of Henry VIII* (1933) and *Catherine the Great* (1934) were lavish British film productions directed by Alexander Korda, but Catherine's story (in which German actress Elizabeth Bergner made her English language debut) of marriage to a faithless husband Peter III of Russia (Douglas Fairbanks Jr) was poignant and sombre, in contrast to the humour of *Henry VIII*. *New York Times* review, 15 February 1934 http://movies.nytimes.com/movie/revie w?res=9D04E5DC1F3DE23ABC4D52DFB466838F629EDE Retrieved 21 May 2011.

† The last lines of 'Guinevere' from Alfred Lord Tennyson, *Idylls of the King*: Vivien, Elaine, Enid, Guinevere (New York: R.H. Russell, 1898).

> Then she, for her good deeds and her pure life,
> And for the power of ministration in her,
> And likewise for the high rank she had borne,
> Was chosen Abbess, there, an Abbess, lived
> For three brief years, and there, an Abbess, past
> To where beyond these voices there is peace.

outbreaks of temper on the part of one parent, or both. The child remembers the dreadful facts of a marriage in which the bond was galling and resisted. The child remembers continual threats of suicide, never seriously intended, but listened to with horror and curiosity. And an adolescence with problems locked up ... Blaming the parents, shutting the parents away from the child, is not enough. The parents were sufferers too. A whole code needs revision and enlarging. The deadletter virtues of the fathers should not be visited upon the children, as any doctor who has come to deal with those problems of childhood knows they are today.

The pit that the mental patient climbs out of is a strange one, and it lies between the patient and the world. It is that sense of unreality, of existing somehow cut off and banished from all normal fact and feeling, that is the hardest barrier. Merely returning to coherence, to the ability to talk and listen, is not enough. The alienated ... sometimes, I know from experience, people whom they loved, and for whom they would have made many sacrifices, mean nothing to them. The first impulse is to turn away from the world altogether. The second is to turn to the person who understands. It is into that pit that the people who expect to have any success with mental cases have to stretch their hands. At present, most of the work is left to overworked doctors – and sometimes, an actual stigma of inferiority attaches to them as well as to their patients, on account of the mental hospital associations – and to untrained girls. Here, for instance, the attendants amongst female patients are mostly girls in their 'teens, sometimes uneducated. Their pay is a little higher than that of domestic servants, but not much. They pass examinations as they go along, and change with seniority from one colour of uniform into another. But their tasks be as much in keeping floors polished, and simply in maintaining

[Final page/s missing]

Select Bibliography

Archives Consulted

Alexander Turnbull Library Wellington (ATL)
Challis, Derek Arden, 1930– . Papers relating to Robin Hyde (c. 1910–2000). MS-Group-1648, Alexander Turnbull Library. Acquired 2009.

Auckland City Central Library (ACCL)
Iris G. Wilkinson Papers. Sir George Grey Special Collections.

Auckland University MSS and Archives (AU)
Iris Wilkinson Papers 97/1.
Poetry Manuscripts c. 1925–37 (AU 1-610)

Derek Challis Collection (DC)
Private Collection transferred to the Alexander Turnbull Library 2009, see above.

Works By Robin Hyde (Iris Wilkinson 1906–1939)

Unpublished Manuscripts Reproduced and/or Cited
'1934 Autobiography'. Sir George Grey Special Collections NZ MS 412A, ACCL.

'1934–35 Journal Fragments'. Rough Diary [printed title]. Exercise Book 12. Derek Challis *(Iris)* calls this '1934 Diary'. DC. Challis, Papers relating to Robin Hyde, MSX-8216, ATL, acquired 2009.

'1935 Journal'. Holograph notebook. Exercise book 13. DC. Challis, Papers relating to Robin Hyde, MSX-8216, ATL, acquired 2009.

'1935 Journal'. TS Copy typed by Gloria Rawlinson. Sir George Grey Special Collections. NZ MS 0837, ACCL.

'1935–36 Journal Fragments' in China Notebook. Holograph notebook, Oct 1935–March 1938. DC. Challis, Papers relating to Robin Hyde, MSX-8206, ATL, acquired 2009.

'1936 Journal Fragment'. Exercise Book 15. Also contains a version of *Godwits*. Challis, Papers relating to Robin Hyde, MSX-8183, ATL, acquired 2009.

'The Cage with the Open Door'. Hyde's original TS, with holograph annotations. Challis, MS-Papers-9110-009, Alexander Turnbull Library, acquired 2009. 'Six Pomegranate Seeds'; 'Lighted Windows', Alexander Turnbull Library.

Untitled essay ['Essay on Mental Health']. Photocopy of Gloria Rawlinson's TS copy of Hyde's original, with annotations. In possession of Mary Edmond-Paul, to be donated to ATL.

'The Unbelievers', 6 vols, Challis, Papers relating to Robin Hyde, MS-Papers-9110-143, MS-Papers-9110-144, MS-Papers-9110-145, MS-Papers-9110-146, MS-Papers-9110-147, MS-Papers-9110-148, ATL, acquired 2009.

Published Stories

Robin Hyde. 'Lonely Street', *Art in New Zealand* 7.3 (1935), 128–33.

For a full list of short stories, see *Lighted Windows*.

Journalism

'Cunning Witches Weave Wily Spells', [Anonymously] *New Zealand Truth*, 11 October 1928, 8.

'Flaming Youth and Free Speech', *New Zealand Observer*, 16 August 1934, 5.

No complete list of Hyde's journalism exists, but for a substantial bibliography see *Lighted Windows*. A range of articles and reviews and other pieces are reproduced in *Disputed Ground* (1991) and on New Zealand Electronic Text Centre (Wellington: Victoria University, 2008) http://www.nzetc.org/tm/scholarly/name-208310.html.

Letters

Robin Hyde wrote many letters, a large number of which are held in public collections. A selection of her letters to John Schroder and J.A. Lee, Pat Lawlor and Downie Stewart (1927–39) are reproduced in Lisa Docherty's thesis ('Do I speak Well?'). Alison Hunt's thesis ('Cage') and essay ('Angel-Guarded Liar' in *Lighted Windows*) reproduce Hyde's June 1933 correspondence with Dr H.M. Buchanan, found in his Psychiatric Clinic notebook 1933. For references to and quotation from many individual letters, see *Iris* and *Lighted Windows*.

Books

The Book of Nadath, ed. and introd. Michele Leggott (Auckland: Auckland University Press, 1999).

Check to Your King: The Life History of Charles, Baron de Thierry, King of Nukahiva, Sovereign Chief of New Zealand (London: Hurst and Blackett, 1936).

—. Reprint (Harmondsworth and London: Penguin, 1975).

—. Reprint (South Yarra: Viking, 1987).

The Conquerors and Other Poems (London: Macmillan, 1935).

The Desolate Star and Other Poems (Christchurch: Whitcombe and Tombs, 1929).

Disputed Ground: Robin Hyde, Journalist, ed. and introd. Gillian Boddy and Jacqueline Matthews (Wellington: Victoria University Press, 1991).

Dragon Rampant (London: Hurst and Blackett, 1939).

—. Reprint. Introd. Derek Challis, Critical Note by Linda Hardy (Auckland: New Women's Press,

1984).

The Godwits Fly (London: Hurst & Blackett, 1938).

—. Reprint. Ed. and introd. Gloria Rawlinson (Auckland: Oxford University Press/Auckland University Press, 1970, 1980, 1984. 2nd edition, 1993).

—. New edition. Ed. and introd. Patrick Sandbrook (Auckland: Auckland University Press, 2001).

A Home in this World, Introd. Derek Challis (Auckland: Longman Paul, 1984).

Houses by the Sea & The Later Poems of Robin Hyde, ed. and introd. Gloria Rawlinson (Christchurch: Caxton Press, 1952).

Journalese (Auckland: The National Printing Company, 1934).

Nor the Years Condemn (London: Hurst & Blackett, 1938).

—. Reprint. Introd. Phillida Bunkle, Linda Hardy and Jacqueline Matthews (Auckland: New Women's Press, 1986).

—. Reprint (Dunedin: University of Otago Press, 1995).

'A Night of Hell', in *A Home in this World,* Introd. Derek Challis (Auckland: Longman Paul, 1984).

Passport to Hell (London: Hurst & Blackett, 1936).

—. Reprint. Introd. and notes, D.I.B. Smith (Auckland: Auckland University Press, 1986).

Persephone in Winter: Poems (London: Hurst & Blackett, 1937).

Selected Poems, ed. Lydia Wevers (Auckland: Oxford University Press, 1984).

The Victory Hymn 1935–1995, ed. Michele Leggott (Auckland: Holloway Press, 1995).

Wednesday's Children (London: Hurst & Blackett, 1937).

—. Reprint. Introd. and afterword Susan Ash (Auckland: New Women's Press, 1989).

—. Reprint (Dunedin: University of Otago Press, 1993).

Young Knowledge: *The Poems of Robin Hyde*, ed. and introd. Michele Leggott (Auckland: Auckland University Press, 2003). Notes online at http://www.nzepc.auckland.ac.ns/authors/hyde

Secondary Sources

Works relating to Robin Hyde

Boddy, Gillian, and Jacqueline Matthews. Ed and introd. *Disputed Ground: Robin Hyde, Journalist* (Wellington: Victoria University Press, 1991).

Bridge, Diana. 'China, Imagined and Actual, in Robin Hyde's *The Godwits Fly*, Two Journal Entries and the "China" Poems'. In Mary Edmond-Paul (ed.), *Lighted Windows: Critical Essays on Robin Hyde* (Dunedin: Otago University Press, 2008), 89–106.

Buchanan, H.M. Case Notes for Iris Wilkinson. Medical Superintendent's Psychiatric Clinic Notebook 1933. YCAA 1090/7. Archives New Zealand, Auckland.

Calder, Alex, 'Violence and the Psychology of Recklessness: Robin Hyde's *Passport to Hell*'. In *Lighted Windows*, 67–72.

Challis, Derek and Gloria Rawlinson, *The Book of Iris: A Life of Robin Hyde* (Auckland: Auckland University Press, 2002).

Challis, Derek. 'The Fate of the Iris Wilkinson (Robin Hyde) Manuscripts'. *Journal of New Zealand Literature* 16 (1998), 22–32; revised New Zealand Electronic Poetry Centre (University of Auckland: New Zealand Electronic Poetry Centre, 2002) http://www.nzepc. auckland.ac.nz/authors/hyde/challis.asp

Clayton, Megan. 'Iris, Read and Written: A New Poetics of Robin Hyde' (PhD: University of Canterbury, 2001).

—. 'Thoroughly Modern Malory: Robin Hyde's Poetic Ciphers and Camelot Codes'. In *Lighted Windows*, 107–18.

Docherty, Lisa. '"Do I Speak Well?": A Selection of Letters by Robin Hyde 1927–1939' (PhD: University of Auckland, 2000).

Edmond-Paul, Mary (ed.). 'Introduction: Dark Torch'. In *Lighted Windows,* 15–28.

—,'Robin Hyde (Iris Wilkinson) 1906–1939'. *Kotare* Special Issue 2007 http://www.nzetc.org/tm/ scholarly/tei-Whi071Kota-t1-g1-t11.html

Hessell, Nikki. 'Novitia the anti-novice: Robin Hyde's Parliamentary Reports'. In *Lighted Windows,* 151–61.

Hunt, Alison. 'Angel-Guarded Liar in a Pleasant, Quiet Room: Robin Hyde's Experiences in the New Zealand Mental Health System of the 1930s'. In *Lighted Windows*, 143–50.

—. '"The Cage with the Open Door": Autobiography and Psychiatry in the Life and Works of Robin Hyde'. (PhD: University of Auckland, 2008).

Jeffreys, Alison. 'Other Pastures: Death, Fantasy and the Gothic in Robin Hyde's Short Stories'. In *Lighted Windows,* 73–88.

—. 'The Short Stories of Robin Hyde (Iris Wilkinson) 1906–1939' (MA: University of Auckland, 2001).

Leggott, Michele. Introduction. *Young Knowledge: The Poems of Robin Hyde* (Auckland: Auckland University Press, 2003).

—, Notes to *Young Knowledge* www.nzepc.auckland.ac.nz/authors/hyde/yk.pdf

Murray, Stuart. 'Robin Hyde' in *Never a Soul at Home: New Zealand Literary Nationalism and the1930s* (Wellington: Victoria University Press, 1998).

Paul, Mary. *Her Side of the Story: Readings of Mander, Mansfield & Hyde* (Dunedin: University of Otago Press, 1999).

Sandbrook, Patrick. 'Robin Hyde: A Writer at Work' (PhD: Massey University, 1985).

Zimmerman, Anne Barbara. 'Godwitting and Cuckooing: Negotiations and Legitimations of

Cultural Identity in New Zealand Literature' (PhD: University of Berne, 1996).

—. 'A Philological Analysis of Robin Hyde ms "Autobiography"', Research Notes, October 1991. Reproduced as Addenda D in Zimmerman, 'Godwitting and Cuckooing'. [Held in] Special Collections, Auckland Central City Library.

Other Works

Appignanesi, Lisa. *Mad, Bad and Sad: Women and the Mind Doctors* (New York: Norton & Co., 2008).

Barrowman, Rachel. *Mason: The Life of R.A.K. Mason* (Wellington: Victoria University Press, 2003).

Brookes, Barbara. 'Shame and Its Histories in the Twentieth Century', *Journal of New Zealand Studies*, Issue 9 (Oct 2010), 48.

Brookes, Barbara and Jane Thomson (eds) *'Unfortunate Folk': Essays on Mental Health Treatment 1863–1992* (Dunedin: University of Otago Press, 2001).

Brunton, Warwick. 'A Choice of Difficulties: National Mental Health Policy in New Zealand, 1840–1947' (PhD: University of Otago, 2001).

Caruth, Cathy. *Unclaimed Experience: Trauma, Narrative and History* (Baltimore: The John Hopkins University Press, 1996).

Crozier, Andrew. *The Causes of the Second World War* (London: Blackwell, 1997).

Dante Alighieri. *Inferno,* Indiana Critical Edition (Mark Musa Bloomington: Indiana University Press, c. 1995).

Ferrall, Charles and Rebecca Ellis. *The Trials of Eric Mareo* (Wellington: Victoria University Press, 2002).

Freud, Sigmund. 'Mourning and Melancholia', Vol. 14, *The Standard Edition of the Complete Psychological Works*, ed. and trans. James Strachey (London: Hogarth Press, 1953–74), 237–60.

Geller, Jeffrey L. and Maxine Harris, *Women of the Asylum: Voices from Behind the Walls, 1840–1945* (New York: Anchor, c. 1994).

Gordon, Beth, Sunny Riordan, Rowena Scaletti and Noeline Creighton. *Legacy of Occupation: Stories of Occupational Therapy in New Zealand 1940–1972* (Auckland: Bush Press, 2009).

Graves, Robert (Introd.). *The New Larousse Encyclopedia of Mythology* (London: Paul Hamlyn, 1968).

Hilliard, Chris. *The Bookmen's Dominion: Cultural Life in New Zealand 1920–1950* (Auckland: Auckland University Press, 2006).

Holloway, Judith. '"Unfortunate Folk": A study of the Social Context of Committal to Seacliff 1928–1937'. In Barbara Brookes and Jane Thomson (eds) *'Unfortunate Folk': Essays on*

Mental Health Treatment 1863–1992 (Dunedin: University of Otago Press, 2001).

Hubert, Susan J. *Questions of Power: The Politics of Women's Madness Narratives* (Newark: University of Delaware–Associated UP, 2002).

Jensen, Kai. *Whole Men: The Masculine Tradition in New Zealand Literature* (Auckland: Auckland University Press, 1996).

Jones, Lawrence. 'The Novel'. In Terry Sturm (ed.). *The Oxford History of New Zealand Literature* (Auckland: Oxford University Press, 1991).

Jones, Lawrence. *Picking up the Traces: The Making of a New Zealand Literary Culture, 1932–1945* (Wellington: Victoria University Press, 2003).

King, Michael. *Frank Sargeson: A Life* (Auckland: Viking, 1995).

Lee, Hermione. *Virginia Woolf* (London: Vintage Books, 1999).

Lemprière, J. *A Classical Dictionary* (1878) (London: Routledge and Kegan Paul Ltd, 1963).

Oppenheim, Janet. *'Shattered Nerves': Doctors, Patients and Depression in Victorian England* (Oxford: Oxford University Press, 1991).

Porter, Roy. *A Social History of Madness: The World Through the Eyes of the Insane* (New York: Weidenfeld and Nicholson, 1987).

—. *Madness: A Brief History* (Oxford: Oxford University Press, 2002).

Rapp, Dean. 'The Discovery of Freud by the British General Public, 1912–1919', in *Social History of Medicine,* vol. 3, no.2 (August 1990), 217–43.

Rusden, G.W. *History of New Zealand* (Melbourne: Chapman and Hall, 1883).

Sandbrook, Patrick. 'Robin Hyde: A Writer at Work'. (PhD: Massey University, 1985).

Scott, David (ed.). *The Story of Auckland Hospital 1847–1977* (Auckland: Medical Historical Library Committee of the Royal Australasian College of Physicians in New Zealand, 1977).

Scull, Andrew. *The Most Solitary of Afflictions: Madness and Society in Britain, 1700–1900* (New Haven and London: Yale University Press, 1993).

—. *Hysteria: The Biography* (Oxford: Oxford University Press, 2009).

Shephard, Ben. *A War of Nerves: Soldiers and Psychiatrists in the Twentieth Century* (Cambridge, Mass.: Harvard University Press, 2001).

Showalter, Elaine. *Hystories: Hysterical Epidemics and Modern Media* (New York: Columbia University Press, 1998).

—. *Inventing Herself: Claiming a Feminist Intellectual Heritage* (New York: Scribner, 2001).

—. (ed.). *These Modern Women: Autobiographical Essays from the Twenties* (New York: The Feminist Press, 1978).

—. *The Female Malady: Women, Madness and English Culture 1830–1980* (New York: Pantheon Books, 1985).

Stansfield, T.E Knowles. 'The Villa or Colony System', *The Journal of Mental Science*, vol. LX, no. 248 (1914).

Styles, Jennifer. 'Men and the Development of Psychiatry in New Zealand in the 1920s and 1930s' (MA: University of Canterbury, 1997).

Tennyson, Alfred. 'The Lotos-Eaters', *Poems, Chiefly Lyrical* (London: Effingham Wilson, Royal Exchange, 1830).

Thompson, Neil (ed.). *Loss and Grief: A Guide for Human Services Practitioners* (Hampshire: Palgrave, 2002).

Walter, Tony. *On Bereavement: The Culture of Grief* (Buckingham: Open University Press, 1999).

Williams, Wendy Hunter. *Out of Mind, Out of Sight: The Story of Porirua Hospital* (Porirua: Porirua Hospital, 1987).

Wood, Mary. *The Writing on the Wall: Women's Autobiography and the Asylum, 1868–1932* (Urbana: University of Illinois, 1994).

—. 'A Wizard Cultivator: Zelda Fitzgerald's *Save Me the Waltz* as Asylum Autobiography', *Tulsa Studies in Women's Literature* 11 (1992), 223.

Index

Gray, Theodore 31–2, 49
Greece 219
Grey Lodge, *see* the Lodge (Grey Lodge)
Grey, Sir George 200–1, 215
grief 58–9
Griffin Press 198, 287–8

Hamilton 11, 120
Hankey, Sir Maurice 219
Hanmer, *see* Queen Mary Hospital, Hanmer
Springs
Hardcastle, Aroha 195–6, 252, 280
'Haroun,' *see* Sweetman, Harry ('Haroun')
'Haste Thee Nymph' (RH, short story) 182
Hawthorn, Gwen (later Mitcalfe; 'Jezebel') 11,
20, 43, 45, 78–83, 89, 112, 114, 124, 130,
138, 159, 221, 223, 227–8, 236, 293
Hawthorn, Olga 81–2, 124, 125
Hay, Beula (née Jenkin) 165, 221, 244
Hewlett, Maurice 86
Hillyer, Jane, *Reluctantly Told* 296–7, 301
Hitler, Adolf 218–19
Hokitika Mental Hospital 50
Holbein, Hans 96; 'Man in the Biretta' 127
Holloway, Kay 198
Holloway, Ronald 41, 195, 198, 252, 258, 261,
262–4, 280, 287, 288, 289
Holmes, Charles and Violet 104
Holmes, Oliver Wendell 94
Holtby, Winifred 286, 289
'Homage to Dis' (RH, poem) 92
A Home in this World (RH, non-fiction) 12, 37,
41, 43, 45, 48, 219, 239, 295
Hong Kong 13, 252, 261, 295
Hotel Rossville, Eden Terrace, Auckland 161
Houses by the Sea (RH, poetry) 44
Hunt, Alison 14, 15, 21, 42, 47, 48, 49–50,
53, 55, 64, 65, 91, 102, 120, 142, 170, 193,
196–7, 204, 223, 239, 269, 270–1, 295,
296–7
Hurst & Blackett 12, 14, 188, 217, 228, 266

Hutson family 11, 12, 144, 165–6
Hy-Brasil (Breasil) 71
Hyde, Christopher Robin: birth and death 10,
48, 105, 116–17, 191; Hyde tells about
indirectly, by taking baby's name 57; Hyde
tells Buchanan about 55, 173, 224; Hyde's
grief after death 58–9, 67, 95, 121, 122,
123, 147, 148–9, 150–1, 250–1; Hyde's
pregnancy 10, 18, 110–16, 124, 127; secret
child 54, 55, 56, 148, 173, 174; society's
attitude to unmarried mothers 39, 54
Hyde, Frederick de Mulford (Cedric) 10, 56,
105–10, 111–12, 113, 114, 116, 118–19,
121, 122–3, 221, 224; parents 123–4
Hyde, Robin
children, *see* Challis, Derek Arden
(Gerard); Hyde, Christopher Robin
family and early life: Aunt Louise 72, 79;
birth 10; death of parents 43; disaffection
40, 57; effect of parents' arguments
74–5; family's finances 18; family's lack
of knowledge of Hyde's second baby
(Derek) 56; father's flute 66–7; holiday
at York's Bay 235–6; and Hyde's mental
illness 20, 27, 28, 48, 57, 74–5, 235;
judgmental attitudes 18, 37; 'Laloma,'
Northland, Wellington 11, 69, 74, 125–6,
127, 159, 291, 293; matriculation 85–6;
Newtown, Wellington 10, 66, 258; parents'
relationship 66, 67–8, 74–5; 'Robin Hood
Cottage' 66, 258; Wellington Girls' College
78–9, 82–4, 85–6; World War I 68–9; *see
also* Wilkinson, Edna; Wilkinson, Edward;
Wilkinson, Hazel; Wilkinson, Nelly;
Wilkinson, Ruth Saxon Louvain
finances: debt to Milne and Choyce
Department Store 102–3; and holiday in
Rotorua 105; independence from family 18;
on leaving *New Zealand Truth* 138; during
pregnancy with Derek and immediately
after birth 153–4, 159, 202; during

248–9, 251–2, 257, 267, 273–5; Hyde's
isolation 182, 183; Hyde's self-discharges
12, 143, 144, 193; Hyde's smuggling of
drugs into 52–3, 55, 56, 224; occupational
therapy 35, 49, 50; writing therapy 50, 296;
see also Buchanan, Henry; Tothill, Gilbert
London 13, 14, 17
'Lonely Street' (RH, short story) 210–11
Long Grove Mental Hospital 33, 49
love, Hyde's views on need for 203–4, 206,
215, 233, 239
Lovell, P. 252, 258
Lowry, Robert ('Bob') 198–9, 262–4, 287–8
Lutoslawski, Wincenty 246

MacDonald, Ramsay 218
Mackay, Jessie 150
Macky, John 193
Macmillan and Company 12, 188, 232
MacMullan, Mrs 248
Madden, Norm 25
Magistrate's Court, Auckland 288
Maheno 10
Malory, Thomas, Sir, 'Morte D'Arthur' 230–1
Mander, Jane 38, 280
Maning, Frederick 278
Mansfield, Katherine 216, 278
Marama 10, 112
Mareo, Eric 289
Marris, Charles A. 11, 12, 210–11
Mason, Ron (R.A.K.) 66, 198–9, 287, 288;
'The Beggar' 273
materiality 227
Matthew 99, 104, 136; 13:12, Parable of the
Talents 132, 207
McKeefry, Father 245
McLean, John Gordon (Mac) 11, 22, 161, 170,
173, 218
McPhail, Mrs J. 276
men: asylum patients 24; mental illness 24, 26,
27; sexuality 29

mental hospitals 33; attendants 306; patient
classification 33; regimes of good
behaviour, reward and punishment 32, 35,
49; stigmatisation of patients 20, 33, 34,
300, 301, 302, 304; United States 301;
voluntary admissions 33, 58, 302; *see also*
asylums; mental illness; psychopaedic
hospitals; voluntary villas; and names of
individual institutions
Mental Hospitals Department 31
Mental Hygiene Movement 297
mental illness: 'acute' and chronic 33–4;
borderline recoverable 17, 18, 25–9, 32,
34–5, 188; familial patterns and social
attitudes precipitating 188–9, 204, 305–6;
fear of 124; and feelings of shame 39;
and gender roles 24, 35–6; humanisation
19; Hyde's views on need for love 203–4,
206, 215, 233, 239; Jung's 'celebration
of social consciousness in recovering
neurotics' 270; men 24, 26, 27; physical
and hereditary degeneracy argument 24–5,
28, 31; psychopharmacological treatment
19; public attitudes to 20, 33, 34, 300, 301,
302, 303; 'riddles of a disordered mind' 19;
women 26, 27, 29, 35–7; *see also* asylums;
depression; Hyde, Robin, mental illness;
hysteria; mental hospitals; mood disorders;
neurasthenia; psychiatry; psychotherapy
Mercer, Cecil William 224
Mew, Charlotte 257
Milne and Choyce Department Store 102–3
Milner, Ian 66
Mitcalfe, Gwen (née Hawthorn; 'Jezebel') 11,
20, 43, 45, 78–83, 89, 112, 114, 124, 130,
138, 159, 221, 223, 227–8, 236, 293
Mitcalfe, Percy 12
Mitchell, Silas Weir 27
Mitchison, Naomi, *Cloud Cuckoo Land* 192
'the Mob' 64, 66
modernism 31, 176–7, 178, 227

to Hyde at the Lodge 142

Rea, Lorna, *The Happy Prisoner* 93

Reade, Charles, *The Cloister and the Hearth* 227

relation to time and society 36–7

repetition compulsion 59

Richmond, Dorothy 235, 236, 242

Ricoeur, Paul 42

Rilke, Rainer Maria, *Notebooks of Malte Laurids Brigge* 218

Rivers, W.H.R. 30

Roper, Richard 235

Rostand, Edmond, *Chantecler* 209

Rotorua 10, 11, 105, 106, 116, 118–20

Rotorua Sanatorium 105

'Rough Diary,' *see* Journal Fragments, 1934–1935 ('Rough Diary')

Rutter, Edward Owen, *Chandu* 213

Sandbrook, Patrick 14, 63, 295

'Sarah' (RH, poem) 247–8, 249

Sargeson, Frank 18, 66

Savage, George 20–1

Schreiner, Olive 73

Schroder, John 11, 95–6, 127, 131, 150, 170, 221, 238

Scull, Andrew 23. 24–5, 30, 31, 37

'Seaborn' (RH, poem) 150

Seacliff Mental Hospital 24, 49, 130

Seager, Samuel Hurst 166

sensitivity 208

Shakespeare, William 75, 82, 96, 155, 177, 304; see also *Antony and Cleopatra; As You Like It*

Shanghai 13

'She' (RH, poem) 150

Shelley, Percy Bysshe 165, 176; *The Cenci, A Tragedy in Five Acts* 96; *A Defence of Poetry* 66

shell-shock 30–1, 33

Shephard, Ben 27

short stories of Robin Hyde 216, 223, 228, 269; 'The Cage with the Open Door' 41, 61, 198, 269–90; 'God Rest You, Merry Gentlemen' 226, 251; 'Haste Thee Nymph' 182; 'Lighted Windows' (unpublished) 206–7; 'Lonely Street' 210–11; 'My Countrymen' 175, 184; 'Six Pomegranate Seeds' (unpublished) 209, 249; 'Sweet William' 198; 'Unicorn Pasture' 12, 198, 245, 258, 269

Showalter, Elaine 28, 31, 35, 36, 38

Simon, Sir John 218

Sinclair, Upton, 'Journal of Arthur Stirling' 246

Singapore 13

'Six Pomegranate Seeds' (RH, unpublished short story) 209, 249

Skilton, Hazel 49

Skinner, Mavis 239

Smee, Mary (later Dobbie) 47, 246, 250

social Darwinism 25

'Sodom' (RH, poem) 139–42

Spielrein, Sabina 51, 52

Spinoza, Baruch (Benedictus) 131, 134

spiritualism 67, 130, 151

Stark, Freda 289

Stark, James Douglas ('Starkie') 220, 221, 222–3, 225, 227, 228, 231, 232, 233, 241, 245, 267

Stephen (Woolf), Virginia 20–1, 28, 50, 120, 227

Stewart, Peggy 248

Stewart, W. Downie 12

stigma: asylum and mental hospital patients 20, 33, 34, 300, 301, 302, 304; expression of female sexuality and emotions 37, 54; mental hospital doctors 306

stoicism 56

Stronach, Elsie 267

Stronach, Jane 267

Sun (Christchurch) 11, 19, 95, 210–11, 238

'Sweet William' (RH, short story) 198

Waitomo caves 91, 209, 249
Waley, Arthur 60
Walker, Geoff 44–5
Wanganui 11, 80, 146
Wanganui Chronicle 11
Webb, Mary, *Gone to Earth* 84
Wednesday's Children (RH, novel) 13, 14, 47, 271
Weir Mitchell cure 27
'The Well in the Forest' (RH, poem) 244
Wellington 10, 11, 97, 100, 124–8, 144, 158–9, 199; 'Laloma,' Hyde's home in Northland 11, 69, 74, 125–6, 127, 159, 291, 293; neglected garden with pool, visited with Sweetman 76, 87–8
Wellington Girls' College 78–9, 82–4, 85–6, 209
'Wellington Hills' (RH, poem) 181
Wellington Public Hospital 97–100
Wellington Zoological Gardens 99–100
Wells, H.G. 289
Whangaroa Harbour 12, 293
Wilkinson, Edna 44, 74, 223
Wilkinson, Edward 43, 66; Hyde's relationship with 18, 69, 75, 83, 86, 125, 240–1, 291; Hyde's will 223
Wilkinson, Hazel 44
Wilkinson, Iris, *see* Hyde, Robin
Wilkinson, Nelly 43, 44, 103, 104, 105, 118; Church of England 124, 128; Hyde's relationship with 10, 12, 18, 68, 72, 82, 111, 112, 116, 121, 122, 123, 124, 128, 148, 158, 221, 226, 239, 242, 258, 291; Hyde's will 223, 258

Wilkinson, Ruth Saxon Louvain 128, 223
Wilson, Woodrow 265–6
wistaria dream 94–5
Wolfe Home (Main Building, Auckland Mental Hospital) 26, 34, 194, 203, 204, 212–13, 214, 215, 219, 236, 238, 251–2, 299; in 'Essay on Mental Health' 302–3, 304, 305; Hyde transferred to 12, 17, 53, 56, 65, 133, 156–8, 196–7, 224, 242, 299; Hyde's fear of 100, 106, 212, 248
women: asylum patients 24; career women 36, 38; 'feminine moral code' 99, 203; mental illness 26, 27, 29, 35–7; sexuality 38, 39–40; social attitudes to 'new woman' 37–40; stigma around expression of sexuality and emotions 37; unmarried mothers 39, 54, 58, 203
Women's Mirror 10
Woolf (Stephen), Virginia 20–1, 28, 50, 120, 227
World War I 30–1, 59, 68–9, 282–3
writers, modern 176–7, 178, 227
Wyndham Street, Auckland 278–9

York Retreat 23
York's Bay, Wellington 235

Zimmerman, Anne Barbara 63–4

Otago University Press titles by and about Robin Hyde

Nor the Years Condemn
Robin Hyde
Wednesday's Children (reprint forthcoming)
Robin Hyde
Her Side of the Story: Readings of Mander, Mansfield & Hyde
edited by Mary Paul
Lighted Windows: Critical Essays on Robin Hyde
edited by Mary Edmond-Paul